Harry —

Blessings

Always —

Rocco A. Errico

8-3-03

Facsimile of one of the few surviving Aramaic texts of the New Testament with the exception of the Book of Revelation and a few Epistles. It was found in the ruins of an ancient Assyrian Church, in Persian (Iranian) Kurdistan. Since the publication of Dr. George M. Lamsa translation of the Four Gospels from Aramaic, 1933, these manuscripts have greatly increased in value

Showing Portion of Ancient Aramaic New Testament MS.
Recently Placed at Early Sixth Century CE.

Showing Portion of Page of Newly Discovered
Old Aramaic (Syriac) New Testament MS.
(Now in possession of George M. Lamsa Estate)

Showing Portion of Psalm 7 from Codex Ambrosianus Fifth Century CE.

THE GOSPEL OF MATTHEW

Chapter 1:1-15

Eastern Estrangela Aramaic Text

Sixth Century CE Manuscript

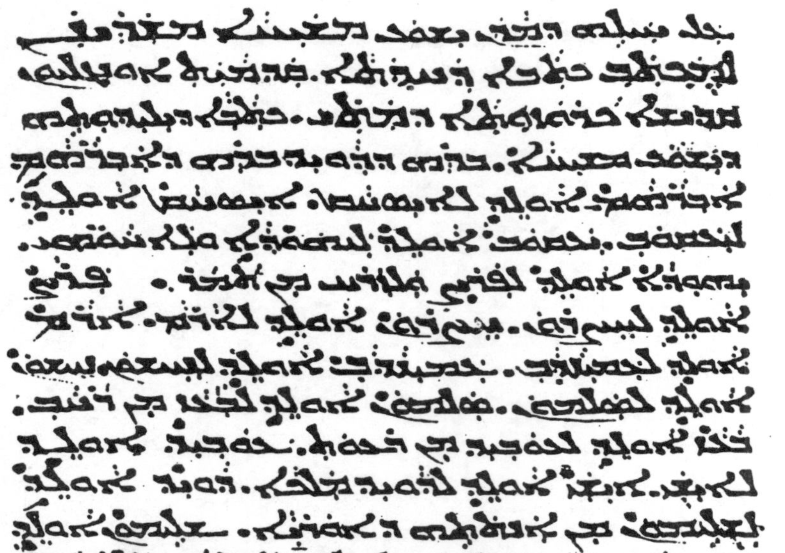

ARAMAIC LIGHT
ON THE
GOSPEL OF MATTHEW

Aramaic New Testament Series – Volume 1

Other books in print by Rocco A. Errico:

Setting A Trap for God: The Aramaic Prayer of Jesus
Let There Be Light: The Seven Keys
And There Was Light
The Mysteries of Creation: The Genesis Story
The Message Of Matthew: An Annotated Parallel Aramaic-English Gospel of Matthew
Classical Aramaic—Grammar Book 1

Spanish publication:
La Antigua Oración Aramea de Jesús: El Padrenuestro

Other books in print by George M. Lamsa:

The Holy Bible from the Ancient Eastern Text
New Testament Origin
The Shepherd of All—The 23rd Psalm
The Kingdom on Earth
Idioms in the Bible Explained & A Key to the Original Gospels

ARAMAIC LIGHT
ON THE
GOSPEL OF MATTHEW

A COMMENTARY ON THE TEACHINGS
OF JESUS FROM THE ARAMAIC AND
UNCHANGED NEAR EASTERN CUSTOMS

Aramaic New Testament Series — Volume 1

ROCCO A. ERRICO / GEORGE M. LAMSA

Noohra Foundation, *Publisher*
1045 E Don Diego Ave
Santa Fe, New Mexico 87501

First Edition 2000

ISBN: 0-9631292-6-0

May 2000

As a token of appreciation for your
generous support and unwavering interest in furthering
the Aramaic work, I dedicate this commentary to you
Ms. Nell E. Clement

CONTENTS

THE COMMENTARY

FOREWORD
by Rocco A. Errico

AN INIMITABLE COMMENTARY

Aramaic Light on the Gospel of Matthew is a distinctive and incomparable commentary for several reasons. First, it is the only writing that provides access to a clearer understanding of the Semitic, New Testament, Near Eastern times. This understanding illuminates difficult and puzzling passages of the New Testament and offers unparalleled insight into the character and behavior of the people.

Dr. George M. Lamsa, the coauthor, was a native Aramaic speaking Assyrian and came from an area of the Near East where the people were still living and practicing much of the ancient Semitic customs and manners. He grew up in that part of the ancient biblical land from which Abraham migrated to Palestine. Dr. Lamsa's family lived a simple pastoral life, as did his ancestors during the time of the patriarchs. Even to this day these Aramaic speaking people converse in idioms and parables, some of which would be difficult for Westerners to comprehend.

Second, through this work we can venture into the New Testament intelligently and empathetically and into the ambience in which it first took form. We then can enjoy a genuine intellectual as well as a spiritual relationship with those Semites who aspired ardently and sincerely in their own manner to contribute great spiritual truths for the upliftment of humanity.

Third, the commentary acts as a Near Eastern guide, revealing to the Western mind a more intimate view of the socio-religious and psychological environment of the period. It reveals to us the man Jesus, his teachings, apostles, disciples, followers, and opponents in the light of his own language, people and times.

DR. LAMSA'S ORIGINAL COMMENTARY

When Dr. Lamsa wrote *Gospel Light*—a commentary on the four gospels (Matthew, Mark, Luke and John)—his publisher and his friends advised him to comment only on the most difficult and important verses. They especially asked him to elucidate passages of Scripture that had become obscure through translation and misunderstanding of Near Eastern word meanings, idioms, and culture. While he was preparing *Gospel Light,* Dr. Lamsa was constantly cognizant of the size of the book. He was writing this commentary during the depression and he knew that if the manuscript was too large, the publishers would reject it.

When *Gospel Light* made its appearance in 1936, it received worldwide acclaim and publicity. This recognition brought requests from various regions in the United States and Canada for a commentary on the remainder of the New Testament—Acts to Revelation. In the subsequent years, Dr. Lamsa completed three more works on the Bible: *New Testament Commentary, More Light on the Gospel* and *Old Testament Light.* Then, during the time Dr. Lamsa and I were collaborating (1965-1970), we were inundated with requests for further commentaries on holy Scripture. In the early 1970's we drafted additional material on the Bible but these works were not completed.

Now, with the kind and generous permission of Dr. Lamsa's niece, Mrs. David (Nina) Shabaz, I have been editing, expanding, annotating and preparing Dr. Lamsa's previous volumes in a new format. I am also adding information derived from my continual research in the Aramaic language and am completing the comments that Dr. Lamsa and I had only drafted. *Aramaic Light on the Gospel of Matthew* contains over 50% new material.

FORMATION OF THIS COMMENTARY

Dr. Lamsa and I had worked together for ten years before he passed from this earthly life on September 22, 1975. I have been lecturing, writing, teaching and continuing the Aramaic work since his passing. Before Dr. Lamsa became ill, he told me how he wanted to rewrite his previous commentaries. He also wanted to present each gospel as a complete work (in separate volumes) and not scattered through several volumes as they were then. I have complied with his last wishes. This is the beginning volume of the New Testament series based on the Aramaic language and on the ancient, Semitic, cultural habits of Near Easterners.

Aramaic Light on the Gospel of Matthew is not a commentary founded on contemporary academic analysis of Scripture. In other words, it does not use critical source/historical and literary methods of interpretation. For example, I do not differentiate between the voice of Jesus and the voice of the early Church traditional teachings that developed after Jesus' crucifixion. (These teachings were put on Jesus' lips and added in the gospels.) Occasionally, in the footnotes, I do make reference to some of the modern, scholarly material on the gospels.

The reader must keep in mind that this commentary works with the received text—that is, with the gospels as we now have them in their present forms—and does not attempt to provide the reader with source/critical studies. I use laymen's language and not theological, specialized terminology. As much as possible, each comment is written in story form. This style is maintained throughout the volume.

All scriptural excerpts are from the King James Version of the New Testament. I have also quoted scriptural passages from *The Holy Bible from Ancient Eastern Manuscripts* by Dr. George M. Lamsa. Each quotation is identified as the "Lamsa Translation." There are other passages of Scripture in the body of the comments that I have translated directly from the Aramaic Peshitta text. These citations are identified as "Aramaic Peshitta text, Errico."

Most of the time, when referring to Semites in the comments, I refer to Near Eastern Semites and not Westernized Semitic peoples. I also have attempted as much as possible to avoid a collision with denominational interpretations and theological implications. However, in certain scriptural passages cited in this volume it became unavoidable. Apparently some biblical interpreters have unwittingly formed and established monumental dogmas and confusing notions on verses that were only idioms, metaphors or customs. The expressions in the gospels and most of the New Testament are Semitic and, therefore, we must understand them from their Near Eastern, cultural viewpoint.

According to Scripture, God, through revelation, had told the prophets to write in a plain and simple language (see Deuteronomy 27:8 and Habakkuk 2:2). But, because of translating from one language to another, adding and omitting from Scripture, and a lack of understanding of the Near Eastern customs and psychology by translators, Scripture has suffered many losses. Thousands of passages that were once clear in the original language became obscure and the subject of theological controversies. Both the literalist interpreter and the modern thinker have contributed to a misunderstanding of Scripture, not through a fault of their own, but because the Bible comes to us from a culture distinct from our forms of thinking.

OUR CHANGING WORLD

The world has made great changes in the past 2,000 years. Customs and manners that existed in Jesus' day and withstood change until the middle of the twentieth century in certain areas of the Near East have either disappeared or are gradually disappearing. Originally, a remnant of people in the mountain vastness of Kurdistan had kept the ancient biblical customs and language alive. Today, the language in which Jesus, his apostles, and disciples first proclaimed the glorious gospel of the kingdom of God is spoken only by small, surviving clusters of Aramaic speaking people in different parts of the world.

Nevertheless, the ethical teachings of Jesus and the Hebrew prophets have not changed. The central truths remain the same as of yore and are just as practical for today's world. For example, in our modern Western style of living we hardly ever see an ox or a donkey fallen under a burden on a highway, except in third world countries. But we see cars and trucks stalled on our highways and drivers needing help from those passing by. Therefore, if Jesus' gospel had been written today, it would read: "If you should see a motorist stranded on the road, do not pass by. Give aid to your neighbor." Nor can we imagine an ox with its mouth muzzled, threshing wheat under its feet. However, there are thousands of laborers who receive very little pay and are often restrained from eating of the crops that they raised for their landowners. Jesus' gospel addressed problems such as these.

We can apply his practical teaching for the needs in our present society. But the main barrier to surmount is the lack of knowledge of the idiomatic language, customs, parables, and similes whereby Jesus so aptly and ably illustrated and illumined his gospel of the kingdom. People in Jesus' day understood the new message he taught because they knew the issues and problems which were prevalent. Jesus' gospel of the kingdom was to empower the people to solve and overcome the difficulties and challenges they were facing. His teaching was revealed and written to a simple and illiterate people who spoke in unobtrusive ways and counted on their fingers. They would not have understood complicated theological theories or commentaries.

As another example, Jesus' disciples and followers knew very well that even giving a child or a thirsty traveler a cup of water was a tremendous favor in the Near East. That simple act merited a reward, because in those lands water was scarce; people had food, but they often retired at night dying of thirst. Who would think of granting a reward to a person for a glass of water in America or Europe where water is abundant.

ANCIENT AUTHORS

The authors of the four gospels were not concerned about order, sequence and time. Their main interest was to record the precious teaching of their master, so that they could impart it to their followers. Each portion of the gospel writing was transcribed on separate scrolls which were later compiled by the evangelists and placed in the order they wanted. Each book was compiled in its own way for its distinct use among the early community of believers. For instance, Mark's gospel is almost an identical copy of Matthew's earlier scrolls. Nearly everything in Mark is in the gospel of Matthew. But some of the material may have been put in a different order. Nevertheless, all of the four gospels give us some idea of the times in which the events took place during Jesus' ministry.

ACKNOWLEDGMENTS AND FINAL WORD

My very sincere and heartfelt thanks and appreciation to Ms. Sue Edwards, Ms. Ann Milbourn, and Ms. Linetta Izenman for their constructive suggestions and assistance in preparing this manuscript for publication.

These comments on the Gospel of Matthew are the only works based solely on Aramaic and the Near Eastern Semitic culture. They were written not to leave the impression that we have not understood Jesus' gospel of the kingdom but to present a clearer picture and setting in which that gospel comes to us. May this commentary be a light and guide to those who seek to understand more fully the eternal truths which were once spoken by the Semitic, Galilean prophet—Jesus of Nazareth.

To all the readers of this commentary, I say to you: *taybootha washlama dalaha nehwoon amhon hasha walmeen.* "The grace (loving kindness) and peace of God be with you now and always!"

Rocco A. Errico, October 22, 1999.

FOREWORD
By George M. Lamsa[1]

This volume is the result of many questions asked by men and women who have attended my lectures on Aramaic. Letters of inquiry have also come from ministers and laymen of many Christian denominations and other faiths who have read my translation of *The Gospels from Aramaic*[2] and other books on this subject. Many of these people expressed the desire to have, in writing, Aramaic interpretation of the passages that I had explained in my lectures. They also wanted other obscure and important passages in the Gospel narrative explained from my knowledge of ancient Semitic customs. Many lovers of the Bible who value truth more than pride and sectarian dogmas are ready to welcome any light thrown on the teachings of Jesus and any suggestion that makes them clearer.

In this work no attempt is made to discuss theological issues nor to describe distances, localities or dates. This has already been done by others who have made a thorough study of these subjects. When I first wrote this book [1936], I had to think in both Aramaic, my mother tongue, and English, my adopted tongue.

Near Eastern and Western scholars agree Aramaic was the language of Jesus and his disciples. However, not all Western scholars believe that the New Testament was written in Aramaic first before Greek. Nevertheless, the antiquity and originality of the Eastern Aramaic text is always defended by Near Eastern, Semitic Christians of all denominations. So far not the slightest evidence contrary to this assumption has been discovered.

I pray God this work will prove helpful to all lovers of the teachings of the beloved Lord and Master-Teacher of Galilee, Jesus

---

[1]Dr. Lamsa's foreword appeared in the 1936 edition of *GOSPEL LIGHT*. I have edited and expanded only a small portion of his foreword with excerpts from some of his other writings.

[2]Dr. Lamsa's translation of the four gospels—published 1933.

of Nazareth. I thank God for preserving my people and their ancient language to the present day. I pray that this work will help the readers of this book to better understand the gospel message especially in these days when Christianity is challenged and unity is needed.

I also pray that denominational and creedal differences will be overlooked. Let us unite in one accord for the common purpose of understanding Jesus' message of the kingdom—a message which is the cornerstone for a human society wherein harmony and peace may reign on earth. May God make us worthy partakers of this glorious, heavenly kingdom.

FOREWORD
by John Peabody Harrington, D.Sc.
Ethnologist
Smithsonian Institution, Washington, D.C.[1]

Miracle of miracles to me is the survival of the language of Christ through all the vicissitudes of the centuries even down to our own time, as a vernacular and literary tongue, and the power of a native reared to speak this tongue to interpret the gospels, the Acts of the Apostles, and other writings of the New Testament with floods of newer and truer light. It is indeed as if this language were a precious bit of amber which has embedded in it and thus preserved throughout the ages some bit of prehistoric life which otherwise would not be known.

Hidden away in the mountains of Kurdistan and Mesopotamia this tongue, almost exactly in the form spoken by the Master two thousand years ago, has escaped by miracle indeed being trampled under foot by conquering armies of Greeks, Persians, Romans, and Turks, to carry with it and have embedded in it, like the specimen embalmed in ancient amber, the life and thought and customs unaltered of people who lived in the time of Christ and in that period before his life which laid the foundation for the Jewish and Christian faiths.

Lamsa's claims that customs, manners and languages in his country have not changed since the time of Jesus are strongly supported by recent facts brought to light in Ethiopia. Ancient tribes with their unchanged customs and languages are just brought before the attention of western scholars. The unbroken dynastic descent of Emperor Haile Selassie I of Ethiopia may seem unbelievable to westerners, but it is a fact and unbroken tradition to the people of Ethiopia. This is because of isolation. It is true that our civilization is

---

[1]This foreword appeared in *GOSPEL LIGHT* when it was first published in 1936.

changing every day, but Ethiopians and Assyrians have been for centuries isolated in their mountain regions cut off from the rest of the world; then again, what to us looks "old," to them is sacred and valuable, their very life is based on their ancestry and their ancient customs and traditions which they tenaciously wish to carry on to future generations.

No foreigner to Dr. Lamsa's Assyrian nationality, however learned or studious even if he spent his life among the mountaineers, could do the present task of interpreting the New Testament to the western world with quite the fidelity and back-ground that comes from one raised on an Assyrian mother's knee. Speaking both the Christian and Jewish dialects of modern Assyrian of the region, he knows the language of Christ even as the apostles knew it and has the feeling for nicety of expression which is lost or which has been overlooked in many of the passages of the Greek translation which has hitherto been the means of communication between the words and times of Christ and our western civilization. This has indeed been a task to tax all the knowledge and linguistic knack of this comparatively young Assyrian who has consecrated his life to this service for mankind.

It will be noted in the following pages that Dr. Lamsa has touched only on the passages that have not been fully understood.[2] To many of these he has given new life—a brilliant interpretation taken from the standpoint of his own oriental [Semitic] life. Words have survived, every word a bundle of meanings which combine with the meanings of other words to form a fabric as delicate as that of an oriental rug and as impossible for western factory-made learning or machinery to imitate. The survival of the personal mechanism to feel for and interpret is in itself as great a miracle as that of the survival of the language.

It has been a popular fallacy that the so-called modern dialects of Assyrian, which is but another name of Aramaic, have become

---

[2]This statement, of course, only applies to *GOSPEL LIGHT* when it was first published.

bastardized, and that it is impossible for any language to maintain itself without the most fundamental changes during a period of two thousand years. Let whoever wishes to believe this do so. When we actually take the Aramaic words recorded in the New Testament and compare them with the modern, we are astounded to find them unchanged. In fact, Dr. Lamsa makes an interesting point that any literary language, such as that in which the old Assyrian gospels are written, is of necessity more or less artificial and flowery, so that the modern language such as Dr. Lamsa himself talks is more like the daily speech of Christ and his disciples than like any embellished literary form of the language. The colloquial then and now is the sea, the literary is the surface agitation and foam.

Even to those interested principally in Judaism, Lamsa's writings, as those of a speaker of a pure Semitic language, have a fundamental appeal. The gospels were written for Semitics. Lamsa gives us the semantics of Semitics. To all who love the rich spiritual life and theology of the Jewish people, Lamsa will have almost as much claim to approach as to Christians. The mountain Assyrian with his Christian religion is as purely Semitic, religion and all, as could be his brother of Jewish or Mohammedan culture and faith.

Greek came into the story of the New Testament merely because it was the European language spoken nearest to the Semitic territory and the only one which has spilled over liberally into that territory. Jews and Jewish Christians in Alexandria, Egypt, which has since the earliest times had large Semitic and Greek population, realizing that they were fast giving up their Aramaic tongue, translated their "biblia" or scriptures with little preparation into the Greek language as the Septuagint. Saint Jerome in the fourth century wrote the Vulgate. Further European translations were based on Greek and Latin, with some scholarly recourse to Hebrew; Aramaic in its modern form was used not at all. The miracle of its discovery and utilization as a new key to the understanding of the Scripture will constantly impress the reader of Dr. Lamsa's fact filled pages.

INTRODUCTION
Aramaic New Testament Series

Throughout the centuries, people of different countries have attempted to portray the life and teachings of Jesus as though he came from their lands and ethnic backgrounds. Europeans have depicted Jesus with light hair and blue eyes. Abyssinians have interpreted him as having curly hair, a dark face, and clad in nomadic attire. Hindus have portrayed him as a learned mystic with an ascetic face, meditating in the shadow of the temples. Russians have imagined Jesus like themselves.

A SEMITIC VIEW OF JESUS

Semites, however, truly claim Jesus because he was a genuine son of the Near East. He was born and reared among Semitic peoples. Jesus was an Aramaic speaking Semite. Their customs and manners played an important part in his life and teaching. They, therefore, know and understand him far better than others. Scripture prohibits making pictures of any sort; nevertheless, they visualize him through their mind's eye. They picture him as a Near Easterner: dark olive complexion, bright brown eyes, full bushy beard and mustache, strong body and masculine features. Some even picture him as six feet tall.

When Jesus spoke or taught, it would be with extravagant expansiveness and vivid, gripping imagery. Being Semitic, he would also impress his listeners with exaggerated speech. At the same time, he told his stories with utter simplicity and an uncommon portrayal of certain human relations. His style of storytelling was poetic, humorous and, at times, filled with tension. He was fully human, revealing passionate and loving feelings. On other occasions, he showed irritability and great sorrow. All this is typical of Near Eastern temperament.

One of the most amazing facts about Jesus is that, regardless of his ethnic background, he appeals to people of all nationalities. His spiritual genius and nature and his practical teaching that transcends all human boundaries, reveal him as he actually was—a man without a country. Nevertheless, people throughout the world claim him as their own. All racial characteristics retire into the background in the unique drama of his life. No forms of prejudice or human limitations can interfere with his universal, all-encompassing message. Although he was born in a poor home and brought up in a small village, Jesus appeals to the rich and poor, to the conqueror and conquered. Nothing has been able to overshadow his influence throughout these many centuries.

THE DESCENDANTS OF THE ANCIENT ASSYRIANS

There are certain aspects in Jesus' life and teaching that the descendants of his own race could best explain, such as their own Semitic life-style and Near Eastern traditions. It is this phase of his teachings and sayings that this New Testament series endeavors to illustrate. What we have written in this commentary is based on customs and practices that have remained undisturbed from early biblical times up to the eve of World War I. As strange as this might seem, a fragment of that ancient Semitic civilization had survived, without change, in Mesopotamia and Kurdistan until the early 1900's. In the rugged mountainous country north of Iraq, European nations discovered a small, feeble remnant—the descendants of the once mighty Assyrian nation and Ten Northern Tribes of Israel.

Since the fall of Nineveh in 610 B.C.E., empires have risen and fallen. New nations have been born and old nations have perished. Invading armies of Greeks, Persians, Arabs, Mongols and Turks have fought their battles for supremacy upon the plains of Arbela (Mesopotamia). The sound of the triumphant trumpets of the Greek victors in the plains of Arbela did not disturb these Assyrian descendants. Nor were they aware that nomad Arab forces had defeated the Persians at the battle of Kadisia in 637 C.E and that the Persian Empire had fallen before the Moslems after the historic battle of Nehaband in 642 C.E. The waves of conquest continued to flow, but nothing seemed to interfere with the independence of these Assyrian tribes. None of the conquerors attempted to invade the seclusion of these warrior people. They knew very little of the changing history that was taking place in the plains south of their mountain fortresses. Interestingly, until about 1910 the Assyrians called the Turks, *Rhomayeh*, meaning "Romans." They thought these people belonged to the Christian Roman Empire because the Turks invaded Asia Minor by way of Europe and not by way of Mesopotamia.

The survival of these descendants of the ancient Assyrians, their language and customs is nothing short of a miracle of divine providence. Semitic culture and languages have elsewhere either been radically altered or replaced by those of the conquering forces. Even the Jews, in spite of their tenacity in holding to tradition, were unable to withstand the unavoidable changes. Their ancient language went dormant and the old customs were no longer practiced. Their biblical teachings, written by simple men for uncultured people, became a mystery and had to be interpreted with the aid of commentaries.

Dr. W.A. Wigram, a noted English scholar, spent over ten years as a missionary and researcher in Kurdistan. Concerning the survival of the descendants of the ancient Assyrians and their customs, he writes:

> A strange survival in an isolated corner of the world, these last representatives of the ancient Assyrian stock have hitherto kept up the most primitive of Semitic customs to an extent that can hardly be paralleled elsewhere, even in Mesopotamian marsh districts. As an ancient and fossilized Church, they had also preserved ecclesiastical rites and ceremonies which have either perished altogether elsewhere, or else have survived only in almost unrecognizable form. . . . Here are a people who, in the time of the beginning of the Christian era, are found living in the lands where, in the year 600 B.C., the Assyrian stock had been established since history began; nor is there any record of any considerable immigration into, or emigration from, that land in the interval.

Their own traditions affirm that they are of the old Assyrian blood, with a possible intermixture of certain Babylonian or Chaldean elements. . . . It was only natural that this old Semitic stock, living where nothing had ever occurred to disturb their habits of life, should keep up the old Semitic customs. They still lived, or did live till the changes of the Great War brought about an alteration, the life of the Old Testament. Bible customs, or those that we call such, were, of course, not peculiar to the Hebrew, but were the common heritage of all the stock to which he belonged and a part of the atmosphere of the land.[1]

THE ARAMAIC LANGUAGE

To this day, Assyrians and Chaldeans still speak the Aramaic language not only in Kurdistan, Iraq and other areas of the Near East but also in the United States and in different countries. However, the younger generation in the United States is losing their mother tongue. This was the language that Jesus and his disciples spoke throughout Galilee. It became the vernacular of northern Palestine long before the Chaldean captivity because the area had been repopulated with Assyrians brought from Edessa and other regions beyond the Euphrates. In 721 B.C.E., the Assyrians carried away the ten tribes of Israel into Nineveh and scattered them throughout Mesopotamia (Northern Iraq, Afghanistan and Pakistan). Hebrew was almost completely lost as a language. Jews in northern Mesopotamia, Kurdistan and Persia still speak and pray in an Aramaic dialect known as *Leshana Galoth*, "the language of captivity." The dialect spoken in Persia (Iran) is related to the Chaldean or Southern Aramaic.[2]

---

[1]Dr. W. A. Wigram, *THE ASSYRIANS AND THEIR NEIGHBORS*, pp. 177, 178, 185.

[2]The towns where Jews speak Aramaic are: Sindur, Amedia, Barwar, Zakho, Bohtan in Mesopotamia; Bashkala and Diza in Kurdistan; Urmiah and other towns in the province of Adurbajan in Persia (Iran). In other regions, Arabic and other languages have replaced Aramaic.

Aramaic was destined to become Israel's vernacular tongue; but before this could come about it was necessary that the national independence should be destroyed and the people removed from their own home. These events prepared the way for that great change by which the Jewish nation parted with its national tongue and replaced it in some districts entirely by Aramaic, in others by the adoption of Aramaized Hebrew forms. . . .The dialect of Edessa which owing to the Bible version made in it, became the literary language of the Christian Arameans—bearing pre-eminently the title of Syriac—was certainly also employed in ancient times by Jews.[3]

Such a change was inevitable. Aramaic had long before become the language of the Near East. The Edessan dialect was the *lingua franca* and all literary works were written in this tongue. This was largely due to the long continued influence and power of the Assyrian Empire. Even after the fall of Assyria, the Chaldeans and Persians used this language for purposes of commerce and communications. There were other Aramaic dialects such as Western (Syriac), Chaldean and Hebrew, but these dialects were chiefly used in speech and had only a local interest. The Jews and Syrians could not have engaged in commerce and diplomacy without the knowledge of northern Aramaic. The high officials of King Hezekiah requested that the ambassador of the Assyrian king speak to them in Aramaic.[4] This occurs today in situations where there are many dialects in a language and the most expressive of them is used for literary and commercial purposes.

Palestine was a small country and its inhabitants were chiefly herdsmen. Their vocabulary was limited to their local needs. The smallness of the Palestinian kingdoms is illustrated by the fact that its subjects sought the advice of their rulers in business and other practical affairs. For example, Saul sought the advice of the prophet

---

[3]W. Bacher on "Aramaic Language among the Jew." The *JEWISH ENCYCLOPEDIA*, vol. II, copyright by Funk & Wagnalls Company.
[4]See 2 Kings 18:26; Isaiah 36:11.

Samuel in locating his father's lost donkeys. At that time, Samuel was the ruler in Israel. Solomon's wisdom and judgment were sought to decide on the parentage of an infant.

However, this was not the case in the great empires of Assyria, Chaldea and Persia. The kings of these kingdoms were worshiped as deities and the common people could not approach them. In these ancient lands, a high civilization existed thousands of years before the arrival of the Hebrew patriarch, Abraham. Aramaic was, at that time, a literary language; Hammurabi's code of law was written in that language. During and after the exile, the Jews made extensive use of this language. Josephus and other writers also wrote in Aramaic.

Aramaic has continued to the present day with some slight variations between the written and the spoken forms. There is no such thing as modern Aramaic. Language is a process and cannot be invented in a day or night. Differences exist between the literary and the vernacular because writers, in the process of time, improve and beautify the written language while the colloquial remains more or less in its original form. The vernacular of any language is, therefore, the older form. For instance, when the people of Anatolia, who speak Turkish, go to Constantinople or Ankara, they are not able to understand clearly the Turkish speech that the people use there. This is because the people of Constantinople and Ankara borrow many of their expressions from Arabic and European languages.

It is indisputable that Aramaic has continued unchanged to the present day. The greatest evidence in support of this is that the same Aramaic words retained in the Greek version of the New Testament are still in use both in the vernacular and written forms of the language. It is significant that all Aramaic literature, from the earliest centuries to the present time, is written without the slightest variation. This is further illustrated by the maintenance of the ancient customs as well as the costumes worn by the Assyrian people in Kurdistan. There is an amazing similarity, as shown in the clay tablets made centuries before Christ, between the Assyrian ancestors in the facial likeness and head gear and that of the present day Assyrian. Again, concerning the language, Dr. Wigram writes:

One thing is certain, that the Assyrians boast with justice that they alone of all Christian nations still keep as their spoken language what is acknowledged to be the language of Palestine in the first century, and that therefore, they alone among Christian nations, if we except a few villages that may still exist in Lebanon, use regularly the language of Christ. . . .[5]

ANCIENT BIBLICAL CUSTOMS

It is clear that the Assyrians have preserved what might be called the background of the biblical culture that existed before Nineveh was built and Abraham had migrated to Palestine. They are the direct descendants of the people who laid the foundation of the great civilization that made history. In that part of the ancient world some of the people still lead nomadic lives. Tents are made of the hair of goats and continue to be the home of the roaming tribes. Today, however, they too are disappearing.

Houses in the mountains of Northern Iraq are built in the same style as they were in the days of Hammurabi. The people still use sheep and goatskins as containers. Oxen that are used for threshing have their mouths muzzled so that they may not eat any of the scarce wheat. The earthen oven, dug in the houses and heated with grass gathered from the fields by women, has been continuously used. Sheep and goats are separated as in the ancient days. The old-fashioned earthen lamp, now as then, is lighted with butter and not oil.

Two women usually operate the hand grinder to grind wheat. These people still employ the ass's millstone to extract oil. Burdens are carried on the backs of men, women and animals as they have always been throughout the centuries. Laborers are roused in the morning by the crowing of the cock that announces the hour for work

---

[5] Dr. W. A. Wigram, *THE ASSYRIANS AND THEIR NEIGHBORS*, p. 181. However, there are also over one million Chaldeans and Syrians who speak and use regularly the language of Jesus. In 1950, a community of Jews speaking the Edessan form of Aramaic had migrated from Northern Iraq to Israel.

and for prayer just as in biblical days. In this area where clocks are unknown, time is still measured by the falling shadows of the sun.[6] At night a servant sits at the door of the house looking for the return of the master and neither can tell the hour because time cannot be measured in the darkness.

Spiritual healers and doctors with their medicinal herbs go about as of yore. The tribal blacksmiths and silversmiths continue their trades secretly. Scribes, still, with reed pen in hand, copy manuscripts that they place on their right knee, holding their body upright, supported by their left knee. Styles and fashions of dress have not changed because Near Easterners wish to perpetuate the ways of their ancestors. Each tribe follows after its own customs and practices. Even in Bagdad, an ancient city that had not escaped the invading armies of Mongols and the West, has preserved almost intact her ancient civilization—that is, until the middle of the twentieth century. In 1933 a special article on Bagdad reported:

> Bagdad bazaars are much the same as in Bible times. . . . Sheep may yet be slain to seal a vow and men know the covenant of bread and salt. Sabaean silversmiths, who con the stars, ply their trade now as in the days of Father Abraham.[7]

In contrast with this, one is surprised to see today in Palestine and Syria such modern devices as automobiles, department stores, hotels, fast food concessions, news stands, lunch counters and other innovations. One can also hear new Jewish settlers speaking various European languages as well as American and British English.

JUDAISM, JESUS' TEACHING AND THE GOSPELS

Jesus' gospel of the kingdom and his movement, which spread throughout Palestine, cannot be understood without a thorough

---

[6]See 2 Kings 20:9.

[7]National Geographic Magazine, p. 265, September 1933.

knowledge of Judaism and its Semitic background. These two religious movements did not develop along parallel lines from two distinctive sources of thought; one derives from the other. Judaism represents the seed; Jesus' kingdom movement, later becoming known as Christianity, was the flowering of that seed. Jesus, himself, was an Aramaic speaking Semitic Jewish Rabbi—but not a Rabbi as we now understand the role of a Rabbi. He was known as *Rabbi Eshoa bar Yosep*. The origin of most of the problems in the four canonical gospels can be traced to our not understanding Jewish customs embodied in biblical culture and common to all Semitic people. It is this Semitic atmosphere that connects the gospels with the Hebrew Scriptures and the messianic promises.

Western culture penetrated into the holy land because of the European conquests during the Crusades, the establishment of the Latin kingdom in Syria, and the close commercial relations between the people of Syria, Palestine and Europe. Although the ancient way of life has almost entirely disappeared from Palestine, except in a few isolated areas and small country towns, it remained undiluted among the Assyrian descendants in Mesopotamia and Kurdistan.

The four gospels are not difficult to understand and religion is not so complicated as some people seem to think. These four books belong to the simplest and most direct literature that a human being has ever penned. Most people have been taught to think of religion as something mysterious; otherwise, it could not be termed "religion." This view was common in early times because of the scarcity of books. The owner of a book became the sole authority in interpreting its contents. Later, when books became available to anyone who wished to purchase them, this situation changed. Today, Bibles are given away free. Many people have broken away from established traditions; they think for themselves and are satisfied only with facts.

The reason we have a problem in understanding the gospels is largely due to the rapid changes of customs and manners throughout Europe and the United States—changes which are totally alien to so much of the biblical customs and ways of thinking. Added to this is the difficulty caused by so many translations of Scripture. For example, the King James Version is based on earlier English translations. Then, we must realize that Greek versions of the gospels do not adequately express Semitic thought; Greek cannot fully carry the manner of speech that is characteristic of Semites.

Modern inventions are products of the Occidental mind and cannot be easily understood by the people of the Near East. They need the help of Western people. The same holds true with a Near Eastern religion, which Christianity originally was. The Bible was conceived in the minds of Semitic prophets and written primarily for the guidance of their people. Westerners need help from the Near East to fully grasp its modes of thinking and speaking.

Semitic Christianity preceded Greek and Roman forms of Christianity by many years. Jesus and his disciples were Galileans and his first followers were Galileans, Jews, Syrians, and Assyrians. All these peoples were closely held together by ties of lineage, language and culture. They were all Semitic. It was natural for Jesus' movement to take root in its own native ground; from there it expanded eastward and westward.

GREEK CULTURE

Greek culture and literature are, undoubtedly, the basis of European civilization. Greece has always served as a clearing house for Semitic ideas and religions as well as for commerce. Greece inherited three thousand years of Near Eastern arts and sciences through the fortunes of war and trade.[8] *Christianity entered Europe via Greece; therefore, Greek became the major language of the New Testament and theological notions in Asia Minor and the Western world.* It is true that Europe received its culture and religion by way of Greece, but the Greeks imported them from Asia only after their defeat of the Persians and their conquest of the East. Previous to this,

---

[8]See Walter Burket, *THE ORIENTALIZING REVOLUTION: Near Eastern Influence on Greek Culture in the Early Archaic Age.*

the Persians carried Near Eastern culture to Europe during their conquests of various regions in Greece.

It was the Greeks who copied the Near East and not the reverse. In Assyria and Chaldea, centuries before the Greeks were even known as a people, writing was common among the Semites. They were mining gold and silver, weaving silk and cotton, building temples and establishing their systems of priesthood. These Semites had a diversity of inventions: the wheel, the horse-drawn wagon, coinage, letters of credit, craft, industries, law, government, the calendar, the clock, libraries, schools, cosmetics, income tax, beer, to name only a few.[9]

It is a matter of history that when the Greeks conquered Persia, they were amazed by the wealth and the art of gold and silver craft they found in the luxurious palaces. The countries of Chaldea and Persia were so far beyond Greece in culture that Alexander the Great decided to make Babylon his capital; to further the alliance, he married the daughter of Darius the Persian King.

ARAMAIC AND GREEK ALPHABETS

The Greeks also borrowed their alphabet from the Near East. Its characters still retain the original Semitic names and, to some extent, the original forms that were derived from Semitic objects. A few examples: the first letter, *alpha*—Greek, *alep*—Aramaic, is an Assyrian word for ox and the character *A* represents the head of an ox. The ox was an Assyrian god; the first letter in the Aramaic word for "God," *Alaha*, is *alep*—"a." The second character, *beta*—Greek, *beth*—Aramaic, is the Aramaic letter *B* which resembles the structure of a one-room, ancient Assyrian house. The Greeks divided the shape of the letter in two because the Greeks had two-story houses. *Gamma*—Greek, *gamal*—Aramaic, is the third letter *G*. In Aramaic

---

[9] See Will Durant, *OUR ORIENTAL HERITAGE: The Story of Civilization,* Chapter vii "Sumeria: Orientation—Contributions of the Near East to Western civilization."

it resembles a camel's hump or saddle. There are twenty two letters in the Aramaic and Hebrew alphabets. It was this alphabet that entered Europe via Greece.

Even the Armenians, who are recognized as one of the ancient Christian people, used the Aramaic alphabet and language in Church services from the second century to 500 C.E., when Mesrop invented the present Armenian alphabet. Previous to the fifth century, Armenian Christianity was closely allied to the Assyrian Church. Many of its leaders and writers were Assyrians. The Armenian Church continued using the Near Eastern Aramaic Scriptures until the Monophysite controversy; then for political reasons, the Armenian Church became allied with the Church in the Byzantine Empire.

GREEK AND ARAMAIC INFLUENCES

Greek culture, philosophy and religions had no influence on Jesus and his immediate disciples or early Jewish followers. Palestinian Jews resisted every influence not Semitic. Greek customs and manners were forbidden. During the reigns of Trajan and Hadrian, the Jews were not permitted to learn Greek or use Greek ceremonies. The first part of the Talmud and the Mishnah emphatically declared it was worse for a Jew to learn Greek than to eat swine flesh. With only a few exceptions, Palestinian Jews strictly observed these laws. They jealously preserved their religion, customs and language from contamination. Renan, the famous French scholar and archeologist, who spent many years in the Near East in research work for the imperial Government of France, says:

> It is not probable that Jesus knew Greek. This language was very little spread in Judea beyond the classes who participated in the government, and the towns inhabited by pagans, like Caesarea. . . . . Neither directly nor indirectly, then, did any element of Greek culture reach Jesus. He knew nothing beyond Judaism; his mind preserved that free innocence which an extended and varied culture always weakens. In the very bosom of Judaism he

remained a stranger to many efforts often parallel to his own.[10]

Nearly all Jewish literature from the fourth century B.C.E. to the ninth century C.E. was written in Aramaic. In all parts of the world Jews, generally, continue to use prayers composed in Aramaic. The liturgies of ancient Christian Churches in Syria, Palestine, Iraq, and Iran are also written in Aramaic. The Greek language was not used for such purposes. There are no traces of Greek customs and culture east of the Euphrates. If Greek influence had been strong in the Near East during the first and second centuries, the Greek word *Christos* would have been used instead of *M'sheeha*, "Messiah," in the Near Eastern text of the New Testament, and the Aramaic word *shleeheh*, "sent ones or messengers," would have been *apostolos* in the text. But this was not the case.

The Greeks Hellenized many Aramaic names. Bar-Hebrews, the famous Near Eastern historian of the twelfth century, noted this fact and said that the Greeks changed the forms of many Aramaic nouns and did not pronounce them as given in the originals. For instance, *Nokh*, derived from Aramaic *Noha* meaning "rest," becomes *Nokaus* (Noah) in Greek; *Yacob*, derived from Aramaic *yqb* meaning *"heel,"* becomes *Jacobus* in Greek; *Bar-soma*, from Aramaic *bar* meaning "son" and *soma* meaning "fasting," is pronounced *Bar-somos* in Greek. The Aramaic name *Eshoa* or *Eshoo*, from the Hebrew *Yehoshua* meaning "to help, save," in Greek becomes *Iesus* (Jesus). *Kuria*, "town," becomes *korios*; *paracleta*, from Aramaic *prak* meaning "to save or comfort," becomes parakletos;

We find a few Greek words in early Aramaic, but these were in common use: *estrategy* (soldiers), *estadawata* (miles), *costonaries* (guards). Some Jews used Greek names, but this does not necessarily mean they spoke Greek. When the Jews were in Chaldea, they adopted Chaldean names. This same practice is carried on today. Jews adopt the personal names in the language of the countries in which they live. (Dr. Lamsa adopted the English name "George" when he

---

[10]Ernest Renan, *THE LIFE OF JESUS*, pp. 90, 92.

entered the United States. His name was simply "Lamsa." George M. Lamsa was the full name he used in America. The "M" stands for his tribe, "Mamisho.")[11]

The Jews in Alexandria spoke Greek because they didn't understand Aramaic. This explains why Philo, the Jewish philosopher, also wrote in Greek. The Jews translated their Hebrew Bible into Greek for the Jews who understood neither Aramaic or Hebrew. The name of this translation is "Septuagint." They did not use this Greek translation of the Hebrew Bible in Palestine, where it would not have been understood and where the original text was in common use. Interestingly, Semitic Christians in various areas of the Near East did not use or accept the Greek Septuagint. This is still true today. The Near Eastern text of the Hebrew Bible, known as the Peshitta, is the authorized text of the Assyrians, Chaldean Roman Catholics, Jacobites and other Semitic groups of Christians. All these Semitic people strongly support the antiquity and originality of the Peshitta text of the Hebrew Bible despite their theological differences.

The Septuagint was rejected partly because it contained the books of the Apocrypha; these books were not included in the Jewish Canon. This question was debated at the Jewish Council of Jamnia in 90 C.E. and settled in favor of the Palestinian decision. It was only after St. Jerome made the Latin Vulgate in the fourth century C.E. that the Roman Catholic Church accepted the Apocrypha books as canonical.

THE GOSPELS IN ARAMAIC

If Jesus had written the gospels, they would have told the story differently. But the gospels were written by Galileans, in their own northern Aramaic dialect, for use among their own Semitic speaking people. Their lord was a Galilean who spoke Galilean Aramaic and,

---

[11]For more details on this particular custom see George M. Lamsa, *THE GOSPELS FROM ARAMAIC*, "Introduction," p. xvi, 1933.

inexperienced as these Galileans were, they would not have attempted to record this sacred material in an alien tongue. They did not have access to Bible manuscripts and commentaries. But they did their best to record the sayings, parables, and works of their master-teacher that they had heard and learned by heart.

The gospels were written for the followers who had seen and heard Jesus and for those who were to follow them. The simple folk around the lake of Galilee were the people to whom this new teaching made its appeal. They were the likely ones to welcome an account, written in their language, that contained the words and works of their beloved teacher. The Jews in the South would not as readily accept this strange Galilean gospel.

Jerusalem was an international city and many languages and dialects were spoken there, as was seen in the days of Pentecost. The people of other nationalities would not have been interested, at this time, in the life of a man who had met with a horrible death and whose teachings were not understood. And, except for the Galilean merchants who had become followers of Jesus, the Jews in Jerusalem and other prosperous and cultured centers were satisfied with their own religion and were not ready to welcome anything that tended to disturb long-established traditions.

Dr. F. C. Burkitt of Cambridge made the following remarks:

But our Lord and his first disciples spoke Aramaic; there is nothing to suggest that they were acquainted with the current Greek version. In the Synagogues they would hear the Scriptures read in the original Hebrew, followed by a more or less stereotyped rendering into the Aramaic of Palestine, the language of the country, itself a cousin of Hebrew. A faithfully reported saying therefore of Jesus or of Peter ought to agree with the Hebrew against the Greek, or at least ought not to acquire its point and appropriateness from a peculiar rendering in the Greek. . . . Apart from questions of language and purely literary criticism, the three Synoptic Gospels might be translations from the Aramaic. The main ideas of the Synoptic Gospels, the fundamental phrases round which move the thoughts belonging to the Gospel, all have their explanation and illustration from contemporary Judaism. The kingdom of God, the Christ or Messiah, the Day of Judgment, treasure in heaven, Abraham's bosom—all these are Jewish ideas entirely foreign to the native thought of the Graeco-Roman world.[12]

Had the gospels been written in the Chaldean dialect, the contents would have been quite different. Take, for example, the Greek word *logos* that appears in John 1:1, Greek version. This word *logos* is a direct translation of the northern Aramaic word *miltha*, meaning "word, utterance." It is not a translation of the Southern Aramaic (Chaldean) word *memra*, meaning "sentence."

What seems obscure in the gospel becomes quite lucid when translated from the Near Eastern text written in northern Aramaic. Dr. Gustav Dalman was cognizant of the influence of northern Aramaic in Palestine. He writes:

> The spread of Aramaic in the original Hebrew Palestine must already have begun in the year 721 B.C., when Samaria was peopled by Mesopotamian colonists. Through the influence of the Babylonian and later, the Persian Governments, it continued to spread. . . . finally reaching Southern Palestine, when the leading classes were deported from there and supplanted by the alien element. The Judean exiles on their return made a last attempt to preserve their native language[13]

Dr. C.F. Burney of Oxford University is equally explicit on this point:

> Even in the pre-exilic times (2 Kings 18:26) Aramaic was the *lingua franca* of international communication. It must have been widely used, along with Babylonian, in the Neo-Babylonian kingdom. Cuneiform tablets of the late Assyrian, Neo-Babylonian

---

[12]Dr. F. C. Burkitt, *THE EARLIEST SOURCES FOR THE LIFE OF JESUS*, pp. 25 and 29.

[13]Gustave Dalman, *JESUS—JESHUA*. Studies in the Gospels, p. 8.

and Achaemenian periods, bear Aramaic dockets; and scribes or secretaries were employed for the purpose of writing Aramaic upon parchment along with those whose business it was to write Babylonian in cuneiform upon clay tablets. . . .The mass of the people who did not read books came more and more to speak Aramaic exclusively and to lose the knowledge of Hebrew.[14]

The earliest gospel recording was probably written 15 years after Jesus' crucifixion and resurrection. There is no reason to date it later. The synoptic gospels—Matthew, Mark and Luke—as we now have them were probably compiled at a later date, but all dating is conjectural. Some scholars date them between 45 to 60 C.E. and others date them around 70 to 85 C.E. The gospel of John has a very late date circa 90 C.E. Regardless of the dating, the earliest gospel that contained Jesus' sayings, parables and works of healing was probably between 42 and 45 C.E. Aramaic writing was common. The sacred Hebrew Scriptures were in circulation. The traditions of the Jewish elders were also in writing and circulating. (Dr. Lamsa believes that the gospel writers Matthew and John were witnesses who had seen and heard Jesus. They were Galileans who accepted him from the beginning. The Semitic Galileans were Jews by faith and not by race. These men remembered what he had said and done.) [15] Dr. Lamsa makes the following suggestion:

> Had the gospel been written in 60 or 90 C.E., writers could not have mastered the extensive material, especially if they were writing in Greek without a knowledge of Aramaic and without Aramaic documents. For example, how could a modern day Japanese reproduce Abraham Lincoln's Gettysburg address with no knowledge of English and without a copy of it? It is more reasonable to suppose that the gospels were written early in

---

[14] C. F. Burney, *THE ARAMAIC ORIGIN OF THE FOURTH GOSPEL*, p. 21.

[15]Today almost all New Testament scholars reject the notion that any gospel writer was an eyewitness. Near Easterners who have not come under the influence of Western scholarship believe that Matthew and John were eye witnesses in spite of the fact that redactors (editors) reworked their gospels.

Aramaic and in their native setting. Later, Jewish and Syrian Christians translated them into Greek just as translations are made today on the mission field. These translators knew the Koine or vernacular Greek but they were not sufficiently familiar with Greek idioms and they thought their own Aramaic idioms would carry the same meanings in Greek. This is why translators render literally such Semitic idioms as "he breathed on them" which means in Aramaic "he gave them courage, or he encouraged them."[16] Today when a foreigner thinks in his own language and speaks in English, his idioms become just as meaningless.[17]

The gospels contain only an outline of the teaching of Jesus and do not go into details for two reasons. First, the issues were still fresh in the minds of the people who were contemporaries. Second, when Jesus preached, he did not explain the issues but answered the questions directly. For example, if an American in the 1930's had addressed an audience with issues concerning prohibition repeal, N.R.A., or oil, the American speaker would have taken it for granted that his audience understood what the basic issues were. A writer does the same thing. However, fifteen years later, a highschool girl or boy reading a book on these issues would need to have them further explained.

If the gospels were written very late in the first century, the writers would have had to explain in detail the issues that were prevalent during Jesus' ministry. Furthermore, if they were originally written in Greek, they could not have retained their Semitic style. The Greek translation of the gospels retains approximately 42 Aramaic words and expressions and explains some of their meanings. But there is not a single sentence in the Near Eastern, Peshitta New Testament that is not in Aramaic and no explanations of word meanings exist in the text.

Interestingly, it is in the New Testament epistles that one comes in direct contact with Greek culture, philosophy and manners totally

---

[16]Jn. 20:22.

[17]George M. Lamsa, *GOSPEL LIGHT*, "Introduction," p. xxx, 1936 ed.

alien to Semites. St. Paul denounces many foreign practices such as idol worship. Some cultural practices were revolting to Semitic people, especially to those who were not in touch with the Graeco-Roman world.

COMPARISON OF TEXTS

The obscurities in the Greek and other versions of Scripture are due to mistranslations of Aramaic words having diverse meanings and to misunderstanding Near Eastern parables and allegories. The original writers were not responsible for these obscurities because they are not found in the Aramaic. For example, Shakespeare cannot be held responsible for mistranslations of his works and plays by the people of the Near East who are unfamiliar with Victorian English idioms and customs. When those who are familiar with the idioms and terms of speech in both Aramaic and English translate scriptural text then these biblical "obscurities" are clearly understood.

According to the Greek text, translated in the King James version, Luke 14:26 reads: "If any man come to me and *hate not* his father, and mother, and wife, and children, and brethren, and sister, yea, and his own life also, he cannot by my disciple." The Aramaic Peshitta text reads: "He who comes to me and *does not put aside* his father, and mother. . . ."[18] This is more in keeping with Jesus' teaching about loving and honoring one's parents.

Missionaries today put aside their parents to go to the mission field but this does not mean they hate them. The Aramaic word *saneh* has many meanings in Aramaic. It does mean "to hate, despise, dislike," but it also means "to stand up, to put out (a light), to snuff out (a candle), *to set to one side*, and a threshing floor." Through confusion of meaning the translator chose the harsh word instead of the more appropriate word.

As another example, in Mark 10:30 we read: "But he shall

---

[18]Lamsa translation.

receive an hundredfold now, in this time, houses, and brethren, and sisters, and *mothers*, and children, and lands, *with persecutions*; and in the world to come eternal life."[19] The Aramaic text reads: "Who shall not receive now, in this time a hundredfold, houses and brothers and sisters and *maidservants* and children and fields and *other worldly things*, and in the world to come life everlasting."[20] Again, the confusion over meanings occur. The Aramaic word *amhatha*, means "maid servants" and the word *emhatha*, means "mothers." Therefore, the better rending is "handmaidens or maid servants." Again, in the same passage of scripture we have a problem with the Aramaic word *radhoopya* from the Semitic root *rdp* which means "to chase, banish, pursue, follow, and persecute." A proper translation would be "pursuits" and not "persecutions." This is in accord with the teaching of Jesus, who told his disciples and followers what they would receive from adhering to his gospel of the kingdom.

In Luke 14:5, the King James version reads: "And answered them, saying, Which of you shall have *an ass* or an ox fallen into a pit, and will not straightway pull him out on the sabbath day." The Aramaic text reads: "And he said to them, which one of you, if *his son* or his ox should fall into a pit on the sabbath day, would not immediately pull and bring him out?"[21] The Greek translator confused the Aramaic word *breh*, "his son," for *hmareh*, "his donkey." The translator probably thought that the first part of the word was blotted out since the word that followed "son" was "ox." So, he thought the original word was "ass." However, Near Easterners, in their parables or sayings, are more likely to link a human being with an animal for emphasis rather than link two animals in their proverb.

---

[19]King James version.
[20] Mk. 10:30, Aramaic Peshitta text, Lamsa translation.
[21]Aramaic Peshitta text, Lamsa translation.

THE PURPOSE OF THIS COMMENTARY

The Aramaic New Testament series, Volume 1, beginning with the Gospel of Matthew, is not a critical commentary discussing textual matters. The material pertaining to textual criticism is extremely extensive and cannot be dealt with even briefly in this volume or in the volumes that follow. This commentary is based upon the knowledge of Aramaic and ancient customs that have survived unaltered in Dr. Lamsa's native country and home. The purpose of this work is to bring enlightenment to as many passages of scripture as possible and to transport the reader into a Near Eastern setting. Also, we trust that the thousands of earnest Bible students and seekers of truth will welcome such help. The aim throughout this book is to illuminate and strengthen the teaching of Jesus with greater clarity and insight.

We also wish to say that in no comment do we deny the efficacy of Jesus' power to do anything miraculous. The issue never is *could he* but *did he* perform certain things. Jesus always refused the demands that were made on him to perform some sort of sign (magic). He did not pose as a magician.

Jesus revealed to humanity a loving, all-inclusive presence he called Father. This was his only theology, if one might call it that. Through his powerful and endearing ministry, Jesus opened the eyes of the blind, cleansed the lepers, healed the physically, emotionally and mentally ill, and raised the dead. And, in the final outcome, he triumphed over death and the grave and we join with the voices of his early followers the wondrous declaration, "he is risen!" But we insist that Jesus never worked any magic or wonders so that he could persuade people. He would not and did not change stones into bread or pull bread and baskets out of the air to prove his powers. His divine mission and miraculous powers are still being demonstrated in the lives of his faithful followers today. The healing power of God still flows through his magnificent gospel of the kingdom, healing thousands of souls. The ever-present ministry of the Christ has healed and comforted untold numbers of broken hearts. Men and women have surrendered to his teaching over the centuries. Herein do we find the greatest miracle of Jesus' mission of the kingdom, that it has never lost its power even to the present day. The living Christ abides forever, healing and transforming the hearts and minds of women, men and children all over the world.

Rocco A. Errico and George M. Lamsa

ABBREVIATIONS

HEBREW BIBLE:

Gen.	Genesis
Ex.	Exodus
Lev.	Leviticus
Num.	Numbers
Deut.	Deuteronomy
1 Sam.	1 Samuel
2 Sam.	2. Samuel
1 Chron.	1 Chronicles
Ps.	Psalm
Prov.	Proverb
Isa.	Isaiah
Jer.	Jeremiah
Ezek.	Ezekiel
Mic.	Micah
Zech.	Zechariah
Mal.	Malachi

NEW TESTAMENT

Mt.	Matthew
Mk.	Mark
Lk.	Luke
Jn.	John
Rom.	Romans
Heb.	Hebrews

OTHER ABBREVIATIONS

B.C.E.	Before the Common Era
C.E.	Common Era (A.D.)
K. J. V.	King James Version

INTRODUCTION
The Gospel According To Matthew

MATTHEW'S NAME

According to Near Eastern tradition, the gospel of Matthew was the Aramaic preaching and writings of the apostle Matthew who originally penned Jesus' teaching. In Aramaic *Mattai* is the shortened form of the name *Mattith-yah(u)* and comes from the Semitic words *natan*, "he gave," and *Yah(u) "Yahweh."* Today the name has come to mean "gift of Yahweh" or "gift of God." In some gospels Matthew is referred to as Levi.[1]

Near Eastern Christians have always believed that Matthew and Zaccheus are the same person.[2] Zaccheus means "victorious." Matthew was a native of Galilee and a tax collector at Capernaum and later at Jericho. It was the policy of the Roman provincial government to transfer tax officials from one place to another and this system was applied in the Near East also.

THE ORIGIN OF THE GOSPEL

As a tax collector, Matthew could read and write. These were indispensable qualifications for his post. His experience in this office reveals itself in the arrangement of the material in his gospel. It is probable that he first prepared a list of the sayings of Jesus, then a list of his important deeds. Jesus' sayings would have been in demand for healing purposes as they still are today among Semitic believers. Thus, Matthew supplied this demand for the words of Jesus when he was traveling with his master and then after his lord's death. Sometime after Jesus' resurrection, additional material had to be added in the

---

[1] See Mk. 2:14; Lk. 5:29 and the gospel of Peter 60.
[2] Lk. 19:2.

1

form of scrolls. He created a detailed outline of Jesus' teaching, correlating all his material by naming localities where they had traveled, the time, the occasion, and other items of information.[3]

Matthew's gospel emphasizes Jesus as the Messiah/Christ and God's kingdom which was at hand. He attempted to convince the Jewish people that Jesus was the Messiah and that the ancient biblical prophecies were fulfilled in Jesus. Matthew, a Galilean, defended his master before the Jewish religious authorities of his day who denounced his lord even after his death.

In the Aramaic Near Eastern Peshitta text, scribes appropriately titled all four canonical gospels as *Karozootha d'Mattai, Markos, Lukas, Yohannan*—"The Preaching of Matthew, Mark, Luke and John." By these titles, we understand that these writings present each writer's own view or version of Jesus' teaching and ministry. It is obvious that the scribe who assembled Matthew's scrolls had given them the title "The Preaching of Matthew" and was responsible for editing, additional materials and narratives such as the birth and genealogy of Jesus. The issues concerning Jesus' ancestry and birth arose later, especially after the resurrection. However, the early community of disciples and followers were concerned only with what Jesus said and did and not about where and how he was born. Up until the beginning of the twentieth century, Near Easterners did not record dates of birth and death and in many regions they still do not record these dates. Births and deaths were always connected with important events, such as wars, special taxation, persecutions, and the rise or fall of rulers and kings.

AUTHORSHIP

In the Near East, authorship is understood differently than in the

---

[3]Today, New Testament scholars believe that it is improbable that the gospel in its present form was the work of an eyewitness apostle. However, Dr. Lamsa did not concur with this concept.

Western world. A book written about the preaching of Matthew or a compilation of Matthew's writings would be known as the Book of Matthew. The reason for this is that the scribe or copyist would not consider himself an author of the material he wrote or compiled. The writings that appear on these scrolls never contain the name of the author or the copyist, especially in the case of sacred literature. For instance, if Joshua had written a book about Moses, the name of the manuscript would be the Book of Moses, but it would not include Joshua's name. As another example, the books of Moses and Joshua give the details of the death and burial of both these Hebrew leaders. But, how could they have recorded their own deaths? What happened was this: Moses and Joshua had possession of the tribal records. But after their deaths, scribes arranged these accounts in the best chronological order possible with supplementary material.

DIFFERENCES IN THE CANONICAL GOSPELS

The differences between the four canonical gospels are largely due to the nature of the material, oral sources, difficulties in obtaining complete sets of scrolls from which to copy, and the locality for which the text was produced. Also, scribes had no access to new material owing to their isolation. Another problem was that certain material that would have appealed to some Semitic communities, like the Jews in Judea, would not have interested other communities, such as Galileans and Syrians. Some would even find the material objectionable. This is the reason that Mark and John omitted the account of Jesus' genealogy and his birth narrative. However, Matthew omitted the story of Jesus and the Samaritan woman at the well because the Jews, at that time, despised the Samaritans. Therefore, a favorable account of a discourse between Jesus, as a Jewish prophet, and a Samaritan woman would have been unacceptable to the Jews. On the other hand, John seized the opportunity to convince the Samaritans and Gentiles that Jesus not only declared his gospel of the kingdom to Jewish people but to Gentiles also.

This practice of omitting and adding material in sacred books was and is common in the Near East. For instance, in Flavius Josephus *"The Antiquities of the Jews,"* a Christian scribe added to Josephus' history a detailed account of Jesus' death and resurrection that reads exactly like the gospels.[4] Also, Aramaic manuscripts, some of which were written in the fifth century C.E., were published by Roman Catholics, Anglicans and Presbyterians in the early 1900's. These publications based on the ancient manuscripts vary according to the beliefs of those who use them. For example, Roman Catholic authorities omit what is not doctrinally acceptable and insert what was formerly rejected by the original author as heresy. Anglicans omit the names of some Near Eastern Church Fathers because they had denounced such credos as "Mary, mother of God" and "God died on the cross." These early Church Fathers said that Mary was the mother of Jesus and was not the mother of God. They also taught that Jesus died on the cross as a man. The original authors are not responsible for these later changes made in their writings. Presbyterians did not change anything but printed accurately from these ancient scrolls.

There is no doubt that at least one of the apostles wrote the basic material that was the basis for two of the gospels (Mark and Luke), and that writer was Matthew. Writing was common at that time.[5] Epistles were exchanged between Christians of Antioch and the Apostles of Jerusalem and between Paul and the churches in Asia Minor. Eusebius quotes Papias to the effect that Matthew wrote his gospel in Hebrew—that is, Aramaic. He further says that Matthew

---

[4]For an account of Josephus and interpolations by Christian scribes, see A MARGINAL JEW: Rethinking the Historical Jesus, John P. Meier, "Josephus," pp. 56-88.

[5]See Acts 15:23. "Behind much that has been written about the synoptics in the past eighty years there have been two almost wholly unspoken assumptions. The firs is that the period of oral transmission was relatively long, we now know, from Qumran preeminently, of quite extensive literary activity in the period." C. S. Mann, *MARK: A New Translation with Introduction and Commentary,* "The Date of Mark's Gospel, p. 73, Anchor Bible, Doubleday, 1986.

and John were the only apostles who left recorded comments.[6] Tradition all over the Near East verifies this.

According to tradition, Matthew's gospel was placed first when the scrolls were compiled because it was the first written document. The early followers of Jesus ought to have known which was the first document and who was its author. Had they known that dispute would have arisen over authorship of these gospels, they would have handed down to us written evidence of dates and other facts. We must also realize that in the ancient Near Eastern world many religious authorities who opposed Jesus' movement burned much of the early literature. Then, during the ten persecutions against Christians much of their writings were also destroyed. Nevertheless, the information that these writings contained was handed down orally.

MODERN THEORIES

New Testament experts hold the theory that Mark, not Matthew, was the first gospel. They theorize that our present gospel of Matthew is a copy of Mark's gospel with modifications. They also think that many Matthean passages not found in Mark come from early Aramaic collected sayings of Jesus known as Q (Quelle, a German word meaning "source"). This is pure hypothesis.

There are other scholars who suggest that the Apostle Matthew may have been the original author not only of his own gospel but that his material formed the basis for the writings of Mark and Luke—that is, assuming he gathered Jesus' teachings together in a collection similar to the scholarly notion of a Q document. Recently, a research team of scholars have written a book showing that Luke's material for his gospel came originally from Matthew and not Mark or Q writings.

In recent years, advocates of the Two Gospel Hypothesis have been challenged by colleagues to take up a matter which had

---

[6]Modern scholars dispute Eusebius' statement about John and Matthew.

received only passing attention, namely, the origin of the Gospel according to Luke. For many years partisans of this hypothesis have deemed it to be more important methodologically to tackle the question of the relation of the Gospel of Mark to the other two Synoptic Gospels. To this end, considerable time has been spent amassing evidence to show that the Two Gospel Hypothesis can give a plausible account of Mark's composition. A logical outcome of our efforts have been the conclusion that neither Matthew nor Luke was composed on the basis of Mark or Q. Our results have aroused considerable interest. . . .[7]

Most scholars accept the dating of Matthew's gospel in its present form somewhere between 75 and 95 C.E. But most dating for the gospels is conjectural. The original Matthew was probably between 40-45 C.E. A minority of scholars believe all three synoptic gospels were written before 70 C.E. Some biblical historians suggest that the gospel of Matthew was written in Galilee[8] and others teach that it was composed in Antioch.

---

[7]*LUKE'S USE OF MATTHEW, BEYOND THE Q IMPASSE:* A Demonstration by the Research Team of the International Institute for Gospel Studies, Edited by Allan J. McNicol, with David L. Dungan and David B. Peabody with a preface by William R. Farmer, p. 1. See also David Laird Dungan, *A HISTORY OF THE SYNOPTIC PROBLEM: The Canon, the Text, the Composition, and the Interpretation of the Gospels,* Part three, "Current Trends in Understand How the Gospel Were Created," pp. 368-391.

[8]See J. Andrew Overman, *MATTHEW'S GOSPEL AND FORMATIVE JUDAISM: The Social World of the Matthean Community*, Fortress Press, Minneapolis 1990.

THE GOSPEL OF MATTHEW
INTRODUCTION TO
Chapters 1 and 2

THE INFANCY NARRATIVE

New Testament scholars refer to chapters one and two of Matthew's gospel as the "Infancy Narrative." These biblical academicians understand the "Infancy Narrative" not as a biographical tradition but as a "religious" tradition—that is, a theological approach to the messiahship of Jesus of Nazareth. Each episode that occurs in these two chapters has been subjected to much historical and scholastic investigation. Scholars recognize these first two chapters as a "theological prologue" to the gospel of Matthew. They do not perceive them as historical events. (It is very important to keep this understanding in mind when reading the commentary of the first two chapters. And regardless whether the birth narrative of Jesus is historical or not, it is still based on Near Eastern customs.)

These scholars also suggest that a scribe or scribes added the "Infancy Narrative" much later in the developing Christian tradition in the first century. For example, verse 18 of chapter one reads, "Now the birth of Jesus, the Messiah/Christ, was in this manner." When we contrast it with verse one of chapter one, "The ancestral record of Jesus, the Messiah/Christ. . . ," we clearly see that verse 18 begins a completely separate origin of Jesus, distinct from the genealogy which precedes it (vv. 1-17). And when we compare the infancy narrative in the gospel of Luke, we have yet another almost distinct story.[1]

---

[1]For an in-depth study of the infancy narratives in Matthew and Luke, I refer you to my bibliography under the heading "Infancy Narratives." The comments in chapters one and two of this book work only with the Near Eastern Aramaic culture, customs, and language that lie behind the "Infancy Narrative." This book is not a critical source/historical/literary/academic analysis of the Gospel of Matthew.

7

CHAPTER 1

THE ANCESTRY OF JESUS

The book of the generation of Jesus Christ, the son of David, the son of Abraham. Mt. 1:1.

The Aramaic text reads: "The ancestral record of Jesus (*Eshoa* or *Eshoo*) the Anointed (Messiah), the son of David, the son of Abraham."[2] Near Eastern people considered a document that listed ancestors to be very important. One of the many styles for beginning a book was to open with an ancestral table. Semitic writers recorded numerous genealogies throughout the Hebrew Bible.

The scribe who authored Matthew's genealogy divided it into three sections, each with fourteen generations: Section (1) Abraham to King David; Section (2) Solomon to Yokanyah; Section (3) Shelathel to Jesus. In I Chronicles 1:34-3:24, from the Aramaic Peshitta text, we can find the list of names recorded in the first two sections. However, the third section lacks one name. Three sections of "fourteen" generations was an artificial construction and the writer accomplished it through the omission of names. The scribe included ancestral names to prove that Jesus was a descendant of the royal family of David. He also traced his lineage back to Abraham and he wanted to refute any slander concerning Jesus' birth.

"Son of David" is a royal, messianic title. The bearer of this designation was to be the final successor of King David. It was he who was to restore Israel as a free and sovereign nation. "Son of Abraham" is a broader and less restrictive title than "son of David." A "son of Abraham" was to bless all nations and not just Israel.[3] In other words, "son of David" is more nationalistic in its implication, but "son of Abraham" is more universal in its application.

---

[2] Mt. 1:1 Aramaic Peshitta (pronounced P'-sheet-ta) text Errico.
[3] See Gen. 12:1-3.

THE SONS OF TAMAR

And Judas begat Phares and Zara of Thamar; and Phares begat Esrom; and Esrom begat Aram; Mt. 1:3

In biblical days the Hebrews were polygamists like many other Near Eastern Semites. Usually wealthy and noble men married several wives. Poorer class men also followed this custom. In every case, people would give the name of the mother with her son's name. Understanding this Near Eastern custom explains why, in many places throughout the Hebrew Bible, the name of a mother is recorded in connection with the kings of Israel and Judah.

It often happens, as well, that a father may have several sons who bear the same name but were born from different mothers. Therefore, three or four of his boys may have the name Simon but are distinguished from one another by connecting the sons with the names of their mothers. Interestingly, if a boy named Zara dies and another son is born to that same mother, he too might carry the name Zara.

Matthew's genealogy lists Thamar's[4] name because she gave birth to Judah's sons Phares and Zara who were to be distinguished from the sons of Judah's first wife, Bathshua.[5] This follows Near Eastern tradition when recording parentage.

The genealogy mentions three other women besides Thamar. They are Rahab, Ruth, and Bathsheba. Verse five of the Aramaic text records Rahab and Ruth: "Salmon fathered Boaz from *Rahab*; Boaz fathered Obed from *Ruth;* Obed fathered Jesse." Verse six reads: "Jesse fathered King David; David fathered Solomon from the *wife of Uriah* [Bathsheba]." Take note that it reads "wife of Uriah" and not "wife of David."[6] Again the scribe singles out the mother from the

---

[4]More properly the name is *Tamar* in Aramaic and Hebrew and not *Thamar* as in the King James Version. "*Tamar*" in Hebrew means "a palm tree."

[5]For the complete narrative of Judah and *Tamar*, see Genesis, Chapter 38. For the wife of Judah before *Tamar*, see vv. 2, 12, and 1 Chron.2:3.

[6]See 2 Sam. 11:1-27.

9

other wives of the different ancestors.

MARY THE MOTHER OF JESUS

And Jacob begat Joseph the husband of Mary, of whom was born Jesus, who is called Christ. Mt. 1:16

Part A—MARY AND JOSEPH. Matthew's gospel traces Jesus' genealogy from Abraham to Joseph. The author of the genealogical table in this verse used two grammatical forms of the Aramaic verb "to beget," *awlidh* (masculine) and *etthilidh* (feminine). This verb also means "to generate" and "to cause to be born." Throughout the entire lineage, the scribe used the masculine form of the verb. But when he recorded Joseph in the genealogy, he changed the verb from masculine to feminine: "Jacob begat Joseph, the husband of Mary, of whom was born (*etthilidh*) Jesus."

The reference to Mary in the ancestral line shows that Mary, and not one of Joseph's other wives, gave birth to Jesus (see comment on "The Sons of Tamar"). In Scripture when a scribe recorded the name of a king with his mother's name, it was to single out that particular mother from any of the other wives of his father.

If Joseph had no other wives except Mary, the scribe would have used the verb *awlidh* just as he had used it throughout the genealogy. Verse 16 would then read as "Joseph begat Jesus." But because he recorded Mary's name, he used the feminine form of the verb, *etthilidh*, instead of *awlidh*. Again, this indicates that Mary, and no other wife of Joseph, is the mother of Jesus. In many regions of the Near East where people still practice polygamy, whenever a son is mentioned, Near Easterners will also refer to his mother.

Part B—THE CHRIST. Christ is a title and not a proper name. The expression "Jesus Christ" didn't come into use until the middle of the first century C.E. During Jesus' ministry and for sometime after his crucifixion, people referred to him as Jesus of Nazareth.

M'sheeha is the Aramaic term for our English word "Christ."

Christos is the Greek form. In English we drop the Greek ending "*os*" from the word "Christos." *M'sheeha* means "messiah," "anointed," "the consecrated one," or the "appointed one." And, by inference, it means a God-ordained individual. It comes from the Aramaic root *mshakh* and means "to anoint, consecrate, ordain and to smear with oil." Kings, priests, and prophets were anointed with oil into their respective offices.[7] Israel's kings were known as "the Lord's anointed ones."[8]

Oil symbolizes light and light signifies understanding. God's light was to shine through Jesus as the Messiah/Christ. According to John's gospel, Jesus said, "I am the light of the world." This anointed light (understanding) was to be poured upon his disciples, followers, and the world so that all nations might know God's all-inclusive reign of peace and justice.

MARY'S ESPOUSAL TO JOSEPH

Now the birth of Jesus Christ was on this wise; When as his mother Mary was espoused to Joseph, before they came together, she was found with child of the Holy Ghost. Mt. 1:18

The Aramaic text reads: "Now the birth of Jesus, the Anointed (Messiah) was like this: When Mary his mother was promised to Joseph, before they lived together, she was found pregnant by the Holy Spirit."[9] *Mkeera* usually translates into English as "betrothed," "engaged" or "promised." Its verbal root *makhar* means "to barter," "to bargain," "to purchase," or "to acquire for a price."

Most Near Eastern countries still maintain many ancient marriage customs. A remnant of Assyrians and other ancient racial descendants, whose civilization and social life have remained unchanged, continues

---

[7]See Ex. 28:41; Lev. 4:3, 5 and 16; 1 Sam. 2:10,35; 1 Kings 19:16.
[8]See 1 Sam. 24:6.
[9]Mt. 1:18, Aramaic Peshitta text, Errico.

to preserve old Hebrew marriage customs. Brides are paid for just as Jacob had paid for his two Assyrian wives by serving his uncle Laban for fourteen years (Genesis 29:15-28). The bride's father receives the dowry in the form of money or animals. Negotiating for a bride is the same as one would bargain for other articles. What determines the amount of the dowry depends on the prospective bride's social standing, beauty, weight, and health.

Marriage customs in Syria, Egypt, Palestine, and other regions of the Near East differ from the Hebrew custom. In some areas the bride's father pays the groom for marrying his daughter by furnishing an expensive trousseau.

Usually Near Eastern men do not court women as we do here in the West. There is no intimacy of any kind until a couple are married. Men commonly marry women whom they have never known or seen. Parents of the prospective bridegroom arrange a match. If the parents do not make the match, a professional matchmaker under the orders of the parents will find a suitable woman. Near Eastern parents mostly think about the physical stamina of the future wife and not about physical beauty. They feel that the value of a wife depends upon her ability to work, care for the home, and to bear children.

When a matchmaker finds a bride, he or she informs the parents immediately. Then a group of elders and noblemen selected from the town are sent to the house of the prospective bride to bargain about the dowry. After the hearty reception and lavish entertainment, the bride's father again greets the guests. He says to them: "You have come over my eyes. My house is yours." The chief bargainer then responds: "We are honored by you. We are here to seek your hand." This strange phrase "we are here to seek your hand" means we are here to enter into a relationship. To this the father modestly and humbly replies: "My daughter is a pair of shoes for your feet."

Now the business of bargaining begins and may continue for at least five or six hours, sometimes with heated and even bitter remarks. If the parties cannot reach any satisfactory agreement, they will drop the entire matter, either temporarily or permanently. Meanwhile, the matchmaker has another party in mind and will send the delegation there in the hope of a better arrangement.

Negotiating is not always easy for the bride's father. Frequently the father demands a high dowry for his daughter on the principle that the higher the price the greater the honor for him and his family. Nevertheless, once the parties agree and the parents pay the dowry, preparations for the wedding begin. Thus the bride automatically becomes the wife and property of her husband.

In the Near East it is not unusual for men to marry girls who are only nine or ten years of age. In some cases, parents arrange these early marriages because of inheritance laws. In other cases, when a father dies leaving a young daughter, often the family will give her in marriage to one of her nearest relatives. It doesn't matter if she may be under age and her prospective husband may be an old man. The family has to do this to protect property rights. Invariably, orphan girls marry at a very young age because they have no means of support.

Sometimes parents of both the bride and bridegroom make secret oral agreements when the girl is young. The parties involved sacredly keep and respect these pledges. The bridegroom promises to honor his newly wedded child wife and to treat her as if she were his own sister. She lives and sleeps with him but retains her virginity until she arrives at the marital age, when she then becomes his full-fledged wife. Then, two elderly women will witness the token of her virginity on behalf of her parents in the presence of the bridegroom's mother. This is very important. If the two witnesses discover that the girl is not a virgin, her husband can obtain an annulment on the grounds of deception.

Many Near Eastern people still carefully follow this ancient biblical custom to protect the wife from future reproach in case her husband decides to divorce her. Furthermore, the family will always keep this token of virginity as long as the wife lives. "If any man take a wife, and go in unto her, and hate her, and then give an occasion of speech against her, and bring up an evil name upon her, and say, I took this woman, and when I came to her, I found her not a maid. Then shall the father of the damsel, and her mother, take and bring forth the tokens of the damsel's virginity unto the elders of the city in the gate. And the damsel's father shall say unto the elders, I gave my daughter unto this man to wife and he hateth her. And, lo, he hath given occasions of speech against her, saying, I found not thy daughter a maid; and yet these are the tokens of my daughter's virginity. And they shall spread the cloth before the elders of the city. And the elders of that city shall take that man and chastise him."[10]

Generally, Westerners do not know about these Eastern marriage customs because Near Easterners do not discuss them publicly. They regard such customs as sacred secrets. In the past, even missionaries who had lived all their lives in the Near East knew very little of these private domestic affairs that occurred daily. Only the parents and relatives who are concerned in a marriage affair know of these things.

In the case concerning Mary, evidently the dowry had been settled and the amount given to her family following the usual custom. The people now recognized that Mary and Joseph were married. But according to Matthew's narrative, the family had given Mary to Joseph when she was a young girl. If Mary had been only Joseph's intended and was living with her parents, then Joseph could not have found out that she had conceived a child. There would have been no grounds for divorce.

By the manner in which the author tells the birth story, we understand that Joseph had married Mary when she was a child bride in terms of the contract mentioned above. But to his surprise and dismay he discovered that she was pregnant and questioned her fidelity. Upon considering the situation carefully, he decided to divorce her secretly to avoid the tragedy of having her stoned to death. Stoning was the capital punishment for adultery according to the laws of Moses.[11]

In this dilemma, the angel of the Lord appeared to Joseph in a dream and revealed to him that Mary was not only pure but was exceptionally favored of the Lord, for she was to be the mother of a holy one. Immediately, Joseph's worries and suspicions disappeared. He accepted Mary as his lawful wife and kept the entire happening a

---

[10]Deut. 22:13-18, K.J.V.
[11]Deut. 22:21.

secret.

Joseph would have had to keep the matter a secret because the people of Nazareth would not have believed him. As far as the people of Nazareth were concerned, they always thought that Jesus was the son of Joseph. The gospel of John confirms this thinking: "And Philip found Nathaniel and said to him: We have found that very one of whom it was written by Moses in the Torah and by the prophets, and he is Jesus, *the son of Joseph*, who is from Nazareth."[12]

We must always keep in mind that when the birth story was added to Matthew's gospel, quite some time had passed. Interest in the early life of Jesus did not occur until Jesus had become famous. The birth story of Jesus serves a theological purpose and does not necessarily describe a complete historical event. Nonetheless, the customs and style of writing in the narrative follow Near Eastern convention. Many parts of the tradition are probably legendary. Irving M. Zeitlin, Professor of Sociology at the University of Toronto, says concerning legend: "Where the Hebrew scriptures are concerned, too sharp a dichotomy between legend and history is bound to be misleading. For legends frequently contain historical elements. And even in the absence of such elements, legends may prove to be extraordinarily valuable for what they reveal about the culture and consciousness of the people."[13] This same notion applies to the New Testament and especially to the infancy stories concerning Jesus.

A RIGHTEOUS MAN

Then Joseph her husband, being a just man, and not willing to make her a public example, was minded to put her away privily. Mt. 1:19

Kena is an Aramaic word meaning "pious," "gentle," "quiet,"

---

[12]Jn. 1:45, Aramaic Peshitta text, Errico.
[13]Irving M. Zeitlin, *ANCIENT JUDAISM*, "The Patriarchs and their God" p. 36.

"humble," "righteous." Near Easterners use this word to characterize a man who is meek and lowly in manner and usually does not interfere in other people's affairs. This word also describes an individual who, generally, is retiring and does not engage in quarrels and gossip.

Joseph was a pious and kind man. He didn't want the townsfolk to know that Mary, his wife, had conceived a child. He knew that they would not believe his story about an angelic visitation and a miraculous conception. The community would have made Mary a public example for other women of Nazareth by stoning her to death according to the laws of Moses.

Joseph attempted to avoid this tragedy and began to find a way to divorce her secretly. He wanted to put her away on some minor charge. Often in the Near East, men divorce their wives for no real legitimate reason so no one suspects that these wives may actually be accused of adultery.

However in Joseph's case, when the angel appeared and revealed to him Mary's conception, Joseph was relieved. He dropped the entire matter and the affair remained a secret between Mary and Joseph. The people of Nazareth knew nothing about what had taken place. When Jesus was born, everyone believed that he was Joseph's son. Evidently, this incident was never made public until Mary had died.[14]

DREAMS, VISIONS AND CONCEPTION

But while he thought on these things, behold, the angel of the Lord appeared unto him in a dream, saying, Joseph, thou son of David, fear not to take unto thee Mary thy wife; for that which is conceived in her is of the Holy Ghost. Mt. 1:20.

Part A—DREAMS AND VISIONS. "Dream" in Aramaic is *ḥelma*. It derives from the Semitic root *ḥlm*, "to dream." Hebrew and

---

[14]For a detailed study of the genealogies and Jesus' birth story see Raymond E. Brown, *THE BIRTH OF THE MESSIAH*, Doubleday, 1977 &1993.

Arabic use this same root for their word "dream." Interestingly, *ḥlm* also means "to heal, make whole, make well or sound, restore to health." Near Easterners believe that God's guidance and revelation can come through dreams. They place a great deal of trust in dreams of angelic visitations and messages.

Dreams and visions play a major role in the lives of Semitic peoples, especially among the Hebrews. For instance, when God revealed himself to the patriarchs and prophets, it was usually through dreams and visions. (However, this was not the only means for spiritual guidance and communication.)

A verse in the book of Numbers tells us: "And the Lord said to them, Hear now my words! If you are prophets I, the Lord, will reveal myself to you in a *vision* and will speak to you in a *dream*."[15] When King Solomon prayed for wisdom, the scribe who chronicled the King's reign reports: "In Gibeon the Lord appeared to Solomon *in a dream* by night and God said, Ask that I shall give to thee."[16] "For God speaks once; he does not speak a second time; through a dream, and through a vision of the night, when sleep falls upon men, while in deep slumber upon the bed, then he opens the ears of men. . ."[17] The recorded appearances of God and angels in the Hebrew Bible usually occurred in the minds and hearts of the people while they were sleeping or in a deep trance.

Part B—CONCEPTION. Near Easterners, especially the Hebrews, believed that for conception to happen it takes three powers—the man, the woman, and God. For example, when Rachel was having difficulty in becoming pregnant she said to her husband, "Give me children, or else I die." Jacob became angry with Rachael and he said to her, *"Am I in the place of God,* that I have prevented you from having a child?"[18]

Story after story in the Hebrew Bible tells about God's involve-

---

[15]Num. 12:6, Aramaic Peshitta text, Errico.
[16]1 Kings 3:5, K.J.V.
[17]Job 33:14-16, Aramaic Peshitta text, Lamsa translation.
[18]See Gen. 30:1-2.

ment with conception. These stories also tell us how God opens wombs for pregnancy and closes wombs to prevent pregnancies. This was the belief of the people.

The following quote is not a critical examination of Jesus' birth story from a rational Western point of view; nor should we understand it as an attempt to prove the narrative. Rather, these comments from a native Syrian reflect the typical Eastern, spiritual attitude toward human reproduction and birth:

> In a more literal sense we always understood the saying of the psalmist, "Children are a heritage from the Lord." Above and beyond all natural agencies, it was He [God] who turned barrenness to fecundity and worked the miracle of birth. To us every birth was miraculous, and childlessness an evidence of divine disfavor. From this it may be inferred how tenderly and reverently agreeable to the Syrian ear is the angel's salutation to Mary, "Hail, Mary, thou that art highly favored, the Lord is with thee; blessed art thou among women!—Behold thou shalt conceive in thy womb and bring forth a son" (Luke 1:28, 31).
> A miracle? Yes! But a miracle means one thing to your Western science, which seeks to know what nature is and does by dealing with secondary causes, and quite another thing to an Oriental [Near Easterner] to whom God's will is the law and gospel of nature. The Oriental [Semite] does not try to meet an assault upon his belief in miracles by seeking to establish the historicity of concrete reports of miracles. His poetical, mystical temperament seeks its ends in another way. . . But the story of Jesus' birth and kindred Bible records disclose not only the predisposition of the Syrian mind to accept miracles as divine acts, without critical examination but also its attitude toward conception and birth—an attitude which differs fundamentally from that of the Anglo-Saxon mind. . . Back of all these social traits and beyond the free realism of the Syrian in speaking of conception and birth, lies a deeper fact. To Eastern peoples, especially the Semites, reproduction in all the world of life is profoundly sacred. It is God's life reproduc-

ing itself in the life of man[19]and in the living world below man.[20]

A VIRGIN

Behold, a virgin shall be with child, and shall bring forth a son, and they shall call his name Emmanuel, which being interpreted is, God with us. Mt. 1:23

In this verse the scribe quotes Isaiah 7:14. The Hebrew text uses the word *almah* (*ha-almah*) and it means an adolescent girl, one of marriageable age. It does not necessarily signify "virgin." *Bethulah* is the Hebrew word for "virgin," although *almah,* "young woman," sometimes has the same meaning as "virgin."

In Aramaic the word for young girl is *alemta.* The Peshitta text uses the Aramaic word *b'thulta,* "virgin," for the verse in Isaiah and in Matthew. In this instance the Hebrew word *almah* is more accurate. Doubtless this word was changed when the Assyrians had adopted Christianity. Nevertheless, the Aramaic word *b'thulta* can also mean an unmarried woman who may be young or old.

When Isaiah spoke these words, the Assyrians were invading Palestine and had carried the ten tribes of Israel into captivity. The Assyrians were also threatening to invade the kingdom of Judah, for they already had devastated the countries around Jerusalem. Invading forces had defiled many women.

Isaiah depicts a brighter future for the restoration of Judah. The Assyrian and Chaldean empires would disappear and Israel would be restored to her former glory. Peace and prosperity would reign. There would be virgin girls in Israel and the nation would again be sanctified

---

[19]See Genesis 1:26-27. According to Gen. 2:7, God breathes into Adam's nostrils (literally—face) the breath of life and this is what makes humans different from animals. The biblical author infers that a human's superiority lies in the fact that he became a living being through the breath of God.

[20]Abraham M. Rihbany, THE SYRIAN CHRIST, "Birth of a Man Child," pp.20-25.

to God. The prophet Isaiah meant that a child, a chosen one, would be conceived and born of a woman who was a virgin until she was married. It would be improper for a king to marry a widow because in such cases their sons could not ascend the throne. God would now be with his people through this child.

Emmanuel means "with-us-is-God." Evidently, the scribe tells us that the son of Mary and Joseph is to have the name "Jesus" but at the same time, their son will be the fulfillment of the *Emmanuel* (God with us) prophecy from Isaiah. This boy will be the bearer of the divine presence among the people. Although the prophecy of Isaiah (7:14) had to do with the political and national problems of the times and not exactly with the birth of the Messiah, the gospel redactor (editor) placed a spiritual emphasis on this prophecy in regard to Jesus' birth.

THE NAME JESUS

Then Joseph being raised from sleep did as the angel of the Lord had bidden him, and took unto him his wife; And knew her not till she had brought forth her firstborn son; and he called his name Jesus. Mt. 1:24-25.

The Aramaic text reads: "Then Joseph woke up from his sleep, he did as the messenger of the Lord had commanded, and he took charge of his wife. And he did not know her until she gave birth to her firstborn son; then she named him Jesus."[21]

Yeshoa or *Yeshua* (pronounced *Eshoa*) is the Northern Galilean Aramaic form of Jesus' name. This name was a common and popular one in biblical lands during the first century. (See Colossians 4:11.) Our English form of Jesus' name comes from a shortened classical Aramaic/Hebrew form of *Yeshua*. In English we use the name Joshua. The Semitic letter *yoth* "*y*" becomes "*j*" in Latin. English carries over the Latin root. Its full rendering is *Yehoshua*. The Semitic root *ysha* means "to help, aid, save, rescue, and deliver." "Jesus" means

---

[21]Mt. 1:24-25, Aramaic Peshitta text, Errico.

"Yahweh helps," or more precisely, "help, Yahweh!"

This name was popular because of Israel's great national leader and hero, Joshua. He led the conquest of Palestine and helped to settle the twelve Israelite tribes in the land of Canaan. Whenever Israel felt the need of God's intervention, many of its people would name their male children "Joshua," that is, "Jesus—Deliverer, Yahweh rescues." The Hebrews, more than any other race of people in the world, were aware of God's power. He had saved and delivered Israel many times when the people were in difficult straits. They always turned to God when they found human help alone was of no avail in overcoming great challenges.

For centuries, the Hebrews had been longing for a great savior to deliver them from their oppressors. Prior to the Assyrian and Chaldean captivities, these tribal people had relied on men like Samson, David, Solomon, and other great leaders to save them from the Philistines, Idumites, Ammonites, Moabites and other small kingdoms that surrounded them.

During the eighth century B.C.E. Assyria and Chaldea (Babylon)—two great imperial powers which lay east of the River Euphrates—were confronting Israel. The small army of Israel and its allies could not defeat these two powerful nations with their large armies, abundant military supplies, and weapons of war. At that time Israel's army was equipped only to fight for a very short period of time.

Israel's leaders saw a different kind of world before them. They saw imperial kingdoms that were larger than the smaller powers such as Moab, Ammon, and Edom whose kings ruled over a few hundred square miles or less. Now they realized that only God could aid them in defeating the awesome armies of Assyria and Chaldea. These Israelite leaders recognized that they needed a savior—a great deliverer like the one Isaiah had predicted. "For to us a child is born, to us a son is given; and the government will be upon his shoulder; and his name is called Wonderful Counselor, The Mighty One, The

Everlasting Father, the Prince of Peace."[22]

Such also was the belief in Palestine during the first century C.E. The people of Israel were hoping for salvation through the appearance of a great savior. God and his anointed (the Christ) would save them from the great Imperial Power of Rome. Roman forces had come to Palestine not only to plunder silver, gold, and other material goods but to annex the land and crush the hopes of Judaism. Israel realized that only God could overthrow such a military power whose legionnaires occupied all the lands around the Mediterranean sea.

Jesus, the true deliverer, was the fulfillment of this great hope. According to the narrative, the angel of the Lord had told Joseph to name the child "Jesus." This child was destined to save his people from their sins. "She will give birth to a son, and you will call his name Jesus; for he will save his people from their sins."[23] "Sin," *htaya*, in Aramaic literally means "to miss the mark." "Save," *hyah*, comes from the Aramaic root *haye*, "life" and "vitality." Thus, "to save" in this verse means "to revive, recover, restore, give life or resuscitate."

Jesus, through his deeds and teachings, was to revive and restore vitality to his people who were missing the mark and had lost their way. "Jesus" is the human name of the great deliverer, who was not only to give life to Israel but to all nations. Global peace and happiness was to come about through Jesus' method and plan of salvation which he based on the Torah (Mosaic law), the prophets, and God's active presence in the world.

---

[22]Isa. 9:6, Aramaic Peshitta text, Lamsa translation.
[23]Mt. 1:21, Aramaic Peshitta text, Lamsa translation.

CHAPTER 2

MAGI

Now when Jesus was born in Bethlehem of Judea in the days of Herod the king, behold, there came wise men from the east to Jerusalem. Saying, Where is he that is born King of the Jews? for we have seen his star in the east, and are come to worship him. Mt. 2:1-2.

According to the narrator of the infancy story, Jesus was born in Bethlehem, probably in 4 B.C.E.[1] It was about this time that the magi came seeking the "King of the Jews."

M'gusheh is the Aramaic word for "Magi." Its root comes from the Chaldean/Persian word *magno,* meaning "receptive." Interestingly, it is from this root that we derive our English words *magnetic* and *magic,* conveying the impression of greatness through wonders. In Aramaic a *m'gusha* refers to a fire-worshiper, magician, wizard, and a priest of the Persian religion.

The Magi were not kings as we usually assume. They were Chaldean priests who worshiped the sun and were schooled in the art of magic, enchantments, fortune telling, astronomy, and astrology. These men were the great astronomers of their day; they studied the stars and planets in connection with their temple worship. Their investigations of the heavens enabled them to divide the years into months, weeks, and days. Their religion demanded a thorough analysis of the universe and its celestial bodies. (Near Eastern tradition teaches

---

[1]Bethlehem means "the house of bread." It was a small town six miles south of Jerusalem in the state of Judea. Bethlehem was well known as the seat of the family of David (see Ruth 1:1,4:11; 1 Sam. 16:1; and Mic. 5:2). Most New Testament scholars think that Nazareth was more likely the birth place of Jesus. He is called Jesus of Nazareth and not Jesus of Bethlehem (see Jn. 1:5). Herod the Great an Idumaean, became governor of Galilee in 47 B.C.E.. Then in 40 B.C.E., Antony and Octavius made him king of Judea. Herod was also a friend of Julius Caesar.

that when the wise men came from the East, they were supposed to have come from the smaller Aramaic-speaking kingdom of Urhai or Edessa.)

Zoroaster, the famous Eastern prophet, had predicted the coming of a Great One. According to Eastern tradition, Zoroaster retired from the world at an early age. While he was sheltered in a lonely cave, he received divine visions revealing spiritual principles and laws of correct moral life almost equal in beauty to those of the Christian faith. As a result of some of these visions, Zoroaster predicted that from the East there would go forth from among his followers Magi—members of the priestly cast—who, under the guidance of a divine light, would be led to the coming Ruler of the world.

Magi based their predictions on the appearance of new and unusual stars. These Magi had seen a strange star in their country and they saw it again when they were in Jerusalem. According to the gospel writer, the appearance of this star at the time of Jesus' birth was clearly a fulfillment of the Zoroastrian prophecy. The great Deliverer was now born.

The gospel scribe does not tell us how many Magi were present. Early Near Eastern tradition among the Assyrians and Chaldeans informs us that there were twelve. In later Christian traditions the number became three because of the three gifts given to the child. (See Matthew 2:11). Then, at an even later date, these Magi became three kings. This tradition is based on Psalms 72:10 and Isaiah 49:7.

The expression "for we have seen *his star* in the east" refers to a Near Eastern belief—that every human being has his or her own star. Easterners embrace the notion that everyone's personal star holds the secret to his or her destiny. This personal star guides and watches over the individual throughout the entire life span. When a person is kind, they say "his star is attractive." When two people care for each other, they say "their stars are in harmony." The star the Magi saw symbolized the appearance of the Messiah/Christ. It also represented the peace and assurance his kingdom was to bring on earth.

24

FOLLOWING THE STAR

When they had heard the king, they departed; and lo, the star, which they saw in the east, went before them, till it came and stood over where the young child was. Mt. 2:9.

"And lo, the star, which they saw in the east, went before them, till it came and stood over where the young child was." This is a Semitic style of speaking. The star was not moving. It means that the Magi went in the direction of the star; that is, its position directed them.

In those ancient days, and even today in areas where people know nothing about the compass, travelers depend on the stars as one would on a compass. Near Easterners consider the stars as guides and companions—the wondrous display of God's power, wisdom and glory.

"The heavens tell the story of God's glory and the firmament manifests his handiwork. Day after day pours forth speech and night after night declares his understanding. There is no speech, also no words whose sound is unheard. Their joyful message has gone out throughout the land and their words to the end of the world. Above the sun, among the heavens [literally—'among them'] he pitched his tent."[2]

Stars still guide nomad tribes traveling hundreds of miles in the expansive Arabian desert. Shepherds understand the seasons of the year by the position of the stars. They also determine the changes of pasturage for their flocks and coming shortage of water by the stars' positions.

Before the advent of Western roads and technology, caravan leaders followed certain routes through the position or direction of the stars. Native automobile drivers crossing the Arabian desert would find travel difficult without the help of the stars. A little error in direction, now as then, would mean a loss of a party or caravan.

---

[2]Ps. 19:1-4, Aramaic Peshitta text, Errico.

The desert is a level waste without well-defined routes. Shifting sand quickly obliterates imprints of camel hooves and automobile tires. There are no other signs upon which a traveler may depend for direction while traveling in the desert except the stars.

A Near Easterner giving a stranger directions for travel will say: "Take that star in your hand until you come to the oasis. Then drop that star and take another in your hand until you reach your destination." This means "follow straight in the direction of the first star until you reach the oasis. Then take another route by looking at another star." Another way of giving directions would be: "Take this road in your hand until you come to the town."

In many areas of the Near East today, people know little of the nature or size of the stars. The naked eye cannot reveal the immeasurable distances between the stars. Though they are familiar with the planetary movements, they do not know about their orbits, form, and size. The stars appear small from the earth, so many people believe that these stars are small but powerful.

Hebrew prophets and learned men considered the stars to be simple lamps hung in the sky for the sake of beauty and adornment. They thought the stars were created for the benefit of the earth. This ancient and curious opinion concerning stars is still prevalent among many bedouins. Near Easterners who have not studied in European and American schools scorn the idea that the stars and planets are larger than the earth and that they are independent units. Neither do they believe that the earth turns on its axis.

In the early 1920's at a conference of Assyrian priests and tribal chiefs, gathered around their patriarch, Dr. Lamsa asked the most learned priest how large he believed the sun, moon and the stars were. The venerable priest's reply was prompt, simple, and emphatic. He said: "The sun is as large as a Persian melon but very powerful. An angel takes care of it, bringing it out in the early morning from heaven to lighten the earth; and in the evening, he wraps it up in a large handkerchief and puts it in his pocket. The moon and stars are as large as apples." The priest became very indignant and thought that Dr. Lamsa was a heretic when he told him the sun was many times larger than the earth.

The ancient Assyrians and Chaldeans had a higher understanding of astronomical knowledge before the fall of their empires. After the collapse of their sovereignties, there was a gradual decline in the science of astronomy and so it continued until the first century C.E. Astronomy practically disappeared as a science. The superstitions of astrologers and soothsayers had completely supplanted the ancient school.

It is no wonder that the Magi were surprised to see the same star that they had seen in Mesopotamia, 400 miles away, standing over the house in Bethlehem where the young child was. By this time in history, these men had an awkward and limited knowledge of celestial bodies. They believed that the star had either walked or disappeared and appeared again. Of course, if the Magi had been in Cairo, they would have seen the same star there, too. Some Easterners believe a star seen from one city could not be seen from another.

When one stands on the street or on a housetop in Jerusalem and looks up at the stars in the direction of Bethlehem, the stars will appear to be lower in the heavens and sitting just above the houses in Bethlehem. However, if one were looking up at the stars from the plains, the stars would not appear lower. Jerusalem is built on the top of a mountain[3] and Bethlehem is in the valley. Also, when one looks at the stars from a distance toward the horizon, they appear to be touching the ground. The Near Eastern star-studded heavens can easily mesmerize the mind of a traveler in the desert.

THE STAR OF BETHLEHEM

When they saw the star, they rejoiced with exceeding great joy. And when they were come into the house, they saw the young child with Mary his mother, and fell down, and worshiped him: and when they had opened their treasures, they presented unto him gifts; gold, and frankincense, and

----

[3]More precisely, Jerusalem is on the top of seven hills.

myrrh. Mt. 2:10-11.

Part A—SEMITIC BELIEF. This story of "the star of Bethlehem" agrees so easily and beautifully with Near Eastern thought and temperament. Semites feel deeply within their hearts that the heavens reveal the glory of God and that the stars tell many wondrous things to the human family. The ancient song writer also sings of the omniscience of God: "He tells the number of the stars; he calls them all by their names. Great is our Lord, and of great power: his understanding is infinite."[4]

These people see the stars as messengers of good and evil, objects of the highest ideals or the "crudest superstitions." Every community has a "stargazer" who can read an individual's fortune and who can "arrest" an absent person's star and learn whether things are going well or ill for that person. Israel, at times, put too much trust in the stargazers of the day. (See Isaiah 47:13-14.) Easterners do not think of stars the way we do in the West:

> Beyond all such crudities, however, lies the sublime and sustaining belief that the stars are alive with God. . . .the beautiful story of the star of Bethlehem indicates that to the Oriental [Semitic] mind the "hosts of heaven" are no mere masses of dust, but the agencies of the Creator's might and love. So the narrative of the Nativity in our Gospel sublimates the beliefs of the Orientals about God's purpose in those lights of the firmament, by making the guide of the wise men to the birth place of the Prince of Peace a great star.[5]

Part B—PRESENTING GIFTS. "When they were come into the house, they saw the young child. . .then they opened their treasures and offered him gifts. . . ." When a male infant is born, relatives, friends, neighbors and strangers "parade" into the house—even on the very day of his birth—to bring presents. They want to congratulate the

---

[4] Ps. 147:4-5, Aramaic Peshitta text, Lamsa translation.
[5] Abraham M. Rihbany, THE SYRIAN CHRIST, pp. 36-37.

parents on the divine gift that is now in their keeping. It was because of this custom that the Magi, who were strangers, were permitted to enter with the gifts. The gifts were befitting a king: gold, frankincense and myrrh.

NAZARETH

And he came and dwelt in a city called Nazareth: that it might be fulfilled which was spoken by the prophets, He shall be called a Nazarene. Mt. 2:23.

The name of the town of Nazareth may come from the Semitic root *nzr*, "to watch, keep, guard, protect." Nazareth might have been the home of the Nazarites who appeared from time to time in Israel. These Nazarites lived in seclusion and often separated themselves from people. They did not cut their hair or take strong drink.

The village of Nazareth is situated a few miles south of Cana at the northern end of the plains of Esdraelon. The name of this town is not mentioned in the Hebrew Bible. Probably, the refugees whom King Sargon had transported into this region had built the town.

Dr. Lamsa believed that the writer was making a Semitic play on words with the Hebrew verb *nzr* (*z* spelled with a *zayin*)—"to take a vow, consecrate"—and the Aramaic root *nzr* (*z* spelled with a *tsadeh*).[6] A Nazarite was dedicated to God before he was born. When God answered prayers of childless women, these women often pledged to offer their first born male child to God as a Nazarite. This is how Samson and Samuel became Nazarites.[7] Numbers 6:1-21 describes the law of the Nazarite. Verses 3-8 in the same chapter describe prohibitions for the temporary Nazarite.

The Nazarites were different in that they lived even simpler lives

---

[6]Aramaic and Hebrew retain two "z's" in their alphabets—*zain* and *tsadeh*. Only those who know Aramaic and Hebrew can understand this word play.

[7]See Judges 13:7 and 1 Sam. 1:27

than the common folk. People thought of them as men of God because they were dedicated to God's work. In the Assyrian Church, the order of the Nazarites is still preserved. Bishops and other ecclesiastical authorities are all Nazarites. They do not cut their hair, marry, or use strong drink.[8] "He shall be called a Nazarene" is an Aramaic figure of speech.[9] It is probable that the scribe refers to Jesus' consecration and dedication to God and the Torah.

There is another consideration here. The gospel writer may be making a play on the Hebrew *nezer*—"a branch" in Isaiah 11:1: "And there shall come forth a shoot out of the stem of Jesse and a branch [*nezer*] shall grow out of his roots." This has messianic overtones. A "branch" or "shoot" is another name for the Messiah in Hebrew. This interpretation may well be the gospel writer's intention. However, New Testament scholars do not agree on any one interpretation.

---

[8]See alo Jn. 1:45
[9]A Nazarene also means someone from Nazareth.

CHAPTER 3

JOHN THE BAPTIST

In those days came John the Baptist preaching in the wilderness of Judea, and saying, Repent ye: for the kingdom of heaven is at hand. For this is he that was spoken of by the prophet Esaias, saying, The voice of one crying in the wilderness, Prepare ye the way of the Lord, make his paths straight. And the same John had his raiment of camel's hair, and a leathern girdle about his loins; and his meat was locusts and wild honey. Mt. 3:1-4.

In this verse, the term "wilderness" means an uninhabited region. Nonetheless, we must not think that John the Baptist was in a totally arid area. He was in the section of the Judean desert, near the town of Jericho, where many bedouins and migratory tribes were dwelling. This was in a district where many Jewish families spent their summers with their sheep, making butter and cheese.

Part A—PERMISSIBLE FOOD. John, like many people who were dwelling in this part of the Judean desert, lived on carob and other foods that bedouins eat. In the Sahara desert there is a kind of locust that people do consume. There are also some Arab tribes who eat locusts.

Moses permitted the Israelites to eat certain kinds of insects. In the book of Leviticus we read: "Yet these things you may eat of every flying insect that goes upon all fours, which have legs above their feet with which to leap on the earth; of these you may eat: the locust after its kind and the large winged locust after its kind, But all other flying insects which have four feet are unclean to you."[1]

Dr. Lamsa said that he never saw a Jew, Christian, or Moslem eating locusts. However, there is something more to consider. There is also a small bird that looks like a quail and is very numerous in the

---

[1]Lev. 11:21-23, Aramaic Peshitta text, Lamsa translation.

desert. Some people refer to them as locusts because they "cover the land" like a swarm of locusts. Dr. Lamsa had eaten this type of bird in the Arabian desert. Regardless of what kind of food John ate—locusts, carob, or the quail-like bird—he did eat food that the Mosaic law permitted.

Part B—THE SIGN OF A PROPHET. As to John's attire, he wore the insignia of a prophet.[2] His clothes were made of camel's hair with a leather belt. John patterned his ministry in the same mode as the prophet Elijah. In the book of Samuel, we find a description of the prophet Elijah: "A hairy man and girt with a girdle of leather about his loins."[3] Desert Arabs dressed in coarse clothes made of camel hair. In the old days prophets wore sheepskins as a token of their office, indicating that these prophets were living a rugged life and fighting for religion's true meaning.

In biblical days some kings, princes and queens were opposing the reforms these men of God were proclaiming. Therefore, these kings and princes were constantly hunting the prophets to do away with them and their message. Both Elijah and his disciple, Elisha, spent most of their lives in caves and in the mountains hiding from the rulers who sought them.

The apparel of prophets and men of God was a symbol of extreme sacrifice for the sake of their religion. Jesus said those who are dressed in fine clothes (linen or cotton) are in kings' houses.[4] These prophets took the challenge and were willing to deny themselves the comforts of life. They did this so that they might become examples against the corrupt system of materialism. They also did this to rebuke those who lived in luxury at the expense of their poor subjects, such as King Herod Antipas and the High priests were doing.

Part C—REPENTANCE. John's message was about repentance. The Aramaic text reads: "Now in those very days, John the Baptizer came and he was preaching in the plains of Judea, proclaiming: Turn

---

[2]See 1 Kings 19:13; Zech. 13:4.
[3]2 Kings 1:8.
[4]See Mt. 11:7-8.

to God! Heaven's reign has arrived!"[5] The Aramaic verb *tuwu* means "turn or return." Repentance, *tyawootha*, refers to the action of turning or returning—that is, "turn to, return to God." In Hebrew the word *shuwu*, "repent," also means "return," the idea being that one must return to God and the covenant. According to widely attested Jewish sources "repentance," *tishuva*, meant "return to God, the covenant, and the practice of good works, all of which bring salvation."

John believed that divine judgment was coming to every single person so he called the people to turn to God with good works. (See Luke 3:9-14.) Each individual was responsible to turn to God and do good to others. God's reign was arriving with judgment. According to John, the axe was laid at the root of the tree. Every tree that did not bear fruit would be cut down. However, Jesus' message of God's ruling presence would differ from John's vision of God.

GENERATION OF VIPERS

But when he saw many of the Pharisees and Sadducees come to his baptism, he said unto them, O generation of vipers, who hath warned you to flee from the wrath to come? Bring forth therefore fruits meet for repentance: And think not to say within yourselves, We have Abraham to our father: for I say unto you, that God is able of these stones to raise up children unto Abraham. Mt. 3:7-9.

The Aramaic text reads, "O offspring of vipers." However, Dr. Lamsa suggests that the Aramaic word *akidneh*, which usually translates as "vipers" or "poisonous snakes," really refers to "scorpions." He translates the phrase as "O offspring of scorpions."

It is a Near Eastern belief that when a scorpion is conceived, its father dies. And when a scorpion is about to be born, it eats its way out of the side of its mother causing her death. Therefore, scorpions

---

[5]Mt. 3:1-2, Aramaic Peshitta text, Errico.

come into the world without guidance and protection. Both parents are dead. Scorpions are on their own from the moment of their birth.[6]

John the Baptist declared to the Pharisees and Sadducees that they were like the offspring of scorpions; that is, they were like orphans. He said that they were like the scorpions' offspring and not the scorpions themselves. And like orphans, they were without the guidance of a mother and father.

For a very long period of time, Israel as a nation had no prophets and seers to warn them against the inevitable judgment that was to come. Who, then, could have advised and warned these men to come to the banks of the Jordan? It must have been the divine Spirit!

John, therefore, insisted they should give proof of their sincerity before receiving water baptism. The people knew that judgment was impending, but they had not turned to God to prepare themselves for what was to come. Merely acknowledging John as a new prophet was not an adequate mark of repentance. They had to produce the good fruits of a genuine returning to God and thus absolutely show that they were true sons of Abraham. This was the meaning of John's water baptism. (See Matthew 12:34; 23:33; Luke 3:7-9.)

MIGHTIER THAN I

I indeed baptize you with water unto repentance; but he that cometh after me is mightier than I, whose shoes I am not worthy to bear; he shall baptize you with the Holy Ghost, and with fire. Mt. 3:11.

Part A—THE MESSENGER. When a Semitic prince or governor contemplates a long journey to visit his people, a high official accompanied by servants is sent out in advance. This official will announce the coming of his lord and make preparations for the proposed visit. The mayor and the citizens of the towns that are to be

---

[6]See THE *COMMENTARIES OF ISHO'DAD OF NERV,* Bishop of Hadatha, 850 C.E. in Aramaic, pp. 39-40.

visited will greet and welcome the official party. In the Near East one bestows honor on the coming lord by treating his servants and representatives with great respect and dignity. If anyone shows disrespect to the party, the mayor and his people may be punished and the visit to the town canceled. Therefore, the advance party announcing the royal visit will receive a most cordial welcome.

Sometimes, the townspeople give too much honor to the high official and his entourage. When the representative receives such excessive and unnecessary honor, he becomes uneasy and afraid, lest his lord learn about such an extravagant reception and becomes jealous and displeased. Misunderstanding could occur and the kind remarks of the simple townsfolk could be misinterpreted.

For example, King Saul became jealous of David and began to hate him when the daughters of Israel sang, "Saul hath slain his thousands, and David his ten thousands."[7] It was this that made David flee from Saul and become a wanderer for years. During such receptions some officials reject remarks of praise made about them. Each one responds by saying: "I am nothing. I do not deserve what you say about me. I am only the messenger and one of the least of the servants of my lord. There is one who is coming after me. This honor is due only to him. I am not worthy even to untie the strings of his shoes."

John was only a messenger who was to precede his lord. He was to announce the coming of the Messiah/Christ but some of the people believed John was the Messiah. The people had waited patiently for the coming of a great prophet. Many centuries had passed and there had been no prophet in Judea. Therefore, some of the people greeted John as the great prophet Messiah/Christ.

When John appeared on the banks of the river Jordan, the people were so overjoyed that they forgot there was another who was to follow him. John disclaimed the honor given to him and emphatically stated he was nothing but an agent of the awesome prophet who was coming. He proclaimed he was not worthy to remove the shoes of this

---

[7]1 Sam. 18:7.

great lord.

Part B—REMOVING SHOES. The Aramaic text more correctly reads, "whose shoes I am not worthy *to remove*" and not "whose shoes I am not worthy *to bear*." This has the same meaning as "unloose" that we find in Mark 1:7 and Luke 3:16.

Europeans and Americans take off their hats when entering a home but Near Easterners remove their shoes and retain their hats. It is the worst breach of Near Eastern etiquette to enter and sit in a home wearing shoes. Friends and neighbors take off their own shoes; in some instances, servants remove their masters' shoes. But when an illustrious guest or a stranger enters, the woman or servant of the house will promptly remove the honored guest's shoes, showing a very warm welcome. If the guest is exceptionally distinguished, the master of the house will remove the guest's shoes. The practice of removing shoes is a mark of respect and honor to the guest.

John the Baptist not only denied that he was the Messiah/Christ; he also declared himself unworthy to take Jesus' shoes off his feet. "I am not worthy to remove his shoes" is a Semitic expression signifying humility and submission. John, speaking in this manner, repudiated any messianic claim and announced himself only as the servant of the Messiah/Christ.

Part C—BAPTISM OF SPIRIT/FIRE. "Baptism of fire" is an Aramaic saying. It means "free from sin." Fire purifies metals and burns dross, making the metal shine. In olden days—when the crucible was unknown—fire purified gold, silver, brass, and other metals instead of the chemical solutions that are used today.

Baptism by fire would remove all sins. Baptism by water signifies repentance. Baptism by the Holy Spirit symbolizes sanctification and salvation. Fire also indicates the presence of God. In this passage, fire represents the power of the Spirit that cleanses the inner being. Water only cleanses the physical body. The Spirit cleanses the heart and mind.

Jesus had the power to baptize and to release sins. John the Baptist's power was limited to baptism by water. When the people came to John and confessed their sins, they did not receive forgiveness

36

of sins.

Interestingly, in biblical days, Gentile idolaters passed their children through the fire, burning them alive as offerings to their gods. When the Israelites turned away from their God, they also practiced some of these deplorable sacrifices.

BAPTISM OF HUMILITY

Then cometh Jesus from Galilee to Jordan unto John, to be baptized of him. But John forbad him, saying, I have need to be baptized of thee, and comest thou to me? And Jesus answering said unto him, Suffer it to be so now: for thus it becometh us to fulfill all righteousness. Then he suffered him. Mt. 3:13-15.

"Then Jesus came from Galilee to the Jordan to John, to be baptized by him. But John tried to stop him, saying, I need to be baptized by you, and yet have you come to me? But Jesus answered and said to him, Permit it now, for this is necessary for us so that all righteousness may be fulfilled; and then he permitted him."[8]

Did John really baptize Jesus? Some New Testament scholars have debated the authenticity of this particular episode that began Jesus' ministry. However, most scholars accept Jesus' baptism as authentic.[9] The major purpose of this commentary is not a historical/critical analysis of the episode. The approach is to understand Jesus' baptism from the gospel perspective and its Near Eastern, Semitic setting.

New Testament critics look upon John's refusal to baptize Jesus as a later Christian addition in the gospel narrative. The text implies that John knew that Jesus was greater than he. This is the reason he did not want to baptize Jesus.

---

[8]Mt. 3:13-15, Aramaic Peshitta text, Lamsa translation.

[9]For a full treatment and discussion on the episode see John P. Meir, *A MARGINAL JEW*: Rethinking the Historical Jesus, "The Historicity of Jesus' Baptism by John," pp. 100-106, and "Jesus a Disciple of John?" pp. 116-130.

On the other hand, John was also mindful of Near Eastern formality. Custom of the time dictated that people of high social standing often humbled themselves as a sign of social grace. For example, at a banquet a nobleman will say to one of a lower social status, "Please sit higher than I." However, the man of lower social rank will insist that the nobleman occupy the higher seat. They do this to honor one another.

Although Jesus understood what John was doing, he did not pay any attention to Eastern formality. Jesus knew what his mission was about. He was identifying himself with his people. It was an act of solidarity with the people of Israel. He submitted himself to a baptism of humility.

By submitting to John's water baptism, Jesus also accepted John's message and acknowledged the Baptist's mission. The reported reply of Jesus to John in the gospel was, "Let it be so for now, because it is necessary for us, so that all righteousness may be fulfilled." As I said earlier, despite the fact that much later Christian scribes added to the narrative of Jesus' baptism, his recorded response carries a simple but profound meaning for those hearing or reading the story.

In Aramaic, *kenutha* refers to an authentic "piety"—that is, "integrity." It also means "justice, devoutness, righteousness, godliness, and goodness." It refers, as well, to an ethical justice based on the Torah (Mosaic law). Jesus did whatever was necessary for a just life, one full of integrity, because he was one with the Father.

Jesus showed his humility and meekness by identifying with his people and with John's message. He was concerned only with matters that were beneficial to humankind. Thus, at the River Jordan, Jesus humbled himself and let John baptize him. He revealed the true qualities of God. Through meekness and gentleness Jesus evinced a genuine spiritual leadership.

From the very onset of his ministry, Jesus desired to fulfill the scriptural meaning of justice—that all human beings are equal in God's eyes. He constantly showed this when he ministered to the marginal people of society. He brought God's presence into the lives and homes of the harlots, tax collectors, and sinners. He taught his disciples that the greatest one among them should be the servant. The teaching of meekness that the Hebrew prophets had declared was to triumph over pride and force. Jesus, at his baptism, set the example of true humility and justice. (See Mark 1:9-11; Luke 3:21-22.)

GOD'S APPROVAL OF JESUS' MISSION

And Jesus when he was baptized went up straightway out of the water: and, lo, the heavens were opened unto him, and he saw the Spirit of God descending like a dove, and lighting upon him; And lo a voice from heaven, saying, This is my beloved Son, in whom I am well pleased. Mt. 3:16-17.

Part A—OPENED HEAVENS. "Then when Jesus was baptized, and as soon as he came up out of the water, heaven was opened to him, and he saw the Spirit of God descending like a dove, and it settled on him. And behold, a voice from heaven was saying: This is my son, the beloved! I am delighted with him."[10]

"The heavens were opened" is a Near Eastern expression that symbolizes a communication between heaven and earth. In other words, what was once a mystery or secret was now revealed. Through this Galilean sage and teacher, heavenly truth was to be revealed and realized in a new way. "Opened heavens" is another way of saying that the universe rejoiced because Jesus' presence would remove the chasm (which exists only in one's mind) between heaven and earth.

The dove signifies meekness and purity, as well as peace, harmony, and tranquility. In the Near East, when describing a humble and gentle individual, people often say "He is so good and harmless that even a dove will come and sit upon him," or "He is so meek that a bird will not fly away from him."

Spirit has neither shape nor form, but the Semitic writers of

---

[10]Mt. 3:16-17, Aramaic Peshitta text, Errico.

Scripture symbolized the Spirit as a dove so that common folk might grasp its meaning. The Spirit of the Lord came upon Jesus as a pure, innocent, and harmless bird—a dove. John saw the Spirit while in a moment of trance, exactly as Ezekiel and other Hebrew prophets had seen the throne of God and His habitation in various ways. The apostle Peter, also in a trance, had seen a sheet come down from heaven full of animals—both clean and unclean.[11] Trances were common among the Semites.

Spirit as a dove settling on Jesus meant that God had approved of Jesus and that a new world order of peace and understanding was to replace the old order. Jesus was now ready to embark on his glorious mission. This would change the world and bring humanity to a greater understanding of God, and hence, to a greater understanding of itself and the meaning of life.

Part B—THE BELOVED SON. In the Aramaic language and Semitic culture, the term *bar dalaha*, "son of God" or "child of God," has many meanings. This Aramaic expression may refer to: (1) an orphan; (2) a meek young man (in contrast, people may often refer to a meek older man as "a man of God"); (3) a peacemaker; (4) a good, kind, pious individual; (5) the Messiah. In this passage (v.17) it is a messianic title and means "God's beloved one."

Interestingly, Semites use the Aramaic word *bar*, "son," subtly because it infers "likeness, resemblance, and to be in the image of." Thus, "son of God" signifies "like God" or "God-likeness." The meaning of the term "son of God" depends on its context. Hosea, the prophet, calls Israel, "God's son."[12]

This "special sonship" in Hebrew Scripture and in the New Testament does not refer to a "physical-divine" son but rather to a spiritual relationship between God (Spirit) and the individual designated as "son." Being a son of God, then, is a spiritual relationship between God and a human being that is based on love, respect and doing the will of the Father (God).

---

[11]Acts 10:10-12.
[12]Hosea 11:1.

When Near Easterners called someone "son" or "my son" it was their way of showing affection and it signified that person as a "beloved." In verse 17 "my son" refers to the Messiah. According to the synoptic gospels—Matthew, Mark, and Luke—Jesus was the son of God through God's anointing. Peter declared to Jesus: "You are the Messiah/Christ (the Anointed), the son of the living God!" [13] Paul, the apostle, claims that Jesus was the son of God through the resurrection.[14] The psalmist also refers to King David as God's anointed and calls him God's son. "I will declare the decree: The Lord hath said unto me, Thou art my son: This day have I begotten thee."[15] According to rabbinic interpretation, this verse in the psalms refers to the king of Israel who was anointed of God. The psalmist uses the term "begotten" figuratively. The Jewish concept of the Fatherhood of God has always been spiritual and not physical.

The phrase "I am delighted with him" is the joy of a father delighting in his son. In this case, Jesus was faithfully revealing and doing God's will—that is, the will of the Father. Hence, God was delighted with his devoted and dedicated son.

In verses 16 and 17, the gospel of Matthew describes a psychic happening. This episode is in perfect harmony with the mystical soul expression of the Near East.

---

[13]Mt. 16:16.
[14]See Rom. 1:4.
[15]Ps. 2:7, K.J.V.

CHAPTER 4

THE TRIAL IN THE DESERT

Once John had baptized Jesus, the Galilean prophet immediately felt that the time was right to declare his mission. Thus Jesus had to retreat to the desert and fast so that he could decide his future. He must test himself to see how he would present himself in his new role and ministry. God had appeared to Moses and Elijah and counseled them for their future work when they were in the desert. Now it was Jesus who would be in the desert.

Surrounded by the quiet and mystical radiance of the desert, Jesus communed with spiritual energies that were moving within his being. He was to face an inner contest with dark suggestions that would try to block him from fulfilling his mission. As a true holy man, Jesus had to encounter what the Jewish people call *yetzer hara*—"the evil inclination"—also referred to as "Satan" and "the devil." The desert was the perfect place for his trial. At night the vast star-filled heavens appear to be a glorious decorated canopy stretched out over the desert floor, radiating a soft light and flooding the earth with peace and harmony. It was here that Jesus formulated his gospel.

LED BY THE SPIRIT

Then was Jesus led up of the spirit into the wilderness to be tempted of the devil. And when he had fasted forty days and forty nights, he was afterward an hungred. Mt. 4:1-2.

The Aramaic text reads: "Then Jesus was guided by the Holy Spirit into the desert so that he might be tested by the adversary. And he fasted forty days and forty nights; then finally he became hungry."[1]

---

[1]Mt. 4:1-2, Aramaic Peshitta text, Errico.

Part A—RUHA. In Aramaic the word for "spirit" is *ruha*. It also means "wind." Carried away or led up by the spirit is a typical Aramaic way of speaking. In other words, an inner, spiritual, and powerful impulse guided Jesus into the desert. Whenever Aramaic speaking people want to describe an individual who is suddenly driven to do something, they say: "Wind has entered into him; that is why he acts that way."

The Aramaic verb *naseh*, "tempt," also means "to weigh, try out, prove, test something, or one's self." In this verse "tempt" means "to try out." Near Easterners tempt (try out) oxen and horses before they purchase these animals.

Men often tempt themselves—test their abilities—before they begin a challenging and difficult career. Holy men, or anyone who aspires to leadership, must undergo some sort of testing and endure trials. All ancient literature is filled with such episodes.[2] Jesus had to face his own fears and thoughts. He had to test himself.

The Aramaic word *akelqazar* is usually translated as "the devil" or "Satan." This is not incorrect. However, the word does mean an "accuser, slanderer, adversary." The root meaning is "to gnaw, ridicule." The writer is telling us that Jesus is about to embark on a desert experience and engage in an internal struggle, a battle within his soul. This conflict is externalized as the adversary and three major temptations.

Jesus had come to the conclusion that he should begin his ministry as a prophet. After all, had not the Jews in the South warmly received the ministry of John the Baptist as a prophet? This reception of John greatly encouraged Jesus. Nonetheless, there would be considerable opposition from his family, relatives, and friends. He had to make a decision. He could no longer wait in silence. Thus he went into the desert so that he could decide his future. The Holy Spirit (divine inspiration) filled his heart and mind. The more he examined himself, the more he felt moved by his decision to begin his mission.

---

[2]See Ps. 11:5 and Abraham's testing — Gen.22:1, "And after these things it happened that God tempted (tested) Abraham. . . ."

He knew that he would ultimately triumph regardless of any opposing forces that would seek to deter him.

Part B—WILDERNESS. *Madhbra* means "desert," "wilderness." In the Aramaic text, there is a play on words between the verb "guided," *d-b-r,* and the noun "wilderness," *m-d-b-r.* *Madhbra* is a wild, arid region without trees or inhabitants. In some areas, certain herbs grow during the spring season. The nomadic tribes, who live in tents near the edges of the desert and at an oasis, use these regions for grazing.

Although the desert lacks trees, villages, and the attractions that make life enjoyable and important in populated centers, it has its own majestic beauty. Celestial bodies pour their limitless light of awe-inspiring splendor on the desert. The deep indigo blue heavens with their brilliant stars look like a painted ceiling. It is in these awesome sites that the Arabs and other nomadic people live.

The beauty of the innumerable stars, by their seeming closeness to the ground as one looks out on the horizon, fascinates the human imagination. It reveals an order in the heavens unexcelled by anything on earth. When one lives in these wide open desert spaces, where the vastness of the heavens is contrasted with the smallness of the earth, one can perceive life in its proper proportion to the universe. Being away from the materialism of organized civilization, the desert dwellers feel that God is near and everywhere. They sense God in the natural and mystical radiance coming from the heavens and flooding their abodes. They can feel God's presence there in the desert to a far greater extent than the inhabitants of the cities can. The three major Semitic religions of the world were born in these desert areas. All three leaders—Moses, Jesus, and Mohammed—came out of the desert with their revelations.

Col. T. E. Lawrence, a famous British hero of Arabia, was impressed with the mystic life of the desert Arab and the Syrian people. He lived in obscurity, declining honors and decorations as a reward for his victories. His writings on Arab life were a revelation to the world.

This square of land, as large as India, formed the homeland of our Semites, in which no foreign races have kept a permanent footing, though Egyptians, Hittites, Philistines, Persians, Greeks, Romans, Turks, and Franks had variously tried. All had in the end been broken, and their scattered elements drowned in the strong characteristics of the Semitic race.[3]

Jesus, like many other great Eastern leaders, spent considerable time meditating near the edge of this desert. He needed silence and quietness to overcome certain human ambitions. He had to conquer them so that they would not hinder him from fulfilling his mission. The desert helps to reveal one's inner life. These inner victories are greater than temporal glory that fades like desert grass scorched by the sun. There was no better place than this desert region for Jesus to lay out his plans to establish a universal understanding of God's kingdom. It was here that he could see how to bring a greater realization of God's presence closer to humanity.

Part C—THE NUMBER FORTY AND FASTING. Near Easterners regard the number 40 as a sacred number. It was a well known number. Moses spent forty years in the desert of Midian. It took the Israelites forty years from the time they left Egypt until they arrived in Canaan. Moses and Elijah fasted forty days. And now Jesus fasted forty days.

In many Near and Middle Eastern countries, fasting is a religious demand and is strictly observed. People fast from meat, butter, and byproducts of sheep. Some men, for a period of forty days, fast from everything, eating only the evening meal. Islamic adherents fast during the day and eat at night. Some rich men, who are not willing to fast, hire the poor to do it for them.

Fasting was first instituted so that the rich might have sympathy and understanding for the conditions of the poor. In the Near East, when the rich fast they are very generous in their gifts to the poor. During this season of fasting, they have a taste of poverty and hunger.

---

[3]T. E. Lawrence, SEVEN PILLARS OF WISDOM, p. 37.

Fasting also helps in subduing physical desires, reducing physical strength, and increasing spiritual energies. It is an aid for spiritual insight and character. (See Luke 4:2.)

THE FIRST TEST

And when the tempter came to him, he said, If thou be the Son of God, command that these stones be made bread. But he answered and said, It is written, Man shall not live by bread alone, but by every word that proceedeth out of the mouth of God. Mt. 4:3-4.

Part A—BREAD AND STONES. Near Easterners do not bleach their wheat; therefore, the color of their bread is brown. When they bake their flat bread, these round loaves resemble stones. Hungry travelers who see stones of this type baking in the sunlight along the roadside often wish they were bread.

People recognize a genuine prophet by his miraculous works and when his predictions come true, not by his doctrinal beliefs. They will not accept a man as a prophet unless he can exhibit these extraordinary gifts. When God commissioned Moses to return to Egypt, Moses needed some sort of sign to test his ability as a prophet. So he turned his staff into a serpent. When he was in Egypt, Moses did wonders that surpassed the marvels of the great Egyptian priests who were skilled in the art of magic. The Hebrew prophet Elijah performed many miracles. He increased the widow's flour and oil when she was about to use up her last bit of food. Another time, when Elijah had predicted a drought and fled from King Ahab, ravens came and fed the weary, hungry prophet.[4]

Jesus was feeling the temptation to test his abilities as God's Anointed—Messiah. He had to perform greater miracles than those of his predecessors. He was to embark on the most exceptional mission ever undertaken by a representative of God. The temptation was that

---

[4]See 1 Kings 17:1-16.

if he is truly God's son, he should be able to change those stones that looked like bread into real bread.

However, changing stones into bread would not transform the hearts and minds of people. God had worked many miracles throughout Israel's history, but the people always forgot them and went after other gods. Jesus would have to depend on his heavenly Father to guide him and provide whatever "bread" might be necessary to meet the need. He would not perform just any wonder in order to convince people.

Part B—LIVING BY GOD'S DECREE. "It is written that it is not by bread alone a human being lives but by every word that comes from the mouth of God."[5] Jesus quotes from holy Scripture, the book of Deuteronomy: "And he [God] humbled you and suffered you to hunger and fed you with manna, which you did not know, neither did your fathers know; that he might make you to understand that man does not live by bread alone; but by everything that proceeds out of the mouth of the Lord does man live."[6]

The conclusion that Jesus came to when he felt this test to change stones into bread was that God alone decrees and provides what is nourishing. He was able to counter his negative thought with a biblical quotation. In other words, he squelched the satanic notion. Jesus was to nourish his people and the world with the word of God. He would heal and perform miracles only in response to faith. This is how he would present himself as God's son and Anointed.

THE SECOND AND THIRD TESTS

Then the devil taketh him up into the holy city, and setteth him on a pinnacle of the temple, And saith unto him, If thou be the Son of God, cast thyself down; for it is written He shall give his angels charge concerning thee; and in their hands they shall bear thee up, lest at any time thou dash

---

[5]Mt. 4:4, Aramaic Peshitta text, Errico.
[6]Deut. 8:3, Aramaic Peshitta text, Lamsa translation.

thy foot against a stone. Jesus saith unto him, It is written again, Thou shalt not tempt the Lord thy God. Again the devil taketh him up into an exceeding high mountain, and sheweth him all the kingdoms of the world, and the glory of them; and saith unto him, All these things will I give thee, if thou wilt fall down and worship me. Then saith Jesus unto him, Get thee hence, Satan: for it is written, Thou shalt worship the Lord thy God, and him only shalt thou worship. Then the devil leaveth him, and behold, angels came and ministered unto him Mt. 4:5-11.

Part A—THE TEMPLE. Jesus, in his imagination, sees himself on one of the pinnacles of the temple.[7] What a spectacular manner in which to present himself as God's special holy one. If he would jump from the temple, God would send his angels to protect him. He would not receive any injury. The angels would stop him from even dashing his foot against a stone. In this second temptation, the conclusion that Jesus reached was that he was not to test God. He would not purposely put himself in danger and expect God to save him because he was God's son. He put down the satanic notion for a second time.

Part B—HIGH MOUNTAIN. The writer uses the term "high mountain" figuratively. It means a high point in human aspiration. This temptation was by far the most alluring of the three. The reason for this is that the devil—deception, negative thought, or anything contrary to truth—offered Jesus the greatest rewards known to human beings. It could easily have diverted him from his true course. Satan offered everything that the human imagination can comprehend and embrace. This third and last notion presented the kingdoms of this world and all their wealth.

Jesus, through the energy of his mind and emotions, went to a high mountain. This means Jesus reached the summit, the highest point in human imagination. Now he could see the splendor, power, and wealth of the worldly kingdoms. He did not literally go to any

---

[7]There exists a rather late rabbinic source that records: "When the Messiah reveals himself he will come and stand on the roof of the Temple!" Taken from Rabbinic Works — PESIKTA RABBATI, ed. M. Friedmann (Vienna, 1880), p. 162 a.

mountain. This is a literary device to explain an emotional and mental state of heart and mind.

The location of the so-called Mount of Temptation in the holy land is a wasteland hundreds of feet below sea level. There are no kingdoms or large cities nearby, but small hamlets, sheep folds, and Arab camps. The only town close to it is the humble little town of Jericho.

Jesus, in this temptation, saw himself working with the high priest or with the learned men of his religion. He could work things out with the high officials and those in power. But, he immediately realized that if he should start to cooperate with them, he would have to be faithful to them. In other words, he could not have participated with these authorities without bowing down to them and accepting their teaching. His path and infinite understanding of God were quite different from their teachings. He knew that new wine could not be contained in the old goatskins but must be put in new containers. Jesus' teaching was so contrary to the doctrines of the elders and to the political and materialistic concepts of that day that it could not blend with them. In his understanding of God's kingdom, people were to serve and worship only God.

Part C—ANGELS MINISTERED. When Jesus' ordeal in the desert was over, Matthew tells us, angels approached him and ministered to him. The Aramaic word for "angel" is *malakha*. It means "messenger, minister, counselor, emissary."[8] Angels—that is, God's messages or thoughts—were supporting and strengthening Jesus during and after his struggle with powerful negative forces. At the end of his desert experience, Jesus was hearing from his Father's emissaries. His mind and heart were now filled with clear and uplifting thoughts.

When the writer says "Angels ministered to him," it meant that God's counsel took care of Jesus. Angels can only minister to an individual's soul—to guide, and strengthen him or her during temptation. Angels have no physical form to minister to a person as

---

[8]See Ps. 104:4, Heb. 1:7.

49

a servant does.

God counseled Jesus during his trial in the desert. In other words, Scripture came into Jesus' mind to counter the false notions that had crept into his soul. God prevailed and Satan (falsehood) was defeated. God's angels (counsel) are always ready to assist those who trust in him. Near Eastern belief holds that angels are constantly ministering to humanity.

In the Near East, people believe that every person has an angel resting on his right shoulder to guide him. Easterners often say that one's angel has gone before him or her to prepare the way. They also believe that children have guardian angels.

GALILEE OF THE GENTILES

The land of Zabulon, and the land of Nephthalim by the way of the sea, beyond Jordan, Galilee of the Gentiles. The people which sat in darkness saw great light; and to them which sat in the region and shadow of death light is sprung up. Mt. 4:15-16.

Galilee comes from the Aramaic word *gal*, "to take captive." *Galutheh* in Aramaic means "captivity." In 721 B.C.E., Shalmanesar and his son Esarhaddon carried away the ten northern tribes of Israel into captivity and settled them in Assyria. Then they brought a large mixed Assyrian and Chaldean population to settle in Samaria and northern Israel.[9] These new settlers spoke Aramaic, worshiped their own gods, and practiced their own customs. They also accepted the God of Israel as their chief god because he was the god of the land where they were dwelling.

The Jews in the south called the descendants of these early settlers Galileans—that is, foreigners. Although they worshiped Israel's God, they still carried on some of their idolatrous practices. "They feared the Lord, and served their own gods, after the manner

---

[9]See 2 Kings 17:23-24.

50

of the nations whom they carried away from thence."[10] The Jews always despised them and looked on them as the descendants of the people who had conquered them and destroyed their country. They would have nothing to do with them.

When the tribe of Judah returned from Chaldea (Babylon) and began to rebuild the temple and the wall of Jerusalem, the Galileans who were descendants of the early Assyrian settlers were living in the cities of Samaria and the North. These settlers came down to Jerusalem and offered to share in the rebuilding of the temple and the restoration of the tribe of Judah. But Zerubbabel and other Jewish leaders rejected their offer on the grounds that they were foreigners and had no part in the ancestral inheritance.

The Galileans gave many reasons why their offer should be accepted and tried to prove that they were Jews by faith although not by blood. They said that since the days when the Assyrian kings brought their forefathers to settle in Galilee, they had been worshiping the God of the land. But the Jews told the Galileans that although they had been worshiping their God, they could not be admitted to the Jewish race.[11] In the book of Ezra, Israel referred to the Galileans as adversaries, but this was probably a sentiment of prejudice.

The Jews in the South raised this same question during the time of Jesus. They said, how could the Messiah/Christ come from Galilee? Their Scripture clearly declared that the Messiah/Christ would come from Bethlehem and from the tribe of Judah.

Seven hundred years had elapsed since the days of the captivity, but the Jews had never forgotten the horrors of the Assyrian invasion. They continued to regard Galileans as Gentiles and pagans. They would not tolerate a prophet who came from that region. This racial hostility and resentment was intense in the days of Jesus. The Roman invasion had made the Jews feel bitter toward all foreigners, especially toward foreign teachers of religion.

They feared foreign teachers because their teachings might

---

[10]2 Kings 17:33 K.J.V.
[11]See Ezra 4:2-3.

weaken the Jewish faith upon which their racial solidarity rested. Such racial feelings expressed through religion still prevail in the Near East to this very day. Arabs believe that all Islamic holy men and leaders must be Arabs. No matter how qualified a Turkish Muslim may be in piety and learning, the Arabs would question his authority as a religious leader on racial grounds.

"The people who are sitting in darkness have seen a tremendous light and those who are sitting in the region and in the shadows of death, light has dawned upon them!"[12] The reference here is to the Gentiles who were living in Galilee. The Assyrian kings had settled these people in the territories of Zebulun and Naphtali in 721 B.C.E. The light of Jesus' gospel shined first upon the Jews, Galileans, Gentiles, and then upon other nations of the world.[13] The light was symbolic of the Messiah/Christ and his teaching. According to rabbinic literature, one of the names of the Messiah was "Light."

SYNAGOGUE

And Jesus went about all Galilee, teaching in their synagogues and preaching the gospel of the kingdom, and healing all manner of sickness and all manner of disease among the people. Mt. 4:23.

Kenushta in Aramaic means "a meeting place." "Synagogue" derives from the Greek word *synagoge*—"gathering, assembly." During Jesus' time, the *kenushta* was the Jewish public meeting place for non-sacrificial worship.

The Hebrew phrase *ohel moed,* "tent of meeting," more closely approximates the meaning of the Greek word *synagoge.* Most scholars believe that the synagogue originated in Chaldea (Babylon) during the exile. Some biblical experts consider the text in 2 Chronicles 17:9, "And they (Levites). . .went about throughout all the cities

---

[12]Mt. 4:16, Aramaic Peshitta text, Errico.
[13]See Isa. 9:1-2.

52

of Judah and taught the people," as a possible clue to the beginning of the synagogue as an institution.

Then again, these scholars cite Ezekiel 11:15-16 as the first hint to the origin of the synagogue because of the Hebrew words *mikdash meaht* which translates as "little sanctuary."[14] Be that as it may, when the synagogue did appear, it was an assembly and form of ceremonial worship where prayer, confession, and fasting were practiced but not animal sacrifice. As the institution developed, Jewish men started reading and interpreting scriptural passages during the gatherings. At these synagogue meetings the leaders began to promote and maintain the concept of the one universal God.[15]

---

[14]See also Ezek. 14:1 and 20:1.

[15]See Azriel Eisenberg, *THE SYNAGOGUE THROUGH THE AGES*, New York, Bloch Publishing Company, 1974.

CHAPTER 5

THE CONSTITUTION OF THE KINGDOM OF GOD

This very important section of Matthew's gospel, chapters 5-7, contains Jesus' basic teachings. Biblical interpreters have given various titles to these three distinct chapters—"The Sermon on the Mount," "The Messianic Torah," and "The Constitution of the Kingdom of Heaven." Jesus used four modes of communication with his fellow Semites: (1) He spoke in short sayings which at times had a cutting edge. (2) He told stories that imaged God and the kingdom in a new way. (3) He healed physical illnesses. (4) He taught, healed and celebrated God's presence with the outcast of society.

This portion of Matthew's gospel consists of Jesus' sayings. Early Christian scribes have undoubtedly reworked some of his sayings. Again, the purpose of this commentary is to present the Aramaic Near Eastern culture and language. It is not a critical commentary.

Knowing the Semitic idioms, language, and religious and cultural context of Jesus' teaching is extremely helpful in understanding much of the Master-Teacher's sayings. These utterances express his own distinct views and interpretation of the Torah (Mosaic law) and his deviation from some of the traditions of the times, the teachings of the elders and the oral law. Jesus expressed his understanding of truth in his emphasis on meekness, justice, peace, purity of heart, compassion, love of self, neighbor, enemy, and devotion to God's presence in the world. His teaching, based on a practice of authentic piety, is in perfect harmony with the spirit and heart of Hebrew Scripture, its prophets, sages, and song writers (Psalmists).

Jesus' magnetic, charismatic presence and powerful words reached into the very souls of his listeners and ignited the hearts of his disciples, followers, and people. At the same time, he angered those who did not accept or realize what he was all about. To them he was too revolutionary! They probably felt that he was undermining ancestral, cultural, and long-held religious values. There is no doubt, however, that Jesus was meeting the needs of those who longed for God's kingdom and its genuine reign of justice.

Jesus pronounced joy—that is, blessings—on the poor, the humble, the mourners, the seekers of justice, the compassionate, and those who were persecuted for the sake of justice. He encouraged doing good works taught in holy Scripture. He had the deepest respect for the Torah and came to fulfill it, although his critics thought otherwise. "Do not imagine that I have come to nullify the Torah (law) or the prophets. I have not come to nullify but to fulfill."[1] This meant he came to enact the spirit of the law and not the letter of the law.

Jesus taught his disciples to practice the spirit of the Torah by helping them to see beyond the traditions of the elders and man-made rules and regulations. Faith, prayer, giving, fasting, healing, forgiving, and more are all a part of Jesus' sound, spiritual and practical ethics recorded in these three chapters. According to his parables, which are a part of his gospel, he brought the image of God as Father to a new meaning. God was a loving presence now active in the world in spite of the violence and inharmonious conditions.

THE SETTING

And seeing the multitudes, he went up into a mountain; and when he was set, his disciples came unto him. And he opened his mouth, and taught them saying: Mt. 5:1-2.

Matthew creates the setting for the collected teachings of Jesus. "And seeing the multitudes" is a linking phrase to 4:25, "And there followed him great multitudes of people." The notion of the mountain intends to give us the impression that a new Moses has appeared. Jesus will reveal his messianic Torah just as Moses gave the law on Mt Sinai.

The author gives us a Semitic picture of Jesus acting as a rabbi, giving his torah to his *talmeedeh*—"disciples." It is the writer who

---

[1]Mt. 5:17, Aramaic Peshitta text, Errico.

55

makes these teachings intended for the disciples: "his disciples came unto him." In Luke we have an entirely different setting. Jesus is on the plain and not on the mountain. He is standing when he teaches.[2] This was the usual custom until about the middle of the first century C.E. After that time Jewish teachers began to "sit and teach."

Jesus moved away from the crowds, and his disciples followed him up the mountainside. Then his disciples drew close to him and Jesus opened his mouth and taught them. "He opened his mouth" is an Aramaic Semitic idiom. It means "to speak." It is not literally describing the physical act of opening one's mouth.[3] Sometimes it means the teacher has removed his hand from his mouth and is ready to speak. Now that Jesus is ready, he says in Aramaic, *"Toowayhon l'miskayneh brooh, dilhon hee malkutha dashmayah."*

POOR IN PRIDE

Blessed are the poor in spirit: for theirs is the kingdom of heaven. Mt. 5:3.

The Aramaic text reads: "Blessed are the humble, for theirs is the kingdom of heaven."[4] In Aramaic the word "spirit," *ruha*, has many meanings. In this verse "spirit" means "pride" and refers to those who are poor in pride. It also refers to the humble, the unassuming, and those who are free from racial pride and prejudice. Jesus usually addressed his message to the poor, oppressed, and underprivileged people. Commonly, the pious poor where those who surrendered to God and were awaiting God's reign on earth.

Both Matthew and Mark tell us that Jesus went throughout all of Galilee proclaiming that God's kingdom was at hand.[5] Jesus taught that

---

[2]Lk. 6:17-20.

[3]See Ps. 38:14.

[4]Mt. 5:3, Aramaic Peshitta text, Lamsa translation.

[5]Mt. 4:23, Mk. 1:14-15.

God's reign was present despite the fact that Rome, a Gentile power, was ruling in Palestine. In this verse, Jesus further declared that the kingdom of heaven belongs to the humble.

Semites were proud of their ancestry and social standing. Those who were rich and belonged to nobility were reluctant to serve under others. Some people in the Near East, although poor and uncultured, were highly respected and honored because of their ancestry. These people were exempt from particular levies and burdens that others had to bear. Certain Near Easterners would rather starve than do any manual labor because their ancestors were never employed in that type of work. This kind of pride frequently reduced them to poverty and destitution.

The Jews were proud that they were Abraham's children. Abraham was the founder of their race and a servant of the living God. The people of Israel believed that Yahweh, their God, was the creator of the universe and that the gods of the other nations were not gods. Therefore, when their enemies defeated them and took them captive, they often despised their conquerors.

Israel had endured many hardships and changes. Its national glory had vanished. For nearly 500 years, the Israelites were living under a foreign yoke and there was little hope for the nation's restoration. Some Pharisees, priests, and scribes, to console themselves, lived in their past glory. However, there was nothing they could boast about except an unrealistic national pride.

These men tried to make others accept the idea that their nation was too good to consent to foreign rule. They believed that their nation was so holy that they should have no dealing with other nations. They also felt that the people should have enough pride not to take orders from officials of foreign lands whose gods were inferior to their God.

According to Jesus' teaching, God's kingdom was now arriving and the "poor in pride"—"the humble"—would participate in this heavenly reign. This kingdom belonged to them. But those who were holding to false pride would keep themselves from participating in God's dawning kingdom.

Blessed are those who have no racial prejudice and are accepting of others. Jesus knew that before his nation could find peace, it would have to learn to be meek and unassuming. The people had to be humble and tolerant before they could expect tolerance from their foreign rulers.

Matthew's gospel uses the expression "kingdom of heaven" exclusively. The other two synoptic gospels, Mark and Luke, use the term "kingdom of God." Matthew uses the word "heaven" euphemistically. He substitutes the word "heaven" for "God." Nonetheless, the meaning is the same. "Kingdom of God or heaven" refers to God's sovereignty, God's reigning presence.

The Aramaic word *toowayhon* usually translates as "blessed" but it also has other meanings: happy, content, blissful, delighted, fortunate. "Delighted" suggests great happiness, prosperity, and abundant goodness. I translate the first beatitude as, "Delighted are those who surrender to God because heaven's reign belongs to them!"[6]

The gospel author uses the expression "poor in spirit" with a specialized meaning and not just in the sense of those who possess nothing. Luke's gospel says, "Blessed are the poor." In Judaism of the last two centuries B.C.E., the term "poor," according to rabbinic sources, had practically become a synonym for "pious" or "saintly." The poor were the ones who surrendered to God and let God guide them in everything. They were humble and relied totally on God and not on material possessions.

THE MOURNERS

Blessed are they that mourn: for they shall be comforted. Mt. 5:4

In countries where wars, revolutions, and persecutions frequently occur, mourning is common. Among these unfortunate people, one often sees women with their hair cut, heads bowed down, and dressed in black. And the men will have their heads covered with black cloth

---

[6]Mt. 5:3, Aramaic Peshitta text, Errico.

and their faces expressing deep sorrow. Even little children share in the sorrowful events that are constantly taking place. Seldom does one see or hear joy and laughter in these homes.

Galilee was a center of insurrections; Galileans were a warlike people. They were the descendants of the Assyrians and had retained their strong tribal characteristics. These people made repeated attempts to free Palestine from its Roman yoke but failed miserably. The Jews in the South did not help them. Judas, the Galilean, started a revolt and gallantly fought the Roman legionaries. The Roman soldiers defeated his uprising and killed him.[7]

Pilate and Herod vehemently tried to stamp out these revolts so that they could win favors from the Roman emperor. Some Jewish leaders also betrayed their own people so that the Roman officials would bestow special favors on them. Pilate had mingled the blood of some Galileans with their sacrifices. (See Luke 13:1.) The Galileans mourned the death of their heroes and loved ones who lost their lives trying to free their country from alien rule.

In the new kingdom, God's presence would comfort the mourners. Their sorrow was to be changed into joy and the oppressors would be no more. These people came to Jesus and complained of the injustice and suffering that they were enduring. He cheered them: "Blessed are those who mourn for they will rejoice." They were soon to become citizens of the new kingdom and participate in the eternal presence of their God. Joy and happiness awaited them. The Kingdom of God was at hand. (See Luke 6:21; John 16:20.)

THE MEEK

Blessed are the meek: for they shall inherit the earth. Mt. 5:5.

Near Easterners commonly use the Semitic proverb: "The meek shall inherit the earth." It refers to a type of person who does not

---

[7]See Acts 5:37.

retaliate. This proverb describes a person who is free from a grasping temper that leads to disputes and quarrels often ending in bloodshed and murder. The meek are those who practice nonresistance and submit to injustice even at great inconvenience. They seldom protest to their rulers but in their supplications always remind God of their heavy burdens.

It was customary in the Near East that when a man died or was killed in war leaving no male heir, the meritorious meek would inherit his property. Landlords invariably preferred to lease their vineyards and farms to men of good character, who were responsible and reliable. Therefore, the meek were ultimately blessed and rose in power and prosperity. Undoubtedly, Jesus knew of cases where the Romans executed Galilean rebels and confiscated their property and gave it to those who were not seditious. In this beatitude, Jesus stresses the quality of meekness that brings contentment and satisfaction. This saying goes against the spirit of chronic restlessness that creates disturbances and violations of the law.

We must not confuse meekness with weakness. The meek are gentle and do not reward evil for evil. These people bend like trees during a heavy storm and survive, while the proud and arrogant perish. Meekness is a sword of the spirit that destroys hatred and removes fear and enmity. In the new kingdom, its citizens will be armed with the weapons of the spirit—meekness and loving kindness. These weapons will triumph where the sword and force have failed.

JUSTICE

Blessed are they which do hunger and thirst after righteousness: for they shall be filled. Mt. 5:6.

The Aramaic term *kenutha*[8] means "justice, piety, devoutness, righteousness, godliness." It is an ethical justice based on the Torah.

---

[8]*Kenutha* pronounced Kay-noo-tha.

Exploitation of the poor and injustice prevail almost everywhere. When government officials levy heavy taxation, people begin to hunger for true justice. To console themselves during times of extortion and mistreatment, Near Easterners dream of kind rulers and honest officials in the place of their present harsh leadership.

Judges and other government leaders do not judge people in accordance with what they have done, but according to class and money. Therefore the unjust often crush the poor and confiscate their property. These mistreated people grow tired and become indifferent to political parties and reformers. So they continually pray for the establishment of God's rule throughout the land.

Justice is the foundation of all world religions and democratic institutions. Peace, progress, happiness, harmony, law and order without justice are impossible. Justice is another name for truth. In Aramaic "justice" and "religion" mean "balance" and "equality." The universe is established on laws and true equations that bring an equilibrium that lasts forever.

Nations that have flaunted justice have eventually fallen. Justice may come slowly, but it will always catch those who have violated it. Jesus assured those who were hungering and thirsting for justice that they would find satisfaction. God's reign had now come to open the way for the people. When we hunger and thirst, we will seek what we hunger and thirst for. Jesus' teaching about God's kingdom brought an understanding of true justice among his disciples and followers.

THE COMPASSIONATE AND THE SINCERE

Blessed are the merciful: for they shall obtain mercy. Blessed are the pure in heart: for they shall see God. Mt. 5:7-8.

Mrahmaneh refers to the merciful, the compassionate. It comes from the Semitic root *rhm*, "to love, delight in, to be kind, friendly." The compassionate were those who performed deeds of mercy. This was practical compassion.

Jesus was aware of universal law. He knew that those who were kind, charitable, and compassionate would in turn receive kindness, charity, and compassion. For those who give, it will be given to them; to those who open their doors to strangers, doors will be opened to them. Jesus blesses those who are merciful and compassionate. These are the people who participate in God's kingdom. Where would the world be without merciful men and women who constantly share with those who are in need? The principle of giving and receiving is inherent in nature. The wise Creator set this pattern for all life to function in harmony. When this principle is broken, all life is disturbed.

"Pure in heart" is an Aramaic idiom. It refers to a sincere, contrite individual. It also means a person with a clear mind. A clear heart and mind perceives God. To see God is to know the ever present divine presence—God's immanence. When the mind and emotions are clouded one does not perceive the good that is present. The mind is the mirror of the soul. A spotted mirror cannot reflect a clear image and it is the same with the mind. Thus, when the mind is filled with hatred and resentment, it cannot reflect goodness. All of humankind's actions, good or bad, begin in the mind. When the mind is clear, it reflects the goodness of God and then we can see God.

The pure in heart are the pious and innocent men and women who never think of harming other people. They feel the presence of God constantly. They know that God is good. The genuinely pious reflect that image of God wherever they may be.

WORKERS FOR PEACE

Blessed are the peacemakers: for they shall be called the children of God. Mt. 5:9.

The term "peace" in Aramaic is *shlama*. It means "to surrender." In the ancient Near East, when one person greeted another with *shlama lakh*, it carried the idea of "I surrender to you." Today, it simply means "hello." When the one who was greeted accepted the salutation, the reply would be: "I surrender to you," "Be at peace," or "Be in tranquillity." The enchanting power of this ancient greeting inspired confidence and removed all fears and doubts from the minds of strangers who had exchanged greetings. Thus, by surrendering to one another, they would find peace. When everyone surrenders, there is no one else to yield and entrust themselves to but God.

Peacemakers sat at the gates of the city, acting as judges and working to reconcile people who had grievances. They settled quarrels and managed to calm disputing friends. They admonished those who were using force to settle matters. Until the turn of our century, there were not many government-appointed judges in the Near East. But there were always peacemakers working hard to bring peace to both neighbors and strangers. These men received no compensation.

Most people preferred going to peacemakers rather than traveling long distances to find the few judges that the government had appointed. In those bygone days when judges received no salary, they relied on gifts and bribes for their livelihood. So the people would rather not risk appearing before these men who were eagerly awaiting their prey. These judges would often keep the disputants in jail until they had parted with their last penny. Jesus told his followers that they needed to settle with their adversaries while on the road and not to appear before judges. (See Matthew 5:25-26.)

PURSUED AND PERSECUTED

Blessed are they which are persecuted for righteousness' sake: for their's is the kingdom of heaven. Blessed are ye, when men shall revile you, and persecute you, and shall say all manner of evil against you falsely, for my sake. Rejoice, and be exceeding glad: for great is your reward in heaven: for so persecuted they the prophets which were before you. Mt. 5:10-12.

Jesus knew that his new and practical teaching would undermine the prevailing concepts of religion, law, and order. Like new wine in an old wineskin, this new teaching would burst asunder old relationships, patterns of thought, and ways of living. His teaching would create problems in the family. He also knew that those who believed in force—the mighty, the proud, and the greedy—would oppose the gospel of God's kingdom. Those in power would pursue, persecute, imprison, and slay his followers. Jesus' teaching contradicted all that the material world and its institutions stood for.

In the new world order that the Hebrew prophets had heralded and Jesus had envisioned, all men and women would be equal citizens of the kingdom of God. Participants in this kingdom would share God's light; racial and class barriers would be eliminated and national boundaries obliterated. People would pray for one another, help those in need, and forgive those who had offended them. Laborers would learn to love their employers and remain loyal to them. Employers would be faithful and fair to their workers. Love would motivate all work.

Love alone can create a just and universal social order. Love is impartial, inclusive, and universal. Despite this fact, the new gospel was like a sword. It would divide people and there would be reproach and persecution. Many would reject the powerful truth and ideas that Jesus taught. His followers would suffer, but great is their reward in heaven. A heavenly reward means a reward that never dies; it is eternal. It is an Aramaic way of speaking that means your reward is assured. The enactment of God's kingdom, through Jesus' disciples and followers, would live forever. Generations to come would bless, praise, and remember them because these men and women dared to reveal and live a new way of life.

SALT OF THE EARTH

Ye are the salt of the earth: but if the salt have lost his savour, wherewith shall it be salted? It is thenceforth good for nothing, but to be cast out, and to be trodden under foot of men. Mt. 5:13.

From time immemorial, salt has been a precious element. Centuries ago when salt was scarce and modern methods of processing were unknown, salt became a medium of exchange, just as gold and silver are today. Our term "salary" derives from the Latin word *sal* which means "salt." In those days, they paid their soldiers and workers in salt.

No food would have any flavor without mixing a little salt with it. But when salt loses its savor it becomes useless. There are two kinds of salt—sea salt and earth salt. Sea salt never loses its savor. But when salt is mined from the earth, it must be kept dry so that its savor may be preserved. When Easterners carelessly store their salt and it loses its savor, they will throw the salt on their roof tops. Then men and women working and children playing on the housetops will trample the salt under their feet.

The Hebrew Bible tells that God had called Israel as a nation to be a spiritual leader for other nations. Israel's prophets had been teaching their people and God's word had been guiding them, but for many years the people of Israel had lost their way, and the Gentile nations had trampled them. The people of Israel were the precious salt of the earth to savor the nations of the earth. These people had God's word and the idea of a universal kingdom based on peace and justice. Jesus spoke directly to the people and admonished them not to lose their savor. They were to be examples of living in the kingdom of God right now regardless of the world's condition.

LIGHT OF THE WORLD

Ye are the light of the world. A city that is set on an hill cannot be hid. Neither do men light a candle, and put it under a bushel, but on a candlestick; and it giveth light unto all that are in the house. Let your light so shine before men, that they may see your good works, and glorify your Father which is in heaven. Mt. 5:14-16.

The Aramaic word for light is *noohra*. Metaphorically, it also means "teaching, enlightenment, brilliance, intelligence." Near Easterners refer to good and pious people as "light." They also thought

65

of the Torah, God's word, and the teaching of their prophets as "light."
And, they referred to God's presence as "light."

Israel's light was buried under so many commentaries and other
man-made ordinances that no one could see it. Many religious teachers
had pretended to be concerned about minor laws so that they might
break the more important ones. Thus, while condemning others, they
illegally escaped condemnation themselves.

Faith, forgiveness, humility, meekness, peace, justice, love, and
purity of heart are the "light" of the human soul and need to shine in
the world. When they do shine in the world, the human family sees that
the kingdom of God has truly arrived. Jesus' disciples were to carry out
and act on the teaching of their lord.

ENACTING THE TORAH

*Think not that I am come to destroy the law, or the prophets: I am not
come to destroy, but to fulfill. For verily I say unto you, till heaven and earth
pass, one jot or one tittle shall in no wise pass from the law, till all be
fulfilled. Whosoever therefore shall break one of these least commandments,
and shall teach men so, he shall be called the least in the kingdom of
heaven: but whosoever shall do and teach them, the same shall be called
great in the kingdom of heaven.* Mt. 5:17-19.

"Do not expect that I have come to weaken the law or the
prophets; I have not come to weaken but to fulfill."[9] The Aramaic word
nishreh means "to untie, loose, weaken." Recently installed governmental officials, when establishing a new regime, usually assure the
people that the new laws will be easier and the taxes reduced.

Generally, founders of new religions condemn or disparage the
principles and practices of established faiths. Exacting ceremonies and
religious demands are abolished or modified so as to gain the favor and
support of the people. It appears that no movement, religious or

---

[9]Mt. 5:17, Aramaic Peshitta text, Lamsa translation.

political, can be started or be successful without some criticism of the old systems.

Jesus was a new prophet. His teaching deviated from the recognized leaders of his day. Many were accusing him of organizing a different faith. Others felt that his teaching was undermining the influence of the law and the prophets because he refused to comply with certain ordinances and traditions. Then, there were those who thought of him as a troublemaker.

False rumors were spreading that Jesus' teaching was aimed against the Torah (law) and against the teachings of the holy prophets. Jesus' enemies, and even some of his friends and followers, had mistakenly interpreted some of his remarks against the teaching of the elders. Men at the synagogues, who did not understand the new gospel, said that Jesus had come to destroy their religion by weakening the law and the prophets. The new insights that Jesus taught were not intended to weaken the law and the prophets. These teachings were meant to bring out the spiritual meaning of Scripture. In reality, what Jesus advocated was the enactment of the law and prophets.

God had given to Moses a simple and clear law. It was a light to the world. Man-made interpretations and false doctrines cannot obscure or destroy it. As long as there is "heaven and earth" there will be law to guide and govern humankind. It is the spirit of the law that counts and gives life and not the letter of the law. No, not even a *yodh* (the smallest letter in the Aramaic and Hebrew alphabets) or a line will pass away from the law until all is enacted.

GENUINE RIGHTEOUSNESS

For I say unto you, That except your righteousness shall exceed the righteousness of the scribes and Pharisees, ye shall in no case enter into the kingdom of heaven. Mt. 5:20.

Many scribes and Pharisees read, analyzed, and taught the law but did not live up to its principles. They showed their piety (righteousness)

67

through their literal knowledge of the law and through their outward observances. Some of them preached piety and justice but defrauded the widows and embezzled the property of orphans that was entrusted to them. Many of them prayed long prayers publicly to impress the people with their piety. They concerned themselves with the law's minute ordinances but disregarded the important matters, such as justice and mercy. They failed to reach the inner meaning and depth of the law and its true application for daily living.

Jesus' disciples and followers were to go beyond a literal analysis of the law. His disciples were to practice and reveal the inner meaning of the law and the prophets. God had given the law to help people in their relations with one another, not to burden them. When humanity enacts the inner depth—the spirit—of the law, the kingdom of God hastens into manifestation. The phrase, "And ye shall in no case enter the kingdom of heaven" means that unless one was actually practicing the principles of the kingdom one would not be participating in God's sovereign presence. "Enter" means "to participate." Jesus' adherents were to demonstrate God's kingdom on earth.

SURPASSING TRADITIONAL TEACHING

Ye have heard that it was said by them of old time, Thou shalt not kill; and whosoever shall kill shall be in danger of the judgment: But I say unto you, that whosoever is angry with his brother without a cause, shall be in danger of the judgment: and whosoever shall say to his brother Raca, shall be in danger of the council: but whosoever shall say Thou fool, shall be in danger of hell fire. Mt. 5:21-22.

The Aramaic text reads: "You have heard that it was said to those who were before you: You will not murder; and anyone who murders deserves the judgment of the court. But I am saying to you that anyone who is angry with his brother for no reason deserves the judgment of the court; and anyone who says to his brother, 'spit' (*raqa*) deserves the judgment of the congregation; and anyone who says *lilla* is

68

sentenced to anguishing regret *(gehenna* of fire)."[10]

"You have heard" means "you have received a tradition." The next phrase, "that it was said to those who were before you," introduces a scripture: "thou shalt not murder."Anyone committing murder deserves whatever penalty the court decides. According to Jesus' interpretation of the law, one needs to recognize what motivates murder. For example, Jesus knew that Near Easterners look upon an offensive and defamatory word like *raqa*,"spit," as precipitous of murder. Some men would slay the offender who spoke such a word to anyone or who actually spit in another's face.

Part A—EXPECTORATING. *Raqa* is an Aramaic noun and comes from the Semitic root *raq* "to spit." In the Greek text of Matthew, the translators did not translate this word from Aramaic into Greek. Hence, there is no English rendering of this Aramaic term in our New Testament based on the Greek text.

During heated arguments and controversies, Near Easterners often expectorate in each other's faces. Merchants and prospective customers, after long bargaining and arguments concerning price, may spit in each other's face when they fail to agree. Spitting almost always initiates serious and dangerous quarrels. One often says: *"raqa arek na bapek*—I will spit in your face." Expectorating is the most contemptible action one can take in Near Eastern society. Many people still engage in this despicable habit in Egypt, Syria, and Palestine. It is an abusive and insulting practice.

Just one offensive word or an action such as spitting will usually evoke an explosive quarrel that could lead to murder. It is better to conquer one's anger than to let it escalate and lead to murder. One can control a fire when it first starts, but once it is blazing, it is uncontrollable. Jesus wanted to stop trouble before it began. He taught that the most important way to prevent murder is to examine the causes leading to it. Making offensive remarks to another can and often does lead to unnecessary loss of life. Interestingly, a sect of devil worshipers near Mosul, Iraq, forbids spitting under any circumstance. This restriction

---

[10]Mt. 5:21-22, Aramaic Peshitta text, Errico.

is their protest against people of other religions who spit in each other's faces. And it is against those who, when making a mistake, spit on the devil saying: "*po elek satana*—I spit on Satan."

Part B—THOU FOOL. *Sakhla* is the Aramaic word for "fool." However, the Peshitta text uses the Semitic word *lilla* and not *sakhla*. Saying the word "fool" is not offensive among Near Eastern people. They use this word *sakhla* without any implication of insult.[11] Brothers often call each other *sakhla* without a thought of offending. However, *lilla* is an offensive but antiquated Aramaic term. To call someone *lilla* is worse than an insult because it reflects on that person's character.

In the ancient Near East, among certain Aramaic speaking clans in the mountains of Kurdistan, and also at the turn of the twentieth century, the term *lilla* referred to men who performed household duties that a woman would do. Most Near Eastern fathers would consider it a disgrace to mind the children in the absence of their wives. At such times, they call on their women neighbors to help them. *Lilla* also means "nursemaid."

Near Eastern men will also call a coward, a woman. They say this because women usually do not fight. So the term *lilla* has another meaning and refers to someone who is a coward. No full-blooded Easterner would tolerate such a term being said to him. Today, among certain Aramaic speaking people, *lilla* describes someone who is incredibly stupid. It is an extremely offensive word.

Part C—HELL FIRE. The Aramaic expression *gayhenna dnoora* is usually translated as "hell fire." *Gayhenna—Gei Hinnom* in Hebrew—derives from the infamous valley of *Ben Hinnom*, southwest of Jerusalem.[12] After the fall of the northern kingdom of Israel, Assyria made the southern kingdom of Judah pay tribute. In 2 Chronicles 28, we read that the Judean King Ahaz (735-715 B.C.E.) took some of the precious temple silver and gold ornaments to appease the King of Assyria. Ahaz worshiped and offered sacrifices to idols. In the valley of *Hinnom* in Jerusalem, the king also condemned his son to the flames

---

[11]See Mt. 7:26; I Cor. 15:36.
[12]See Jer 19:2.

as a sacrificial offering to pacify the gods. It was because of these horrible atrocities and practices that the valley, *Gei Hinnom*, became a Semitic term for "hell." During the time of the New Testament, the Hinnom Valley became a place to burn rubbish and the bodies of plague victims.

Jesus used the phrase *gayhenna* or *gayhenna dnoora*, "hell fire," (Matthew 5:22, 29, 30) idiomatically to indicate deep regret, mental suffering, torment, or destruction. This inner, psychological condition is a result of making grave offensive remarks against one's brother that could lead to revenge and murder. In verses 29 and 30, the term "hell fire" means that practicing certain habits would lead one to utter torment and destruction.

RECONCILE WITH YOUR BROTHER

Therefore if thou bring thy gift to the altar, and there rememberest that thy brother hath ought against thee; Leave there thy gift before the altar, and go thy way; first be reconciled to thy brother and then come and offer thy gift. Mt. 5:23-24.

Quarrels and disputes are common between brothers because they live in the same house. Wives and servants usually help bring about the unrest between the brothers and contribute to the altercations. Then, when the brothers separate and their families live apart, further troubles arise because of property divisions. Reconciliation and peace become nearly impossible. At times two brothers living under the same roof may never speak to each other.

In this verse, the word "brother" means a neighbor, a member of the same race or faith. Generally, reconciliation between brothers, neighbors, or members of the same faith takes place during feast and holy days. A few days before the feast a group of townspeople known as peacemakers begins making peace between quarreling parties. They settle the differences, divide the properties, and urge them to forgive each other and reconcile.

When the efforts of peacemakers fail, the final hope for reconciliation rests on the words a priest will speak during the services on that holy day. On such occasions, the priest reads absolution and prays to God, asking forgiveness for his people. He then asks the people to forgive each other so that they may receive forgiveness from God. This is done before giving holy communion. Communicants who have not been on good terms rush to kiss each other.

If the priest discovers that certain brothers or neighbors have not settled matters, then the priest will refuse to give them communion. Some men, before the conclusion of the service, will leave the church to find their adversaries and make peace with them. They will kiss them and reconcile with them so that they may return and participate in holy communion.

Jesus recommends that one should leave even the most sacred gift on the altar and go in search of an enemy and reconcile with that person. Love and peace are greater than all temples and sacrifices because God is love. Without peace between people love cannot find expression. One must reconcile with a brother or neighbor first in order to know full peace with God. When there is peace with one's brother and neighbor there is no cause for abuse, so to reconcile with an enemy and subdue one's anger is far greater than offering a gift to God.

SETTLING WITH AN ADVERSARY

Agree with thine adversary quickly, whiles thou art in the way with him; lest at any time the adversary deliver thee to the judge, and the judge deliver thee to the officer, and thou be cast into prison. Verily I say unto thee, Thou shalt by no means come out thence, till thou hast paid the uttermost farthing. Mt. 5:25-26.

In many areas of the Near East, there are few courts and judges. One reason for this is that most Semites prefer to settle their differences by arbitration or through peacemakers who are chiefly bishops and priests. When such efforts fail they turn to government officials and justices of the peace who are stationed at capitals of provinces or at some far distant points. In such cases men have to make long journeys to seek justice. In olden times prophets and men of God were the arbitrators, peacemakers and judges who looked after the political and spiritual welfare of the people. Samuel was this type of judge to whom all Israel came.[13]

Even today in most countries of the Near East, the disputants journey for two, three, or more days in search of justice. In many instances the parties concerned travel together, stop at the same inn, eat and converse with each other during their journey. They may have fought with each other or perhaps even wounded one another, but on the long journey in search of justice, they have to be friendly. They could meet bandits on the road who might rob and kill them and they would have to protect and fight for each other. Often on the weary and tiresome journey, their troubles and differences are forgotten. Friendly conversations take the place of resentment and hatred. They will speak gracious words to each other instead of cursing one another. Love and sympathy will dominate their relationship.

Thus while on the way to the judge, men who have been enemies for months suddenly become friends. They talk over their differences and suggest remedies to each other. Such attempts and discussions would have been impossible if the men were at home. Usually friends and enemies would have interfered and prevented a reconciliation. But on the tedious journey, they have time to think things over and are free to make agreements without others interfering.

Questions that were difficult to settle at home now appear to be easy. They apologize to each other, admitting their ignorance of facts or blaming others for their quarrel. So while they walk together, they enter into friendly relations and can settle their differences to the advantage of both. Besides, they now can avoid the loss of time and expense necessary to present their cases before the officials of justice.

Two men may start on a five day journey to a judge and return

---

[13]1 Sam. 7:15.

home unexpectedly on the first or second day. On their arrival in the town, one of them will kill a sheep and give a banquet in honor of the other, inviting friends to share in the reconciliation without having to go before a judge. At the banquet, each of the two men asserts the blame was his own.

However, on such a journey, if neither one was willing to yield, both would have to face the judge and experience many hardships. Generally, judges have few cases during the year. Since their support comes from complainants, they can become like spiders patiently waiting for their victims to fall into the web. A trifling affair is made into a big case requiring months and sometimes years to settle.

Justice is often executed not according to guilt but wealth. If both parties are poor, the case is promptly dismissed with a few rebukes. But if the disputants happen to have money or other wealth, the case may never be settled until the last cent is gone and all property sold. Some judges are so cruel and unjust that they will immediately put both parties in prison, desiring to obtain money quickly. Relatives and friends will have to sell the disputants' properties, pay enormous bribes, and meet other expenses, hoping to gain liberty for the imprisoned. Freedom only comes when the judge knows that nothing more can be sold and the prison cell has to hold other unfortunates.

Jesus had seen many men lose their property and receive severe punishment for little differences that could have been easily settled out of court. According to Jesus, reconciliation with an enemy is important. It is better to settle a problem while it is small and perhaps lose a little than to not reconcile and lose it all.

VOYEURISM

But I say unto you, That whosoever looketh on a woman to lust after her hath committed adultery with her already in his heart. Mt. 5:28.

"Yet I am saying to you that anyone who looks at a woman so that he may desire her, right then commits adultery in his heart."[14] Near Eastern women have always covered their faces with a veil. They resent non-family men looking at them. Some women are even shy in the presence of their own husbands if they are not wearing a veil. It would be a disgrace for a woman to dress or undress before her husband, or worse, for a stranger to see her.

Men and women seldom meet socially. A woman's body is a mystery to Near Eastern men. It is on this account that men will try to see a woman secretly. "Looking at a woman" does not mean to look at her face but to make an attempt to see her body.

Houses in the Near East are built close to each other. Only walls separate them. Women usually bathe in the house or courtyard so there is little chance for privacy. Often when women bathe, men hide themselves on the housetops and other places so that they might see them bathing.

King David, from the roof of his palace, saw Bathsheba bathing in her courtyard. He immediately lusted after her, had her brought into the palace and committed adultery with her. She, of course, became pregnant. To avoid problems with Uriah, her husband, King David brought him home from the battlefield. However, Uriah did not sleep with Bathsheba during his stay in Jerusalem. Then David had Uriah sent to the front lines of the battle. He also had given instructions in a letter that read: "Set Uriah in the forefront of the battle, and then retire from him that he may be smitten and die." After Bathsheba's husband was killed, King David married her.[15]

Jesus goes directly to the heart of the situation rather than to its results. He censures looking at a woman that is deliberate and lustful.[16] The adulterous act is done in the mind first. Action follows the desire to commit adultery. It is this kind of "looking at a woman" that Jesus refers to in his teaching.

---

[14]Mt. 5:28, Aramaic Peshitta text, Errico.

[15]See 2 Sam. 11:2.-17.

[16]In the West, we refer to men who do this kind of looking as "peeping Toms."

75

THE EYE AND THE HAND

And if thy right eye offend thee, pluck it out, and cast it from thee: for it is profitable for thee that one of thy members should perish and not that thy whole body should be cast into hell. And if thy right hand offend thee, cut it off and cast it from thee: for it is profitable for thee that one of thy members should perish, and not that thy whole body should be cast into hell. Mt. 5:29-30.

Part A—THE EYE. The eye is the symbol of desire and envy. It is the unspoken but understood language of the Near East. Thus the reference here is to envy. The eye with its varying shades of light gives expression to the countenance; in turn, the heart influences both the eye and the countenance. This unspoken language of the eye is a fearful menace to many superstitious Semites.

Near Easterners often say, "cut your eye from my boy," which means, "don't envy my boy"; or they say, "do not cut your eye from my family while I am away," meaning "look after my family while I am absent from them." At times when sheep or cattle die, their owner might blame a neighbor whose "evil eye" had brought the misfortune.

If a woman with a reputation of having an "evil eye" enters a home where there is a handsome lad, his mother will smear his face with charcoal to avoid the spell of that evil eye. In the Near East one must say: "What an ugly child." This saying dispels the work of an evil eye. In other words, if you admired a child who later becomes sick, you will be blamed for putting the "evil eye" on that child. This is one reason why some of the faces of children are seldom washed. Among the Semites, "safety first" is more important than sanitation.

Jesus' counsel to "pluck out the envying and coveting eye" is an Aramaic idiom. It means that if one has the habit of envying another's property, stop the habit before it brings you to stealing. It is better to lose one of your eyes than become a slave to envy that will lead to hell (destruction). Semites deem the right eye, hand, and foot more important than the left eye, hand, and foot. In biblical lands, when governmental authorities catch thieves, bandits, and criminals they will punish them by cutting off their hands or feet. And finally, with too many offences, the thieves will lose their heads.

Part B—THE HAND. "Cut off your hand" is an Aramaic saying. It has no reference to actually cutting off a hand. People often say to each other, "cut off your hand from my vineyard" meaning "don't gather grapes from my vineyard." "His hand is too long" refers to a thief. "Shorten your hand" means "do not steal." As with "plucking out your eye," "cutting off your hand" denotes cutting out a habit that leads to destruction. The hand is mentioned because it is the agent by which the mind and body do their work.

Part C—FALLING INTO HELL. The Aramaic text says: "For it is better for you to lose one of your members, and not have your entire body fall into hell." This is typical figurative Aramaic speech. It implies that the evil act which the hand or eye is doing is greater than the loss of the eye or hand. One can do without the things he or she may be coveting, or wanting to steal, rather than lose one's entire life and suffer mental and emotional regret. It is better to sacrifice the lesser for the sake of the greater.

"Hell," metaphorically, means "mental suffering, anguish, and regret." In the Near East, people do not understand the term "hell" literally. Some teachers in the West and those influenced by Western religious teachers believe God would burn human bodies or souls as a punishment. Indeed, burning by fire was a form of Babylonian capital punishment. Near Easterners often say, "he burned me; I have been in fire for a long time" meaning "I have suffered mental agony because of him." One must not take these expressions literally. Mental suffering goes on forever and ever. It is far worse than fire. On the other hand, no human body could withstand being burned forever and ever. A body can be turned into ashes in four hours, but mental suffering never seems to end and is truly hell. (See Matthew 18.9.)

The public understood these terms. Galileans who spoke northern Aramaic were not puzzled by these remarks which sound so harsh to Westerners. Nor did they require explanations, because these expressions of speech were in current usage and still are current in Aramaic speech and thought.

DIVORCE

It hath been said, Whosoever shall put away his wife, let him give her a writing of divorcement: But I say unto you, That whosoever shall put away his wife, saving for the cause of fornication, causeth her to commit adultery: and whosoever shall marry her that is divorced committeth adultery.
Mt. 5:31-32.

"It has been said that whoever divorces his wife, must give her divorce papers. But I say to you that whoever divorces his wife, except for fornication, causes her to commit adultery; and whoever marries a woman who is separated but not divorced, commits adultery."[17] Near Easterners do not recognize nor practice civil marriages. The only sacred bonds between a man and his wife are the blessings of the priest and the payment of the dowry. At times it takes from three to seven days to celebrate a wedding feast, but it only takes a few minutes for a man to divorce his wife.

Most Near Easterners consider marriage a sacred institution. It must, therefore, not be mixed with politics or courts as is the case in other countries. Near Eastern women look upon marriage as a lottery and feel resigned to their fate. They have no say in their marriage nor do their parents ask for their consent. Consequently, they have nothing to say when the divorce question arises. The sole authority is invested in the man, who exercises unlimited power over his wife or wives.

Descendants of the ancient Christians who still adhere to the Mosaic Code are the oldest branch of the Semitic (Assyrian) race. Divorces among them are very rare and the attitude of the men toward their wives is quite different from that of other neighboring Semitic races. They are more tolerant and, to some degree, their women exercise a certain freedom equal to Western women. No doubt, this change took place when Christianity was adopted as the religion of the country.

It is very important to know that the Peshitta text of this verse

---

[17]Mt. 5:31-32, Aramaic Peshitta text, Lamsa translation.

uses two Aramaic words, whereas the Western text uses only one. *Nishbook* is one word and it means "to leave." The other word is *nishreh*, "to divorce." Today, if a man marries a woman who is left (separated or abandoned), the church will excommunicate both the man and the woman. But if a woman who has been left by her husband obtains a decree of *shiriana* "divorce" (meaning the loosening of the bond), she can marry again. The church considers this remarriage lawful.

To gain a clearer understanding of the divorce question, we need to study the divorce customs among those influenced by Semitic religions and culture—that is, non-Christian Semites such as the Jews in Mesopotamia and Persia, the Arabians, and the non-Semitic races such as the Kurds and Persians. Ancient biblical law still fully governs these races. Some of these peoples divorce their wives for no criminal or moral reason but for other cultural considerations.

For example, men may divorce their wives for not bearing any children, for not working hard enough, for not having found favor in their husband's eyes, or for looking at other men. If any religious authorities should intervene to stop the divorce, a small bribe of a lamb, chicken, or two pounds of sugar would be sufficient to appease some of these authorities. The men can now obtain religious approval for the divorce.

For unknown ages, Near Eastern women have been degraded and regarded as man's property, at times even bought and sold in open markets. Divorces are so easy and frequent that religious laws have been instituted to help remedy the situation. For example, laws have been enacted that say: If a husband puts his wife away for no reason and then regrets it and wants to take her back, the woman will first have to marry another man for two or three months. After the two or three months of marriage, she then may obtain a divorce before she can return and remarry her first husband. This, of course, is very humiliating for the first husband.

However, people have found ways to get around this strict law. In Kurdistan, for instance, if a Kurd should divorce his wife for no legitimate reason and then later desire to remarry her, the woman is immediately betrothed and married to a male goat or an ox. After the marriage, the animal is killed and the woman becomes a widow. When her mourning days are fulfilled, her first husband may remarry her.

Jesus condemned the laxity of the divorce law and attempted to strengthen it. He did not try to change the Mosaic law that allowed divorce based on the grounds of adultery. What Jesus condemned was the abandonment of wives by their husbands in arbitrary ways. Jesus saw husbands mistreating and humbling their wives and putting heavy responsibilities on them. He knew women were equal to men and that their tasks in life were just as important as men's.

Jesus was the first prophet to champion the rights of women and to give them equality with men. According to Jesus, no woman should be deserted or divorced except on the grounds of adultery. He condemned the injustice that was committed against women of his day. Women of all countries and creeds admire and honor Jesus for his teaching about women. (See Matthew 19:3; Mark 10:2; Luke 16:18.)

SWEARING

Again you have heard that it hath been said by them of old time, Thou shalt not forswear thyself, but shalt perform unto the Lord thine oaths: But I say unto you, Swear not at all; neither by heaven; for it is God's throne: Nor by the earth; for it is his footstool: neither by Jerusalem for it is the city of the great King. Neither shalt thou swear by thy head, because thou canst not make one hair white or black. But let your communication be, Yea, yea; Nay, nay: for whatsoever is more than these cometh of evil. Mt. 5:33-37.

Swearing in the name of God, holy men, and sacred places and things is an integral element in Semitic speech: "For men swear by one who is greater than themselves; and in every dispute among them, the true settlement is by oaths [swearing]."[18] Scripture is filled with examples of swearing in the name of God. (See Genesis 21:23-24,

---

[18]Heb. 6:16, Aramaic Peshitta Text, Lamsa translation

Romans 9:1). The writers of Scripture tell us that even God wasn't free from this Semitic mannerism. (See Genesis 22:16, Isaiah 62:8, Hebrews 3:11 and 6:13.)

In a very natural and spontaneous manner a speaker will turn his eyes and lift his hands toward heaven and say, "By God, what I said is right and true!" or "Let God witness to the truth of my words!" Apparently swearing had lost its original sacredness and become meaningless. Jesus encouraged truthful and straightforward conversation without the need of swearing.

In the Near East merchants and business people do not work with fixed prices as we do in the West. Therefore, buying and selling is a complicated business. Each merchant has his own prices and quotes them to each customer as he pleases. The customer is afraid of being cheated and has his own idea of what the price should be. For example, if one decides to buy a pair of shoes or a garment, it means a day's loss and much exhaustion because of mistrust and incessant bargaining before making the purchase.

When the price cannot be settled by bargaining, merchants and their customers generally take oaths by temples and holy names in proof of their sincerity. They take an oath saying: "By God and all his holy angels, this pair of shoes cost me six dollars but you can have them for three dollars." When such oaths are ineffective, they then resort to swearing such as: "If I lie to you I am the son of a dog or an ass. The shoes cost me three dollars but I will let you have them for a dollar and a half." To all of this the suspecting customer replies: "By my only son's head, I will not pay you more than a dollar." If this fails the merchant is apt to spit in the face of the customer.

People swore or took oaths in the name of God and the holy temple because they believed in sacred oaths and in a Higher Power, but they swore falsely. They used the name of God to cover their dishonest actions and to further their own interests. The problem was that people no longer took this kind of swearing seriously because it had become so common; to the contrary; the one who swore by the Lord's name or by his own head was looked upon with great suspicion as a liar and cheat.

Instead of this conventional cross play, waste of time and temper, Jesus here insists on directness and frankness in dealing with one another. He knew that a man who is cheated will in turn cheat others. And if oaths are uttered with sacred names and deception is being practiced, the person being deceived will do the same in transactions with others. "Yes, yes and no, no" is the only successful and straight-forward method in business. The Semites were only now learning that such a method is far superior to their traditional system. Whatever people practice will also come back on them.

NONRESISTANCE

Ye have heard that it hath been said, An eye for an eye, and a tooth for a tooth: But I say unto you, That ye resist not evil: but whosoever shall smite thee on thy right cheek, turn to him the other also. Mt 5:38-39.

Part A—MOSAIC LAW. There was a time when the Israelites were living a semi-nomadic life. The people were illiterate and uncultured and the penalty for breaking the law was severe. There was no other way to rule over the unruly who constantly lied, quarreled, fought, and stole from one another. It was this kind of behavior and these harmful deeds that made Moses write such a strict law as "an eye for an eye and a tooth for a tooth." Moreover, force, at that time, was the only law that these people knew.

In the first century c.e. life was different. The people in Judea were educated and aware of God's word. There were now synagogues and teachers in every town and the public heard the law and the prophets read to them continually. They understood that recompensing evil for evil would only multiply evil and increase hatred and vengeance; an eye for an eye would result in more murders and injuries. But when one does not resist evil, he puts an end to its power. When one turns his cheek, no one will smite him again.

Part B—EVIL. The term "evil" in this verse refers to an injustice. In the Near East people are forced into hard labor. Those in power generally oppress the poor. Property is confiscated unjustly. Resistance in such cases usually results in heavier burdens, violence, and even murder. Nonresistance is the only weapon with which the poor can defend themselves. Politicians, government officials, and the rich are always friendly and kind toward those who willingly carry their burdens without complaining. On the other hand, those who offer resistance are treated as rebels and made to pay heavy penalties. The reference here is probably to government officials and soldiers who misuse their authority and against whom resistance is futile.

Part C—AN IDIOM. "Turning the other cheek" is an Aramaic idiom. It means "learn to take the wind out of the other person's sails," "settle a problem while it is small." Often, when we resist an injustice, we augment the problem. "A soft word turns away wrath."[19] These verses are not a restriction against self defense but rather a remedy against strife and vengeance. Jesus encouraged peace and harmony in human relationships.

COAT AND CLOAK

And if any man will sue thee at the law, and take away thy coat, let him have thy cloke also. Mt. 5:40.

Petty bandits and robbers commonly take a victim's garments and shoes by force. Clothes are also stolen from homes and the fields. When the courts bring a man who is under suspicion to trial, the court takes his good upper garments as a bond. Innocent men are often mistaken for bandits and taken before government officials. If the court finds them guilty and they have no money, they are stripped of their clothes.

Creditors also accept clothes as collateral for loans. When people fail to pay their loans, creditors are willing to accept the garments in lieu of payment. If a man should resist surrendering his robe, he will be

---

[19]Prov 15:1, Aramaic Peshitta Text, Lamsa translation

forced not only to surrender his robe but other clothing as well and then the court will punish him. But, the man will not be naked if he surrenders his shirt and robe because Near Easterners wear many undergarments and robes, one over the other in summer and winter alike. Frequently, a man wears all the garments he owns because the number of clothes he wears determines his social standing in the community.

The idea is to not resist the one who wishes to sue you and take your robe. Show your adversary you are willing to work things out. One does this by saying "you may take my undergarment (shirt) also." By doing this, one may not lose anything. This is in accord with the biblical custom and culture of the time.

OBEYING ORDERS

And whosoever shall compel thee to go a mile, go with him twain.
Mt. 5:41.

Merchandise, food supplies, and building materials are carried on the backs of animals and men. In some isolated regions, roads are so narrow and difficult that men become the only means to carry on the transportation of such goods. Where animals of burden are scarce, men and women carry wheat on their backs 20 or 30 miles or more. During the winter months, in certain areas, men are the only means of transportation.

In times of war or peace, when army regiments are transferred from one place to another, they will draft men and animals to carry their military supplies. If roads are inaccessible for the animals, men do it all. The army officers evenly divide the work among the people from various towns en route to their destination. The people of one town carry the supplies as far as the next town. They are notified in advance so that they may be ready. On some occasions the journey is not more than one or two miles.

Those who gladly respond to the summons and willingly take the supplies are released as soon as they arrive at the next town. But the officers will punish those who resisted them or those who failed to report in proper time. They will compel them to carry the supplies for two or three days instead of just going a mile or two. When harsh officers approach and ask gentle and humble men to carry supplies for a mile, they generally reply. "I will be glad to go two miles, my lord." These officers will usually respond by giving them lighter burdens and releasing them as soon as possible.

Jesus had seen Roman officers recruiting men to carry food and military supplies during the revolutions and wars in Syria, Palestine and Persia. It is quite probable that he had to submit to orders as well. In the eyes of Jesus, nonresistance was the only way to combat mistreatment from others. Meekness and gentleness were ultimately to bring happiness and peace. Resistance only increases one's burdens.

SHARING

Give to him that asketh thee, and from him that would borrow of thee turn not away. Mt. 5:42.

When helping others, giving assistance to those in need, and lending to neighbors in difficulty, we show care and compassion. "And to those who give, to them it will be given and to those who lend to the needy, people will lend to them." Jesus is simply saying "learn to share what you have with others."[20] There is a Near Eastern saying: "Do not refuse your neighbor's request, for tomorrow you may be in want."

LOVE YOUR ENEMIES

Ye have heard that it hath been said, Thou shalt love thy neighbor, and hate thine enemy. But I say unto you, Love your enemies, bless them that

---

[20]See Lev. 25:35.

curse you, do good to them that hate you, and pray for them which despitefully use you, and persecute you; That ye may be the children of your Father which is in heaven: for he maketh his sun to rise on the evil and on the good and sendeth rain on the just and the unjust. For if ye love them which love you, what reward have ye? Do not even the publicans the same? And if ye salute your brethren only, what do ye more than others? Do not even the publicans so? Mt. 5:43-47.

Part A—LOVE. "You have heard that it was said, that you shall be friendly to your neighbor and hate your enemy."[21] According to the Hebrew Bible, Moses encouraged the Israelites to be friendly toward their neighbors and also to strangers in the land. (See Leviticus 19:18, 33-34.)

The imperative form of the word "love" in verse 43 means to be friendly. It comes from the root *ḥab* meaning "to warm, kindle, set on fire." In Hebrew the word is *aḥeb*. In the Semitic languages of Aramaic and Hebrew, this word has many shades of meaning. Here it does not refer to sentimentality or ardent affection but rather to being warm towards, kindly, amicable—that is, "to be well-disposed toward." "If thine enemy be hungry, give him bread to eat; and if he be thirsty, give him water to drink."[22] Anyone, then, actualizing this kind of attitude and disposition toward an "enemy," in reality, has no enemy. Jesus constantly stressed the highest ideals in every individual so that humanity may practice peace and reconciliation. Hatred and vengeance only breed more hatred and vengeance, but love nourishes and encourages the finest in human beings.

When you love your enemies and pray for those who hate you, you release the potent force that is hidden within every human being. This power of love is stronger than any armor of the flesh. It conquers that which weapons of war have failed to conquer and heals the wounds that refuse healing. Love is a bonding force , not only between you and your loved ones, but between you and all individuals. Love

---

[21]Mt. 5:43, Aramaic Peshitta text, Errico.
[22]Prov. 25:21, K. J. V.

knows no boundaries and racial distinctions. Love is exactly like the air we breath, the water we drink and the rays of the sun that shine on all of God's creation. It is limitless and its source is eternal.

Jesus was a practical teacher. He based his entire message on the principles of God's kingdom manifesting on earth. At the beginning of his ministry, Jesus announced that the kingdom of God was present.[23] He demonstrated the ever-present power of the kingdom through his own deeds and actions of forgiveness and healing. "And if by God's spirit I am healing the insane, then the kingdom of God has come to you."[24]

Jesus emphasized love as the major key for the manifestation of God's reign on earth. He taught love not as an ideal to hope for, but as a practical means to win over anyone who was opposing God's counsel, loving presence, and sovereignty. Jesus knew that love, not sentimentality, is the only powerful antidote for all human ills. It does not matter what the ills may be: physical, emotional, mental, political, or spiritual. He instructed his disciples to apply this principle of love when facing their persecutors and enemies. Teaching his disciples to "love their enemies" was not a form of introverted aggression; it was a courageous expression that was to transform the hearts and minds of people everywhere. The wisdom of love in action through human beings expresses God's presence on earth.

Part B—"HATE" NOT IN THE SCRIPTURES. The quote "hate your enemies" is not in the Hebrew Bible. It may have been in a commentary, a marginal note, or in some other writings on the law of Moses. It is not scripture and Moses never taught any such law. If it were a scripture Jesus would have said "it is written."

Many Bible readers have blamed Moses for this citation, not understanding that the scribes and the elders wrote many commands and ordinances that are not based on the laws of Moses. Marginal notes were often copied and put in the text and words added or omitted. Moses admonished Israel not to tamper with holy Scripture. "Ye shall

---

[23]See Mk. 1:15-16.
[24]Mt. 12:28, Aramaic Peshitta text, Errico. See also Lk. 7:18-23.

not add unto the word which I command you, neither shall ye diminish ought from it." Jeremiah accuses the scribes of falsifying the sacred word. "How do you say, we are wise, and the law of the Lord is with us? Lo, surely the lying pen of the scribes has made it for falsehood."[25]

In Leviticus we read: "thou shalt not hate thy brother in thine heart; thou shalt not bear the grudge against the children of thy people, but thou shalt love thy neighbor as thyself."[26] The Aramaic word for neighbor is *qareewa*, "kinsman, relative, neighbor"—that is, one of your own flesh and blood. Some of the Jewish scribes and elders probably believed that these admonitions were limited to the Jews only; therefore they concluded that they could hate those who were not of their race, especially those who were their enemies. Many tribal people against whom the Jews fought, such as the Moabites, Ammonites, and Edomites, were their kin. These were all members of the same race and spoke the same language.

In those early days, when the law read "eye for an eye, and a tooth for a tooth," members of one tribe hated the members of another regardless of race and kinship. They would fight each other to the death. During wars they would even massacre little children. Israel itself fought against members of its own tribes. Moses admonished Israel to help its enemies. If an Israelite should see an enemy's ox fallen under its burden, he should offer help.

According to Jesus, all races are neighbors. He wanted his disciples and followers to extend their kindness and sympathy not only to their relatives, friends, neighbors and people of their own race and faith, but to people of all religions. Jesus' way was to embrace all nations and peoples.

Part C—CURSING. "Bless anyone who curses you." Cursing, here, means to pronounce curses—that is, to invoke evils, misfortunes, proclaim calamities upon someone. Near Easterners feel that their personal enemies are God's enemies and, as such, they deserve ruin and utter destruction. An Easterner may hurl at his enemies such cursing as:

---

[25]Jer. 8:8, Aramaic Peshitta Text, Lamsa translation
[26]Lev. 19:18, K.J.V.

"May God burn the bones of your fathers; May God exterminate your seed [offspring] from the earth; May God cut off your supply of bread; May your children be orphaned and your wife widowed." The Psalmist in Psalm 109:5-20 records line after line of the ancient style of cursing. Jesus exhorted his disciples to bless those who were cursing them.

Part D—A BENEVOLENT FATHER. Ancient belief held that only the righteous prosper and the wicked do not. The people believed that God blesses the just but the unjust receive no blessings.[27] Jesus taught that God as a father blesses the good and the bad, the just and the unjust. Central to Jesus' teaching is his stance that God desires mercy and compassion above all religious ordinances and sacrifices because the Lord God is compassionate. (See Matthew 9:13, Hosea 6:6, and Micah 6:8.) God is detached from humankind's formal arguments over moral world order and is associated with the goodness, powers, and mystery of the natural order of life. God's laws call on humanity to behave justly, with compassion, true judgment, and discernment.

PERFECTION

Be ye therefore perfect, even as your Father which is in heaven is perfect. Mt. 5:48.

The Aramaic word *gmeera* means "complete, whole, mature, perfect, thorough, finished, inclusive, rounded out." This verse does not refer to being perfect in character as God is perfect. It refers to being perfect or complete in understanding. Jesus knew that no one could be perfect like God.

Near Easterners call a learned person *gmeera biolpana*, meaning that he is acquainted with every branch of learning. *Gmeera bnamosa* means one who is well versed in the law. When a young man reaches

---

[27] See Job 20: 4-7,12, 14; 27:13-14,16-18.

the age of maturity, people will refer to him as a *gmeera*—a man of understanding.

Jesus wanted his disciples and followers to have a complete understanding of God's kingdom. They were to be open and receptive to all people and to treat everyone in the same manner as God would. They were not to be exclusive but all-inclusive, just as God lets his rain fall on the just and unjust and lets the sun shine on the good and the bad. They were to be wise, pure, alert, gentle, and courageous. "Therefore, be inclusive even as your Father who is in heaven is inclusive."[28]

---

[28]Mt. 5:48, Aramaic Peshitta text, Errico.

CHAPTER 6

GIVING ALMS IN SECRET

Take heed that ye do not your alms before men, to be seen of them: otherwise ye have no reward of your Father which is in heaven. Therefore when thou doest thine alms, do not sound a trumpet before thee, as the hypocrites do in the synagogues and in the streets, that they may have glory of men. Verily I say unto you, they have their reward. But when thou doest alms, let not thy left hand know what thy right hand doeth. That thine alms may be in secret: and thy Father which seeth in secret himself shall reward thee openly. Mt. 6:1-4.

Zedhqatha is the Aramaic word translated as "alms." It means "a right, a rule, a just or righteous act, a right or proper thing to do." This Aramaic term means an act of goodness that involves the giving of money.

In the ancient land of Palestine, unjust rulers had reduced many people to poverty level. Taxes and heavy tributes had devoured their substance. These circumstances forced the people into accepting alms, which was extremely embarrassing for them. Many would prefer hunger to stretching forth their hands and asking alms. It often happens that a recipient feels embarrassed in the community because the giver has told his relatives and friends. At times, the elders will announce the almsgiver in the synagogue and it will be discussed in the market places.

"Let not your left hand know what your right hand is doing" is an Aramaic way of saying "let no one know that you are giving alms." God knows and sees a good deed even when the person does it secretly. There is no need to let anyone know about alms giving. In Jesus' day, many rich men gave alms to the poor to bring attention to their piety. Even today certain religious organizations publish a donor's name in the newspaper and install a plaque in the church in the donor's memory. Some would not give unless they were assured of public recognition.

Jesus said when you give alms, don't blow the trumpet before you; that is, don't publicize your giving. Those who find recognition for their giving have already received their reward from the people who praise their names in the synagogues, street corners, and market places.

There is another possible rendering of the phrase "do not sound the trumpet before thee." *Qarna* means "horn, a horn of an animal, trumpet." In Hebrew the word for "horn" or "trumpet" is *shofar*. Some rabbinic textual experts suggest that the Aramaic verse may have read "do not pass [instead of sound] the horn before you." They used the *qarna* or *shofar* as an offering plate.

SECRET PRAYERS

And when thou prayest, thou shalt not be as the hypocrites are: for they love to pray standing in the synagogues and in the corners of the streets, that they may be seen of men. Verily I say unto you, they have their reward. But thou, when thou prayest, enter into thy closet, and when thou hast shut thy door, pray to thy Father which is in secret: and thy Father which seeth in secret shall reward thee openly. Mt. 6:5-6.

Part A—PRAYING SECRETLY. Semites understand God as spirit. Mortal eyes cannot see God. Spirit knows neither time nor space; it is omnipotent. God's power and presence are everywhere and everyone can feel them. Moses covered his face when he talked with God. Elijah heard the still small voice of God. In the course of time, God became localized; that is, people could only reach the divine presence in certain sacred places in the cities or certain shrines erected in high places.

Near Easterners frequently pray publicly. Some pray near a brook or stand near a mosque or a church wall; others pray in churches during the hour of prayer. There are those who pray secretly in a little room apart or in a corner of the house. Almost all Near Eastern

Semites today believe that God is present wherever they may pray and that, though they do not see God, God sees them.

They also believe that when they pray, the spirits of departed loved ones are around them. During prayers, they petition God for things they need. If the petitioners are sincere, they believe that God will grant their requests. The Pharisees and priests, who were religious professionals, prayed in public so that others could see them and consider them pious men. They received only the people's praise as their reward and not the true blessings of God. Jesus speaks of true, sincere petitioners praying in secret.

Part B—CLOSET. Near Eastern houses have a small adjoining room that the people call *tawana,* "inner room." This is where the family keeps their supplies and valuables. A small door built in the wall connects this inner room to the house.

There is virtually no privacy in these houses because many families live under the same roof. People change their clothes with no curtains around them. There are no dividing walls. Within the same house and at the same time, some may be praying, sleeping, drinking, singing, and eating. A priest may be saying grace or performing a religious ceremony in one area of the home while men and women in another part may be arguing quite loudly with each other.

Some men prefer to pray outside on the roof, but this place is also a playground and thoroughfare; others seek a brook for quietness. People who pray so that their neighbors and strangers may see them stand in conspicuous areas. Near Easterners have no prayer books; they recite their prayers from memory. When praying they usually stand and move their lips rapidly. People can hear indistinctly their mumbling utterances. In market places, shopkeepers pray in their tiny shops, placing their coats under their knees. At times they rise to praise God, then kneel again to pray.

Jesus did not like this outward form of prayer. He knew that these men were praying so that others might see them. (These men also thought people would consider them religious and honest.) He suggested that men should enter the *tawana,* "inner room," where no one would see them. There would be no disturbance and they could say their prayers in secret to the Father who sees in secret but rewards openly.

PRAYER

But when ye pray, use not vain repetitions, as the heathen do: for they think that they shall be heard for their much speaking. Mt. 6:7.

Ṣlotha is the Aramaic word for prayer. It also means "adjustment." Its Semitic root is *sla* and means "to lay a snare, to incline, to turn toward, to array, to set a trap." In the mountains of Kurdistan, Near Eastern hunters set wooden traps to catch an animal. They usually retire from the place where they have placed the trap so that the animal may not see them. The process requires patience, quietness, diligence, and watchfulness. This is true for prayer also.

Prayer is neither a reminder to God of what we need—as though the divine presence had forgotten us—nor is it a formal act of mere outward reverence to impress God. Prayer is an attitude of spirit to prepare us for what we need and qualify us to receive what God has provided. In prayer we also express our gratitude.

God knows our needs and is always ready to grant sincere prayers. We must be prepared to receive divine messages and admonitions. In prayer we become aware of God's presence. When we petition for certain things, it is through prayer that we can discern between what is appropriate and what is inappropriate for us.

THE LORD'S PRAYER — Introduction

This simple and direct prayer that Jesus composed contains the essence of his teaching. It is a capsule summary of the message he taught and preached throughout his entire ministry. It is also the essential kernel of the Hebrew Scripture. Jesus' prayer is a brief synopsis of his beliefs about God, humankind, and the world. His method of prayer is succinct, earnest, and devotional.

Jewish historians inform us that there are many parallels and similarities between the language of this prayer and that of the Hebrew Scripture and rabbinic prayers. According to these scholars, a few of the sources would be: (1)Various prayers that are recited on Mondays and Thursdays, before returning the Torah scrolls to the ark; (2) The *kaddish;* (3) The "short prayer" of the early *Tanna;* (4) The *Shemoneh-Esreh,* "Eighteen Benedictions," and in certain Talmudic prayers. However, when we consider the Lord's Prayer in its entirety, it is original and singular. This prayer reflects Jesus' own religious genius, creativity, and insight.

This style of prayer belongs to a certain genre of prayer. Jewish scholars refer to this genre as the "Short Prayer." It does not belong to the liturgical Hebrew form of prayer. It has its own style, originality and variety. The Lord's prayer is meant to be a pattern for prayer; that is, one's prayers should be short and contain the same ideas that Jesus presented to his disciples.

Jesus' instruction about prayer may be summed up in two words: *be sincere.* The time, place, or number of words are not essential but an open, trusting, and receptive heart and mind are indeed necessary for communing with God. Jesus shifted the emphasis of all prayers and changed the meaning of prayer and worship. Forgiveness takes the place of vengeance; love takes the place of hatred. The kingdom, power, and glory (song and praise) belong to God only. God is a loving parent, protector, and provider at all times.

Through Jesus' inspiring and beautiful prayer come some specific but simple realizations: (1) God's presence is like a loving parent who is forever present and concerned about the welfare of the entire human family. (2) We are all children of a gracious heavenly presence that has provided for us in all ways. (3) God's sovereign presence (kingdom) and will are to be expressed on earth. (4) We must understand the value of forgiveness, both for ourselves and for others, even as our heavenly Father forgives all who ask for forgiveness. (5) God, as a benevolent parent, helps us not to enter into temptation but delivers us from error. (6) God alone has the kingdom, power, and glory to accomplish all that we need. (7) God is the same throughout all ages.[1]

ABBA—FATHER

Our Father which art in heaven. Hallowed be thy name. Mt. 6:9

Part A—DIVINE PARENT. The word for "father" in Aramaic is *abba*. Calling God "Father" was Jesus' way of endearing God to people. He revealed God as a loving parent and not as an almighty, awesome deity. The use of the term "father" was not meant to categorize God as a male deity. It was an affectionate term.

Jesus' concept of God as a parent ("father") was not gained so much from his knowledge of holy Scripture but rather from his experiences as a youth. He had seen caring shepherds searching after water and grass for their sheep. He also knew that shepherds so loved their sheep that they would risk their lives for them. If shepherds would do this for their sheep then God as a father would do even more so for humankind. Jesus saw parents pouring their love out on their children. If human parents loved their children in such a manner how much more would the heavenly Father, who is the source of eternal love, do for all humanity.

As an example of the use of "father" as an endearing and affectionate expression, Near Easterners may address a guest, a close friend, or a faithful servant as *babi*, "my father." It expresses not only endearment but also trust. To call an individual "father" is the highest honor one can bestow on another.

An Assyrian who is proud of his earthly father and his ancestors will say: "I am son of my father; I will do what he commands." There is nothing more dear to him than his traditional family ties. On the other hand, if the relationship on the maternal side is more important, or if the father had died while the family was young, people will call

---

[1]For a devotional and in-depth study of the Lord's prayer see Rocco A. Errico, *Setting A Trap For God:* The Aramaic Prayer of Jesus.

96

these children "sons of their mothers." This is the reason that Jesus, at times, is referred to as "the son of Mary." It is supposed that Joseph had died when Jesus was a little over twelve years of age.

Jesus, having lost his father at a young age, relied on no one but his unseen universal Father. His faith in God as a protector became stronger and more vital, while dreams of his earthly father vanished. Jesus understood God not only as the Father of the Jewish nation but as the Father of Galileans, Gentiles, sinners, and outcasts of society. He discarded all mystical worship of God in ceremonies, sacrifices, temples, and intermediaries. Long prayers were not necessary. God can be approached through a short, sincere prayer, simply addressing God as "Our Father." Jesus' imagery of God as a heavenly Father revealed God as the Father of all humanity.

Part B—HALLOWED BE THY NAME. One may also translate this Aramaic phrase *nithqadash shamkh* as "Let your name be set apart (set aside)." *Qadeesha* means "pure, holy, a holy one, or saint." It comes from the Semitic root *qdsh* meaning "to hallow, sanctify, consecrate, set apart for a specific purpose, to dedicate for a holy use or cause, to be distinct."

During Jesus' time, and no doubt even before his time, people were using God's name falsely. Jesus reminded his disciples and followers to keep God's name holy—apart from abusive deeds and unjust transactions. God's name represents all that is good and wholesome. God's name is distinct; that is, God's presence has the set purpose of enlightening the entire human family in all the ways of good and well-being.

God is holy and is apart from all error and evil. But this holiness doesn't mean that God is unapproachable, distant or aloof. God is dedicated to the good of all humanity, for humanity is God's image and likeness. The prayer is directed to Abba—Father—and not a deity. Whether the prayer speaks the name, will, power, or glory, it is always connected to the Father.

DAILY BREAD

Give us this day our daily bread. Mt. 6:11

In Aramaic the text reads: "Provide us our needful bread from day to day."[2] The Aramaic word *laḥma,* "bread," does not refer just to actual bread but also to food in general. No Near Eastern household would be without bread, although other foods are abundant, while entertaining guests. When a man invites a stranger to eat with him, he says: "Come eat bread with me." This means come and dine with me.

Wheat is the staple food supply. It is carefully stored for lean times. People live in fear that days of lack may come. No matter how abundant their supplies may be, they always predict famine and hardships. This fear causes such a troubled state of mind that people lose faith in God. They begin to think that either God's power is limited or that God has forgotten them during their times of misfortune. They do not recognize that fear, greed, hoarding, and conflicts have created the misfortune.

"Give us our daily bread" does not mean that God has forgotten to supply this urgent need but that we should be satisfied with our supplies from day to day. If God meets our every day needs, then why should we store our food supplies in fear of lack or fear of depression. Jesus knew that God always meets these needs just as parents supply their children's needs.

"Needful bread" refers to supplying needs. Near Easterners treat bread with the utmost respect because they literally, in the name of God, plant and harvest the precious seed, scatter the sheaves on the threshing floor, grind the grain into flour and bake the daily bread in a "God-centered" consciousness. The prayer for "needful bread from day to day" reflects a deep, inner gratitude and acknowledgment of the Provider of all "good and perfect" gifts.

---

[2]Mt. 6:11, Aramaic Peshitta text, Errico.

CANCELING DEBTS

And forgive us our debts, as we forgive our debtors. Mt. 6:12.

We may also translate this verse from Aramaic as: "Forgive us our offenses, as we have forgiven our offenders."[3] Or we may translate it as: "Free us from our offenses as also we have freed our offenders." We may also render the phrase as: "Untie or release us from our offenses. . . ."

Haubain literally means "our debts." This term is peculiar to the Aramaic language in its own Semitic, early Palestinian context. Here in the prayer, the word "debt," *hauba,* is a metaphor for "sin, error, guilt, fault, offense, mistake, trespass, transgression." The term *hayawein* literally signifies "debtors" but denotes "sinners, offenders, transgressors." We also find this peculiar use of the Aramaic term *hauba,* "debt," for "sin and guilt" in the Dead Sea Scrolls.

Shwaqan usually translates as "forgive" and "pardon." But it has other meanings such as "to free, remit, untie, cancel, loosen, release." With the distinctive Aramaic term meaning "debt," *shwaqan* carries the idea of "remittance" or "canceling" a debt.

Forgiveness revitalizes our hearts and emotions. It releases inner tensions and mental agonies that plague our minds and souls. When we release others, we release ourselves. When we forgive, we live in self-compassion and self-acceptance. Forgiveness is one of Jesus' major teachings. It is the only way we can love our enemies, bless those who curse us, do good to those who hate us, and pray for those who persecute and oppress us.

LEAD US NOT INTO TEMPTATION

And lead us not into temptation, but deliver us from evil: For thine is the kingdom, and the power, and the glory, for ever. Amen. Mt. 6:13.

---

[3]Mt. 6:12, Aramaic Peshitta text, Lamsa translation.

The Aramaic text reads: "And do not let us enter into tempta-tion."[4] Aramaic speaking people often say: "Do not let us be in need," or "prevent me from making a mistake." When a husband goes on a journey, his wife's last remark to him is: "do not leave us in want."

Talan comes from the Aramaic root *al*. This root has many meanings. *Al* as a verb denotes "to enter, attack, fight, wrestle, contend." It also means "to have intercourse." When the root *al* appears as a preposition, it can signify "on, in, by, upon, over, above, alongside, on top of." In this phrase of the prayer, *talan,* means "to enter—thus, the meaning "And do not *let us enter into* temptation." Jesus used this same word when he told his apostles: "Awake and pray *that you may not enter into* temptation."[5] It is the same word but in a different verbal form—*tiloon.*

The Aramaic term *nisyona* refers to trials, luxurious or worldly living, or things that may obscure spiritual sight. For example, the love of money had tempted Judas when he betrayed his Master for thirty pieces of silver. God did not tempt Judas. God leads no one into temptation. "Let no man say when he is tempted, I am tempted of God; for God cannot be tempted with evil, neither does he tempt any man."[6] God guides those who look to him for wisdom and directs people away from materialism that would entrap them.

Pasan, "deliver us," more precisely means "part us" or "separate us" from evil. The word "evil," *beesha,* has many meanings in Aramaic such as "bad, error, mistake, difficulty, trouble, an evil inclination." Some interpreters believe it refers to "the evil one"—Satan. However, Satan is an externalization of an internal inclination toward a wrong—evil, error, deep trouble.

Hila, "power," also means "might, energy, force, strength." *Tishbohta,* "glory," also signifies "song and praise." The Prayer's conclusion is missing in many ancient manuscripts of the New Testament but one can find this particular phrase in Hebrew Scripture

---

[4]Mt. 6:13, Aramaic Peshitta text, Lamsa translation.

[5]Mt. 26:41a, Aramaic Peshitta text, Lamsa translation.

[6]James 1:13, Aramaic Peshitta text, Lamsa translation.

(see I Chronicles 29:11 and Psalms 45:6). The Aramaic term *amen* means "to make firm." It refers to anything that is true, lasting, never-ceasing, eternal, perpetual, and faithful.

TREASURES

Lay not up for yourselves treasures upon earth, where moth and rust doth corrupt, and where thieves break through and steal. But lay up for yourselves treasures in heaven, where neither moth nor rust doth corrupt, and where thieves do not break through nor steal: For where your treasure is there will your heart be also. Mt. 6:19-21.

Until the twentieth century, most Near Eastern countries did not have banks and safe deposits. People buried their coins of silver and gold and other valuables in the ground to keep them safe from bandits and robbers. They also hid costly garments and perishable goods in secret places constructed in the walls of their homes. These valuables may escape thieves but they are frequently exposed to moths and rust. The ground is invariably damp and insects infest their houses.

Near Easterners usually dream that some day they may discover buried treasures. Therefore, when they plow or dig foundations for buildings, they always hope to uncover a hidden treasure. If they should discover a treasure, it becomes their property no matter to whom it belongs. People bury their treasures secretly at night; the identity of the owners is unknown. Besides, the owners always deny they possess any treasure to avoid lending money to people and to escape the payment of unjust taxes.

Only the person who buried the money knows the hidden place. If that person dies, the treasure is virtually lost to the family. According to the unwritten law, the treasure becomes the property of any finder. Sometimes they find coins that are very old and have no exchange so they will bury them again or melt them secretly for jewelry. If a man happens to find a treasure in his neighbor's field, he hastens to buy the field in order to get possession of the treasure. In any case, if the government finds out about the discovery of the treasure, the officials will confiscate it and perhaps fine or imprison the finder for not giving it to the government.

While some men secretly bury their money, others openly search for it. The owner of the treasure is always worried about his money. He is afraid someone may discover his hiding place. His thoughts and feelings are also buried with his treasure. "Treasures in heaven" refers to good deeds, works of kindness that never perish. Those who put aside treasures in heaven are free from the worry of material things. Earthly treasures are temporal. We can lose and people may steal our earthly treasures, but treasures stored in heaven are handed down from generation to generation. The one who lays up these heavenly treasures (deeds of kindness) lives forever in them.

A PURE EYE

The light of the body is the eye: if therefore thine eye be single, thy whole body shall be full of light. But if thine eye be evil, thy whole body shall be full of darkness. If therefore the light that is in thee be darkness, how great is that darkness! Mt. 6:22-23.

The Aramaic text reads: "The lamp of the body is the eye; if, then, your eye is pure (clear) your entire body is also lighted. But, if your eye is diseased (bad) your entire body will be dark. If, then, the light which is in you is dark, how much more will be your darkness!"[7]

There is a contrast between the Aramaic terms *pesheeta*, "pure, clear, simple, normal," and *beesha*, "bad, evil, sick, diseased." A person with a "pure eye" is a one who has no evil intention or ulterior motive. In modern Aramaic, people refer to a crafty and devious individual as having "salty eyes." This expression, "salty eyes," is comparable to our American idiom, "shifty eyes." A "bad eye" refers to a crafty, evil person. The Aramaic phrase "if, then, the light that is

---

[7]Mt. 6:22-23, Aramaic Peshitta text, Errico.

in you is dark, how much more will be your darkness!" means: "if a shifty, cunning person calls the crooked things he does "good" (light) how much worse are the things he calls "bad." Aramaic expressions of speech such as these can be difficult for us to understand.

TWO MASTERS

No man can serve two masters: for either he will hate the one, and love the other; or else he will hold to the one, and despise the other. Ye cannot serve God and mammon. Mt. 6:24.

There is nothing that a Near Eastern servant despises more than having to work for two brothers who become his masters. Some servants prefer unemployment. They do not want the responsibility of working for two masters.

Near Eastern family ties remain unbroken even after the death of the parents. Brothers, their wives, and their sisters live in the same house. They will work together and eat from the same dish. The family property, frequently, remains undivided. Usually brothers will attempt to keep peaceful relationships between themselves but at times, quarreling wives and children will disturb their brotherly relationship. Sometimes wives indulge in gossip which may result in strained family relations and weaken family unity. Then, brothers become bitter toward each other. They will take sides with their wives and children. Discrimination in the distribution of food and clothing, as well as jealousies and suspicions, will also create domestic troubles.

Under such trying situations, the task of servants becomes confusing and challenging. What one wife orders, the other wife may indignantly forbid. If any servant shows a courtesy or preference for one side of the family, the other side becomes angry. Experienced servants are aware of this. These servants will study the situation and soon learn to know which side to favor (love) and which side to disfavor (hate). They will become attached to the brother whose wife is gentle, kind and from whom they expect better treatment. This is

103

vital for the servants because it is the women who give them their portion of food. Some servants side with the oldest brother and his wife and despise the younger. However, shrewd servants do their best to pretend they favor both families.

Just as a servant cannot work well with and please two masters, so one cannot serve God and worldly riches and pleasures at the same time. Some Pharisees and priests were scrupulous about their religion and its sacred laws, but they were also lovers of gold, silver, and animal sacrifices and other revenues that they derived from people in the name of God. The reality of the situation is that these people were really worshiping earthly things and religion was only a facade. Temple treasures and profits were more important and sacred to them than the true worship of God. The followers of Jesus were to put God first and not the need of worldly things.[8]

THE GRASS AND THE OVEN

Wherefore, if God so clothe the grass of the field, which to day is, and to morrow is cast into the oven, shall he not much more clothe you, O ye of little faith? Mt. 6:30.

In Aramaic and Hebrew the word for an oven or a fireplace is *tanura*, deriving from two Semitic words—*tan*, "place," and *nura*, "fire." The oven referred to in this verse is a large, deep, round hole dug in the center of the house. It is about three feet in diameter, five feet deep, and lined with baked clay. People construct an underground air passage, about five or six feet away, and connect it at the bottom of the oven to keep the fire burning. Some houses contain as many ovens as the number of families living in the house.

They use the *tanura* for cooking, baking bread, and heating the house. The families burn grass and manure that the women gather from the fields. Once the oven is lit, dry grass is steadily added until

---

[8]See Lk. 16:13.

104

the inside of the oven is well heated and turns white. Pots containing food are then lowered with iron hooks into the oven. The dough is rolled until it becomes very thin and flat like a piece of cardboard. It is then clapped on the smooth clay inside the oven. When cooking and baking are finished, a large wooden cover is placed over the oven so the children will not fall into it. A hot, burning oven is a frightful place in the center of the home. When mothers scold their children, they may tell them that they will put them in the oven if they don't behave.

Jesus refers to this type of grass that the women gather for the oven. What he emphasizes is that even grass that is one of the least important plants of God's creation has known God's care. God clothed it with beauty. How much more important are human beings who are God's image and likeness? If God cares for the field grass which today is and tomorrow will be used to heat people's ovens, how much more does God care for humanity (God's children) for whose benefit grass, flowers, and birds were created?

WORLDLY PEOPLE

Therefore take no thought, saying, What shall we eat? Or, What shall we drink? Or, Wherewithal shall we be clothed? (For after all these things do the Gentiles seek:) for your heavenly Father knoweth that ye have need of all these things. Mt. 6:31-32.

The Aramaic text reads: "Now then, do not be concerned or say: What will we eat, or what will we drink, or with what will we be clothed? Because the people of the world are looking for all these things. Yet your Father who is in heaven knows that you also are in need of all these things."[9] The Near Eastern text reads *ammeh dalma,* "worldly people," and not "Gentiles." The phrase refers to those who have no regard for religion and holiness and who value the pleasures of this life only. It refers to anyone, whether Jew or Gentile. National-

---

[9]Mt. 6:31-32, Aramaic Peshitta text, Errico.

ity and religion make no difference. A worldly person can be anyone who puts materialism above spiritual matters. At that time, many people sought material possessions and other comforts of life. They believed that life consisted only of treasures, luxuries, and power. They were not concerned with justice and mercy and took little thought of the life to come.

Jesus encouraged his disciples to seek after the spiritual things of life and not just material gains that worldly people pursued. His disciples were facing a different way of life, filled with difficulties and struggles. At times, they would be hungry, thirsty, and even persecuted. These disciples could not denounce riches and accumulate them at the same time. They must seek first God's kingdom. God would supply all their needs. "But first you look for the kingdom of God and his justice and all these things will abundantly be given to you. Now do not worry about tomorrow because tomorrow will take care of itself. Enough for the day is its own trouble."[10]

---

[10]Mt. 6:33-34, Aramaic Peshitta text, Errico.

CHAPTER 7

CRITICISM AND MEASURING

Judge not, that ye be not judged. For with what judgment ye judge, ye shall be judged: and with what measure ye mete, it shall be measured to you again. Mt. 7:1-2.

Part A—JUDGING. "Judge not" means not to judge the habits, weaknesses, and actions of others. Jesus realized that everyone has character defects and shortcomings. What he censures are the gossip, criticism, and slander of others that usually result in quarrels.

In the Near East, before the days of books, newspapers, theaters and other forms of entertainment, people spent much time gossiping and criticizing each other. They watched every move and action of others. Often people will condemn others for practices of which they themselves are guilty. Therefore, no one has any right to judge others.

Part B—MEASURING. Many primitive Near Eastern areas do not have standard measures. Small and large weights and varied measuring yardsticks are still used as in the past. The merchants use their arms for measuring dry goods. Large and small stones and pieces of bricks are their weights. They also measure wheat with a wooden box.

Part C—THE BOUNTIFUL MEASURE. In the marketplace, one of the most intriguing transactions to watch is that of the measurer. It is he who gives the "good measure, pressed down, shaken together, running over." The motto is: Friendship must forever mingle itself with business. Each liquid, such as milk and oil, must run over at least a little into the buyer's vessel because it is understood "for what measure you measure, it will be measured to you." A Near Easterner carries grain in the skirt of his garments much as a woman sometimes carries things in the folds of her apron. The grain is sold in this manner:

As soon as the merchant and buyer agree on the price, the seller spreads an ample cloak on the ground and pours the golden grain on it in a heap. Then the seller kneels by his little mound of wheat. While calling upon the name of God, he thrusts the square wooden measure (box) into the heap of wheat. Semites consider grain sacred; thus, the selling of it must be accompanied by pious language. When the measurer tosses the first scoop into the skirt of the buyer's cloak, he intones, "Blessing." That means "measure number one." Then he says, "From God," which means "two." He counts out the remaining scoops—"three, four" and so on. When the measurer first thrusts the measuring box into the wheat, he will whirl the wheat around, lift it slightly and let it drop several times. Then with the palms of his hands, he will pack it firmly down. Again he will whirl it, press it, and shake it up, until the wheat overflows the rim of the container.

Part D—MEASURING YARD GOODS. In the Near East they also measure cloth by their arms. However, measuring by arm is impractical and complicated for business because some men have long arms and others have short ones. It is not unusual to find a partnership of two merchants, one with long arms to buy and the other with short arms to sell. When customers see that a merchant has short arms, they complain and insist on having the articles measured with their own arms. Or, they may also bring a friend who has longer arms. Of course, the merchant will object strenuously to this transaction and yields only if his customer refuses to buy.

Greater difficulties arise when they measure borrowed articles by arm. For example, when these yard goods are returned, the person who had originally measured them may be away. This leads to long disputes and arguments between the parties concerned and they will have to settle the case by taking oaths. The lender, when borrowed things are returned, insists on generous measurement, saying that he had measured generously when the articles were borrowed. The borrower denies this and claims that the first lender measured short. This puts the new lender at the borrower's mercy.

This is also true of weights and wheat measures. Some families have several sizes of the measure (box). When they buy, they use larger measures but when they sell, they use smaller ones. It often happens that a stranger will bring cheese and butter to the house of a prospective customer and he will have to trust the customer for the weight or the measure; if not, he could lose the sale.

Everyone is aware of light weights and crooked measuring practices. Therefore, an Easterner counts on rendering the same to his neighbors when they, in turn, come to borrow or buy from him. Thus with the measure they have measured, it is measured to them. So he who cheats is cheated and he who has given generously, to him it is given generously. In the end, if one cheats no one gains.

Jesus knew of these practices. He had seen people arguing and taking oaths and even going to court over measures and weights. Perhaps even he had been cheated. He had watched crooked wheat dealers not filling and shaking the measure for the flour and the dry goods dealer measuring with short arms. This idea works the same with human relationships. How one measures and shares with others is very important. Through this simple custom, Jesus emphasizes the joy of abundant, generous sharing from a true spiritual life.

FAULTFINDING

And why beholdest thou the mote that is in thy brother's eye, but condsiderest not the beam that is in thine own eye? Or how wilt thou say to thy brother, Let me pull out the mote out of thine eye; and, behold a beam is in thine own eye? Thou hypocrite, first cast out the beam out of thine own eye; and then shalt thou see clearly to cast out the mote out of thy brother's eye. Mt. 7:3-5.

The Aramaic text reads: Why, then, do you notice the straw in your brother's eye, but the plank which is in your own eye you do not see? Or, how can you say to your brother: Let me take the straw out of your eye; and behold! a plank is in your own eye? Hypocrite! First take the plank out of your own eye; and then you can see how to take the straw out of your brother's eye."[1] In typical Aramaic speech, Jesus uses exaggerated, humorous imagery. This style of speaking emphasizes the contradiction of faultfinding. One needs to pay attention to one's own faults and begin to correct them.

PEARLS BEFORE SWINE

Give not that which is holy unto dogs, neither cast ye your pearls before swine, lest they trample them under their feet, and turn again and rend you. Mt. 7:6.

Most Near Easterners consider dogs as unclean animals. But swine are an abomination to members of some religions in the Near East. Today Eastern Moslems and Jews do not eat pork and both despise dogs.

According to Semitic custom, the less a wise man speaks the more people honor him. His fame will spread everywhere. Generally, a wise man converses with other wise men and he does not like answering questions of men who are not his equal. Some learned men avoid discussing deep subjects in the presence of uncultured people. They would rather sit quietly and listen to the foolish talk than say something that the people would not understand.

During debates when theological and philosophical questions are discussed, heated and bitter words are usually exchanged. No one is willing to admit to being wrong. When one argues with a learned man and fails to defend his position, he will verbally attack the wise man. He does this so that he may avenge his honor. Generally, men of wisdom are tolerant towards each other, and when their position is not correct, they accept the verdict of others.

Jesus warned his disciples not to discuss theology and philosophy with people who would not understand. Misunderstanding would create disputes and could culminate in a fight, possible injury and

---

[1]Mt. 7:3-5, Aramaic Peshitta text, Errico.

murder. The unlearned persons, like swine, would tread the pearls under their feet. His disciples were to preach a simple gospel using illustrations from daily life and parables that the people could understand.

ASKING: BREAD—STONE, FISH—SNAKE

Ask, and it shall be given you; seek, and ye shall find; knock, and it shall be opened unto you: For every one that asketh receiveth; and he that seeketh findeth; and to him that knocketh it shall be opened. Or what man is there of you, whom if his son ask bread, will he give him a stone? Or if he ask a fish, will he give him a serpent? Mt. 7:7-10.

In many areas of Palestine and Arabia nomadic life still continues. Many people prefer the outdoor life. Their homes are tents woven from the hair of goats or structures built of rough stones. The houses are loosely built with large holes and cracks in the walls. Birds and even snakes build their nests in the ceiling, which consists of brush and straw. It is a common sight to see snakes crawling along the ceiling and dropping to the floor. They come from the fields in search of food. When fish is baked, it is placed in a basket. Its aroma often draws snakes and insects to the basket. It is very common when taking out a fish to get hold of a snake that has crawled into the basket.

People who live in tents keep the bread in a pile of stones around the tents so that one is apt to pick up a stone for bread, which it closely resembles in shape and size. They eat whenever they are hungry during the day or night. When children cry at night, parents quiet them with bread or other foods. As there are no lamps, they have to be careful not to give a snake for a fish or a stone for bread. A Near Easterner often says to his enemy: "If you come to my house, I will set before you snake bones and stones."

Jesus used this illustration to show that if a father who can make mistakes is careful about what he gives his children, how much more would the heavenly Father be concerned about bestowing good gifts to those who trust him. (See Matthew 7:11.)

EVIL OR IMPERFECT?

If ye then, being evil, know how to give good gifts unto your children, how much more shall your Father which is in heaven give good things to them that ask him? Mt. 7:11.

The Aramaic term *beesha* has many meanings: "evil, bad, error, rotten, cruel, unreal, imperfect, immature, misfortune, envy." For example, in Aramaic one refers to bad advice as "evil counsel," unripe figs as "evil figs," and fruit trees that are not bearing as "bad trees." The Aramaic text reads: "And if, then, you who make mistakes know how to give proper gifts to your children, how much more will your Father who is in heaven give beneficial things to those who ask him."[2]

In this text, the term *beesha* means "imperfect," "immature." Jesus did not use the word collectively in the sense that all those who were listening were evil, but that they were not perfect. People make mistakes because of imperfections. According to the King James Version, Jesus addressed the people as "being evil," as if they were doing bad things. This saying of Jesus does not mean that the people were evil. But, "being evil" simply means not perfect—one who is capable of making mistakes. No human being is perfect, and yet in spite of our imperfections, we want to see our children receiving gifts that are beneficial and not harmful.

THE GOLDEN RULE

Therefore all things whatsoever ye would that men should do to you, do ye even so to them: for this is the law and the prophets. Mt. 7:12.

---

[2]Mt. 7:11, Aramaic Pshitta text, Errico.

This important portion of holy Scripture is rightly called "The Golden Rule." It is the core of the law and the teaching of the prophets. When humankind learns to practice the principle of this powerful saying, there will be no need for laws because evil will cease. Envy, covetousness, murder, adultery, and all forms of violence that cause the human family to fail will come to an end.

If people would only place themselves in the position of the other whom they oppress, cheat, or mistreat, they would come to the realization that they would not like such treatment. Moreover, they would respect the rights of other people just as they expect others to respect their rights. The law of compensation is an immutable principle. All acts rebound on the person who initiates them. Those who take the sword perish by the sword, and those who oppress are oppressed. All great imperial powers who violated this principle were measured with the same measure when they were conquered and oppressed by others. Injustices that they had committed were done to them also.

THE NARROW DOOR AND ROAD

Enter ye in at the strait gate: for wide is the gate and broad is the way, that leadeth to destruction, and many there be which go in thereat: Because strait is the gate, and narrow is the way, which leadeth unto life, and few there be that find it. Mt. 7:13-14.

The Aramaic text reads: "Enter in through the narrow door, for wide is the door and broad is the road which leads to destruction, and many are those who travel on it. O how narrow is the door and how difficult is the road which leads to life, and few are those who are found on it."[3]

Part A—DOOR, NOT GATE. Near Eastern church doors and doors of houses are very narrow and low. When entering the houses

---

[3]Mt. 7:13-14, Aramaic Peshitta text, Lamsa translation.

one must bend down to pass through these low and narrow portals. This is very uncomfortable but it cannot be helped. The doors of sheep folds are also narrow and low. This is for security and protection from an enemy. When an intruder attempts to rob a house or sheep fold, both defender and attacker will fight for possession of the door.

The scripture refers to an entrance (door) of a building or to a sheep fold that may or may not have a roof or covering. A gate refers to an entrance into a garden or vineyard. Such gates are generally larger than the doors into buildings or sheep folds. Gates have to be bigger than doors into the homes because animals laden with burdens have to pass through.

We must bend to enter the door into God's kingdom. The gospel of Luke reports Jesus as saying, "strive to enter in through the narrow door."[4] The principles of God's kingdom do not function like the kingdoms of this world; therefore we must strive to participate in God's eternal kingdom. But once we strive and enter through the narrow door, we find eternal peace and happiness.

Part B—THE ROAD. In Palestine there were several roads that travelers could use. The wide road was the popular highway on which caravans would travel. It was an easier route for the traveler because water and other comforts were available. This road was a shorter route but it was also where robbery and murder took their toll. Unwise travelers and the foolish often chose this road.

There was another path that wise men took because they sought safety first. It wound around steep mountains and hills, far away from the main road, where thieves could not lie in wait to murder and plunder. It was a long and difficult road, but travelers could reach their destination safely.

Jesus referred to these two roads to illustrate the way to the kingdom or the way to devastation. The narrow path led to the kingdom. The broad highway that many people traveled led to serious loss. The path that leads to life is narrow and difficult and few will

---

[4]Lk. 13:24, Aramaic Peshitta text, Lamsa translation.

travel this road. Traveling the narrow road that leads to the kingdom of God on earth, we must be prepared to overcome the challenges that may hinder us from reaching our destination.

FALSE PROPHETS

Beware of false prophets, which come to you in sheep's clothing, but inwardly they are ravening wolves. Mt. 7:15.

The word prophet in Aramaic and Hebrew is *nabia.* It comes from the Semitic root *nba* meaning "to bubble up, pour forth, spring forth with a flow of words under excitement of inspiration, to foretell, to announce the news." Prophets were not only seers who predicted future events and who called for divine justice upon the disobedient, but they were also statesmen and leaders of their times. They understood the political and spiritual situations of their day. From this knowledge they were able to predict the future and present their conclusions. Isaiah and Jeremiah were prophets and outstanding statesmen. During wars, revolutions, and other national emergencies these prophets were counselors to their kings.

Near Easterners are believers in prophecies and are mystically inclined. Future events are revealed in a vision during the night when a prophet is asleep. At night the mind is restful and at peace and its range of power is more penetrating. During sleep, the mind does not register time and there is nothing to block inner sight. God spoke to Samuel and Daniel during the night and revelations came to them.

Throughout the religious history of Israel, there were always two classes of prophets—the prophets of God and the prophets of Baal. False prophets and seers have always tried to imitate the works of God's prophets. Egyptian magicians duplicated almost every feat that Moses had enacted. Moses warned his people against false prophets who would come in the future.

Jesus cautioned his disciples against false prophets and christs who would do great signs and wonders to mislead people. The works of real prophets have lasted forever and their predictions have been fulfilled. Magical performances of false prophets have been temporal and unreal. In fact, in all expressions of life we find the authentic mingled with the inauthentic. Often, we cannot distinguish between the genuine and the false. Fruit trees may produce fruit that looks good, but the test of the fruit is in the eating.

BY THEIR FRUITS

Ye shall know them by their fruits. Do men gather grapes of thorns, or figs of thistles? Even so every good tree bringeth forth good fruit: but a corrupt tree bringeth forth evil fruit. Mt. 7:16-17.

In some regions of Near Eastern countries two trees of the same species may grow side by side, but the quality of the fruit can be different. Aramaic speaking people call good trees *ilana tawa* and bad trees *ilana beesha*. A native knows the difference between the good and bad trees, but a stranger can be fooled until he tastes the fruit of the trees. The fruit of the "bad tree" looks fine but its taste is bitter. Walnuts grown on a bad tree are hard to break even with a hammer. It is even difficult to extract the kernel of the nut. Thus, the fruit of a tree tells one how good the tree really is.

Jesus warned against false prophets who give the appearance of being truthful and trustworthy. Appearances can be misleading and deceptive. The fundamental character and deeds of a person reveal whether that person is a true or false prophet.

BAD TREES CUT DOWN

A good tree cannot bright forth evil fruit, neither can a corrupt tree bring forth good fruit. Every tree that bringeth not forth good fruit is hewn down, and cast into the fire. Mt. 7:18-19

Cultivated and productive soil was very scarce in the Holy Land.

Wheat crops were poor, so communities depended on fruit trees for their living. The people valued trees, but they only planted fruit trees. Near Easterners cut down and use for kindling every fruit tree that does not bear edible fruit. All decayed trees are also destroyed so that there may be space to plant productive fruit trees.

Land owners also cut down trees that simply provided shade and aesthetic beauty and used them for fuel. Sacred trees were the exception. The notion of certain trees being sacred came from ancient pagan rites. Sick people decorated the branches of these trees with shreds of cloth, and travelers did the same, as offerings. Many ill people sought the shade of these sacred trees for rest and healing. No Semite dared harm the branches of these trees or pick up dry wood from them for fuel.

Matthew reports Jesus making this figure of speech about unproductive trees to show that people who do not produce good works will be cut down and removed. In reality, unproductive and wicked behavior will eventually remove and destroy itself. God does not reward or punish.

I DO NOT KNOW YOU

Not every one that saith unto me, Lord, Lord, shall enter into the kingdom of heaven; but he that doeth the will of my Father which is in heaven. Many will say to me in that day, Lord, Lord, have we not prophesied in thy name? and in thy name have cast out devils? and in thy name done many wonderful works? and then will I profess unto them I never knew you: depart from me, ye that work iniquity. Mt. 7:21-23.

In ancient biblical days a greater part of the education of priests concerned magical feats, soothsaying, and divinations. These men were not interested in uplifting the people, but they gloried in the wonders that they could perform. The book of Exodus records the struggle between the Egyptian wonder workers and the signs that Moses and Aaron performed. During Jesus' day, healers, wonder workers, and those who practiced magic confused the general public.

The reference here is made to some of Jesus' followers who, in the future, would boast of the great power and wonders with which they were endowed through the teaching of their lord. Nevertheless, throughout his teaching, Jesus placed great emphasis on the works of love, justice, and compassion rather than on prophesying and performing wonders. He also taught visitation of the sick, giving to the poor, and feeding the hungry. There would be many so-called prophets who would make predictions in Jesus' name but they did not represent the true teachings of the Christ. They were false prophets and teachers who would mislead many of the faithful.

In the days of the kings of Israel, hundreds of prophets made predictions in the name of the Lord God, but God had not sent them. They prophesied with, "Thus says the Lord," but the Lord had not said so. These false leaders and prophets preyed on the people, defrauded the innocent, and cheated the widows through their erroneous predictions.

Jesus knew that, in the years to come, some of his followers would do what the adherents of other religions were doing; that is, they would neglect to minister the truth of the kingdom, meet the needs of the people, and would only glory in their high ranking positions and power. These teachers and leaders would become workers of iniquity and depart from the teaching of their Lord. Hence, it would be they who separated themselves from their lord because they no longer represented (knew) him.[5]

FOUNDATIONS

Therefore whosoever heareth these sayings of mine, and doeth them, I will liken him unto a wise man, which built his house upon a rock: And the rain descended, and the floods came, and the winds blew, and beat upon that house; and it fell not: for it was founded upon a rock. And every

---

[5]See Lk. 13:26-27.

118

one that heareth these sayings of mine, and doeth them not, shall be likened unto a foolish man, which built his house upon the sand: And the rain descended and the floods came, and the winds blew, and beat upon that house; and it fell: and great was the fall of it. And it came to pass, when Jesus had ended these sayings, the people were astonished at his doctrine: for he taught them as one having authority, and not as the scribes.
Mt. 7:24-29.

Many towns and villages in the Near East are built on mountain slopes. Sometimes a valley will divide a town. Houses are built on rocks, and in some cases one of the walls of the house is hewn out of the rock. These houses withstand storms because they are very secure. Other houses, because it is much easier and owing to the lack of space, are built near the edge of the valley on the sand. There is little fear of floods because these regions are usually very dry and floods seldom occur.

Nonetheless, at times during the rainy season, the dry valley can turn into a roaring river, so a house that is built on the sand can be swept away. In addition to this, houses built on the river banks will be inundated, the walls will crumble, and the structure will collapse. The raging water is so strong it may even reach the houses that are built on the rock. But these homes can withstand the torrent because they are on strong foundations.

This is a picture of how people build their lives. Some will build their lives on a foundation of truth (Jesus' teaching) that holds firm like a rock and others will build their lives on misleading doctrines and teachings that shift like sand. Rains, floods, and winds represent opposition, temptations, and persecutions which are bound to come but which only those who build on a solid foundation will endure.

Jesus spoke and taught from a direct inner knowledge of Scripture. He did not teach like the Scribes and Pharisees who followed the traditional manner of speaking by quoting the authorities from whom the traditions were being transmitted. His style of presentation was indeed rare and stunned the listeners.[6]

---

[6]We may reasonably suppose that the teachings in Mt. 5-7 are the direct, spiritual ethics of Jesus himself, and not just those of the primitive church. (These teachings, of course, may have gone through some editing, but they do go back to Jesus.) Some New Testament experts also suggest that these sayings are not "a collection of unrelated sayings of diverse origins." They also propose that the utterances of Christ as a tradition were faithfully memorized, repeated, and passed on among the churches. It is typical of Semitic peoples to memorize complete teachings and pass them on from one generation to another. Jesus taught in a deliberate poetic style so that his sayings could be remembered easily. See JESUS AND THE JUDAISM OF HIS TIME, Irving M. Zeitlin, chapter 8, "Jesus' Originality and Creative Genius," pp. 99-100.

CHAPTER 8

PROPER TESTIMONY

And, behold, there came a leper and worshiped him, saying, Lord, If thou wilt, thou canst make me clean. And Jesus put forth his hand, and touched him, saying, I will; be thou clean. And immediately his leprosy was cleansed. And Jesus saith unto him, See thou tell no man; but go thy way, shew theyself to the priest, and offer the gift that Moses commanded, for a testimony unto them. Mt. 8:2-4.

The fourth verse in the Aramaic text reads: "Jesus then said to him, Look, why are you telling it to men?"[1] Most of Jesus' healing took place in public. At times, while he was resting or eating, sick people were brought to him for healing. In the Near East there is little privacy.

Many families live in one house and when an honorable guest or a holy man is entertained, all people, including the curious and the beggars, gather around the guest. Relatives and friends usually accompany the sick that are brought to the home. These people will frequently talk about the healer, either praising or denouncing him.

The man healed of leprosy was talking to those who were around him after his healing. He had been praising Jesus and was no doubt explaining how other healers and doctors tried to heal him but were not successful. This kind of conversation was not wise. It would create jealousy and hatred among the relatives and friends of other healers and doctors in the crowd who had congregated in the home.

Jesus saw that the man was talking too much so he instructed him to go to the priest, show himself for testing of the leprosy, and obtain a testimonial according to the law of Moses. Leprosy was a contagious disease and dangerous. A leper, when cured, had to be examined

---

[1]Mt. 8:4, Aramaic Peshitta text, Lamsa translation.

by the priests, who had the sole authority to pronounce him clean.[2] Since this healing took place in the midst of the crowd, Jesus would not have told him not to tell it to anyone, as the King James version translates the verse, but he was showing that he complied with the hygienic laws of Moses by reminding the cured leper to report promptly to the priests to be declared "clean."

On some occasions Jesus did warn his disciples not to speak of certain things in public. For example, he forbade them to declare that he was the Messiah or the Son of God. Such declarations would have been dangerous to his cause at the beginning. He also told some people whom he had healed to tell it to no one because he did not want to create any needless disputes. This had happened when he had healed the blind man. (See Mark 5:43 and John 9:13.)

THE CENTURION

For I am a man under authority, having soldiers under me: and I say to this man, Go, and he goeth; and to another, Come, and he cometh; and to my servant, Do this, and he doeth it. Mt. 8:9.

Part A—GREAT FAITH. When this Roman centurion sought Jesus to heal his son he was reluctant to invite him to his house, not because it was not good enough for Jesus, but because he was not Jewish. "My lord, I do not deserve that you should enter under my roof, but only say a word and my boy will be healed."[3] This is a typical Semitic saying. The centurion, a Gentile, knew the Jewish tradition that any Jew entering a Gentile's house would be declared unclean. Thus, the centurion politely asks Jesus to speak a word rather than enter his home. He also thought Jesus might be a religious extremist and so be unwilling to enter his house and break bread with him.

In the Near East, even to this day, people hesitate to enter homes

[2]See Lev. 14:1-3.
[3]Mt. 8:8, Aramaic Peshitta text, Errico.

and break bread with members of other faiths. A native often goes to a missionary and says, "My boy is sick but just give me a little medicine for I do no want to trouble you to come to my house."

This centurion had a strong faith in Jesus' ministry and power to heal. He knew Jesus could heal his son by a word of command. He was a captain in the army and he did things by command. He also recognized that Jesus was a prince of a spiritual kingdom. His realization was that Jesus had unlimited powers and his words could accomplish in the realm of the spirit exactly what the soldiers under him were doing by simply complying with his orders. The centurion derived his authority from Caesar, an earthly prince, and his words were obeyed. How much more would be the power of Jesus who derived his authority from God, the ruler of heaven and earth.

Part B—THE TERM LORD. The Roman centurion called Jesus "my lord." In Aramaic the word for "lord" is *mara*. It also means "sir, master." Near Easterners use this term when addressing a superior. In the first century C.E., people employed the term "lord" in everyday language. For example, a wife may call her husband "my lord"; a son could also address his father as "my lord." It was used not only to address a superior or ruler but also to address an outstanding teacher, holy man, healer, and a worker of miracles.

Jesus' disciples, when speaking to their master, used the term "lord." Matthew records this Aramaic form of address to indicate the teaching and religious aspects of Jesus' ministry and personality. Jewish historians consider Matthew's use of "lord" as more authentic and faithful to the original Aramaic genre of story-telling. This fact is well attested by extra-biblical evidence and its usage was very common in the first century.[4]

SEATED WITH ABRAHAM IN THE KINGDOM

And I say unto you, That many shall come from the east and west, and

---

[4]See Geza Vermes, JESUS THE JEW, "Jesus the lord," pp. 103-128.

shall sit down with Abraham and Isaac and Jacob, in the kingdom of heaven. But the children of the kingdom shall be cast out into outer darkness: There shall be weeping and gnashing of teeth. Mt. 8:11-12.

The power and recognition of the kingdom of heaven (God) was to emerge from Israel—that is, from the Hebrew religion that was revealed through Abraham, the Mosaic Law, and the Prophets. This evolving kingdom was to become a universal state, embracing all races and nations. According to the book of Genesis, God had told Abraham that through his seed (teaching) all nations of the earth were to be blessed.[5]

Israel was God's nursery where the seeds of the kingdom had been planted. And from this nursery the entire earth was to be filled with the fruitful trees of truth. But, as time passed in Israel, the people lost their universal concept of the kingdom and were led to believe that the political restoration of the Davidic kingdom was sufficient for their salvation. However, no nation can live in peace and security while surrounded by nations that lack the same light of God.

Jesus, in this instance, predicted that people of various ethnicity from all over the world would come and dine with the Hebrew Patriarchs in the kingdom of God. All the just would enjoy the fruits of this kingdom and share the light of God together. This entire verse (11) points to a universal celebration. Jesus refers to the great banquet of the just that was to be extended to the entire Gentile world. According to the prophet Isaiah, the Messiah was to be a light to the Gentiles even to the ends of the earth.[6]

Jesus had been greatly impressed with the Roman centurion's faith. "When Jesus heard it, he was amazed, and he said to those who accompanied him, Truly I say to you that not even in Israel have I found such faith as this."[7] This Gentile centurion was enjoying the fruits of the kingdom when his boy was healed.

---

[5]See Gen. 12:1-3.
[6]Isa. 49:6.
[7]Mt. 8:10, Aramaic Peshitta text, Lamsa translation.

"The children of the kingdom will be put out into outer darkness" refers to those for whom the kingdom was destined but who did not recognize that the kingdom had arrived. "Outer darkness" means "ignorance." God does not put anyone "into outer darkness." This is an Aramaic figure of speech meaning some will choose to remain ignorant (in the dark). People disqualify themselves through their own blindness and willfulness. Nonetheless, many may be surprised when they see Buddhists, Moslems, pious Jews, society's marginal people and outcasts participating in God's kingdom. "Weeping and gnashing of teeth" is another Semitic idiom meaning "disappointment and overwhelming regret." Those who rejected God's loving, all-inclusive presence would suffer remorse and wonder why they had acted so foolishly. (See Luke 13:28-29.)

PETER'S MOTHER-IN-LAW HEALED

And when Jesus was come into Peter's house, he saw his wife's mother laid, and sick of a fever. And he touched her hand, and the fever left her: and she arose, and ministered unto them. Mt.8:14-15.

One afternoon when Jesus had finished teaching, he went to Simon Peter's home at Capernaum, a small fishing town near the lake of Galilee. Peter's wife was absent and his mother-in-law happened to be sick with fever. In the Near East fever is not considered a serious illness. Men and women stricken with fever do not stop working. They harvest, milk, care for sheep, cook, and do every kind of work while feeling feverish. If they are not working they will sleep, hoping that the fever will pass.

The sound of feet and the conversation of guests as they entered the house had awakened the sick woman. There was no one to entertain an unexpected and popular guest, the master of her son-in-law. Jesus entered and stood beside the sickbed, gazing at the woman. He took her by the hand and raised her from the bed. The fever began to leave her. Feelings of warmth and joy filled her body, for she was more than glad to take care of the master *malpana* (teacher). The unexpected coming of Jesus made her forget she was sick. She lost every thought of herself; her mind was occupied solely with the presence of the beloved guest. She rose up quickly and began preparing food. Her fever left her and she was healed.

JESUS—THE HEALER

When the even was come, they brought unto him many that were possessed with devils: and he cast out the spirits with his word, and healed all that were sick: That it might be fulfilled which was spoken by Esaias the prophet, saying, Himself took our infirmities, and bare our sicknesses. Mt.8:16-17.

Jesus soon found that he must minister to people's bodies as well as to their souls, the body being just as important as the soul. Prophets had healed the sick, cleansed the lepers, and raised the dead. Even in obscure towns, healers were speaking words of comfort to the sick, mentally ill, and the dying. Why not he? He expected nothing from those who sought his help. Thus, he would not be embarrassed by their seeking him. He was under no obligation except that of love. He authorized no publicity that would commercialize his healing power. His simple formula for healing was: "Your faith has made you whole."

His work of healing brought fame and made friends for him. It also brought disappointments and aroused enemies. At times, out of hundreds of people who were brought to him, some were not healed. Only those who truly had faith in him were healed. Jesus taxed his powers of endurance by sympathizing with the afflicted. He never pretended that he was the only healer in the world. When his disciples failed to heal a sick individual he told them, "If you have faith as a mustard seed you can remove mountains." No magic—just a little faith.

Near Easterners were accustomed to long prayers, incantations, charms, and the magic of certain healers who perverted spiritual healing into a profitable profession. Men and women often went away discouraged because the words uttered by Jesus were too simple and not like the magical exclamations and complicated prescriptions of professional healers. He used no drums with which to chase away evil spirits, no charcoal to blacken faces, no snakes to frighten those who had fever. He used only words as soft as spring winds, and as free, to those who came to him.

Among those who came to seek his help were many who had evil spirits (possessed of devils). The Aramaic word for evil spirits is *shedeh*. Easterners used this term to describe those who talked endlessly without making sense and those who were demented. Some people, at times, called Jesus *shedana*—"lunatic," "devil"—because he said certain things that they could not understand.

Some of the ill and demented folks, when they faced Jesus and looked into his calm face and heard his persuasive words, found there was something wrong with themselves. They now knew they were ill and needed healing. It is the power of God that radiates from the personality of the healer that cures the sick. Personality is the magnetic instrument through which the divine power passes. The healer is a medium for healing energies. Any doubt in his mind would obstruct the passage of the healing spirit, just as rust between two connecting wires interrupts the electric current. By looking into the faces of men and women, Jesus knew their inner selves. He acted as a catalyst for their healing.

HOMELESS

And a certain scribe came, and said unto him, Master, I will follow thee whithersoever thou goest. And Jesus saith unto him, The foxes have holes, and the birds of the air have nests; but the Son of man hath not where to lay his head. Mt. 8:19-20.

Part A—POETIC SAYING. "Jesus said to him: Foxes have holes and the birds of the sky a shelter, but this human being has no place even to lay his head."[8] This saying is Aramaic symbolic speech. "I have no place to lay my head" means "I am a poor man, a man without a home" or "I have nothing to offer you."

Near Eastern houses are so crowded that while travelers and unexpected guests are welcomed and fed, they often have no place to sleep. They are allowed to sit down and lean against the wall or lean on some other object and sleep, but there is no room to stretch their legs and they are not provided any bed quilts. Near Easterners have fixed dates for traveling and do so in large companies so that they will be protected from bandits. But, by traveling with a large number of other people, the houses at these times become overcrowded.

Jesus was an itinerant teacher and such men are not always welcomed in Eastern homes. When he was not received, he had to sleep out of doors. When he was received, if the house happened to be crowded, he had to sleep while sitting up.

Jesus knew the scribe only wanted to follow him because of his popularity. The scribe thought Jesus would be fed and entertained and, therefore, he could share in the hospitality given to the Master Teacher. Judas and some of the other disciples who later forsook Jesus probably followed him for this same reason. Jesus was very frank in admitting his poverty and unpopularity. He wanted to avoid any misunderstanding on the part of prospective followers.

Part B—SON OF MAN. *Breh dnasha*, "son of man," more accurately translated means "human being." Aramaic speaking people used this term in reference to: (1) humankind in general; (2) an individual male; (3) one whose identity is unknown; (4) human beings as distinguished from the animal world.

Jesus frequently referred to himself as *bar nasha* or *breh dnasha*, "a human being." It is an indirect Aramaic style of speech meaning, "I am just a human being." In this manner a Near Eastern speaker shows modesty and humility. In Hebrew the term *ben adam*, "son of man," —a term with which God addresses the prophet Ezekiel—simply means an "ordinary human being." This expression in Hebrew

---

[8]Mt. 8:20, Aramaic Peshitta text, Errico.

128

emphasizes the mortal nature of man even when he has the privilege of beholding the glory of God. It also indicates that whatever spiritual height a human being may reach, he remains "just a man." In this instance, Jesus simply means he is just an ordinary man without a place to lay his head.

BURYING ONE'S FATHER

And another of his disciples said unto him, Lord, suffer me first to go and bury my father. But Jesus said unto him, Follow me; and let the dead bury their dead. Mt. 8:21-22.

This phrase, "permit me to go and bury my father," is Semitic style of speech, especially among Aramaic speaking people. It means "My father is an old man and I must take care of him until his death" or "I am responsible for my father until he dies."

In those days, Semites considered a man of seventy years of age as "dead" because he could not work anymore. Since older people had no insurance protection or banks for savings, an elderly man naturally depended on his son for a living. Also, the highest desire a father possessed was that his son would be with him at the time of his death. An aging father looked forward to the day when he would pronounce a benediction on the family and when his son would close his father's eyes at that final moment. This was the case when Jacob, the Hebrew patriarch, was on his deathbed.[9]

The verse that is troublesome to comprehend is the expression "let the dead bury the dead." Dr. Lamsa suggests that a mistake occurred when Jesus made the statement orally. In Aramaic the word for "dead" is *meeta* and the word for "village" or "town" is *mata*. The difference in the formation and the pronunciation of the word is slight. It is more probable Jesus said, "Let the village (town) bury the dead." Such errors also could easily occur in writing or copying manuscripts.

---

[9]See Gen. 49.

Dots and vowel points were not known when the gospels were first written. Also, manuscripts were often mutilated or blurred. It would have sounded harsh and cruel for Jesus to have said, "Let the dead bury the dead." Besides, this man's father was not dead at that time. Had he been dead, his son would have been busy burying him and Jesus would have been with the mourners. Semites bury their dead very soon after they die.

This follower of Jesus was impressed by the master's teaching but embarrassed by his duty to his aged father. Jesus appreciated what the man told him, so he suggested that under such circumstances, if he wanted to serve in God's kingdom, others in the community would care for his father. This would be consistent with what Jesus said elsewhere: "Seek ye first the kingdom of God and his righteousness; and all these things shall be added unto you."[10] People of the Near East are noted for generosity and hospitality. They not only share food but also bury the dead of the community and look after their aged.

(Among the Assyrian-Chaldean people there is an idiom still in use: *shwoq meetheh dqry meethay*. It is the same expression as Matthew 8:22, but the meaning today is: "Don't become involved in other people's problems. Let them take care of their own difficulties." Jesus could be saying: "Let others take care of their own problems. You follow me.")

JESUS CALMS THE STORM

And when he was entered into a ship, his disciples followed him. And, behold, there arose a great tempest in the sea, insomuch that the ship was covered with the waves: but he was asleep. And his disciples came to him, and awoke him, saying, Lord, save us: we perish. And he saith unto them, Why are ye fearful, O ye of little faith? Then he arose, and rebuked the winds and the sea; and there was a great calm. Mt. 8:23-26.

---

[10]Mt. 6:33, K.J.V.

"And when Jesus went up into the boat, his disciples went up with him. And all of a sudden a violent motion occurred in the sea, so much so that the boat was covered by the waves; but Jesus was napping. And his disciples touched him, awakening him and saying: Our lord, save us, we are perishing! Jesus said to them: Why are you so afraid, you of little faith? Then he stood up and rebuked the wind and the sea; and there was a great calm."[11]

The lake of Galilee, lying deep among precipitous mountains, is exposed, like all mountain lakes, to sudden gusts of wind from all sides. These winds suddenly sweep down the valleys and violently agitate the waters and then depart just as quickly. This is exactly what happened when Jesus was with his disciples in the boat.

Interestingly, there is also some subtle humor in this narrative. Notice the contrasts with "violent" wind storm, the "fearful" and "perishing" disciples with the "napping" Jesus. In the book of Jonah, we have almost the same description: "The LORD (Yahweh) sent out a *violent wind* into the sea, and there was a *terrible tempest* in the sea, so that the ship was in danger of being broken. Then the mariners *were afraid* and cried every man to his god. . . But Jonah had gone down into the inner hold of the ship and was lying down *snoring (napping)*."[12] As one reads further in the story, this ship also was being covered by the waves.

Jesus was a prophet of God and had no fear. His disciples were impressed with his command over the winds. Right at the moment of his rebuke, the winds ceased and all was calm.

COME TO TORMENT US

And, behold, they cried out, saying, What have we to do with thee, Jesus, thou Son of God? art thou come hither to torment us before the time. Mt. 8:29.

---

[11]Mt. 8:23-26, Aramaic Peshitta text, Errico.
[12]Jonah 1:4-5, Hebrew text, Stuttgartensia, Errico.

It is not unusual to see an insane person at the divan of a high government official, nobleman, or even a holy man. On such occasions some people amuse themselves by teasing or tormenting the disturbed individual. Sometimes the lunatic is made to sing, curse, and say many things to entertain the guests. At other times young men will torture them and they become very angry.

Once people begin to show signs of mental illness, they are taken to the priest or a sacred shrine for healing. Priests and holy men threaten the mentally ill by scaring them, especially those who become violent in their actions. They are hoping to drive out the insanity with the threat.

Some Moslem religious healers recommend various forms of torture. They will sometimes brand the insane person with a hot iron. Others, particulary the violent, are threatened with being buried alive. If these threats do not work, they are actually buried for a short while. An opening is left in the ground so that the man can breathe. These treatments are practiced now by only the most primitive Near Eastern tribes. Because of these acts, the insane are always afraid of religious men. In these countries there were no homes for the mentally ill. They would roam the towns and were constantly annoyed and tortured.

When these men saw Jesus traveling with a group of disciples and other people, they were afraid of him. They thought he might prescribe torturing remedies to heal them or that they would be brought before him for entertainment. Banquets are generally held in the evening. This explains their statement to Jesus, "before the time," because he had come on the scene in the morning.

LUNATICS AND THE SWINE

So the devils besought him, saying, If thou cast us out, suffer us to go away into the herd of swine. And he said unto them, Go. And when they were come out, they went into the herd of swine: and behold, the whole herd of swine ran violently down a steep place into the sea, and perished in the waters. Mt. 8:31-32.

Jesus and his disciples crossed from Galilee in Palestine to Gadara in Syria, which was on the other side of the Lake of Galilee. When they arrived at the docking place, they were met by two lunatics coming out of the cemetery. In the Near East, mental hospitals and psychiatric wards did not exist. The mentally ill roamed about and lived in cemeteries located a short distance from the town. Frequently, strangers who were not welcomed by the town people found a resting place in the cemetery also.

These insane men saw the boat docking and when Jesus and his disciples disembarked, they immediately recognized a Jewish prophet. They had probably heard of Jesus and of his miraculous works, since Gardara is separated from Galilee by only a few miles of water. Besides, when a man travels with twelve other men, he is either a religious teacher or a high official and would attract the attention of everybody.

When these madmen approached Jesus, they said to him: "If you heal us, permit us to attack the herd of swine." The swine were feeding by the lake. "Cast out" is an Aramaic phrase meaning "to restore sanity, to remove the cause that produces insanity." Today Aramaic speaking people often say to a healer, "cast out or cut my disease." They also say, "he cut my fever," meaning, "he healed me of my fever." Some healers strike a piece of stone on a metal object to drive out the sickness.

The Aramaic word *al* means "attack" and "enter." Men are said to enter into each other when they wrestle or fight. Semites also say oxen enter into each other when they attack or chase each other. Another example: Assyrians say *la al beh* which literally means, "do not enter into him." But what they are saying is, "do not attack him."

In the Near East when a man has lost his mind, Semites say, "he is under the influence of a devil," "he has turned into a devil," "when he speaks the devil speaks in him." All these expressions relate the idea that the man has become violently insane. We read in the gospel that Satan entered into Judas, but it was Judas and not Satan who bargained with the chief priests to betray Jesus. (See Luke 22:3-4.) In the incident with Jesus, it was the lunatics who conversed with Jesus, and not any devils who were supposed to be in them. No devils would have asked permission to enter the swine and then drown themselves in the lake. They certainly had not asked permission to enter the men.

These mentally ill men were Syrians whose people kept large swine herds, which were an abomination to the Jews. As proof of their conversion to the Jewish faith and in appreciation of what Jesus had done for them, they wanted to destroy the swine. They knew that Jesus was a great prophet and that the God of Israel had more power than the Syrian gods, whose prophets could not heal them. Still today, when people are converted to a different faith, they discontinue the practices considered unclean by the new faith. A Christian cannot become a Moslem and be admitted into fellowship unless he sells or kills his swine and repudiates all customs and practices that Moslems declare unclean.

When Semitic Christians join a Protestant church that upholds temperance, they destroy all their jars of wine as proof of their sincerity. When the apostle Paul preached at Ephesus, the Ephesians who accepted his teaching destroyed the images and burned the sacred books of the pagan religions.[13] The idol-making business began to decline because of Paul's message. The artisans of Ephesus became alarmed, so they met together and decided to expel Paul from the city lest their idol making business come to complete ruin.

When the Gadarenes saw that the lunatics were healed and had become converts to the Jewish faith, and that some of the swine had already been drowned, they became panic stricken. They decided not to allow Jesus to preach in Gadara, fearing his mission would result in many conversions that would destroy their swine industry. They felt their livelihood was more important than the religion of a Nazarene prophet, so they begged Jesus to return to his own country. They did not allow him to go further into their territory. Thus, Jesus returned immediately to Galilee. (See Mark 5:11-12; Luke 8:33.)

---

[13]Acts 19:19.

CHAPTER 9

SIN AND FORGIVENESS

But that ye may know that the Son of man hath power on earth to forgive sins, (then saith he to the sick of the palsy,) Arise, take up thy bed and go unto thine house. Mt. 9:6.

The Aramaic text reads: "They brought to him a paralytic lying on a bedroll. And Jesus saw their faith and said to the paralytic: Be consoled, my son, your sins are forgiven you. Then some of the scribes said among themselves: This person blasphemes. But Jesus knew their thoughts and he said to them: Why are you thinking evil in your hearts? Because, which is simpler to say, your sins are forgiven you or to say, stand up and walk? But so you may know that this human being has authority on earth to forgive sins; he then said to the paralytic: Stand up, pick up your bedroll,[1] and go to your home. So he stood up and went to his home."[2]

The Jewish belief at that time was that sickness was a consequence of sin. Hence a prayer for forgiveness must precede a prayer for healing. But Jesus deviated from the usual form by directly forgiving the paralytic's wrongs (sins). People could forgive any sin or wrong committed against themselves but not for others. Jesus felt moved by the faith of the men who brought the paralytic so he released the paralytic from his sins. But some of the scribes who were

---

[1]The beds in biblical lands are not like the beds in American and European homes. The bed is made up of a quilt and a few rugs. During the day people use the bed or bedroll for reclining while eating or conversing. Generally, Near Eastern homes have one large room. In some localities the entire family sleep on one bed that is spread on the floor. Because of the shortage of bedding, some people invite their guests, who are strangers, to share their bed with them. This kind of hospitality is sacredly respected. As most people do not undress before they sleep, there is no concern about privacy.

[2]Mt. 9:2-7, Aramaic Peshitta text, Errico.

seated around Jesus considered such a remark as blasphemy. They believed that no one could forgive sins but God. These men did not realize that man, himself, is the author of sin and can forgive it.

When the people saw the man rising, taking his bedroll and walking, they were amazed. They began to glorify God for the miracle. To heal a sick man and tell him to rise up and take his bedroll and go his way was greater than to say to him, "your sins are forgiven you." "Then when the crowds saw it, they were in awe and praised God because he gave such authority as this to humans."[3]

PHYSICIAN AND HEALER

But when Jesus heard that, he said unto them, They that be whole need not a physician, but they that are sick. Mt. 9:12.

There are two Aramaic words for "doctor" or "physician." When writing Aramaic speaking people use *asya*, meaning "healer."In common speech they use *ḥakim*. It comes from the Aramaic term *ḥakam*, "to be wise." *Hakima* refers to a "wise man." This word is of Western Aramaic origin. The term *ḥakim* also means "governor" or "mayor" because these officials act as advisors in state matters.

Until the turn of the twentieth century, a Semitic doctor was different from American and European physicians. He was not a graduate of a medical school. He had no medicines nor did he prescribe remedies. His major duties were to see what the trouble was and to advise the patient as to the physical and moral conditions. The healer talked to the patients and encouraged them by saying they would soon recover by the help of God. Near Eastern healers knew nothing about the causes of nervous disorders. They treated such cases with prayer and fasting. The sick were taken to priests and religious healers (and still are today) who would read a portion of Scripture over them and speak some cheerful words about faith in

---

[3]Mt. 9:8, Aramaic Peshitta text, Errico.

God.

There are other doctors who deal with broken bones and wounds. They seldom use medicines but make adjustments to the bones and treat the wounds with herbs. These kinds of doctors emerge from time to time in certain families and the secrets of the profession are handed down from father to son.

In the old days, Near Eastern doctors and healers charged nothing for their services. In some rural areas this is still true. They believe God bestows such powers on them to be used freely. They have received them freely and they must give them freely. These healers and physicians believe that if they charge for their services, the sick man will not be healed. This prevents any doubt in the mind of the healer. If he accepts money, he fears the patient may want it back, especially if the patient does not become well. However, gifts are offered to the doctor (healer) as an offering of gratitude after the sick person is healed.[4] Near Easterners hold doctors in high esteem and they take care of them. This enables the doctors to give their services without charge knowing the people will meet their needs.

One of Jesus' major social activities was associating with "prostitutes, tax collectors, and sinners." He ate with anyone who invited him to break bread. He made no distinction between the religious and sinners. Jesus actually refused to draw any social or religious lines of demarcation. For him, all were invited to celebrate God's presence and enjoy the fruits of the kingdom. Although the religious usually would not associate with those who were considered unrespectable, Jesus opened the door of the kingdom to these outcasts. He brought love, acceptance, and healing to those who were rejected and denied. Religious notions branded these people as "sick" but Jesus, like a good doctor, healed them. They were ready to enter God's kingdom. "Truly I say to you that even the tax collectors and

---

[4]See 2 Kings 5:5-20.

harlots will precede you into the kingdom of God."[5] "Go, learn[6] what this means: Compassion do I desire and not animal sacrifices; because I have not come to invite the just but sinners."[7]

FASTING AND WEDDING FEASTS

And Jesus said unto them, Can the children of the bridechamber mourn, as long as the bridegroom is with them? but the days will come, when the bridegroom shall be taken from them, and then shall they fast. Mt. 9:15.

Fasting is strictly observed in Near Eastern countries. Weddings and banquets are planned in advance so they do not occur during religious fasts. It is irreligious to have feasts during this fasting time because of the accompanying drinking and dancing. Usually people fast from morning to evening. Some fast from meat, butter, and cheese; others, from every kind of food. A wedding or banquet is, therefore, out of the question.

Near Easterners are usually sober and live simply, but during wedding feasts and banquets they indulge in drinking and excessive eating. Social customs, fasting, and other religious observances are put aside for the time being. A complete change takes place; sadness and weariness disappear; enemies become reconciled; poor and rich alike try to make the most of such times. During a wedding feast, people will celebrate day and night for as long as the festivities last.

The bridegroom and bride sit at the head of the banquet table. Nothing is lacking. On these occasions, people's generosity provides abundant food and wine. Neighboring wives carry trays of delicious dishes prepared for the event. Some wedding feasts last three days and others seven. Some of the attendees eat, drink, and even sleep at the

---

[5]Mt. 21:31, Aramaic Peshitta text, Lamsa translation.

[6]"Go, learn" is a Semitic expression used particularly in language of debate or in challenge.

[7]Mt. 9:13, Aramaic Peshitta text, Errico.

bridegroom's house. Beggars and strangers share in the abundance of food. Everybody is joyful.

When the wedding days are completed and the celebration is over, a sudden gloom settles on the village. The bustle ceases when the musicians depart and out-of-town guests leave. Beggars return to begging. Strangers seek lodgings for the night elsewhere. Everything becomes very quiet. Then some men and women begin fasting.

John's disciples and those of the Pharisees fasted according to Jewish tradition, but the disciples of Jesus did not fast at all. Jesus was the bridegroom who was with them only for a brief time. But, while he was with them, they did not observe the traditions of the elders. Soon the time would come when he would be taken from them, like the bridegroom when he takes leave from the wedding guests. Then his disciples would turn to fasting.[8]

NEW CLOTH IN OLD GARMENTS

No man putteth a piece of new cloth unto an old garment, for that which is put in to fill it up taketh from the garment, and the rent is made worse. Mt. 9:16.

In lands where styles are unknown and clothes are worn not for beauty and comfort but for protection of the body, garments are constantly mended and worn until they fall to pieces. It is not unusual for Near Easterners to wear their grandparents' garments. Clothes are handed down from father to son and mother to daughter. Moreover, most of the people prefer to wear the same styles as their forefathers.

Usually an old garment is repaired with a patch cut from a worn-out garment. The old piece of cloth matches better on the old garment than a new piece. However, sometimes a new cloth is used to patch an old garment. Generally, when new cloth is made into a new garment, the leftover pieces and trimmings are kept for future

_____

[8]See Mk. 2:19; Lk.5:34; Jn. 3:29.

patching. Thus, when a woman fails to find an old patch to sew on an old garment, she uses the leftover pieces of the new cloth. The problem is that the new patch does not fit well on the old garment. This new cloth is too heavy for the worn garment to hold and in a few days the new patch begins to pull away, leaving a larger hole than before. Then there is the problem that appears when the garment is washed. The new piece will shrink and the old part of the garment tears under the strain of the washing.

Such is the case of an individual who wishes to receive a new teaching but holds on to the influence of the old beliefs and ideas. The force of the new weakens and shatters the old beliefs. The individual loses everything. An old garment cannot take a new piece of cloth for patching. Jesus' teaching of the law (torah) and prophets contradicted the teachings of the Elders. A new "garment" (understanding) was needed because one cannot patch old traditions with new teachings.

NEW WINE AND OLD BOTTLES

Neither do men put new wine into old bottles: else the bottles break, and the wine runneth out, and the bottles perish: but they put new wine into new bottles and both are preserved. Mt. 9:17.

The Aramaic text reads: "And they do not pour new wine into worn out skins, otherwise the skins will burst and the wine run out and the skins are ruined. But they pour new wine into new skins and both are preserved."[9] Until recent years, the people in biblical lands did not have or use glass bottles and wooden barrels. In some remote regions, such articles are still a curiosity.

"Skins" means goat hide, which many Near Easterners still use today as a bottle or container. The insides of the goat are removed, the legs are tied together, and an opening is made in the neck. The Assyrian and Chaldean people of Northern Iraq still carry water, wine,

---

[9]Mt. 9:17, Aramaic Peshitta text, Errico.

140

milk, and other liquids in goat skins. Bedouins churn milk in the goat skins to make butter.

When new wine is poured into old goatskins, the wine ferments and bursts the skins. Therefore, they store and transport new wine in new skins. The new skins resist the effects of fermentation and both wine and skins are preserved. When a family runs short of new skins, they will carry the new wine in old skins at great risk.

The new gospel of the kingdom, with its fresh spiritual message to humanity, needed new apostles, teachers, and laws. The old traditions and teachings could not express the new ideas. The worn-out cultic, priestly system was to crumble before the power of the new teaching, just as old skins burst with the fermenting of new wine. Men and women were to receive power from the new gospel of the kingdom and be free from "old goatskin" theologies and traditions.[10]

MOURNING

And when Jesus came into the ruler's house and saw the minstrels and the people making a noise, He said unto them, Give place: for the maid is not dead, but sleepeth. And they laughed him to scorn. Mt. 9:23-24.

The Aramaic text reads: "Then Jesus came to the leader's home and saw the singers and the disorderly crowds."[11] Semites mourn with overwhelming grief over their dead. Among the people of the Near East the only suitable conduct at a funeral with which to manifest your respect for the deceased is to show that you are overcome emotionally. If you stood in "respectful silence" while attending an Eastern funeral, it would mean that you had no feeling at all for the departed. This would be insulting to the grieving family.

Near Easterners honor men and women twice: first, at their wedding, when the entire town shares in the joy of the union and helps

---

[10]See Mk. 2:22; Lk. 5:37.
[11]Mt. 9:23, Aramaic Peshitta text, Errico.

to make the wedding celebration a success; later, at death, when all neighbors and friends—even enemies—weep vehemently and lament loudly over their departure. They not only weep over their dead but also slap their faces with their hands, tear their clothes, and even inflict wounds on themselves. Women cut their hair and beat their breasts; men stop shaving as a sign of mourning. King David tore his garments and wept bitterly when the news was brought to him that King Saul and his son, Jonathan, were slain in battle.[12]

The weeping and wailing at a Semitic funeral reaches its highest point when professional singers chant songs of moving lamentations and when men and women eulogize. The relatives of the dead accompany the professional singers. These relatives kiss the deceased and call his name out loud. The singers talk to him as if he were alive, at times even criticizing him and making jokes at his expense. Weeping and wailing would usually start before the person was actually dead. (In ancient days and until the beginning of the twentieth century, Near Easterners would mourn people who were in a coma because they thought of them as dead. They did not understand what a coma was.) Sometimes the wailing is so great and the lamenting so deep that hysteria and disorder might result.

Jesus understood this kind of hysteria and grief. He knew that people looked on death as a calamity. When he entered the house, he commanded the people to leave the sick room and ordered the professional singers to stop making noise. He did not want the little girl frightened by all the crying and lamenting. Jesus told everyone: "The girl is not dead but she is sleeping." This is a Semitic expression that people often use to quiet distressed parents. In Jesus' eyes death was nothing but sleep. To him, the deceased was really alive because the soul was still alive. He took the girl by the hand and addressed her in Aramaic saying: *talita qoomi,* "O, little girl arise." And the little girl stood up.[13]

---

[12]See 2 Sam. 1:11.
[13]Mk. 5:38; Lk. 8:54.

AN HONORABLE TITLE

And when Jesus departed thence, two blind men followed him, crying, and saying, Thou son of David, have mercy on us. Mt. 9:27.

Usually the term "son of David" refers to the Messiah. But in this passage and in many other verses just like it, "son of David" does not necessarily mean the supplicants were calling Jesus the actual blood son of King David or that he was the Messiah. People sometimes used this expression as a way of showing admiration and deep respect to a healer of great reputation or to men of renown.

Near Easterners often called valiant men the sons of famous kings and noble men of the past. This was a great honor to be called "son of David." The blind men who wanted to be healed were asking for mercy and compassion from the Teacher-Healer whose fame had spread everywhere. It was an honorific term that the blind men bestowed on Jesus.

SHEEP WITHOUT A SHEPHERD

But when he saw the multitudes, he was moved with compassion on them, because they fainted, and were scattered abroad, as sheep having no shepherd. Mt. 9:36.

In Near Eastern lands cattle are often left in the fields and mountains to graze alone. It is not so with sheep. Sheep must be led into the pasture and brought back to the fold. They would not go or come back on their own. They are timid and fearful when left alone. Even when under the care of the shepherd, the moment the sheep see a stranger or hear the sound of a strange voice, they become panic-stricken.

The shepherd must constantly watch his sheep and the sheep are always aware he is with them. He leads them into new pastures. During the heat of the day, he takes them under the shade of trees.

When they are thirsty, he takes them to water. The shepherd protects them from wolves, bears, and bandits. David, as a shepherd boy, killed a lion and a bear when they attacked his sheep.[14] If anything happens to the shepherd, his sheep scatter in the mountains and go astray.

The reference is to the people of Israel, who were as sheep without a shepherd. Foreign nations had subjugated them, and their priests had betrayed them. For centuries they had no prophets and seers to guide them. Misrule and persecution had scattered them in foreign lands, and even those who were at home had no genuine leadership. They, also, would soon scatter when the Roman legions under Prince Titus would destroy their holy city, Jerusalem.

---

[14]See 1 Sam. 17:34-36.

CHAPTER 10

APOSTLES CHOSEN AND INSTRUCTED

And when he called unto him his twelves disciples, he gave them power against unclean spirits, to cast them out, and to heal all manner of sickness and all manner of disease. Now the names of the twelve apostles are these; The first, Simon, who is called Peter, and Andrew his brother; James the son of Zebedee and John his brother. Mt. 10:1-2.

Jesus chose twelve because that number represented the twelve tribes of Israel. It was also symbolic of the restoration work of the Messiah for all twelve tribes. (See verse 6.) Part of the messianic restoration work was to heal people's diseases. These men also received authority over *ruḥeh tanpatha*, "unclean spirits." This Aramaic term refers to those who have evil intentions and inclinations, those with mental disorders, the unruly and insane. Jesus knew that his disciples needed more to do than just preach that God's kingdom had arrived. They must be able to demonstrate the power of this kingdom by curing sicknesses and the mentally deranged. The word for "disciple" in Aramaic is *talmeedha* and comes from the root *lmad*, "to put together, compile, learn." Jesus taught them to have authority over illness through faith in God's presence.

The Aramaic text reads: "And he summoned his twelve disciples and gave them authority over mental illnesses that they should cure them and to heal every kind of pain and sickness. Now these are the names of the twelve apostles: The first of them is Simon who is nicknamed Peter and Andrew his brother; and Jacob, Zebedee's son and John his brother;"[1] The word "apostle" is from the Greek language. In Aramaic it is *shleeḥa*, "sent one." Jesus was sending these twelve out to do the work of the kingdom.

"Peter," *Kepa* (pronounced kaypah) is a nickname. The apostle's

---

[1] Mt. 10:1-2, Aramaic Peshitta text, Errico.

proper name was Simon. Also the name "James" is not in the Aramaic text. It is "Jacob." The name "James," which we find in most translations of the New Testament, was a mistake. This name is not known in biblical languages. It was correctly translated as "Jacob" throughout the Hebrew Bible.

BEWARE OF PAGAN PRACTICES

These twelve Jesus sent forth, and commanded them, saying, Go not into the way of the Gentiles, and into any city of the Samaritans enter ye not. But go rather to the lost sheep of the house of Israel. Mt. 10:5-6.

Part A—GENTILE PRACTICES. In Aramaic the word for "way" is *urha*. In this passage it can mean "road, habit, practice." The Aramaic text reads: These twelve Jesus sent out, and charged them and said, Keep away from pagan practices, and do not enter a Samaritan city; But above all, go to the sheep which are lost from the house of Israel."[2] "Do not go in the way of the Gentiles" can also mean "do not practice the customs of the Gentiles."

In the Near East, men and women of different faiths travel the same road in company with each other, converse, and sleep at the same inn. But they do not eat together because the food supply that one group carries may be considered unclean by other groups. For example, some may eat pork, which members of other faiths condemn as unfit and as an abomination. Again, a member of one sect may have two wives, but if he finds a bargain while traveling on the road, he would not hesitate to take a third wife. People of various religions live for generations in the same neighborhood, but they remain loyal to their religious observances of distinctive customs and traditions. Followers of different faiths are known not by their theology but by their customs. Each faith has it own standard of living and its members must faithfully adhere to it.

---

[2]Mt. 10:5-6, Aramaic Peshitta text, Lamsa translation.

146

Jesus' disciples were to travel and preach among the people of their own faith. In most cities, Jews and Gentiles were neighbors; their houses were separated only by a thin wall. The disciples of the new teaching of the kingdom were placed in a peculiar situation. In the eyes of the Gentiles, these disciples were Jews, while the Jews regarded these men as dissenters because they did not observe the traditions of the elders. This created additional problems and made their mission more difficult. Neither Jews nor Gentiles welcomed them at the same inns where they lodged. These challenges would lead to the temptation to lean toward pagan customs. If these disciples adopted some of the Gentile ways, the Jewish leaders would show even greater hostility to Jesus and his followers. The disciples were to carefully follow their own customs. At that time, the Jews detested both Samaritans and pagans (Gentiles). They had to practice the way of the Hebrew prophets—that is, preach first to the people of their own faith. Although they were in a Gentile city, their mission was first to seek and find "the lost sheep of the house of Israel."

The disciples were to strictly observe some of the most important and basic Jewish customs on which the Jewish faith rested. They had to adhere to fundamental principles that distinguished Jews from pagans. This was necessary so that they could win over the Jews to the light of God's kingdom. When one alienates himself from the customs and practices of his own people, he also loses their confidence and hinders the work.

Part B—FORBIDDEN TERRITORY. In Aramaic there are two words for Samaria and Samaritan territory—*Shamrin*, meaning" the city of Samaria" and *Beth-Shamrayeh*, "Samaritan territory." Both the name of the city, which was once the capital of the Northern Kingdom of Israel, and the name of the province are derived from *Shemer*, from which the city site was purchased by King Omri of Israel.[3] The city was built on a hill a short distance from Schechem.

Today, just as in olden days, certain people in the Near East, because of their peculiar customs and religious differences, prefer to

---

[3]See 1 Kings 16:24.

live by themselves in a restricted sector. Such areas still exist in Arabia, Iraq and Iran, and are restricted to members of particular religious sects. There is an ancient community of people near the city of Mosul, in Iraq, known as devil worshipers. They have lived by themselves for centuries. Prior to World War I, they would not permit other people to pass through their territories or visit their sacred places. They traded with neighboring tribes but did not intermarry or have any social dealings with them.

Jesus was not allowed to travel in Samaritan territory, which lay between Galilee and Judea, because his teachings were contrary to the established religion in that region. He often went out of his way and traveled long distances to come to Judea. At times, he passed on the road near certain towns and sent his disciples to buy bread, as when he met the Samaritan woman near the well. On such occasions, a traveler, although a member of another faith, is permitted to drink water and buy bread but cannot lodge in that region. That would be against the religious custom of the area. They would consider themselves or anything the traveler might touch to be defiled. This is one of the reasons Jesus told his disciples not to enter Samaritan territory.

MONEY FOR THE JOURNEY

Provide neither gold, nor silver, nor brass in your purses. Mt. 10:9.

The Aramaic text reads: "Do not accumulate gold or silver or brass in your purses."[4] Since there were no banks, money was carried in purses and belts that wrapped around men's waists. In the Near East, bandits would kill a traveler when finding money on his person. They have to kill the traveler so he will not be able to identify them. A traveler who does not carry any money has nothing to fear. He feels perfectly safe and free while on the road. If he should be in need and

---

[4]Mt. 10:9, Aramaic Peshitta text, Lamsa translation.

robbers encounter him, they will offer to help him and let him go in peace. Near Eastern bandits often share their scanty supplies of food with travelers whom they meet.

Jesus knew that if his disciples went out preaching, uninstructed and unprepared, they would be in danger of falling into temptation. He knew that many men and women would give their wealth and even their jewels for the sake of having their bodies healed, their sight restored, or their loved ones raised from the dead. He knew that his disciples, endowed with the power of healing, would soon accumulate riches and become the prey of robbers who would gladly kidnap them for ransom.

Also, the division of wealth among the disciples could become a problem and could stir rivalry and envy. This kind of difficulty would weaken their ranks and interfere with the progress of their work. In addition to this, there were grave concerns that men seeking only material goods and self-interest would offer themselves for the work.

Jesus understood the mind and psychology of the people of the Near East. These people would not welcome nor trust the teachings of missionaries (sent ones) who are paid for preaching God's word. His disciples were to be ready to lay down their lives for the sake of God's kingdom. The people among whom they labored would feed the disciples. "For the workman is worthy of his food." Near Easterners are hospitable to strangers. They will invite strangers into their homes and will provide generously the food and lodging that is needed. It would not be necessary for his disciples to keep or accumulate anything. The fewer material things the disciples possessed, the fewer difficulties they would encounter.

BAG

Nor scrip for your journey, neither two coats, neither shoes, nor yet staves: for the workman is worthy of his meat. Mt. 10:10

Part A—THE *TARMALA*. The Aramaic word for "scrip" is

tarmala meaning a "bag." It is woven of wool like Oriental rugs and sewed together. Its size is about one foot by one foot and a half. People use the *tarmala* on a journey to carry bread, other food supplies, and some merchandise.

When one left his home on a short journey, he did not expect to find food until he arrived in a town. There were no restaurants where one could stop to rest and obtain refreshments. Bread and food were seldom sold to strangers but if a traveler was welcomed in a home, lodging and food were freely shared with him. However, on long journeys travelers depended largely upon food supplies that they carried in their *tarmaleh* (bags).

A traveler may be stranded on the road or upon his arrival in a town, or he may be unable to find lodging. He also may be welcomed by a poor family who would find it difficult to set bread before him. In this case he eats his own bread, giving a portion of it to the members of the family in exchange for buttermilk and cheese which they will generously share with him.

A traveler with many servants and much baggage is seldom welcome in a Near Eastern home. The family is reluctant to open their doors to such guests because their presence draws the neighbors, who will also have to be entertained. They will not only have to feed the guests but must also replenish their guests' food supplies for the road. Interestingly, a guest with a bag is generally supposed to be going on a long journey. A guest without a bag is usually on a short journey and when asked to eat will decline, saying: "I am not hungry. I'm returning to my own house soon."

Jesus' disciples were not on a journey as merchants and other travelers, with their retinue of servants and bags. They were to be unlike other travelers. The people to whom the disciples brought the new gospel were to welcome, entertain, and take care of their needs just as they took care of Jesus. When the disciples were traveling with Jesus, they lacked nothing. They were received in homes and, at times, entertained lavishly. Now they were to expect the same treatment from the people because they were preaching the same gospel, performing miracles and wonders, as did their master.

150

Jesus, on his travels, did not carry a *tarmala* with food and often suffered thirst and hunger. The disciples once watched him returning from the side of the road disappointed because he could not find any figs to satisfy his hunger. These preachers of the new faith would, at times, suffer hunger to show the people that hoarding and being greedy and extravagant was not the way to live. (See Mark 6:8-9.)

Part B—TWO COATS. In lands where styles do not mean anything, people wear as many shirts as they can afford. Usually what determines the social standing of a man is how many shirts and other garments he wears. When a stranger enters a house, the family judges him according to the number of shirts on his person. Generally, a poor man has just one shirt. If the one shirt becomes soiled, he will remain home until a family member washes and dries it, or he may borrow one from a friend who happens to be sick or not going anywhere. A rich man wears as many as half a dozen shirts and several coats at one time.

Frequently, travelers wear more than one shirt. They do so that they may appear wealthy and so that the home or town they may visit will welcome them and protect them from the cold. Also, Near Easterners have no suitcases or trunks so they must wear everything they own, whether at home or on a journey. They fear that if they leave their garments at home, others will take them and wear them. Before the advent of modern Western nations in the Near East, there were no hotels or inns as we know them. Travelers slept in the clothes they wore. Even when families had opened their homes to them and entertained them as guests, they still would sleep in all the clothes they were wearing. Most hosts were poor and at times received more guests than they could accommodate. They would feed them and give them a mat to spread on the earthen floor for their sleeping quarters.

When encountering travelers on the road, bandits will usually relieve them of their clothes and shoes. These robbers attack men who have more than one shirt. They search very carefully for money and if they do not find any, the robbers beat them and take away all their shirts. Seldom do these bandits attack a man with one shirt. They consider him poor. They search him and let him go. Many Near

Easterners are aware of this. Therefore, when they travel, they let others wear their good garments and they wear a few poor ones so as to mislead the robbers. Jesus knew that if his disciples wore more than one shirt, they would most likely become victims of the professional bandits who preyed on travelers and caravans. The fewer shirts they had, the less trouble they would encounter.

Part C—TWO PAIRS OF SHOES. In Kurdistan, Assyria, and in some other regions where western civilization had not yet penetrated, people still wore woolen shoes. These were manufactured from a piece of woolen carpet that is heavily sewn with thread until it becomes hard like leather. This type of shoe is very comfortable, especially on a journey. Some travelers carry two pairs, wearing one and repairing the other while on the road. Robbers usually relieve travelers of the extra pair and if they resist, they will beat them and may even kill them. In the Near East, it is always better to travel very light so one may avoid trouble on the way.

Part D—LABORER WORTHY OF HIS FOOD. When a Near Easterner hires laborers, he bargains about wages and food. Customarily, the employer provides food for his laborers. Especially during the vineyard and harvest season, employers feed their laborers very generously. They store food stuffs and other supplies for the summer season for the workman, so food is abundant.

When a laborer demands high wages, the question of food becomes an issue for the employer; but when a man is willing to work without a stipulated wage, the employer never discusses the question of food. Men with poor reputations as workers do not generally bargain for wages but work for what they can get.

Among Semites, any type of service performed is worth food. The disciples were worthy of the food they would receive because they were preaching and healing without charge. People gladly welcomed them and gave them food and lodging. Semites are always hospitable to travelers and strangers, especially so to preachers of the gospel. (See Luke 10:7.)

DUST OFF YOUR FEET

And whosoever shall not receive you, nor hear your words, when ye depart out of that house or city, shake off the dust of your feet. Verily I say unto you, It shall be more tolerable for the land of Sodom and Gomorrah in the day of judgment, than for that city. Mt. 10:14-15.

The Aramaic text reads: "Whoever will not welcome you and will not listen to your words, when you leave the house or the village, shake off the sand from your feet. Truly, I say to you that it will be easier for the land of Sodom and Gomorrah on the day of judgment than for that city."[5] "To shake the dust from your feet" is an Aramaic idiom that means "to be absolved of any responsibility." It also means "Have no part in the conduct of people who refuse to welcome guests."

Semites are famous for their generosity and hospitality. They seldom refuse to give food and lodging to a wayfarer. Their motto is "Today a guest knocks at my door; tomorrow I may knock at another's door." Until recent years, many Semites walked barefoot or wore woolen shoes. When a guest would come to a home, the host welcomed him; the guest's shoes would be removed and his feet washed. The sand or dust would fall from his feet inside the house. But when the guest did not receive any hospitality and the host refused to offer lodging, he would shake the sand from his feet at the front door, signifying that this house did not welcome guests.

Many of Jesus' disciples were to be welcomed by the people to whom they were sent to preach and teach. Nonetheless, some families would reject his disciples because their teaching was strange. In the Near East there are some people who believe that they would be contaminated by just touching a member of another religion. Others would refuse to break bread with teachers or preachers whose faith was questionable. Undoubtedly, some Jews, Samaritans, and members of other religions would despise Jesus' disciples because their

---

[5]Mt. 10:14-15, Aramaic Peshitta text, Lamsa translation.

teachings opposed the existing religions and teachings that resulted in hatred, persecution, and discrimination. The gospel of the kingdom of God was all-inclusive. It did not create an insider/outsider, sectarian form of religion.

People who refused these disciples, as well as villages that refused them, would one day regret that they had not opened their doors to God's ambassadors. The figurative terms of speech about judgment simply mean that these people and villages would have greater sorrow and regrets than Sodom and Gomorrah did for their evil doings.[6] (See Mark 6:11; Luke 9:5.)

WISE AND HARMLESS

Behold, I send you forth as sheep in the midst of wolves: be ye therefore wise as serpents, and harmless as doves. Mt. 10:16.

People, generally, think of a serpent as the symbol of wisdom. However, they also consider it as an emblem of wickedness and treachery. Serpents assume the coloring of their native surroundings and they glide in the grass and under objects without anyone noticing them. According to the Eden story recorded in Genesis, it was the serpent that deceived Adam and Eve in the Garden and opened the way for them to transgress God's command.

Usually a serpent will turn aside when it sees someone approaching. A serpent does not invite trouble but when it feels danger, it will attack or attempt to escape to protect itself. When a snake sees danger, it coils and keeps its head in the center of its coil so that its head may be protected. Therefore, the serpent is wise, that is, shrewd.

The dove is the symbol of purity, gentleness, peace, and sincerity. It is a very friendly bird and probably the first domesticated one.

---

[6]Many New Testament scholars believe that Jesus did not actually pronounce this form of judgment on these villages and people. They suggest that these words were placed on Jesus' lips by early church scribes.

Semites often say:, "he is like a dove," meaning he is very unassuming and sincere. Doves are harmless and never attack other birds. As a pet, the dove is faithful to its owner. When Noah sent a dove out of the ark, it returned with a twig in its mouth[7]

Jesus instructed his disciples to be wise as serpents and harmless as doves. They were cautioned to be faithful to their work and avoid the ways of their enemies so as not to invite trouble and danger. He told them to be shrewd and careful so they could protect themselves by relying on God's power and wisdom. The disciples were to travel unarmed and in the event of danger, they were to flee from one city to another. For the disciples to preach purity, peace, and kindness, they themselves must be peaceful, unarmed, and harmless as doves.

Jesus well knew Near Eastern people and the dangers confronting the apostles of a new gospel when traveling. His disciples had to travel among hostile tribes and confront enemies who would persecute them. They would meet men who would betray them. An unarmed and meek person meets less trouble on the road. They are less likely to be robbed. They must learn to rely on God for protection and wear the armor of truth, gentleness, and understanding. The enemy feels this power and knows that they are harmless.

In a world of hatred and violence, one has to be gentle and harmless and depend on God's protection. But, at the same time, one has to be wise. True wisdom, when rightly used, is a gift from God.

FLEE TO ANOTHER CITY

But when they persecute you in this city, flee ye into another: for verily I say unto you, Ye shall not have gone over the cities of Israel till the Son of man be come. Mt. 10:23.

Part A—CITIES OF REFUGE. Biblical systems of law and government still dominate some Near Eastern countries. In some

---

[7]Gen. 8:8-11.

provinces, federal authority is hardly noticeable. The provincial governor and his officials are the only authorities that the people know and recognize. Subordinates exercise full authority in governmental and judicial matters in the districts. There are also some regions and cities that maintain complete freedom and autonomy from provincial and federal rule. Generally, local hereditary chiefs, among whom rivalry and hatred reign, govern these localities.

When a man flees from one city to another, the authorities of that city welcome him and give him protection. Offenses and crimes committed in one city cannot be held against the person in another city. Murderers and thieves often flee to other cities to escape punishment. They share a portion of the spoils with officials in order to secure freedom. In biblical days certain cities were chosen to which murderers could flee for refuge. (See Numbers 35:6; Joshua 21:13-38.)

Part B—WORKING AMONG THE JEWS FIRST. The Aramaic word *tshalmoon* is the second person plural. It comes from the word *shalem* meaning "surrender, convert, finish." The Aramaic text reads: You shall not finish converting all the cities of the house of Israel until the Son of man returns."[8]

The disciples were to work first among people of their own faith as there was much to be done among them. They had to win over and obtain the support of some of the Jewish people before the movement could spread among the Gentiles. This was not an easy task. They were to meet with adversities, oppositions, and persecutions. Their own friends and relatives would betray them to governors and city officials, but the gospel work was to continue until all nations, including the Jews, would accept the message of the kingdom.

Jesus did not mean the disciples were merely to go over the cities of Palestine, because all the cities of Palestine could be worked in a matter of a few months. He meant that they were to win over the Jewish people to the message of the kingdom. When the Jews and all nations come to realize the power and inclusiveness of Jesus'

---

[8]Mt. 10:23b, Aramaic Peshitta text, Lamsa translation.

teachings, then his ideals and principles will become an accomplished fact. His kingdom will be established all over the world and his personality felt in the hearts of all races.

SECRETS

What I tell you in darkness, that speak ye in light: and what ye hear in the ear, that preach ye upon the house tops. Mt. 10:27.

People meet on housetops because public sites for gatherings or meetings are few. Houses are built in a box shape with flat roofs. Children use the flat roofs for a playground, men and women meet on roof tops, and town councils and church meetings are held on the roof. Most secret conversations and gossip are also carried on there.

Where there are no newspapers and other publications, secrets are carried from mouth to mouth. The only way to publish news quickly is to tell the person to whom you speak: "Don't tell anyone." In this way the news becomes important and it spreads from person to person with the same instruction: "Don't tell anyone else." In a few hours the news spreads all over town and everyone is talking about it. The opposite is true when people are free to repeat the news. No one will discuss the matter because it carries no weight.

Jesus told his disciples not to tell the people openly what he was telling them secretly. This was the best way to broadcast the news. However, at certain times, he instructed them not to tell anyone that he was the Messiah. It was dangerous to spread this idea because people thought of the Messiah as a militant and political leader. Besides, this concept would have created disturbances and hindered his gospel work of the kingdom.

"Tell no man," therefore, depends on how one says it. The speaker's voice inflection and the manner in which he delivers the instruction is important. Sometimes the person says it lightheartedly; at other times, in a serious tone.

ENEMIES OF THE SOUL

And fear not them which kill the body, but are not able to kill the soul:
but rather fear him which is able to destroy both soul and body in hell.
Mt. 10:28.

The gospel of Luke says: "But I forewarn you whom ye shall
fear: Fear him, which after he hath killed hath power to cast into hell:
yea, I say unto you, fear him."[9] Most biblical interpreters believe that
Jesus is referring to God. But we believe this is not the case.

Jesus, in this passage, speaks of the enemies of truth, those who
were opposed to the gospel of the kingdom. Many of Jesus' followers
were sooner or later to die for the truth they were representing. They
were teaching that God's kingdom was a present reality. Their Master
had admonished them not to fear those who kill the body only. The
body is the outward form and expression of the soul, but it is not the
essence of life.

Jesus' disciples and followers were warned to be careful,
especially of false teaching, sin (error), and evil forces that can destroy
not only the body but also the soul. Some teachers taught things that
caused the faithful to stray from the truth of the gospel of the
kingdom. They taught them to worship pagan gods and to engage in
practices that succeeded in destroying their souls. Any teaching that
holds to the notion that humans are separate from God places the soul
in hell.

The term "hell" refers to "mental suffering, inner torment."
Misleading dogma and ideas, along with destructive practices, put the
soul in "hell" (mental and emotional suffering). God, being a good and
loving parent, is not the creator of "hell." Human beings create their
own difficulties and their own hell that torment their souls. Also the
memory of an evil deed not rectified creates anguish and torment.
God's presence and power help human beings to overcome their
torments and challenges.

---

[9]Lk. 12:5, K.J.V.

CONFESSING JESUS

Whosoever therefore shall confess me before men, him will I confess also before my Father which is in heaven. But whosoever shall deny me before men, him will I also deny before my Father which is in heaven. Mt. 10:32-33.

Jesus knew there would be divisions and persecutions because of his teachings. This new teaching would create many challenges, conflicts, and hatred among the people, so much so that some of his followers would recant and deny him. Peter was one of the staunch disciples through whom Jesus was to build his followers. Yet, a short while after Peter had confessed Jesus to be the Messiah, he denied his master with strong words, saying he never knew him. Of course, later, Peter repented.

To publicly acknowledge Jesus means to practice his teaching, take up the cross (meet the challenge), and be ready to die for this gospel of the kingdom if necessary. Jesus had told his disciples from the beginning that the road to the kingdom would be narrow and thorny and few would be found on it.

The Aramaic word *nawdey* means "to give thanks" but it also means "to confess," that is, to confess the blessings that the people had received from the Lord. In this passage, Jesus says that those who confess him—those who testify about his teaching and acknowledge his way of life—he too will be acknowledged before God, his father. Those who do not confess him put themselves out of participation in the presence of God (the kingdom) by denying truth.[10]

---

[10]Many New Testament scholars believe that these statements were created after Jesus' crucifixion, when his disciples were forced into either acknowledging their master or denying him. Other N.T. experts suggest that some early Christian prophets, who felt qualified to speak directly for Jesus under the power of the spirit, made these statements and not actually Jesus himself. Later, when the Christian scribes recorded these sayings, they were placed on Jesus' lips. Then again, some scholars believe that Jesus never spoke in the first person singular.

NOT PEACE BUT A SWORD

Think not that I am come to send peace on earth: I came not to send peace, but a sword. Mt. 10:34.

Political leaders invariably promise material prosperity. Prophets predict both peace and vengeance. No leader or prophet could win the public without certain promises of change in the social and political order of things. In countries where persecution and injustice prevail, people always look to a leader to bring peace, prosperity, and change. Usually such revolutionary changes are brought about through the use of the sword.

Jesus did not mean that his mission was to initiate strife and war. But his ideas were so contrary and revolutionary to the social and religious order of his day, they could not be carried out without conflict. His teaching of God's kingdom upset dogmas and traditions and challenged the priestly authority. Because of the differences between Jesus' teaching and those of the culture and religion, divisions would result in the homes and organizations. A son who accepted Jesus' gospel might incur the anger of his father and be thought of as a traitor to his ancestral faith. A daughter might find the same response from her mother if she embraced this gospel. Jesus made it clear that his teaching would create much suffering and persecution from all directions.

Jesus was very emphatic in his declaration to the people that they should not expect his mission to bring immediate peace. He did not make false promises. He wanted his disciples and followers to be aware of the future dangers that would confront them. (Some would even have to suffer martyrdom.) In this manner he eliminated from his ranks all who would come after him for the sake of material gains. He enlisted only those who were ready to renounce everything in favor of this gospel of the kingdom. (See Matthew 10:35-37.)

CONCERN FOR ONE'S LIFE

And he that taketh not his cross, and followeth after me, is not worthy of me. He that findeth his life shall lose it: and he that loseth his life for my sake shall find it. Mt. 10:38-39.

The Aramaic text reads: "And whoever does not take up his cross and follow me is not worthy of me. He who is concerned about his life shall lose it; and he who loses his life for my sake shall find it."[11] The expression "take up the cross" means be ready to meet the challenge and perhaps face death. Most new religious movements in the Near East endure persecutions. Followers of Jesus' gospel would have to meet the challenge of losing their lives for the sake of the kingdom. The notion of the cross was not new to the Jewish people, who had seen many Jewish rebels crucified for their insurrections and defiance against Roman power. Jesus knew his disciples would have to endure hardships, persecutions and death for preaching this new gospel.

The word "findeth" in the King James Version is not a precise translation. Jesus' meaning here is "concerned." He directed this saying toward those who were fearful about losing their lives for the sake of the kingdom. Many would be concerned about the welfare of their families and would avoid identifying themselves with a controversial figure and teacher. Some religious authorities despised the prophet from Galilee. Therefore, the lives of Jesus' followers would be in danger.

However, disciples and followers who were concerned about their lives would deprive themselves of the rich, spiritual life that Jesus revealed. Out of fear, they would exchange the greater for the lesser, the permanent for the temporal. On the other hand, those who would accept the challenge would find the secret of life and realize eternal life. Indeed, many of Jesus' disciples and followers are still living today. Their names are inscribed in the book of life and millions of people read their names from the pages of the Bible. Their earthly

---

[11]Mt. 10:38-39, Aramaic Peshitta text, Lamsa translation.

161

lives have been transformed into life everlasting. Their names are written in heaven, never to be forgotten. "Written in heaven" means "universally and eternally known" and "immortal." This is what Jesus meant when he said, "There are some standing here who shall never taste death."[12]

PROPHETS REVERED

He that receiveth a prophet in the name of a prophet shall receive a prophet's reward; and he that receiveth a righteous man in the name of a righteous man shall receive a righteous man's reward. Mt. 10:41.

When a prophet's prediction was fulfilled, people praised, honored, and emulated that prophet. Then again, a true prophet lives on through his prophecy. People never forget him, just as Jesus said: "There are some who are standing here who shall never taste death."

One who sincerely receives another as a prophet will receive the reward or the blessing of a prophet. The individual will be rewarded for the good deed of receiving this person as a prophet—in other words, for doing an act of charity faithfully, not knowing whether the person was truly a prophet or not. That is the meaning of "in the name of a prophet." And those who receives another as a righteous man will receive the reward or blessing that only a righteous person can bestow.

When a person helps a poor man, that person will be rewarded for this act, whether the one helped was deserving or not. All those who received Jesus' disciples were to be rewarded for their pious acts because it would be the same as receiving Jesus himself. When receiving anyone whether good or bad, the reward remains the same; it is the act that counts. It is just like God, who sends his rain upon the just and the unjust and lets his sun shine on the good and the bad.

---

[12]See Lk. 17:33 and Mt. 16:28.

162

IN THE NAME OF A DISCIPLE

And whosoever shall give to drink unto one of these little ones a cup of cold water only in the name of a disciple, verily I say unto you, he shall in no wise lose his reward. Mt. 10:42.

"In the name of a disciple" means "according to the way, method or teaching of a disciple who had learned from Jesus." What Jesus meant here is that an individual who does even a small deed, such as giving a cup of cold water, and does it sincerely, will receive a reward.

The term "little ones" has two meanings. One meaning is actually little children. In Palestine, children often cry for water and go to sleep thirsty. So doing a kind deed for a child is also important. The second meaning is "the common people," those who have not risen to any prominence in life.

In the Near East, people do favors for men and women of high stations in life because they expect to receive a favor (reward) in return. They entertain those who would, in turn, entertain them. They loan to those who would loan to them. Very seldom would anyone extend favors to the common, insignificant people who cannot repay.

Unfortunately, little children and common people were not welcomed in the presence of prominent and outstanding teachers and leaders. Jesus drew no line between rich and poor, great and small, adults and children. According to Jesus, everyone was a child of God. Acts of kindness and compassion need to be extended to everyone regardless of age, color—race, deserving or undeserving.

CHAPTER 11

JOHN QUESTIONS JESUS

Now when John had heard in the prison the works of Christ, he sent two of his disciples, And said unto him, Art thou he that should come, or do we look for another? Jesus answered and said unto them, Go and shew John again those things which ye do hear and see: The blind receive their sight, and the lame walk, the lepers are cleansed, and the deaf hear, the dead are raised up, and the poor have the gospel preached to them. And blessed is he, whosoever shall not be offended in me. Mt. 11:2-6

"Art thou he that should come?" means "Are you the Messiah?" John, no doubt, was disappointed that messianic events were not happening fast enough. Where was the restoration of Israel's kingdom? Why was he still in prison? If Jesus was truly the Messiah would there not be some sort of change taking place? Or, was Jesus just another messenger like himself? These are some of the reasons John was questioning Jesus and asking him: "Are we to expect another?"

Jesus told the two disciples to report to John the miracles and wonders they had heard and seen. What greater works does one want to see to prove that Jesus was the Messiah? (Healing was one of the signs of the appearance of the Messiah—see Isaiah 35:5-6; 61:1.) When John hears about the good works that Jesus is doing, he will not be disappointed in him. Time confirms everything. The sower patiently waits to see the seeds he planted spring up, grow, and mature. The works of the new gospel of God's kingdom were like newly planted seeds. It takes time before they can break through the earth, develop into plants, and bear fruit.

The last part of verse five reads differently in Aramaic: "The blind see and the lame walk. . .and the poor are given assurance." The Aramaic word *misthabreen* means "to be given hope, assurance, the joyful message."

SOFT GARMENTS

And as they departed, Jesus began to say unto the multitudes concerning John, What went ye out into the wilderness to see? A reed shaken with the wind? But what went ye out for to see? A man clothed in soft raiment? Behold, they that wear soft clothing are in kings' houses. Mt. 11:7-8.

In the Arabah, by the banks of the Jordan, long cane grass (reed) was abundant. "What did you go out in the desert to see? A reed shaken by the wind?" John was like a reed shaken by the wind. He was a man agitated with the problems of his countrymen. He wasn't like Samson and Gideon, strong leaders who judged Israel and brought peace in the land from their enemies. He wasn't even dressed like the princes of this world, wearing soft (fine) garments. He wore a robe made of camel hair and a girdle of skin about his loins. Surely he did not appeal to the masses as a strong leader or Messiah to free them from their enemies.

CLOTHING: Semites have always been sheep-raising people, and because of the abundance of sheep, garments were made of wool. Cotton, linen, and silk garments were scarce and only the rich could afford such luxury in clothing. Although cotton and linen industries are very old among the people of the hills and mountains, the art of spinning and weaving cotton goods is hardly known. Cotton cannot be grown in the mountainous regions.

Nomads know well the art of spinning and weaving woolen garments and rugs that are used both for wearing and for bedding. The fabrics are very rough and warm, but the people are accustomed to them. Cotton goods are manufactured in large cities where cotton industries are known and where wool is scarce. In some isolated areas, even shoes are made of wool and the hair of goats. In such places a cotton garment is very costly.

John was not the only one who wore garments made from the hair of camels. Nomadic people in the Arabian desert also used the same type of garments. Jesus and his disciples probably wore woolen garments. They could not afford to wear cotton or linen.

A MESSENGER

For this is he, of whom it is written, Behold, I send my messenger before thy face, which shall prepare thy way before thee. Mt. 11:10.

The Jews expected the return of Moses and Elijah or one of the great prophets before the coming of the Messiah. These prophets were to come to prepare the way for the Messiah. Nevertheless, centuries had elapsed and none of the prophets had returned.

In the sixteenth century B.C.E., Moses had promised the twelve tribes of Israel that a greater prophet than he would come. He said: "The Lord thy God will raise up unto thee a Prophet from the midst of thee, of thy brethren, like unto me: unto him ye shall hearken:"[1]

Some Jewish interpreters thought that this prophecy referred to Joshua or one of the great leaders who was to defeat the enemies of Israel. Years later they expected a strong and mighty leader who would be different from those of the past, or a prophet greater even than Moses. "Then those men, when they had seen the miracle that Jesus did, said: This is of a truth that prophet that should come into the world."[2]

When Jesus was told that Elijah must return before the coming of the Messiah, he answered that John the Baptist was Elijah. In other words, the spirit (ministry) of Elijah was acting through John the Baptist. For John had denounced King Herod Antipas and his wife, Herodia, just as Elijah had denounced Ahab, the king of Israel, and his wife, Jezebel. John also prepared the way for the coming of the Messiah.

---

[1]Deut. 18:15, K.J.V.
[2]Jn. 6:14, K.J.V.

BORN OF A WOMAN

Verily I say unto you, Among them that are born of women there hath not risen a greater than John the Baptist. . . . Mt. 11:11.

"Born of a woman" is a Semitic idiom meaning "human being." Semites use this term to emphasize a man's weakness against his racial background, title, and pride. It is similar to our English expression "I am only human" or "he or she is only human." "Being human" we are capable of making mistakes but, at the same time, we can reach great heights and do wondrous things in spite of our human weaknesses.

According to Jesus, John the Baptist was the greatest prophet of the old order because he denounced the nobility of his day and repudiated certain Jewish traditions and ancestral pride. One time, while speaking forcibly to the Pharisees, John said: "God can raise children to Abraham from these stones." (See Luke 3:8.) He denounced the old system but then announced the new and coming kingdom. Repentance was more necessary than traditional ancestry and racial pride. From now on, salvation was to be based not on racial ancestry, but on the acceptance of the new kingdom.

The least person in the new kingdom that Jesus had proclaimed and brought into reality would be greater than John the Baptist. John was the son of a priest and was educated by his father. Peter and the sons of Zebedee—Jacob (James) and John—were to surpass John the Baptist in knowledge and greatness. For the first time in religious history the secrets of the kingdom were to be revealed through these illiterate fishermen.

CORRUPTION

And from the days of John the Baptist until now the kingdom of heaven suffereth violence, and the violent take it by force. Mt. 11:12.

The Aramaic text reads: "From the days of John the Baptist until now, the kingdom of heaven has been administered by force, and only those in power control it."[3] This verse refers to the major purpose of the Jewish state and religion which was to prepare the way for God's kingdom. The Jews were the custodians of the kingdom of heaven. But the Jewish faith had suffered much violence and only those who were in power ruled over it. The Roman governor and King Herod had appointed the high priests. Everything was administered by force and controlled by these authorities. The High Priests rivaled each other and exercised complete political, social, and religious power over the people. The system had become corrupt. These men had been selected largely through bribery. Injustice was the chief characteristic of their leadership. Priests and other official religious authorities were more interested in their positions than in leading men into God's kingdom. They were not interested in God's kingdom even for themselves. Prophets and seers in the past had condemned injustices and violence. Those men of God, who had revealed to the people the path of truth that led to the kingdom, met with violent deaths.

Jesus, through his ministry and teaching, had ended this state of affairs by opening the doors of God's kingdom to the people in the midst of corruption. He opened the people's minds to the spiritual meaning of Scripture, exposed the traditions of the elders, and proclaimed the gospel of genuine righteousness. According to Jesus, force and violence are not the hallmark of God's kingdom.

MARKETS, PIPING AND DANCING

But whereunto shall I liken this generation? It is like unto children sitting in the markets, and calling unto their fellows, And saying, We have piped unto you, and ye have not danced; we have mourned unto you, and ye have not lamented. Mt. 11:16-17.

In countries where there are no playgrounds and fields are far

---

[3]Mt. 11:12, Aramaic Peshitta text, Lamsa translation.

away, children play in the alleys, streets, marketplaces, and on housetops. In ancient villages, an alley really is a long entrance connecting several houses that are under the same roof and are only separated by walls. Generally, children use this covered alley as a playground, especially during the rainy season.

Part A—THE MARKET PLACE. In the Near East the marketplace or the square is more than just a place to sell goods. It is a gathering site where business can be conducted as well as the social "business" of gossip and friendly conversation. To a Semite there can be no sort of transaction without a demonstration of hospitality. When one enters a place of business—be it under a tent, in a booth, or in a store—one must be prepared for a friendly visit with the proprietor. The marketplace is also where people tell and retell many parables and exchange proverbs. This kind of social recognition and dialogue is referred to in Jesus' warning to his disciples when he said: "Beware of the scribes who like to go about in long robes and love to be greeted in the marketplace."[4] Scribes were frequent visitors to the marketplaces so that people of all classes could extend them recognition for their special social position. Children also enjoyed gathering here so that they could play their pranks and watch the busy activities of their elders.

Part B—PIPING. "We piped to you and you did not dance, we mourned to you, and you did not lament" means "We have done everything to inform you and you did not respond." Jesus likened the fickle and peevish men of his generation to little boys playing in the squares and marketplaces. In biblical lands, nothing excites children and young people more than the sound of a flute, tambourine, or a drum. At the sound of music, children come running out of their homes to see what is happening. They very seldom have the opportunity to hear music. So when they hear the sound of music, no one wants to miss it or fail to see the musicians playing and dancing. Even older people will leave their food on the table to go and see the musicians. Others will go out with bread in their hands. Also when

---

[4]Mk. 12:38, Aramaic Peshitta text, Errico

one wishes to assemble people, drums, flutes, and tambourines are played. People often say to each other: "I told you to come out. What do you expect me to do, pipe to you?"

Jesus used this expression because many people did not come out to hear him heralding the dawning kingdom of God. They would not celebrate with him God's joyful message and presence. They also did not listen to the voice of John the Baptist when he called them to repentance (to turn to God). Many had refused to respond and had closed their ears to the voice of God. They were reluctant to give up their long cherished traditions in exchange for a new gospel and controversial teaching. Both John and Jesus had encountered a great deal of criticism. (See verses 18 and 19.)

A MADMAN, A GLUTTON AND WINEBIBBER

For John came neither eating nor drinking, and they say, He hath a devil. The Son of Man came eating and drinking, and they say, Behold a man gluttonous, and a winebibber, a friend of publicans and sinners. But wisdom is justified of her children. Mt. 11:18-19.

Part A—JOHN THE BAPTIST. The critical response to John the Baptist and Jesus was not good. Some had accused the Baptist of having a "devil." "He hath a devil" in Aramaic means "he is a madman; he is crazy." John's message cut straight to the heart of the matter (see Luke 3:7-18). He was very outspoken, upbraiding the people, the tax collectors, and the soldiers. Finally, he pointed his finger at the leadership (Herod Antipas and his wife Herodia) which eventually cost him his life. Herod had John beheaded. Many considered John a "madman." A passion had utterly possessed him which made him "crazy" for his cause and took him down the road to his early death. Yet, as Jesus said, he didn't come "eating and drinking," meaning John was usually fasting and didn't live a comfortable life. "Eating and drinking" was a common form of Semitic speech that people still use today. It refers to "being well taken care of." It is

170

comparable to our idiom "to have three square meals a day."

Part B—JESUS' LIFESTYLE. The Aramaic text reads: "Now John came not eating and drinking, yet you are saying: He is a madman! But this human being has come eating and drinking and you are saying: Look at this, a man who eats and drinks wine, a friend of tax collectors and sinners! Yet, wisdom is justified by its works."[5] Jesus did not escape criticism either. The remarks made about him were the opposite of those John had received. Jesus' lifestyle was completely different. He came "eating and drinking." He did not refuse invitations to people's homes; he celebrated with them, ate and drank wine with them, performed healings, and shared the joy of God's presence with them. He also associated with prostitutes, tax collectors, and sinners, eating with them in their homes. His social and religious behavior was not like that of the usual holy man. He didn't openly fast and pray as others were doing. He celebrated God's kingdom (presence) with the common folk, outcasts, and despised people of his day.

The term "son of man" simply means "this human being." Jesus emphasized his humanity; that is why he came eating and drinking. He made no pretension about who he was. He identified himself as an ordinary human being.

Part C—WISDOM AND WORKS. The word "children" is not present in the Aramaic text. This part of the verse reads: "Yet wisdom is justified by its works." It means that wisdom is proven true by its results. Not everything we call wisdom is really wise. We must put it in operation and see its results before we can tell whether it is truly wisdom or folly. A Semitic proverb says: "Foolishness is wisdom to fools, but it is folly to the wise."

CITIES REPRIMANDED

Then began he to upbraid the cities wherein most of his mighty works

---

[5]Mt. 11:18-19, Aramaic Peshitta text, Errico

were done, because they repented not. Mt. 11:20

Verses 21-24 speak of cities that refused to acknowledge the power and presence of God's kingdom that Jesus brought to them. He performed mighty works which revealed the truth that God was among them. If the cities of Tyre, Sidon, and Sodom had these same works demonstrated in them, they would still be standing today. Had the cities that Jesus upbraided accepted his teaching, they, too, would be standing today. These cities were responsible for their own judgment. God does not reward or punish. Whatever we sow, that we will reap.[6]

A SIMPLE GOSPEL

At that time Jesus answered and said, I thank thee, O Father, Lord of heaven and earth, because thou hast hid these things from the wise and prudent, and hast revealed them unto babes. Mt. 11:25.

"Hast revealed them unto babes" means "revealed them to the simple and inexperienced." The teaching of the new gospel, like the teaching of the prophets, was so direct that even little children and the unlearned could understand it. Nevertheless, it was hidden from the understanding of learned men for whom the wisdom of this world remained their guide.

One has to be humble, unassuming, and simple like a child to comprehend the new way of life that Jesus was teaching. Preachers, teachers, and scribes had obscured the pure religion that was revealed to the prophets in a plain and clear manner. They made it difficult to understand with their added traditions and complicated ordinances.

---

[6]Again, New Testament scholars believe that Jesus did not make these judgment pronouncements against these cities. This was not his style of preaching or teaching. His teaching was to "love your enemies" and not to put a curse on them. These scholars feel that these words represent the frustrations of the early followers and leaders who failed to convert the people to the new teaching.

Now simple farmers, shepherds, and common folk would understand the mysteries of God's kingdom. Moreover, these ordinary people, not clergy, would be preaching this new gospel of the kingdom.

SECRETS BETWEEN FATHER AND SON

All things are delivered unto me of my Father: and no man knoweth the Son, but the Father; neither knoweth any man the Father, save the Son, and he to whomsoever the Son will reveal him. Mt. 11:27.

Jesus had utter faith and trust in the unique relationship he knew he had with God as *abba*, "father." According to Near Eastern custom, special family trade secrets of various arts and handicrafts are handed down from one generation to another from father to son. A father will teach and reveal everything to his son. A son will eat, work, and share his life with his father constantly. The father knows his son and the son knows his father completely. The son can do nothing of himself, only what the father has taught him. If one wishes to know the father, he must come to the son. Father and son always work in harmony with each other. They are of one accord.[7]

Jesus worked in complete harmony and oneness with God as his father. Therefore, he could reveal the Father because he knew the Father thoroughly. He had an infinite understanding of God and was able to relieve the burdens of people who did not understand God as a loving father. He was not like other religious teachers who placed heavy burdens on the souls of their adherents.

AN EASY YOKE

Come unto me, all ye that labour and are heavy laden, and I will give you rest. Take my yoke upon you, and learn of me; for I am meek and lowly

---

[7]See Jn. 5:19-20; 10:30; 14:6-11.

in heart: and ye shall find rest unto your souls. For my yoke is easy, and my burden is light. Mt. 11:28-30.

Among Aramaic speaking Semites, "yoke" is a metaphor that refers to taxation and other heavy burdens that an overlord levies on his subjects. Just as the neck of an ox bends under the weight of a heavy yoke, so Semites feel crushed under heavy duties and taxes.

Inhabitants of a village bear the expenses of their lord, maintain his household, provide food and other supplies, and perform services assigned to them. Some are easier on their subjects than others. Some marry many wives and live lavishly at the expense of the villagers. Others live simply and are content with only one wife. Thus, the simpler the ruler lives, the lighter are the burdens of his subjects. In some cases when very heavy taxes are exacted, the misruled revolt. They can no longer carry the yoke of their lord. One can hear people say to one another: "Our yoke has become unbearable." Villagers are happy when the ruler's yoke is light.

When a new ruler succeeds his father, the first thing he does if he is kindly and compassionate is to reduce the taxes and lighten the burdens of his villagers. His subjects continue their loyalty and try to forget the injustice of the former ruler and his servants. Reforms are carried out by cutting down the new ruler's household expenses and dismissing the crafty stewards and servants. The people love such rulers. Semites always pray for good rulers, but some may continue cursing their evil rulers long after their death.

When Rehoboam ascended the throne of Solomon, his father, the people of Israel came to him and asked him to lighten their burdens. After rejecting the counsel of the wise and listening to the advice of his younger counselors, Rehoboam told his subjects that their yoke would be heavier than that of his father. His little finger would be thicker than his father's thumb.[8] (See 1 Kings 12:3-14.)

The Jews were heavily burdened with taxes. There were imperial,

---

[8]The King James Version translates the word as "loins" instead of "thumb. See 1 Kings 12:10.

state, and temple levies. People maintained the state and its officials as well as the temple and the extravagant expenses of its priests. Both temporal and religious rulers lived in luxurious palaces at the expense of the poor. People had to be loyal to both systems.

Jesus had no palaces, temples, sacred shrines or priestly system. He preached and taught about God as a loving father. This God expected no sacrifices or gifts from worshipers. They could approach God with a simple prayer. Men and women were to be freed from the heavy burdens of traditions, dogmas, and misleading teachings. Temporal and spiritual powers were ultimately to be one and God was to be ruler over both. The gospel of the kingdom that Jesus revealed was easy and light.

Jesus, through his teaching, encouraged people and gave them hope of everlasting joy and happiness. His understanding of religion was simple. There would be no intermediary system for worshipers to support nor to pray through so that they might commune with God. He taught people just to come and learn from him. He came to serve and not to be served. He demanded nothing from his followers except that they practice his teaching and turn from evil.

The laws of God were originally given to aid and serve people and not to enslave them. A true religion is not a harsh yoke or a burden but is a blessing. It is a path of joy, peace, and prosperity. Revering and worshiping God is not the same as being afraid of God. The yoke that Jesus bore and taught was easy and light. According to his gospel, God was not an overlord but a loving parent who was constantly mindful of people, caring for them, healing their wounds, and meeting their needs.

CHAPTER 12

PLUCKING EARS OF WHEAT

At that time Jesus went on the sabbath day through the corn; and his disciples were an hungred, and began to pluck the ears of corn, and to eat. Mt. 12:1.

The Aramaic text reads: "At that time, Jesus walked on the Sabbath through the wheat [not *corn*] fields; and his disciples became hungry, and they began to pluck ears of grain and to eat."[1] Palestine is a wheat growing country. People depend mainly on it for their food. Vegetables and other cereal grains are not grown much, but small wheat fields are scattered all over the land. Roads, except for a few military routes, were unknown in Palestine until recent days. Travelers cut narrow, winding paths through wheat fields. Farmers do not like this, but they know travelers must have some passage.

During the harvest season, farmers guard their wheat from travelers and robbers who pluck the wheat, beat it with a stick and carry away large quantities of the grain, but no farmer objects to a traveler taking a handful of wheat to eat. They know that these travelers are often short of bread. The wheat is plucked, rubbed in the hand, then dropped from one hand to the other and the chaff blown away. Now the wheat is clean and ready to be eaten. If there is time and the travelers can find a convenient site, the wheat will be roasted.

Jesus and his disciples often passed through these small fields and plucked wheat to satisfy their hunger and meet their needs. In those days there were no restaurants or eating places. Up until the middle of this century, a traveler found it difficult to buy bread and had to rely on the hospitality of people or had to find fruits for his sustenance. (See Mark 2:23; Luke 6:1.)

---

[1]Aramaic Peshitta text, Lamsa translation.

SABBATH MADE FOR HUMANS

But when the pharisees saw it, they said unto him, Behold, thy disciples do that which is not lawful to do upon the sabbath day. . . . For the Son of Man is Lord even of the sabbath day. Mt. 12:2, 8.

"Then when the Pharisees saw them, they said to him: Look here your disciples are doing things that are not lawful to do on the Sabbath.[2] But he said to them: Have you not read what David did when he was hungry and those who were with him.[3] How he entered the house of God[4] and ate the bread of the Lord's table, that which was not lawful for him to eat, nor for those who were with him, but only for the priests?[5] Or have you not read in the Torah that the priests in the sanctuary disregard the Sabbath and are blameless? But I say to you that someone greater than the sanctuary is here! And if you had known what this means: I desire compassion and not sacrifice; you would not have condemned those who are blameless.[6] Because a human being is lord of the Sabbath.

"Then Jesus departed from there and came to their meeting place (synagogue). And a man was there whose hand had atrophied. And they were questioning him, saying: Is it lawful to heal on the Sabbath?[7] This was so they might accuse him. But he said to them: Who is the man among you who has one sheep,[8] and if it falls into a pit on the Sabbath, does he not take hold of it and lift it out? Then he

---

[2]See Ex. 34:21. Sabbath is equivalent to our "Saturday."

[3]See 1 Sam. 21:1-6.

[4]"The tent of meeting" that housed the ark of the covenant.

[5]See Lev. 24:5-9.

[6]That is, Jesus' disciples.

[7]Rabbinic interpretation permitted healing on the Sabbath (Saturday) providing the life was in danger or there was an emergency that needed immediate treatment.

[8]Common Semitic style of writing and speaking. "One" is not to make a comparison with other numbers. Jesus is simply saying "Who is the man among you who has *a sheep*."

said to the man: Stretch out your hand. And he stretched out his hand and it was made whole exactly like the other."[9]

THE SABBATH. Moses instituted the Sabbath as a day of rest from everyday labors. Israel had been commanded to observe the Sabbath so that as a people they would always remember their slavery in and deliverance from Egypt. The Hebrews, their servants, slaves, strangers, and even their cattle must rest on this momentous day. Sabbath, the seventh day of the week—Saturday—was a great Jewish holy day.[10] In the law of the sabbatical year, the land was to lie fallow.[11] The Sabbath law was the same for everyone, including the land.

The keeping of the Sabbath is the fourth Commandment and is, therefore, an integral part of the Ten Commandments. God gave these Commandments to Moses so that they might serve as a light and a guide to Israel. Sabbath was a day in which God had ceased from all the works he had created. Thus human beings were also to rest one day a week from all their labors. This holy day was ordained for the sake of the people and not for the sake of the Sabbath. The law did not forbid people from doing works of compassion on this holy day, nor did it forbid them from walking, healing the sick, taking care of the wounded, and watering sheep and cattle. Works of mercy are not labor but a joy. God ceased from his works on the seventh day but did not cease from guiding and caring for his creations.

The scribes and elders had changed the simple, spiritual meaning of the Sabbath law and supplanted it with their own interpretations which became a burden for the people. Israel's prophets recommended acts of compassion for the poor and the needy more than sacrifices of meat and drink offerings. So how can the Sabbath be broken by plucking ears of wheat and eating the grain, especially by men who are hungry? Or, how can one transgress the Sabbath if one heals a person's atrophied hand? Jesus reasoned that human beings

---

[9]Mt. 12:2-13, Aramaic Peshitta text, Errico.
[10]See Ex. 20:8-11.
[11]See Ex. 23:10.

178

and life are far more important than the Sabbath. Helping anyone, no matter how small the act—even giving a weary traveler some water to drink—does not break the keeping of the Sabbath. Jesus taught that human beings are the true lords of the Sabbath.

GOD'S SERVANT

And he charged them that they should not make him known: That it might be fulfilled which was spoken by Esaias the prophet, saying, Behold my servant, whom I have chosen; my beloved, in whom my soul is well pleased: I will put my spirit upon him, and he shall shew judgment to the Gentiles. He shall not strive, nor cry; neither shall any man hear his voice in the streets. A bruised reed shall he not break, and smoking flax shall he not quench, till he send forth judgment unto victory. And in his name shall the Gentiles trust. Mt. 12:16-21.

"Behold my servant, I am delighted with him! My beloved one, my being has longed for him;[12] I will put my spirit upon him and he will preach justice to the nations. He will not quarrel, nor will he raise his voice and no one will hear his voice in the streets. He will not break a bruised reed and he will not put out a flickering lamp until he brings justice to victory. And in his name will nations hope."[13]

The term "my servant" refers to the Messiah as a servant of God. Near Eastern emissaries and high ranking government officials were known as "servants of the king." The Messiah was to act as God's spokesman. Matthew, in verses 18-21, quotes the prophet Isaiah[14] who used Semitic figures of speech to describe some of the characteristics of God's ideal servant.

"He will not quarrel, raise his voice, and no one will hear his

---

[12]It is also possible to translate this part of the verse as "My beloved one, my soul has rejoiced in him." However, based on the prime meaning of the Aramaic word, *swhtm*, in this reading "rejoiced" would be second choice.

[13]Mt. 12:18-21, Aramaic Peshitta text, Errico.

[14]See Isa. 42:1-4.

voice in the streets" means "God's servant will not campaign, cry out in the streets, marshal an army nor lead a revolt." When this servant of God appears, everything will be done in an undemonstrative manner. "He will not break a bruised reed and he will not put out a flickering lamp" denote the Messiah's meekness and gentleness. This Anointed one (Messiah) would not hurt even the weakest person but, at the same time, insists on justice being done. God's servant, quietly and unobtrusively, would spread his spiritual influence to all nations of the earth.

Jewish interpretation is divided on whom Isaiah refers to in 42:1. Rabbinic commentators make three suggestions. They believe that Isaiah was referring to himself, Israel, or the Messiah. Other scholars think the allusion is to Cyrus, the Persian King. However, according to Matthew's gospel, "my servant" refers to the Messiah and in particular to Jesus' fulfillment of this prophecy.

BEELZEBUB AND A DIVIDED KINGDOM

And Jesus knew their thoughts, and said unto them, Every kingdom divided against itself is brought to desolation; and every city or house divided against itself shall not stand: And if Satan cast out Satan, he is divided against himself; how shall then his kingdom stand? And if I by Beelzebub cast out devils, by whom do your children cast them out? Therefore they shall be your judges. But if I cast out devils by the Spirit of God, then the kingdom of God is come unto you. Mt 12:25-28.

In Aramaic the name Beelzebub means "lord of the flies." However, some New Testament experts translate Beelzebub as "lord of the high place." The Jews contemptuously altered the name from *zebub* to the Hebrew *zebul*, "dung." In the ancient days, Beelzebub was a popular Canaanite deity. During the time of Jesus, he was "prince of the house of devils." This epithet came to be attached to Satan.

Jesus reasoned that if one devil had healed a man whom another devil had made ill, then Satan was working against himself. If this was the case, then Satan's dominion over sin and suffering would cease (in those days, people assumed that the devil created disease). If Jesus healed the sick through the power of evil, then that malevolent power would no longer be a devil but a rebel against the kingdom of Satan. So Jesus proved that he did not work through the power of Beelzebub. Furthermore, he said "And if I, by Beelzebub, heal the insane, by what do your sons (children) heal?" The term "your children" refers to the disciples of the Pharisees. At that time, there were many men and women who acted as healers and who cast out devils—that is, restored sanity to the mentally ill. How did they do it? Did they heal through the power of Beelzebub? Of course not! They healed by the power that God had given them to destroy evil of any kind, mental or physical illnesses. Nor could Jesus heal the sick by the power of Beelzebub.

Hebrew prophets, centuries before Jesus, healed the sick, cleansed lepers, and even raised the dead. They all performed these miracles in the name of their God and not in the name of Beelzebub. Jesus contradicted the charge of the Pharisees and silenced them with his clever reasoning.

The forces of evil cannot do good, nor can the forces of good act maleficently. Jesus worked through the power of God who had sent him to preach the gospel, heal the sick and open the eyes of the blind. An evil man would not have this power. Jesus brought the realization that God's kingdom was dawning to disrupt and collapse evil (Satan's kingdom). "And if by the spirit of God I am healing the insane, then God's kingdom has come to you."

BINDING THE STRONG MAN

Or else how can one enter into a strong man's house, and spoil his goods, except he first bind the strong man? And then he will spoil his house. Mt. 12:29.

In the Near East, men who have treasures and other valuables are constantly armed. At times, they even sleep with their weapons on them so that no one can enter their homes and plunder their goods without first binding or killing the owners.

In this case, the strong man is symbolic of Jesus, who was armed with God's truth. Jesus told those who were opposing him that if he cast out devils—that is, restored the insane—by the power Satan, it would mean that Satan was working against himself. No devil could have given power to Jesus or possessed him without first disarming him. But this was not true. It was the power of God that healed through Jesus. The spirit of God was Jesus' healing power. Therefore, his enemies blasphemed when they said, "He does these things by the power of Beelzebub." It was a blasphemy against the spirit of God, the holy Spirit. An evil force could not have taken possession of this spiritual power without first winning victory over God. (See Matthew 12:31, Luke 11:20.)

BLASPHEMY AGAINST THE HOLY SPIRIT

Wherefore I say unto you, All manner of sin and blasphemy shall be forgiven unto men; but the blasphemy against the Holy Ghost shall not be forgiven unto men. Mt. 12:31.

Ruḥa, "spirit," in Aramaic also refers to God's healing power. It is this power that passes from the healer to the sick. A healer is the instrument through which the sick person connects with divine power. Any doubt in the mind will interrupt the flow of the spirit just as rust prevents electrical current from passing through connecting wires.

The Pharisees thought Jesus was deriving his power from Beelzebub, the prince of devils. They could not understand how else he could heal. Jesus' actions and utterances were radical and not in harmony with those of the priests and elders. Therefore, they reasoned that he was invoking Satan's power in his healing. The Master-Teacher had heard all these false accusations against him and could no longer hold his peace. He said in effect, "If you blaspheme against God, you will be forgiven because you do not know him. If you blaspheme against the Son, you will be forgiven because you do not know from where he comes. But if you blaspheme against the Holy Spirit, you will never be forgiven in this world or the world to come. For you see with your own eyes that people receive their healing and yet you say it is the spirit of the devil that does the healing. How can this be? One devil cannot create sickness and another heal! A kingdom cannot survive if it is divided against itself. It is from the spirit one receives health and wholeness. But if you call the Holy Spirit satanic, then how can you receive forgiveness from the Spirit that frees you from evil."

Another way to understand Jesus' saying is that any individual or group of individuals who holds a particular state of mind or attitude that attributes evil to the power of good is unforgivable. In Jesus' case, the men called God's healing power evil and their attitude was unforgivable so long as their state of mind exists. This attitude is a stubborn insistence that persists in calling goodness, an evil power and calling light, darkness. Such was the situation among those who were resisting the healing spirit through Jesus' ministry. This deliberate and inflexible attitude itself creates the unforgivable position. The moment this kind of attitude ceases, forgiveness is present.

GOOD TREES—GOOD FRUITS

Either make the tree good, and his fruit good; or else make the tree corrupt, and his fruit corrupt: for the tree is known by his fruit. Mt. 12:33.

The Aramaic text reads: "Either produce like a good tree with good fruits, or produce like a bad tree with bad fruits; for a tree is known by its fruits."[15] We know how healthy and good a tree may be by its quality of fruits. No healthy, high quality fruit tree can produce

---

[15]Mt. 12:33, Aramaic Peshitta text, Lamsa translation.

both good and bad fruits. It either produces good (edible) fruits or bad (inedible) fruits.

This saying refers to the Pharisees who were attributing Jesus' healing power to Beelzebub. They either had to believe in God's healing power or believe that the devil was healing. However, no bad tree can produce good fruit. How can Satan (Aramaic—*satana*) who is a personification of all that is evil heal a person of anything evil? One cannot be both the follower of God and of Satan.

This also refers to those who try to appear righteous but whose works are evil. Some who fast, pray, give alms, and hold high religious offices also oppress the poor and confiscate the property of widows and orphans. Robbers and bandits could not cause as much harm as these false religious types. They hide their crookedness under the guise of holy, religious ceremonies and false devotions so that they can mislead the public. Bandits and thieves operate openly. They are what they are and do not pretend to be something else.

GOOD AND BAD TREASURES

O generation of vipers, how can ye, being evil, speak good things? For out of the abundance of the heart the mouth speaketh. A good man out of the good treasure of the heart bringeth forth good things: and an evil man out of the evil treasure bringeth forth evil things. Mt. 12:34-35.

"O brood of poisonous snakes, how can you speak good things when you are bad? Because from the fullness of the heart the mouth speaks. A good man out of good treasures brings good things, and a bad man out of bad treasures brings bad things."[16]

The men whom Jesus was addressing were like a brood of snakes. These particular men who were accusing Jesus were without prophets and seers to guide them. They had gone so far astray from God's way that they could no longer discern between what was from

---

[16]Mt. 12:34-35, Aramaic Peshitta text, Errico.

God and what was evil. They pretended to be the guardians of God's holy book and teachings. Their minds (hearts) had become so corrupt that they blasphemed by calling God's healing power satanic.

"Treasure," in this instance, is symbolic of the heart or mind. A wise man brings forth words of wisdom from the treasures of his mind, but a foolish man brings forth words of folly. In the Near East, many good and noble men who are admired for their piety and good works possess rich treasures. During banquets, it is their custom to bring out priceless articles from their treasures to show to their guests. On the other hand, evil rich men often bring forth as their treasures imitation articles and display them as though they were costly and precious.

A good man is known by his good words and deeds, while a bad man is known by his bad words and deeds. If a person's heart (mind) is good, he will speak and bring out good things. If the heart is bad, he will see and speak nothing but bad things. These men who saw Jesus healing referred to his healing acts as evil; therefore, they blasphemed against the Spirit of God. Their hearts were evil so they saw nothing but evil instead of good.

RECKLESS WORDS

But I say unto you, That every idle word that men shall speak, they shall give account thereof in the day of judgment. For by thy words thou shalt be justified, and by thy words thou shalt be condemned. Mt. 12:36-37.

"Idle" in this verse means rash or reckless. It refers to remarks that create disputes and result in quarrels. Again, these men who blasphemed against God's healing power would be held responsible for their reckless remarks. Their own rash words and blaspheming remarks condemned them. They were their own judges. They could not recognize God's loving, restoring, healing power through Jesus, so by their own words they would be justified or condemned.

"Idle word" also refers to idle, harmful gossip. Many people of the Near East pass the time gossiping. A casual remark made against someone may thus spread rapidly and in passing from one person to another, the original thought is exaggerated and the words become more inflamed. The person against whom the remark was made will want to retaliate and the originator of the remark will suffer the consequences. Individuals must be responsible for their own speech so that nothing is said that would do damage to another. One whose speech makes trouble will answer for it.

THE SIGN OF THE PROPHET JONAH

But he answered and said unto them, An evil and adulterous generation seeketh after a sign; and there shall no sign be given to it, but the sign of the prophet Jonas: For as Jonas was three days and three nights in the whale's belly; so shall the Son of Man be three days and three nights in the heart of the earth. The men of Nineveh shall rise in judgment with this generation, and shall condemn it: because they repented at the preaching of Jonas; and, behold a greater than Jonas is here. Mt. 12:39-41.

Part A—JONAH AND THE FISH. Jonah had predicted the fall of Nineveh but his prophecy was not fulfilled. According to the Hebrew Bible, God had forgiven and spared the wicked city. Jonah complained because God had not destroyed Nineveh.

Jonah, like other Hebrew prophets, communed with God in dreams and visions. The book of Job reads: "For God speaks once; he does not speak a second time; in a dream, in a vision of the night, when deep sleep falls upon men, while slumbering upon the bed."[17]

According to dream interpretation in the Near East, a fish or whale means trouble, disturbance, and indecision. Being in a fish is a Near Eastern hyperbole that means being in deep trouble or in an extremely difficult situation. It is equal to our saying, "he or she is in a hole or in hot water." Nineveh in Aramaic means a "fish."

---

[17]Job 33:14-15, Aramaic Peshitta text, Lamsa translation.

Jonah was a Hebrew prophet whom God had called to go to Nineveh to rebuke an Assyrian King who was to conquer Palestine and many other parts of the Near East. He was to tell the king that Nineveh was destined to collapse. This was not an easy task for a foreign prophet to do. The weight and seriousness of this mission placed Jonah in difficulties. Therefore, he was reluctant to be a prophet to the Gentiles. For three days he could not understand why God should be concerned about a pagan city. He finally realized that the God of Israel was also the God of the Gentiles. This was a new concept that the priestly school would strongly oppose. Moreover, Jonah was not quite sure that God would destroy such a great city and its people.

The author of Jonah's story portrayed, in figurative and symbolic speech, Jonah's dilemma and his hesitancy to preach to Gentiles. Here are some examples: In the story, the men who threw Jonah overboard into the sea symbolically represented those who advised him not to listen to God's voice. They told him to flee and to let Nineveh perish. The fish that swallowed Jonah represented his quandary. Should he go to Nineveh or not? Then later, when Jonah was in Nineveh, God made a gourd grow to shelter Jonah from the sun's heat. Then God had a worm destroy the sheltering gourd. The loss of the protecting plant made Jonah grieve. This meant that as Jonah had grieved over the withered gourd, so God had pity on the people of Nineveh.

God had appeared in a vision and talked to Jonah just as God had revealed things to Isaiah, Jeremiah, Daniel, Ezekiel and other prophets through visions, figurative and symbolic speech, signs, and metaphors. God is Spirit; therefore, God appeared to the Hebrew patriarchs and prophets in a spiritual manner—that is, in revelations and dreams. When the prophets saw lions, leopards, rams, goats, lambs, cows, eagles, trees, and vineyards, they understood these things as symbols and they saw them in visions. St Ephraim, an early Near Eastern Bible commentator (360 C.E.) in one of his hymns about Jonah, says that this incident took place in a dream or a vision.

The importance of Jonah's revelation is in the miraculous change and repentance of the Assyrian king and his people through the prophecy of a Hebrew prophet. Jonah had difficulty in knowing how to carry out his orders from God. This was a trying and challenging mission for him. Apparently, years later, an Assyrian general gave recognition to the God of Israel and called him Lord. For it says: "The Lord said to me, go up against this land and destroy it."[18]

During this period in Israel's history, the Hebrew prophets taught that their God was using Gentile kings as his agents to carry out his purposes. The story of Jonah emphasizes two major points. It teaches (1) The universality of God and (2) God's interest and compassion upon Gentiles. According to the gospel writer, it also represented the death and resurrection of Jesus that eventually would bring light to the Gentile world

JONAH AND JESUS. Jonah being cast into the sea was symbolic of Jesus' suffering on the cross and his death. The prophet being swallowed by a great fish and remaining in its stomach for three days and nights symbolized Jesus' burial in the tomb. The fish releasing Jonah represented Jesus' resurrection and his victory over death.

Jesus spoke of this incident because he was to suffer and die on the cross. He would be crucified on account of his new teaching and his ideas of sharing God's light and truth with the Gentile world. He saw the Jonah story as a symbolic episode that represented his coming death and victory. Jesus also composed stories that were rich in metaphor and symbolic speech. For example, when he told the parable about Lazarus in the bosom of Abraham and the rich man who was in hell begging Lazarus for a drop of water to quench his thirst, these things were typical Semitic figures of speech. Near Easterners picture the wicked rich, who have acquired their fortunes unjustly, as thirsty and suffering in flames. This, however, is figurative and we are not to understand it literally.

Part B—MEN OF NINEVEH. It is recorded in the gospel that Jesus upbraided the people because of their disbelief in him as Messiah. He had performed many miracles and wonders, but still they rejected him. Jesus related Jonah's experience—how the king and the

---

[18]2 Kings 18:25, Aramaic Peshitta Text, Lamsa translation

people of Nineveh received him, how they repented of their sins, how God spared Nineveh from disaster. But the inhabitants of Jerusalem, being obstinate, were doomed. In the year 70 C.E., the Roman Prince, Titus, destroyed the historic and holy city and its colossal temple.

Interestingly, the descendants of the people of Nineveh had accepted Jesus' gospel of the kingdom while he was in Galilee. Jesus had sent seventy of his disciples to preach his gospel to the lost tribes of Israel.[19] In 722 B.C.E., the Assyrian kings had carried away captive these ten tribes and had settled them in Assyria, Syria, Iran, and other places. Their descendants received the gospel before the people of other races.

Many pagan people revered the God of Abraham, the living God. Some of the Assyrian kings feared Israel's God. When they were subjugating the land of Judah, they claimed that they came with the consent of Yahweh. Isaiah called Assyria "the rod of God's anger," that is, "God's agent."

THE QUEEN OF SHEBA

The queen of the south shall rise up in the judgment with this generation, and shall condemn it: for she came from the uttermost parts of the earth to hear the wisdom of Solomon; and behold, a greater than Solomon is here. Mt. 12:42.

"Queen of the south" refers to the Queen of Sheba. The term "south" is used because some of the territory of the Queen of Sheba was east of the Red Sea and in southern Arabia, which is south of Judea. The Queen of Sheba came to see King Solomon, having heard of his wisdom and understanding. She brought him costly presents so that she might sit at his feet and drink of his wisdom.

According to the gospel writer, a greater one than King Solomon was present and that one was Jesus of Nazareth, but no one paid

---

[19]See Mt. 10:6.

189

attention to him or respected his teaching. On the day of Judgment, the Queen of Sheba would be commended for her pious act in making the long journey to see a teacher who was not as great as Jesus. Thus, her testimony condemned the adulterous generation that sought after signs and who belittled Jesus and did not recognize him as Messiah.

A prophet or a great man is often honored more by alien people than by the people of his own country. It was difficult for Jesus' generation to recognize a poor Galilean peasant as the awesome Messiah, Savior of Israel. However, all of these sayings from verse 39 through 42 are not in accord with Jesus' message of the kingdom.[20]

THE UNCLEAN SPIRIT

When the unclean spirit is gone out of a man, he walketh through dry places, seeking rest, and findeth none. Then he saith, I will return into my house from whence I came out: and when he is come, he findeth it empty, swept, and garnished. Then goeth he, and taketh with himself seven other spirits more wicked than himself, and they enter in and dwell there: and the last state of that man is worse than the first. Even so shall it be also unto this wicked generation. Mt. 12:43-45.

"When the unclean spirit goes out of a man" is an Aramaic colloquial saying and means that a man has been healed. When a person is healed of a certain disease and does not change his way of life but continues to do more evil, the disease that he had will return. But when the disease returns it becomes worse than before. To say that "the evil spirit has returned and found the house empty, swept, and garnished" means that the individual is now ready to become a secure and permanent abode for the illness. "He took seven other spirits more wicked than himself" denotes that the man has a complication of diseases. For example, if the person had been insane, that person may now have heart trouble and other diseases. It does not

---

[20]According to New Testament scholars, the judgment tenor of these sayings is uncharacteristic of Jesus.

literally mean that unclean spirits live in the man as though they had no other dwelling place. It simply means his latter state has become far worse than his former.[21]

A wicked generation only produces more evil spirits (wickedness) in the land. People need to turn to God and change their ways of life so that they can change their state of affairs throughout the land. They must cleanse themselves of evil doing so that no oppressor will covet their land. Good attracts good and evil attracts evil. Troublesome and wicked leaders and oppressors are the results of injustices, exploitations, and unfaithfulness among the people. When a generation is wicked their leaders also are corrupt.

JESUS' RELATIVES

But he answered and said unto him that told him, Who is my mother? and who are my brethren? And he stretched forth his hand toward his disciples, and said, Behold my mother and my brethren: For whosoever shall do the will of my Father which is in heaven, the same is my brother, and sister, and mother. Mt. 12:48-50.

The word "brethren" or "brothers" not only means "brothers and sisters"; in Aramaic and Hebrew it also indicates close relatives.[22] Matthew 13:55 reads: "Is he not the carpenter's son? Is not his mother named Mary, and his brothers, Jacob, and Joseph, and Simon, and Judah?" In this verse "brothers" may refer to the relatives of Jesus. But it may also mean Jesus' actual brothers and sisters.

Regardless, as far as Jesus is concerned, his disciples who left everything and followed him were his mother and brothers. His family did not follow him when he left Nazareth and began to proclaim God's dawning kingdom. His relatives were ashamed of him. They

---

[21]Interestingly, among Assyrian people today, when an unpopular man brings four or five guests with him to a home, these Assyrians say: "he has brought other evil spirits like himself."

[22]See Gen. 13:8, 14:16.

191

said that he had lost his mind. They said this because they were afraid of the synagogue rulers and elders. Had they made a stand with Jesus, they would have been thrown out of the synagogue.

In God's kingdom, true mothers, brothers, and sisters are those who are born of the spirit, have embraced the new teaching, and do the will of their heavenly Father. These are the ones who are closer than any of the relatives who are born of the flesh.

CHAPTER 13

INTRODUCTION TO THE PARABLES

Jesus was a parablist, a teller of stories. Some of his parables were exhilarating and others were offensive. His listeners usually responded to his narratives because they were dramatic, poetic, humorous, and enlightening. Sometimes his stories posed a threat to temporal powers. Jesus' parables also destroyed the divisive and imaginary insider vs. outsider mentality and boundaries that religious, cultural, racial, and political forms of thinking usually create. His message was positive and practical.

The theme of his parables was God's kingdom—that is, God's sovereign presence. The parables acted as lenses so that his followers and listeners could focus on the kingdom. Through the parables, Jesus could bring a realization to the people that God was now present and active among them. His stories changed their concept of God and the now emerging heavenly kingdom.[1]

The English word parable comes from the Greek term *parabolé*.. *Para* means "parallel" or "alongside." The second half of the word derives from the Greek term *ballein* and signifies to "throw, cast, place." A parable, then, is a story we place alongside something else to help clarify its meaning. In Hebrew the word is *mashal;* in Aramaic, *pelatha*. Both these Semitic words carry the same root idea meaning "it is like, similar or it is compared to." *Mashal* and *pelatha* may also translate into English as "parable, proverb, allegory, illustration, riddle, similitude."

A parable is verbal imagery that portrays and illustrates an event or a teaching. The main purpose of a parable is to make an impression and not to construct definitions or establish dogmas. Jesus composed these stories as pure fiction and we are not to understand them in a

---

[1]For a detailed study on parables see Rocco A. Errico, *AND THERE WAS LIGHT*, "The Parables of Jesus," pp. 42-52.

literal sense.

Teaching and carrying on a conversation in parables, proverbs, riddles, and illustrations are characteristic of Semites. Wise men, wazirs, court officials, rabbis, prophets, teachers, and politicians always used parables in their debates and speeches. Merchants and clients, while bargaining, often mention a few parables.

Near Eastern musicians sing parables, proverbs, and riddles as they play their instruments. "I will incline my ear to parables: I will sing my proverbs upon the harp."[2] Speaking in parables was a common way of communication and it remains so to this very day in the Near East. This kind of speech is very precious to Semites. It is poetic, mystical, and social. In the 13th chapter of Matthew, Jesus' discourse on the kingdom is expressed through seven parables. Jesus' basic teaching ministry was composed of sayings and mostly parables. "Jesus spoke all these things to the people in parables; and without parables he did not speak to them."[3]Jesus was an excellent parabler. He could hold his listeners to the last word of his storytelling. The best mode of expressing his teaching was through parables.

PARABLE OF THE SEED

Hear ye therefore the parable of the sower. Mt. 13:18.

According to the Aramaic text, this verse reads: "Now listen to the parable of the seed."[4] The gospel writer did not use the word "sower." *Zara* is the Aramaic word for "seed." *Zarua* is the word for "sower." Both the Western and Near Eastern texts deal with the seed falling in four kinds of soil and not about the sower who was instrumental in planting the seed. This mistake probably came about because the two Aramaic words are similar.

---

[2]Ps. 49:4, Aramaic Peshitta text, Errico.
[3]Mt. 13:34, Aramaic Peshitta text, Lamsa translation.
[4]Aramaic Peshitta text, Lamsa translation.

In the Southern part of Palestine, especially in Judea, it is very hilly and rocky. Small patches of land are like gardens planted on the slopes of mountains. These patches are terraced one above the other. Each field is sustained by a little retaining wall built of stones. Usually the fields are very rocky and people often bring in soil from elsewhere to cover the rocks. Large stones that cannot be removed are allowed to remain. Some stones and rocks are intentionally left in the field to keep the soil from being washed away during the rainy season.

These hilly fields are difficult to cultivate because the soil is poor and there are so many rocks. Some seeds fall on the rocks that are covered only with a thin layer of soil. These seeds sprout but in the heat of the day, the rocks become hot and the plant is scorched. Other seeds fall among the thorns that grow near the edge of the fields. The soil here may be deep, but because thorns grow much faster than the seeds, these weeds choke the plants and, therefore, they cannot produce anything. Some seeds fall on the pathways, but the birds take them and eat them. All other seeds fall at the lower end of the fields where the soil is fertile. It is here that the seeds grow and bring forth a good harvest. (See Luke 8:11.)

God's kingdom is like seed that a sower went out to sow. The first planting failed, the second germinated but failed also, and the third sprouted but failed to make the harvest. Finally the kingdom produces a harvest, some just a normal crop, and some a hundred fold. In God's kingdom there can be both failure and the miraculous. In failure and in daily life there is the miracle of God's activity, the divine presence.

Seeds are small but they have tremendous power. This power causes them to grow into a plant and multiply. This is true concerning the word of God's kingdom. Humans cannot see the word but they can be affected by it. This word/seed of the kingdom contains power and, like a living organism, it transmits itself from one person to another. A good word can change nations, remove boundaries, establish new kings, and revolutionize the whole world. There is little that a word spoken with power cannot do.

RECANTING

Yet hath he not root in himself, but dureth for a while: for when tribulation or persecution ariseth because of the word, by and by he is offended. Mt. 13:21.

When a man changes his religion, he also changes his customs and nationality. For example, if a Christian becomes an adherent to Islam, he must surrender his swine and refrain from eating pork. Moslems do not eat pork. In addition to this, he must renounce other customs that are contrary to his new adopted faith. This same course of action is followed if a Moslem becomes a Christian. However, Christians have fewer restrictions than Moslems.

As religion is the great center of life in the Near East, such changes cannot be effected without persecution and war. Again, if any Moslem confesses his belief in Jesus' teachings openly, his relatives will immediately persecute him and some families may even put him to death. Or, perhaps, reading the gospel of the kingdom or hearing the words of a preacher may affect a Moslem's heart and he may suddenly feel he can give his life for it. But, as soon as his relatives find out he has become a follower of Jesus' gospel, he takes the change of faith more seriously. Fear and threats compel him to recant and denounce his new-found faith.

Persecutions were to arise because of accepting the gospel of the kingdom. This gospel was to do away not only with ancient misleading religions but with their economic institutions, also. Merchants and artisans would not allow their trade and businesses to be endangered by the conversion to a new faith that disregarded material things. Converts themselves were at times disappointed and tired of the seemingly passive faith that they had adopted.

WHEAT AND TARES

Another parable put he forth unto them, saying, The kingdom of heaven is likened unto a man which sowed good seed in his field: But while men slept, his enemy came and sowed tares among the wheat, and went his way. Mt. 13:24-25.

The Aramaic word for tares is *ziwaneh*. It derives from *zana* meaning "to commit adultery." *Ziwaneh* or "tares" grow uncultivated. Although they are carefully separated from the seeds of wheat before they are sown, some tares spring up with the wheat, much to the farmer's dismay. Sometimes tares survived in the ground from the previous harvest. In the spring, wheat and tares grow together; but the tares grow faster and shoot their tendrils over the wheat, preventing the wheat from growing and ripening. At this stage it is very difficult to pull the tares out because their tendrils are wound around the wheat. If they pull the tares, they will lose the wheat. The work of separation must therefore wait until the harvest season.

Many times some farmers throw seeds of tares in the field of another. During the sowing season farmers are very suspicious and afraid of each other, especially those with whom they have had quarrels and troubles. It takes years of hard labor for a farmer to eradicate tares from his wheat fields. When this is done, the farmer rejoices. On the other hand, when a farmer wants to avenge a wrong done to him by a neighboring farmer, he will sow tares at night in his neighbor's field. When the tares spring up, the owner of the field immediately realizes this was a villainous act of an enemy, but he does not know which one of his enemies may have done it. He does not hesitate to retaliate by scattering tares in several fields in the hope his enemy will suffer.

In this parable, wheat represents what is good. Tares denote evil. Good and evil have always existed together. It is difficult to separate them because when trying to remove the bad, the good will also suffer. Good and evil will continue to exist together until the end just as tares and wheat exist together until they are separated at harvest. Farmers will then take the tares and wheat, place them in a smooth wooden instrument, and shake them. Because the tares are round, they roll to one side while the wheat remains in the instrument. When all the tares are separated, they are burned so that no one will scatter them again in the fields, but some of them always remain and multiply very rapidly. After this procedure, farmers store their wheat in their barns.

The meaning of the parable is that true discernment and proper judgment belongs to God. Again, what is ordinary and what is unclean (tares) are associated with God's kingdom. There will be both tares and wheat in this kingdom. But only God can separate them. One must leave matters alone until full maturity occurs. Evil in the end destroys itself. It cannot stand because it has no genuine foundation.

MUSTARD SEED

Another parable put he forth unto them, saying, The kingdom of heaven is like to a grain of mustard seed, which a man took, and sowed in his field. Mt. 13:31.

In Palestine the mustard seed is the smallest of all seeds. It grows wild and people consider it a weed. The mustard seed creates a very potent and hot plant. (Dr. Lamsa said that he had never seen any farmer plant mustard seed.) Eastern Semites never ate the mustard plant because they believed it caused insanity. Nonetheless, at times, they use the seeds for medicinal purposes. Where it grows, it becomes larger than any other plant but never becomes a tree. The text should read that it becomes like a large bush. The plant is about two and a half to three feet in height, and small birds, especially wild sparrows, nest in it. Birds love to make their nests in plants because trees are not abundant. During the very warm hours of the day, one can see birds resting under the mustard plant.

Jesus likens God's kingdom to a grain of mustard seed because it is the smallest seed in the Near East but hot and powerful. Almost everyone thinks of God's kingdom as enormous but, instead, one can easily miss God's sovereign presence because it is so small. This is part of Jesus' humor, making the omnipresent, omniscient, omnipotent

God as tiny as a mustard seed. Nonetheless, it is pungent and potent.

Then again, as grains of mustard seed are round and even, so the truth of the gospel of the kingdom has only one side. The mustard seed cannot be divided in two like some other seeds. So the gospel of the kingdom is based on the truth alone and cannot be divided. The mustard seed is hotter than any other seed. Wherever it grows, other seeds die. Because of its potency, the joyful message of the kingdom was to supplant all and any religious notions and ideologies that separate, alienate, and divide one person against another. This kingdom cannot grow side by side with idol worship and other erroneous, materialistic teaching and philosophies.

Seed, like a word, is one of the most powerful things in the world. In the course of time, it multiples itself rapidly, and the power within it is infinite. Jesus' gospel of the kingdom was like a seed—in this case, a grain of mustard seed. It was proclaimed on the shores of the Lake of Galilee and, in due time, would be carried on wings of the spirit over seas and oceans. It would spread all over the world.

HEAVEN AND LEAVEN

Another parable spake he unto them; The kingdom of heaven is like unto leaven, which a woman took, and hid in three measures of meal, till the whole was leavened. Mt. 13:33.

"The kingdom of heaven" in Aramaic is *malkutha dashmaya.* It means "the kingdom of God." The term "heaven" here is a euphemistic term that refers to "God" and the "universal kingdom." Many believed that the messianic kingdom was to embrace all the kingdoms of this world and restore the throne of David. Jews were to be rulers and the realms of the Gentiles were to be overthrown forever. Nations would have to be subject to Jewish rule.

The prince of peace was to rule over the kingdom of God or heaven. This kingdom would hold both the good and the bad exactly the way Jesus told about it in the parables of the tares and wheat and the good and bad fish in the net. However, this one-liner parable gives us a different picture.

God's kingdom is like a woman doing an ordinary, everyday chore. She is preparing to make bread for the day. This story was a great surprise to his listeners because Jesus likened God's sovereign presence to a woman. She hid or buried the leaven in 50 pounds (three measures) of flour. This is an exaggeration and also a part of Jesus' humor. Then, the woman waited for the dough to rise.

The leaven represents God's presence working secretly. This covert operation was the opposite to the way people were thinking. They thought that when God comes everyone will know this heavenly presence. Things would change magically. Destruction and annihilation would come upon God's enemies. But God's sovereignty works like leaven that is hidden in the dough. It is constantly fermenting the hearts and minds of men and women, secretly working in the kingdoms of this world, and gradually changing them into the kingdom of God, bringing peace and harmony.

SPEAKING IN PARABLES

All these things spake Jesus unto the multitude in parables; and without a parable spake he not unto them. Mt. 13:34.

Speaking in parables is a Near Eastern practice. In countries where people are illiterate, teaching truth is conveyed through illustrations or narratives. A parable is an oral picture that portrays and clarifies an event or a teaching. Parables are familiar to the people and a speaker composes them out of the incidents and experiences of his own life. He first recites an incident corresponding to what he intends to say; as the happening is well known to the people, they easily understand the meaning.

If what the speaker is about to say is of a serious nature, it will be preceded by a parable. This was the case with the prophet Nathan and King David, when the prophet had told the parable about the rich man with many sheep and the poor man with only one lamb. Nathan related this story to make David acknowledge his guilt. Without the parable, David would have been enraged at his court prophet.[5] An Easterner listening to a speaker must understand completely what the orator is attempting to teach. Things partially understood are exaggerated or misconstrued. A wise man, therefore, not only talks in parables but he repeats the same thing again and again until he is convinced his words have impressed the minds of his listeners.

A parable helps people remember what has been said. When buying and selling, people will tell parables to each other. Two men carrying burdens on their backs and going in opposite directions often will stop and engage in conversation. They will tell each other several parables. Statesmen, politicians, and prophets have always used parables in their conversations and heated debates. Parables were the chief medium for communications and Semites still practice this habit today. (See Mark 4:33-34.)

HIDDEN TREASURE AND GOODLY PEARLS

Again, the kingdom of heaven is like unto treasure hid in a field; the which when a man hath found, he hideth and for joy thereof goeth and selleth all that he hath, and buyeth that field. Again, the kingdom of heaven is like unto a merchant man, seeking goodly pearls: Who, when he had found one pearl of great price, went and sold all that he had, and bought it. Mt. 13:44-46.

God's kingdom was like a priceless treasure that the Hebrew forefathers had buried in a field. People would have to search for it and, once it was found, they would have to sell everything to acquire it. Near Easterners usually search for hidden treasures but they cannot be found so easily. One has to work and search diligently to find these buried treasures. So it is with God's kingdom. We must diligently

---

[5]See 2 Sam. 12:1.

search for the reign of God, for it holds peace, justice and tranquillity for all who find it. What Jesus means is that we have to search for truth. This is the only way it can be found and valued.

Jesus compares God's kingdom to a merchant seeking pearls. Pearls, diamonds, and precious stones were not easily acquired in the Near East. In that entire period of antiquity, pearls were highly prized. People went diving in the Red Sea, the Persian Gulf, and the Indian Ocean searching for pearls. Merchants did not sell and purchase precious pearls in an open market. In our country, we display our costly stones and gems in windows of shops and inside glass counters in stores. In the ancient world, people buried their precious gems and stones in the ground.

When a trader wished to purchase a gem, he had to search for it. It was not an easy task. People traded precious jewels secretly. Thus, when a merchant found a pearl, he would risk selling some of his land so that he may purchase the precious gem before others discovered that the jewel was for sale.

In Jesus' parable the trader sells everything that he has for the pearl. This leaves the merchant without any real property except for the pearl. What an ironic twist! He was so eager to obtain the precious pearl that he had to sell all that he possessed. However, the merchant could have sold the pearl and earned even more than he had before. But he would no longer possess the precious pearl that he had so diligently sought. Regardless, Jesus simply ended the story with the purchase of the pearl after the merchant sold all his possessions.

God's kingdom, with its power and presence, is like a precious pearl. And because of its great value, the kingdom becomes a challenge for everyone. First, one must search for it because it is not easy to find. Second, once one finds it, then that one must sell everything to obtain it. The parable makes it very clear that after one finds the presence of God (God's kingdom), and sells all for it, in the end this kingdom really possesses the one who sold all. Ultimately, God's kingdom can never be possessed, controlled, or manipulated. No one will ever have the exclusive rights (ownership) to heaven's rule.

THE NET

Again, the kingdom of heaven is like unto a net, that was cast into the sea, and gathered of every kind: Which, when it was full, they drew to shore, and sat down, and gathered the good into vessels, but cast the bad away. Mt. 13:47-48.

The kingdom of heaven is a universal kingdom that embraces everyone, both good and bad. It is like a fishing net that, after it is cast into the sea and drawn into the boat, contains clean and unclean creatures. This parable is similar to the parable of the tares and wheat. God's kingdom will include many races and people of various beliefs, but not all of them will truly adhere to the teachings of the kingdom. Many are called into the kingdom but only a few will remain loyal. On the other hand, many teachers of the kingdom will be influenced by the teaching of their old religions, traditions, and ordinances.

BROTHERS AND SISTERS OF JESUS

Is not this the carpenter's son? is not his mother called Mary? and his brethren, James, and Joses, and Simon, and Judas? And his sisters, are they not all with us? Whence then hath this man all these things? And they were offended in him. But Jesus said unto them, A prophet is not without honor, save in his own country, and in his own house. Mt. 13:55-57.

The Hebrews were polygamists from the time of Abraham and still are in some Near Eastern countries. In some cases, Jewish law made it mandatory. For instance, if a brother should die leaving a wife and no children, his surviving brother must marry the widow and perform conjugal rights until a male child is born. Thus, even those who were content with just one wife would have to take another wife and raise the child for the deceased brother. On the other hand, men considered their wives as property. Also, men who had many wives were highly respected and were looked upon as wealthy.

Undoubtedly, Joseph had other wives. The brothers and sisters of Jesus who are mentioned in the gospels were not Mary's children but children of Joseph from his other wives. Had they been his own brothers and sisters, they would have stood by Jesus from the beginning and would not have opposed him. They were ashamed of his behavior and remarks concerning his prophetic claims. So Jesus left them and went to towns near the Lake of Galilee.

None of Jesus' brothers or sisters seems to have been present when he was crucified. Jesus placed his mother in the care of John. Had his brothers been his followers, they would have been near at this critical time and Jesus would have asked them to take care of his mother. Strange as it is, in the Near East rivalry and bitterness are stronger between half-brothers than between strangers. (See Mark 6:3.)

"A prophet is without honor in his own house and country." In biblical lands, prophets and men of God are generally rejected and scorned by their own relatives and countrymen. Familiarity breeds contempt. It was difficult for the relatives of Jesus and his own townspeople to accept him because he grew up with them. How could someone who, just a few years or months ago, was working with them in the fields or feeding sheep become a prophet and teacher of their sacred religion? The people of Nazareth had a difficult time believing that God had raised a great prophet from among them. What could a prophet offer to his own people who had seen him living in poverty and carrying the burdens of the oppressors? They could not understand how such a simple man could be the savior of his people.

But in other areas and lands, where people knew nothing about a prophet's early life or history, they could easily honor and respect him. Jesus had to leave his hometown and go to the cities and towns around the Lake of Galilee. These people knew nothing of his background. They were interested in the new teaching that gave hope for the hopeless, a light burden for the heavy laden, and an easier yoke for the oppressed.

CHAPTER 14

DESERT PLACE

When Jesus heard of it, he departed thence by ship into a desert place apart: and when the people had heard thereof, they followed him on foot out of the cities. Mt. 14:13.

The Aramaic word *horba* means "uninhabited place." The word for "wilderness" is *madhbra* and it means a "wasteland" or a "land without water or vegetation." Jesus went to an uninhabited place close to Tiberius.

Until a few decades ago many places around the Lake of Galilee and around Jordan were uninhabited, and a few still are. These were the places to which Jesus and his followers retreated. They were seeking solitude and rest from the crowds of curious men and women who followed him expecting to see great wonders.

All great religions were born in desert lands. Moses spent forty years in the desert, Elijah forty days in Sinai, Paul three years in the desert, and Mohammed, most of his life. One must be in solitude to commune with God. Jesus, as a man, was often disturbed by the opposition which was considerable in the cities. At times, he became fatigued and needed a quiet place to recuperate.

Jesus was not in a mood to meet people at this particular time. Therefore, he went to a place where no one would bother him and his disciples. Even to this day, kings, princes, and religious men seek refuge in isolated places so that they may rest and make important decisions.

FEEDING THE PEOPLE

But Jesus said unto them, They need not depart; give ye them to eat. And they say unto him, We have here but five loaves and two fishes. He said, Bring them hither to me. Mt. 14:16-18.

Interest in the prophet from Galilee was so great that a large crowd of men, women, and children left their villages and hamlets to come and seek the bread of life and cures from this famous healer's hands. They were so attracted to the new teaching and to the hope that it offered the oppressed that they did not go to the towns to procure food supplies for themselves. However, their provisions had been so exhausted that they could not return to their homes hungry, and many might faint from hunger.

The disciples of Jesus found a boy in the large crowd who had five loaves of bread and two fish. Jesus saw that this was sufficient substance to take care of the hungry crowd, so he blessed what was on hand. He knew that the Lord God, who is the giver of all good gifts, would divinely increase the provisions so that the entire crowd could be fed.

Jesus knew that God's supplies are infinite and inexhaustible and that God can meet the needs of his children anytime and any place. Many of these people were seeking God's kingdom, so God would certainly supply their physical needs. No one expected that such a large crowd could be fed with such a scanty supply of food that was at hand.

A marvelous multiplication of bread and fish occurred and the people were fed. The people considered this a wonder simply because the hungry were fed and sent home satisfied. The Messiah/Christ, with his divine power, had met the need and provided sufficient food for those who were seeking the bread of life. In the past, Hebrew prophets also had demonstrated God's power by blessing and increasing the substance of men and women who revered God and were persecuted for the truth.

Nevertheless, some of the people who saw this marvel did not believe in Jesus. They asked him to show them a sign. They even said to him, "What miracles have you performed that we may believe in you?"[1] These men were looking for signs; they wanted some magical performances like those that Moses did when he and Aaron stood before Pharaoh. But Jesus never resorted to any magic or anything that was contrary to God's laws.

The miracle or wonder was that Jesus could meet the needs of the hungry people. How the bread and fish were increased is not relevant. What is relevant is this: The hungry were fed in a desert place and twelve baskets full of fragments of bread and fish were left over. The great need was met, and what at first seemed to be impossible was made possible.

FALSE VISION

And when the disciples saw him walking on the sea, they were troubled, saying, It is a spirit; and they cried out for fear. Mt. 14:26.

Demons and evil spirits play an important part in the lives of Eastern, Semitic people. Belief in unseen spirits is so ingrained that specific religious laws are enacted on their behalf. In some Islamic countries, even to this day, a woman's marriage to a spirit (jinn) is recognized. Men and women hold communion with spirits; some declared that they had seen these spirits.

Fear of spirits is so strong that an innocent man walking at night by the seashore or near a cemetery may be mistaken for a spirit. In Assyria, when a man whom the family cannot identify enters a house at night, he will be tested by sticking him with a large needle so they will know he is not a spirit. The belief is that when a needle touches an evil spirit, it is supposed to change into a donkey.

Jesus's disciples were afraid because of their belief in spirits. But Jesus promptly assured them it was he and not a spirit who was wishing to enter the boat.

---

[1]See Jn 6:1-32.

CHAPTER 15

JEWISH ORDINANCES

Why do thy disciples transgress the tradition of the elders? For they wash not their hands when they eat bread. But he answered and said unto them, Why do ye also transgress the commandment of God by your tradition? For God commanded, saying, Honour thy father and mother: and He that curseth father or mother, let him die the death. But ye say, Whosoever shall say to his father and his mother, It is a gift, by whatsoever thou mighest be profited by me. . . . This people draweth nigh unto me with their mouth, and honoureth me with their lips; but their heart is far from me. But in vain they do worship me, teaching for doctrines the commandments of men. Mt. 15:2-5, 8-9.

Washing of hands and the cleansing of pots, dishes, and spoons were ordinances based on the teaching of the elders. In the past, these teachings were not a part of God's laws. The elders and teachers of the law distracted the attention of the people from the spiritual and moral truths of the law by supplanting the weightier meaning of the word of God with their own teachings and traditions.

"But you are saying, anyone who will say to a father or a mother, whatever you will be benefitted from me is my offering; he does not have to support his father or mother."[1] There are three major points to consider here: (1) According to the Near Eastern cultural tradition, children are to support their parents when their mother and father retire. (2) The fourth commandment reinforces this cultural custom. (3) The Pharisees changed this custom to benefit themselves. They claimed that the money put aside for the parent's retirement could be donated as an offering to the temple thereby exempting the children from their obligation to support their parents. Therefore, according to these blind teachers, to say to one's parents *qorban*—"my sacrifice"

---

[1]Mt. 15:5, Aramaic Peshitta text, Errico.

or "a gift to God"—is far more important than honoring and caring for one's parents.

Man-made traditions and diverse amplifications of the law had nullified God's law and obscured the teaching of the prophets. When one honors his parents, he does everything for them, but the teaching of the elders demanded nothing from the people but lip service and empty words without deeds. Besides, it was easier for the people to wash pots, plates, and spoons than to keep the true meaning of the law and do works of compassion.

UNTRUE TEACHINGS UPROOTED

But he answered and said, Every plant, which my heavenly Father hath not planted, shall be rooted up. Let them alone: they be blind leaders of the blind. And if the blind lead the blind, both shall fall into the ditch. Mt. 15:13-14.

"Plant" in this verse refers to the "doctrine"—that is, the true teaching that God had revealed to Moses and the prophets, the foundation of the Jewish religion. The Pharisees and scribes had supplanted some of the true teachings with their own notions and interpretations of the law.

All teachings that had not come in a revelation from God were soon to be uprooted and subverted by the new and true teaching of Jesus' gospel of the kingdom. This gospel was to be declared and made known regardless of the opposition by some of the Pharisees and scribes who were blind teachers leading the blind.

Jesus' teaching was based on the message of the Hebrew prophets, who in their days had acted as spokesmen for God. Jesus had come to fulfill the law and the prophets—that is, to put these teachings into practice. Truth always replaces deception and misconception. It may take time for truth to be understood, but sooner or later it destroys error.

RACIAL ANTIPATHY

And behold, a woman of Canaan came out of the same coasts, and cried unto him, saying, Have mercy on me, O Lord, thou son of David; my daughter is grievously vexed with a devil. But he answered her not a word. And his disciples came and besought him, saying, Send her away; for she crieth after us. But he answered and said, I am not sent but unto the lost sheep of the house of Israel. . . . But he answered and said, It is not meet to take the children's bread, and to cast it to dogs. And she said, Truth, Lord: yet the dogs eat of the crumbs which fall from their master's table. Then Jesus answered and said unto her, O woman great is thy faith be it unto thee even as thou wilt. And her daughter was made whole from that very hour. Mt. 15:22-28.

Racial and religious feelings are strong in the Near East. Rivalry and hatred dominate. Although people of various races and religions live and trade together, they look upon each other as unclean. Priests of one religion condemn those of other beliefs. Many people will not even tolerate a kind word spoken to them if a religious leader of another faith should extend such sympathy to them.

When Jesus preached in the synagogue of Nazareth, he reminded the people of the famine in Israel when Elisha was sent to the widow of Zarephath in Syria to be fed by her. He was not sent to any widow in Israel. In addition, he also reminded them of Naaman, a Syrian, who was cleansed of his leprosy by the prophet Elijah although many Israelite lepers were not healed of their leprosy. These remarks so enraged the people who were listening to him that they took Jesus to a cliff and tried to throw him over the edge. But, he escaped.

Jesus had no feeling of enmity toward Gentiles though he was a member of the Jewish religion and he did adhere, to a certain degree, to Jewish social customs and manners. A sudden departure from the established traditions would not only have roused the hatred of the Pharisees and priests but would have also weakened the faith of his followers. His motives would not have been understood even by his disciples. People would have repudiated him as a traitor. This is the reason Jesus sent his disciples first to the lost sheep of the family of

210

Israel. They were to be changed first so that barriers could be broken and the principles of a universal brotherhood established.

The lost sheep of the house of Israel were the ten Northern Israelite tribes whom the Assyrian kings carried away captive when Samaria fell before the Assyrian armies in 722 B.C.E. The Hebrew prophets called them "sheep" because at that time Yahweh was the great Shepherd of Israel and the Israelites were his sheep. The descendants of these tribes were praying for the restoration that was to be accomplished by the appearance of the Messiah. It was he who was to gather the scattered people from the house of Israel. These were the people who had been waiting for their deliverance and who would respond to the new gospel of the kingdom.

Gentiles and pagans were known as "dogs" simply because they ate foods that were considered unclean by Mosaic law. They also were considered to be defiled because of some of their cultural customs. The gospel was to be preached first to Jews and to the lost house of Israel and then to the Gentiles and pagans. It was only natural that Israel should hear the gospel first for they had the law, the prophets, and the divine promises of God. Therefore, Jesus had to go to them to invite them to participate in God's dawning kingdom.

The Canaanite woman's faith was so great that she could cross all racial and religious barriers. She was able to reach for healing from a Jewish prophet. She was a Gentile and, therefore, a "dog." Nevertheless, her faith was so powerful that Jesus had compassion on this woman and healed her daughter. Jesus, at first, appears to confirm religious prejudice. But, by granting the woman's request, he gave his disciples two good lessons: (1) He taught his disciples that such religious prejudice does not exist in God's kingdom; this kingdom was ready to receive anyone at any time and place. (2) By healing the Canaanite woman's daughter, Jesus gave assurance to her and all Gentiles that they would receive the blessings of the kingdom.

CHAPTER 16

PHARISEES AND SADDUCEES

The Pharisees also with the Sadducees came, and tempting desired him that he would shew them a sign from heaven. Mt. 16:1.

Part A—PHARISEES. The so-called "sect" of the Pharisees was truly a widespread socio-religious movement within the Jewish State. Its aim was not political. The movement gave birth to most of the outstanding Torah scholars in Judaism. Its recorded historical appearance takes us back to the time of the revolt of the Maccabees in 168 B.C.E. (Maccabee means "one who hammers." See the Apocrypha books 1 and 2 Maccabees for the history of the Jewish uprising against the Hellenizing policy which the Seleucid Syrian King, Antiochus Epiphanes, was attempting to force on Palestine.) The actual revolt was, for the most part, provoked by the high priests who had lost favor with the masses of pious Jews (known as *Hasidim*) because of their scandalous actions both politically and religiously. The final straw was the act of offering swine's blood to Zeus on the altar of the temple. The Jews needed new leadership and the large company of the devout was ready with highly honored scribes, Torah scholars and teachers. The behavior of these new leaders made their opponents nickname them "Pharisees" meaning "Separatists."

"Pharisee" derives from the Aramaic root *parash*, "to separate, set aside, to select." Pharisees were "separatists" who withdrew themselves from others. They were devout nationalists who were wanting to restore political Israel. There is no mention of the Pharisees in the canonical Hebrew Bible. Scribes are often mentioned in the books of Moses. However, the term *sapreh* or "scribes" has been erroneously translated as "officers" in the King James Version.

Scribes and Pharisees worked closely together, and both believed in the resurrection of the body and life hereafter. They also believed in helping their enemies, if they should meet them in distress on the

212

road. They knew that enmity and anger blind one's eyes, but love opens them. They revered the prophets of Israel and were looking for the coming of the Messiah, the Blessed One. The principle idea of the movement was to follow the Torah not only as it is laid out in the five books of Moses—Genesis to Deuteronomy—but to adhere to their forefathers' interpretation of these writings from the time of Ezra, Nehemiah, and the return from Babylon. Therefore, the pious created the oral law, "the tradition of the fathers," which in the gospel is called "the tradition of the elders." They believed in God's omnipotence, human responsibility, free will, and the resurrection. The gospel writers tell us that the Pharisees did not associate with anyone who did not keep the rigorous and demanding standards of purity that they had set and interpreted for the twofold Torah, the written and oral law. The apostle Paul was a strict Pharisee who was drawn to the simplicity of Jesus' teaching and its emphasis on love, meekness, and inclusiveness.

Part B—SADDUCEES. According to the Jewish historian Flavius Josephus, the movement of the Pharisees represented the pious people, but the sect of the Sadducees stood for the affluent. The Sadducees had governed the Jewish state from the time of the Persian period and were formed from the wealthy lay and priestly aristocracy. Sadducees comes from the Semitic term *zadoqayeh*, "righteous ones." This term derives from the name of the faithful priest *Zadoq*, who ministered to King David in Hebron after the death of King Saul.[1] Zadoq's descendants had held the high priestly office in Jerusalem since the time of Solomon. It was the priestly upper classes who were in charge of political affairs during the Hellenistic period. The high priest, with other priests, had formed and directed the Jewish high council that eventually became the Sanhedrin. It was the Sadducees who named the *Hasidim*, "the pious." These pious ones opposed the corruption in the priesthood.

The Sadducees had declared themselves to be the "righteous ones." They were not nationalists, nor did they believe in the

---

[1]See 2 Sam. 8:17 and 1 Chron. 12:23-28.

resurrection. As far as they were concerned, one life was enough. Therefore, they did everything they could to enjoy this life. They were satisfied with the Roman Government and the Herodian dynasty that had been imposed on the Jews by Roman authorities and their cohorts. Thus, many Sadducees were employed in the services of the local and imperial governments.

In his discourses, Jesus reprimanded many scribes and Pharisees, often referring to them as hypocrites and blind guides. But he seldom had any encounter with the Sadducees, for they did not care whether the Jewish religion was reformed or not. Nor did they expect the coming of the Messiah, the great Jewish leader. They were satisfied with the status quo.

WEATHER FORECASTING

He answered and said unto them, When it is evening, ye say, It will be fair weather: for the sky is red. And in the morning, It will be foul weather today: for the sky is red and lowering. O ye hypocrites, ye can discern the face of the sky: but can ye not discern the signs of the times? Mt. 16:2-3.

The Pharisees knew how to forecast the weather. They could discern the times for the rainy season and the dry season because they knew how to read the face of the sky. But they could not foretell the events to come—that is, the true signs of the times.

Their prophets had warned them in advance. The Hebrew prophets had predicted the impending disaster and periods of peace and prosperity, but now Israel had lost the gift of prophecy. They had asked Jesus for a sign. But what greater sign could Jesus give them than the sign of his death and resurrection? The prophet Jonah's story foreshadowed Jesus' rejection, death and burial for three days. This was a feat that had never happened before. No one had ever conquered the grave and death. Jesus would conquer them both and destroy their seeming power forever.

LEAVEN OF THE PHARISEES

Then Jesus said unto them, Take heed and beware of the leaven of the Pharisees and of the Sadducees. Mt. 16:6.

Before women bake bread, they set aside a handful of dough as leaven to be mixed with the next day's supply. This is placed in a large wooden basin and hot water poured over it. When it is dissolved, the flour is mixed with the solution. The leaven causes the dough to ferment, and while it is fermenting, it increases in bulk. Easterners believe the increase is caused by a sacred and hidden blessing in the family leaven. In their eyes leaven is sacred.

When men are on good terms, they bless each other's leaven and are careful not to make the slightest remark against it. But, when men are disputing or fighting, then they curse each other's leaven. One often hears: "Beware of him. He has grown up eating bread made of bad leaven." They also say, "his leaven is bloody." When a man has committed a murder, or is a noted sinner or blasphemer, his leaven is defiled. No one in town will borrow it or touch it. Some men and women are afraid even to eat bread made of such leaven.

The term "leaven" in this instance means "teaching." When people converse with each other, "leaven" may refer not only to a "teaching" but to certain "policies or people." A teaching is like leaven. It permeates human conduct. Good leaven makes the bread good; it increases the dough and makes it taste good. Bad leaven makes the bread tasteless and bad. This is also true of any teaching. The leaven of the Pharisees was like corrupt leaven. They had supplanted the word of God with their own human teachings. Therefore, Jesus warned his disciples about the Pharisees' leaven. It confused and poisoned the minds of the people. Their whole thought was centered on the foolish tradition of the elders that often created schisms, hypocrisy and hatred. The leaven of these doctrines fermented in the Jewish mind to such an extent that many of the people lost their spiritual vision. Many of the Pharisees prayed with their lips but their hands were smeared with the blood of the innocent. Extortion and graft operated under the guise of ecclesiastical authority.

Jesus was careful about his disciples not being misguided and bewildered by corrupt teachings. In the cultural and religious sense of the times, the man whom these disciples were following was neither a holy nor a religious man. Jesus ignored the doctrines of the elders and questioned all religious notions about God. He taught no theology. As the interest of the Jews centered solely around messianic political hopes that the Pharisees and priests had expounded, Jesus' simple disciples could easily have been misled. (See Luke 12:1.)

WHO AM I

When Jesus came into the coasts of Caesarea Philippi, he asked his disciples, saying, Whom do men say that I the Son of man am? Mt. 16:13.

The Aramaic text reads: "What do men say concerning me, that I am merely a son of man (human being)?"[2] Once a man begins a religious career or becomes prominent, he will become the subject of much public discussion. People strive to find out all they can about his ancestry, qualifications, and mission. He is both praised and criticized. Some men describe him as a saint and give him a title appropriate to a holy man. Others may think of him as a new prophet with a new message. And yet others may scorn him and repudiate his claims.

Jesus' popularity was increasing rapidly. The Galileans had already proclaimed him a prophet and king. The Jews in the South were constantly discussing him. Many Pharisees and doctors of the law were challenging his gospel. Some people thought he might be Elijah, Jeremiah or even one of the other Hebrew prophets come back. The Jews believed that Elijah would return to restore the Jewish State. Others openly disclaimed him and considered him only a Galilean peasant and troublemaker.

Jesus had heard all these rumors and knew that people were

---

[2]Mt. 16:13, Aramaic Peshitta text, Lamsa translation.

debating his role in their community. He heard people say that he was only an ordinary man and that no prophet could come from Galilee. He knew that all this had made an impression on his disciples, and he, therefore, wanted to know what they thought about him. He asked them what people said concerning him—whether he was just an ordinary person or a prophet. *Bar-nasha*, "Son of man" in Aramaic, means "an ordinary human being or person." In the Near East a man who holds no credentials is simply known as someone who is just ordinary.

ELIJAH EXPECTED TO COME

And they said, Some say that thou art John the Baptist: some Elias and others, Jeremias, or one of the prophets. Mt. 16:14.

The Pharisees and Scribes taught that the coming of the Messiah would be preceded by either the coming of Elijah, Jeremiah, or one of the other great prophets. God was to send one of them to prepare the way for the Messiah.[3]

In these lands, kings, princes and high government officials send their emissaries in advance to sweep the streets and prepare the way for the arriving powers. According to the teaching of the Pharisees and scribes, the Messiah could not come and walk on the streets of Jerusalem while the pagan Romans ruled both the holy city and the land. They taught that a great prophet would come first to prepare the way and to overthrow the Gentile rule so that the Messiah might hasten his arrival.

Some of the people did not believe that Jesus might be the Messiah; they thought that he was just an ordinary person—no one outstanding. Others thought that he was one of the prophets. But his disciples looked upon him as the coming Deliverer.

---

[3]See Mal. 4:5-6.

PETER'S CONFESSION

He said unto them, But whom say ye that I am? And Simon Peter answered and said, Thou art the Christ, the Son of the living God. And Jesus answered and said unto him. Blessed art thou, Simon Bar-Jona: for flesh and blood hath not revealed it unto thee, but my Father which is in heaven. And I say also unto thee, That thou art Peter, and upon this rock I will build my church; and the gates of hell shall not prevail against it. And I will give unto thee the keys of the kingdom of heaven: and whatsoever thou shalt bind on earth shall be bound in heaven: and whatsoever thou shalt loose on earth shall be loosed in heaven. Mt. 16:15-19.

The Aramaic text reads: "Simon Peter answered and said: You are the Anointed (Messiah), the son of the living God![4] Jesus answered and said to him: Fortunate are you, Simon, son of Jonah, because a mortal did not reveal this to you but my Father who is in heaven. I also tell you that your are a rock (*Kepa*) and upon this rock I will build my church[5] and the doors of *sheol* will not conquer it. I give you the keys of Heaven's sovereign presence and anything you bind on earth will be bound in heaven, and anything you loose on earth will be loosed in heaven."[6]

When Simon Peter (*Kepa*) said, "You are the Christ, the son of the living God," Jesus immediately addressed him as Simon, son of Jonah, because God revealed a secret to him. Then Jesus did a play on words with his nickname *Kepa* (rock or stone). He told him that upon this stone—that is, upon the truth—he would build his church.

Simon's pronouncement to Jesus was the truth. The truth he spoke was firm, hard like a stone, a rock. The term "stone" or "rock" is a Semitic metaphor meaning that truth is so firm and hard that it cannot be changed or altered.

---

[4]"Son of the living God" is a messianic title. "Son" means the "beloved" of the living God.

[5]*Eta*, "church," comes from the root "to celebrate, to throw a party." In this passage it refers to the followers of Jesus forming a universal gathering.

[6]Mt. 16:16-19, Aramaic Peshitta text, Errico.

218

Part A—PETER/*KEPA*. Jesus makes a play on *kepa* (pronounced kay-pah) which was the apostle Simon's nickname. Among Eastern Semites, when an individual receives a nickname, it is because of certain characteristics that individual displays. The apostle's name was Shimon from the root *shma*, "to hear." As a proper name it means "he who hears," "one who is keen, sharp, and perceptive." Shimon was a very popular and common Semitic name. It has a religious significance. Presumably, Simon's friends or townspeople had nicknamed him "*Kepa*" because instead of being quick-witted and alert, which the name Shimon implies, he was slow in his comprehension of matters and situations. Jesus, by making a positive play on his nickname, which had negative connotations, actually encouraged his apostle. "*Kepa*" metaphorically also means "protection, shelter, support."The psalmist declared, "God is my rock"—that is, "God is my support, shelter, and protection." The Apostle Shimon had just made a powerful utterance. He had received a revelation from God and confessed it without hesitation. Simon's confession and quickness in seeing the truth about his master-teacher was heartening to Jesus, so he told him, "You are a rock (a support) and upon this rock (truth) I will build my church." Simon would also be a "rock," "strength and shelter" to the followers of Jesus after the crucifixion. He would help strengthen the brethren and help them build the gathering of followers around the messianic truth of Jesus.

Part B—*SHEOL*, HELL. The word *sheol* probably derives from the Hebrew *shalal*, "to be quiet," or from the Aramaic root *shla*, "to cease." The Semitic concept of *sheol* is that it is a place where people are quiet and inactive, where the souls of the departed abide until the resurrection day, patiently waiting for the sound of the last trumpet. *Gehenna* is the Aramaic word for "hell." When one translates the Hebrew word *sheol* as "hell" this is incorrect.

Many people believed that *sheol* was a place below the surface of the earth and beyond God's jurisdiction.[7] Jesus assured Peter that even the doors of *sheol* (grave and beyond) would not close or stop

---

[7]See Ps. 16:10.

the expansion work of Jesus' followers, teaching his gospel of the kingdom. God has power over everything and this power is everywhere. This idea does away with the thought of dualism and stresses God's omnipotence and omnipresence.

Part C—THE KEYS. In Aramaic speech, "keys" are symbolic of power and trust. When a man trusts his friend, he will give him the key to his house. Or, he may also say to his friend: "You can have the key to my home," meaning "You are a member of my family." Generally, faithful servants are entrusted with unlimited authority. One often hears a master say to his servant, "I give you the keys" meaning "I give you complete authority as overseer of my affairs." In the absence of the lord, such servants have complete control over the entire household. They can buy and sell, lend and collect debts, forgive or discipline workers, and sign and repudiate agreements. "To bind and loose" means "to enact new laws and to repeal others." It also means "to release (forgive) or not release (forgive)."

Peter was a loyal disciple of Jesus. His faith was hard like a rock. He firmly believed that Jesus was the promised one, God's Anointed. Jesus appreciated his loyalty and confession and entrusted him with unlimited power. Peter, as a spiritual father and shepherd of Jesus' flock, would now have the power to judge the people, forgive those who were worthy of forgiveness, and not to free those who did not deserve forgiveness. This power in no way was given to grant favors as earthly rulers do, nor to accept bribes and try to influence God. This power was not to be used for business or politics. By turning to God—that is, true repentance—would Peter know to grant or not grant forgiveness.[8] In reality, only God can give salvation.

The apostle Peter was empowered to make new laws for the new kingdom that would come into full play after Jesus' death. Peter now had the authority to make a new interpretation of holy Scripture and

---

[8]This concept does not mean that God withholds forgiveness but rather that the person who does an evil deed must turn to God and make reparations, if possible, to be released from the offence committed. Peter would be acting as a judge against a crime committed in the community.

to write a new covenant in the hearts of the people. This power was also granted to other disciples who remained loyal to the gospel of the kingdom of God.

CALLING PETER SATAN

But he turned, and said unto Peter, Get thee behind me, Satan: thou art an offence unto me: for thou savourest not the things that be of God, but those that be of men. Mt. 16:23.

Peter thought that when the Messiah came he would conquer all of the Gentile and pagan kingdoms. And since he believed that Jesus was the promised Messiah, he and the other apostles would sit on the vacant throne of David and reign forever. The prophetic concept of a suffering Messiah, which was first preached by Isaiah, was entirely alien to Jesus' disciples. This is the reason that Peter rebuked his master-teacher for making depressing remarks about his death. Peter did not know that the Messiah would suffer humiliation and death on the cross before he could enter into his glory and reign forever in God's kingdom.

On the other hand, Peter, like the other disciples, was interested in the overthrow of the Roman government and sudden coming of the political, Davidic kingdom. Peter was wanting his reward right then on earth. Jesus constantly taught the "kingdom of heaven," not the Davidic kingdom. But, at that time, Jesus' disciples and followers believed they would conquer the Gentile world and sit on literal thrones. Thus, Peter rebuked his master for upsetting them.

The term "Satan" comes from the Aramaic root *sata* meaning "to mislead, miss the mark, slip, slide, deviate from one's course." Peter was trying hard to persuade Jesus that he was not going to die on any cross. The apostle and all the other disciples were brought up in Judaism and were told that the Messiah would reign and live forever. Jesus turned and rebuked Peter because he had told him again and again that the prophecies must be fulfilled and that the Son of Man must die on the cross so that he may enter into his glory. It was from the cross that the Messiah's reign—the reign of love, justice, and meekness—would be established,

Peter did not realize that the high priests, the Pharisees and scribes would completely reject Jesus. Nor did he realize that his master would be condemned to death and crucified by the Romans. He had been close to his master and wanted to comfort him and was not aware that he was offending Jesus by contradicting him.

Jesus was upset at Peter. This is the reason Jesus used a sharp rebuke by calling him "Satan"—"One who misleads." This phrase is very common in Aramaic and Arabic speech. At times, a father may call his own son "Satan" without any malicious intent. (Interestingly, the term "Satan" (Arabic *shitan*) also means an ingenious man.)

HOLY ANGELS

For the Son of Man shall come in the glory of his Father with his angels; and then he shall reward every man according to his works.
Mt. 16:27.

The Aramaic word for "angel" is *malakha,* meaning "counselor, messenger, a representative of God." Angels are spirits and are God's counsel. God, being the eternal Spirit, is everywhere and so is God's counsel.

In biblical days, angels were pictured with wings to signify that God's counsel is everywhere. Wings symbolize God's omnipresence and presence of the Spirit. No matter where one seeks God's counsel, it is always present anywhere and everywhere.

Jesus was rejected, repudiated and crucified with criminals. As far as the world was concerned, he died a defeated man. But, in this saying of Jesus, he implies that his death on the cross was not the end of his mission but the beginning. The day was to come when his kingdom would be established on earth. "Kingdom" in Aramaic derives from the root *mlkh,* "to counsel." God's counsel will triumph at the end. In addition to this, people say in the Near East that when a man suffers defeat or loses his political or economic power, "he is dead." But when he succeeds, they say: "he has come back again."

How Jesus will return no one really knows. Nevertheless, God's kingdom will be fully established on earth and the ideals for which Jesus died will be accepted and practiced universally. Jesus then "will come in glory" in the hearts of believers. The truth is that Jesus had never left his followers and will ever be with his disciples in all ages and dispensations.

SHALL NOT TASTE DEATH

Verily I say unto you, There be some standing here, which shall not taste of death, till they see the Son of man coming in his kingdom.
Mt. 16:28.

"They shall not taste death" is an Aramaic saying which means "their spirits live forever." Jesus refers to those who never die; that is, they die a physical death but their names and souls live throughout the ages. "It is the spirit that quickeneth; the flesh profiteth nothing: the words that I speak unto you, they are spirit, and they are life."[9]

Aramaic speaking people often say, "He will never die." This means the person has achieved a purpose in his life and risen into the realm of the spirit. The sense of happiness and spiritual success destroys the fear of physical death. Spiritual success is truly life eternal. Failure to achieve higher things in life is a true death.

Jesus' disciples had left their homes and occupations. They had denied themselves the comforts of this world and its earthly possessions so that they could achieve life everlasting. Their spirits would live forever because they had exchanged the lesser for the greater—the material for the spiritual.

Both Moses and Elijah had overcome human limitations and had

---

[9]Jn. 6:63, K. J. V.

succeeded in achieving immortality. Although they had departed this physical life, they live securely in the hearts of their followers. The spirit of Christian martyrs and men of God has continued throughout the centuries to live and influence the lives of millions.

Some of the faithful disciples, who were standing listening to the words of Jesus, would never taste death. Their bodies, which were made of earth, would return to the earth, but their souls and their fame would live forever. Today many of these simple and unlearned disciples of Jesus live in the hearts of men and women throughout the world. Those disciples had preached to small groups of people, but since their deaths, their teachings have reached millions and their words are handed down from one generation to another. When they were living, they were hated and despised but later were loved and favored. Their names are inscribed in the gospel message of hope. These simple men surpass the fame of king David, Solomon, and other kings and princes of Israel and Judah.

CHAPTER 17

THE VISION OF THE TRANSFIGURATION

And Jesus came and touched them, and said, Arise, and be not afraid. And when they had lifted up their eyes, they saw no man, save Jesus only. And as they came down from the mountain, Jesus charged them, saying, Tell the vision to no man, until the Son of man be risen again from the dead. Mt. 17:7-9.

On the top of a mountain, Jesus was transfigured before the eyes of Peter, Jacob (James), and John. They also saw Moses and Elijah talking to him. This vision revealed to them that both Moses and Elijah, the two great Hebrew prophets, were in one accord with Jesus. If they had not been in agreement with Jesus' mission, they would not have appeared and stood by him.

The disciples also heard a voice out of a cloud saying: "This is my beloved son, in whom I am well pleased. Listen to him." Now the disciples believed what their master-teacher had told them about his coming judgment, condemnation, and suffering on the cross. The Lord God had revealed this secret to them. But the disciples became afraid when they heard the heavenly voice. The news of their master's death was a great shock to them. They were afraid that the death of their leader would end his mission. They would be left bereaved and helpless. As far as they were concerned, the death of their prophet-teacher meant only one thing—the end of his mission. They could not see anything beyond death, nor could they see victory after the cross.

These simple men, like other Jews, had not understood the prophecies concerning the Messiah, his rejection, and death. Now they were to keep it a secret because no one would believe it if they told them. Some of the disciples and followers of Jesus had already left. They could not see how a dead Messiah/Christ could save Israel.

EPILEPSY, FIRE AND WATER

Lord, have mercy on my son: for he is lunatick, and sore vexed: or ofttimes he falleth into the fire, and oft into the water. Mt. 17:15.

Part A—FIRE. Epilepsy is quite prevalent in the Near East and its victims are exposed to unfortunate accidents by fire or water. When this epileptic boy had his seizures, he would fall into the fireplace. Such accidents were very common because Eastern homes contained one or several ovens dug in the floor for the cooking of food and the baking of bread. The ovens were often left uncovered and sometimes members of the household, as well as strangers, would fall into them and would usually sustain bad burns. This is what happened to the epileptic boy in his own house.

Part B—WATER. There are some towns that are situated near valleys, where brooks, streams, and small rivers run through them. In the springtime, water usually overflows and crossings become dangerous. Most towns do not have bridges. People cross the rivers by wading in the water. Stones are placed at some points in the streams so that people can step from one stone to the other. Women and children often fall and are carried along by the current. Parents are in constant fear of the water for their children. At times, epileptic children fall in the water while crossing and drown. Friends and neighbors usually help the feeble and aged cross the streams.[1]

PRAYER AND FASTING HEAL

Then came the disciples to Jesus apart, and said, Why could not we cast him out? And Jesus said unto them, Because of your unbelief: for verily I say unto you, If ye have faith as a grain of mustard seed, ye shall say unto this mountain, Remove hence to yonder place; and it shall remove; and nothing shall be impossible unto you. Howbeit this kind goeth not out but by prayer and fasting. Mt. 17:19-21.

---

[1]See Mk. 9:22.

226

Faith, fasting and prayer can perform any miracle or wonder. But faith must be absolute to work. A healer must believe with all his heart and mind. Then a little faith, like a grain of mustard seed, will heal the sick and restore the insane. A mustard seed is a very small seed, but it is potent. Faith is the substance of all things that have come to pass. Without faith no one would move or do anything.

Fasting helps the spirit to transcend physical energies and raises our spiritual understanding. While a man fasts, his physical power diminishes, but his spiritual power increases. To perform such a miracle as "casting out the devil" (healing epilepsy), one needs tremendous spiritual strength and a strong faith in God, who is the creator of health and who has power over any illness (demon).

Jesus' disciples were just students. They were not sure of their powers and, therefore, had some fear about their ability to heal. These novices had always relied on Jesus when they were confronted with strange and difficult diseases.

JESUS PAID HEAD TAX

And when they were come to Capernaum, they that received tribute money came to Peter, and said, Doth not your master pay tribute?
Mt. 17:24.

The Aramaic text reads: "Would not your master give his two coins?" Peter replied "Yes." The reference was to a head tax that every male had to pay. It consisted of two coins of silver, and no one was exempt from this levy. The only ones who were probably exempt from paying this tax were the high priest and a few privileged Jewish officials who were in the service of Rome. Usually people are taxed in their homes. When people are traveling, the tax collector has no authority to collect taxes from them. Therefore, many people go to other towns to escape making payment. Because the government has no birth certificates or papers to identity people, the tax collectors' work becomes difficult and expensive.

It seems that the tax collectors were having a hard time finding Jesus and his disciples in their native towns because they were constantly traveling. On this occasion the tax collectors encountered them in Capernaum and took advantage of the situation, trying to collect the tax. Jesus could have deferred payment on the grounds that he was traveling. He could have told them to see him when he returns to Nazareth, his home town. But, he knew this would cause them delay and annoyance, so Jesus told Peter to make the payment.[2]

TAXES

He saith, Yes. And when he was come into the house, Jesus prevented him saying, What thinkest thou, Simon? Of whom do the kings of the earth take custom or tribute? Of their own children, or of strangers? Peter said unto him, Of strangers. Jesus said unto him, Then are the children free. Mt. 17:25-26.

In these countries taxes are collected from workers, strangers in the land, and the poor. Kings, princes, and the noble and rich are exempt from taxes. This exemption also applies to their sons and peers. It would be an embarrassing situation for a tax collector to call on a rich man and ask him to pay taxes. For centuries these men have been looked upon as the nobles and princes of the realm and, therefore, not subject to the ordinances and laws of the land. Some of these men are even allowed to collect taxes from the people for themselves and to conscript workers for their fields without pay. This practice still continues in many areas of the Near East today and is the cause for revolt against the rich.

Jesus knew the customs and manners of the land and, therefore, was willing to comply with them so that he and his disciples would not offend the officials.

---

[2]See Mk. 12:14.

TAX MONEY SUPPLIED

Notwithstanding, lest we should offend them, go thou to the sea, and cast an hook, and take up the fish that first cometh up; and when thou hast opened his mouth, thou shalt find a piece of money; that take, and give unto them for me and thee. Mt. 17:27.

Jesus had to pay taxes like other citizens of the kingdoms of this world. To Peter and other Jews, it was unthinkable that the Messiah, the King of Israel, should pay head tax to a foreign ruler who was oppressing the people. There were times when Jesus and his disciples were without money, and on some occasions, even without food and lodging. But Jesus, with his absolute faith in God, knew that God would always meet their needs and provide their tax money.

This episode, however, expresses another puzzling Aramaic figurative saying that cannot be easily translated into other languages. "You will find a shekel in the mouth of a fish" means "you will quickly catch a fish and sell it for a shekel." Near Easterners often say: "There are ten dollars in the horn of my ox," meaning "my ox can be sold for ten dollars." They also say: "There is a dollar in each one of my lambs." This means each lamb can be sold for a dollar. Also, when things are easily and unexpectedly acquired, they say: "I have found the money."

The tax collectors demanded that Jesus and Peter pay their head taxes. They had no money, so Jesus directed Peter to the source of supply. In this land, taxes may be paid in kind. Animals, grain, cheese, butter, fish, and other products are exchanged in the market places and are accepted for taxes. Peter was a fisherman by trade. Jesus assured him that the first catch would be worth a shekel. This was sufficient to meet the taxes for both of them. The fish was either sold to someone else or given to the tax collector.

Families who cannot pay in cash provide food and lodging for tax collectors as payment. As taxes are often levied by local officials without the knowledge of the central government, tax collectors are glad to accept whatever they can exact from the people.

The miracle, in this instance, is that Peter, when divinely directed by his master, caught a large fish which was enough to pay the taxes. No doubt, Peter was surprised when he caught the fish so quickly. At times, it takes the entire day to catch a single fish in the Lake of Galilee. But Jesus, through his inner guidance, told Peter where to catch the fish.

Regardless, the miracle is that the tax money was supplied and the tax collectors were not offended. This comment on the Aramaic figurative speech does not in the least depreciate the efficacious power of Jesus, who healed the sick, cleansed the lepers, raised the dead and performed great works for the benefit of others.

CHAPTER 18

LIKE LITTLE CHILDREN

And Jesus called a little child unto him, and set him in the midst of them, And said, Verily I say unto you, Except ye be converted, and become as little children, ye shall not enter into the kingdom of heaven. Mt. 18:2-3.

Little children are free from many habits that adults have acquired. They are natural and trustful because they know nothing about deception and diplomacy. They usually say what they mean and believe what they hear. There is no fear and worry about the future. Children know that their parents will take care of them and will not fail to meet their daily needs no matter how poor they are. This is the trust a child has in loving parents. A child also knows nothing about his race, religion, and the importance of his family. The mind of a child is like film that will take any image to which it is exposed.

People are to trust their heavenly Father like little children trust their parents. They must do away with greed and selfishness because God, as a father, will never fail to provide for their needs. They must trust God just as a little child trusts its mother and never questions her wisdom.

A true convert to God's kingdom has to surrender everything that he has learned in exchange for the truth that he has now accepted, like the merchant who had found the precious pearl of great price and sold everything he had so that he could purchase the pearl. A new convert has to become like a child in order to learn the new teachings. People who are set in their ways are difficult to teach and to change. Most of them are satisfied with what they know. They also believe it is too late to learn a new teaching. However, children are humble and ready to respond to their relatives, as well as to strangers. They have faith in everything and they know no evil.

OFFENCES

Woe unto the world because of offences! For it must needs be that offences come; but woe to that man by whom the offence cometh!. . . . Take heed that ye despise not one of these little ones; for I say unto you, that in heaven their angels do always behold the face of my Father which is in heaven. Mt. 18:7,10.

Offences and persecutions are bound to come because of people's behavior. But some people bring offences on themselves; therefore, as offenders, they suffer more. In biblical lands children are not treated as tenderly as they are in the West. And when children draw near holy or prominent men, they are rebuked and chased away. At times, children do approach their elders to listen and to learn, but their presence at such meetings is usually not welcome.

Near Eastern Semites for many centuries have believed, and still do believe, in guardian angels. They say that everyone—man, woman and child—has a guardian angel, who protects and warns him or her of danger. The guardian angel also warns the individual when he or she is inclined to do evil. People also believe that the guardian sits on one's right shoulder, and the devil on the left. The term "angel" means "God's counsel."

Angels ministered to Jesus while he was experiencing his temptation in the wilderness. In the Hebrew Bible, we read that God's angels appeared to Jacob, Gideon, Samson's parents, and many others. In the New Testament they appeared to Mary, Joseph, and to the apostles. God's counsel is always with those who seek to do his will.

Jesus loved little children and wanted to have them seated close to him, listening to his words. He knew they were pure in their minds. One must be like a child, innocent and harmless, in order to enter (participate) in God's kingdom. Interestingly, most prominent Near Eastern men would have shunned these little ones, but Jesus took them in his arms as the true examples of God's children.

LOST SHEEP

How think ye? If a man have an hundred sheep, and one of them be gone astray, doth he not leave the ninety and nine, and goeth into the mountains, and seeketh that which is gone astray? And if so be that he find it, verily I say unto you, he rejoiceth more of that sheep, than of the ninety and nine which went not astray. Even so it is not the will of your Father which is in heaven, that one of these little ones should perish. Mt. 18:12-14.

A good shepherd is constantly conscious of his reputation, so when one sheep has gone astray from his flock, he feels that all his sheep are lost. Therefore, he leaves the flock, his duty at the camp, and begins searching for the lost sheep. He will not rest until he finds that sheep. God is like a good shepherd, supplying all the needs of the flock, binding their wounds, and searching for those who have gone astray.

God does not reject anyone but constantly seeks those who have lost their way and rejoices when they are found. So it is that God, as a father, always cares for his children. A parent's heart and mind will also be with the child who has gone astray and is more than happy when the errant child returns.

RECONCILE WITH YOUR BROTHER

Moreover if thy brother shall trespass against thee, go and tell him his fault between thee and him alone: if he shall hear thee, thou hast gained thy brother. But if he will not hear thee, then take with thee one or two more, that in the mouth of two or three witnesses every word may be established. And if he shall neglect to hear them, tell it unto the church: but if he neglect to hear the church, let him be unto thee as an heathen man and a publican. Mt. 18:15-17.

Those who had entered the kingdom—that is, were participating in the new way of life—were to behave differently as citizens of God's kingdom. They were to be examples to everyone in the community.

Therefore, all grievances and offenses were to be settled among themselves. They were to shun the usual court systems of unbelievers because earthly judges do not conform to the ways of God's kingdom.

The Aramaic text of verse 17 reads "tell it to the congregation" instead of "tell it to the church" as rendered in the King James Version. The term "church" was a later usage; the followers of Jesus did not know this term in the early stages of the movement. *Eta* in Aramaic means "group, assembly, gathering, congregation" that was composed of elders and town counselors who generally arbitrate disputes, settle quarrels, and pass judgment on legal matters.

Nomads, as well as inhabitants in small country places, are governed by a group of elders selected from among themselves. These elders are also members of the chief's cabinet who advise on tribal matters. They sit in judgment and pronounce sentences of punishment.

In the wilderness, Moses chose a group of elders to act as judges, but important cases were submitted to him as chief justice.[1] This custom still prevails in areas of the Near East where the Patriarch acts as chief justice, and the bishops and ministers as judges. Smaller cases are arbitrated by lay members. The assembly was the court, empowered to judge the followers of Jesus, to execute justice, to extend mercy and forgiveness, and to convict those who refused to accept its decisions.[2]

WORTHY AND DESERVING

Again I say unto you, That if two of you shall agree on earth as touching any thing that they shall ask, it shall be done for them of my father which is in heaven. Mt. 18:19.

---

[1] See Ex. 19:25; Deut. 22:18.

[2] Many New Testament scholars agree that these verses were composed at a later date when a community of believers was formed. The dictates put on the lips of Jesus were relevant to that time when his followers had to have methods of dealing with errant actions. Jesus' followers used the ancient methods of solving these challenges and problems.

The Aramaic word *nishtwon* means "worthy of" or "deserving" and not "when two of you *shall agree* on anything," as translated in the King James Version. It means the prayer of a group of people or a congregation will be granted if two among them are worthy. If no one is deserving, the request will not be granted.

When Abraham appealed to God on behalf of the people of Sodom and Gomorrah, God told him that if there were ten men who were righteous in those cities, he would spare them. According to the biblical writer, not even one was found, so fire destroyed those cities.

God grants requests to those who ask if they are worthy of what they ask. The term "worthy" or "deserving" refers to those who have the ability to be responsible for the thing they are requesting. As an example, no father would give a child something dangerous if he knew the child could not handle it or care for whatever is being requested.

When people are working in the interest of God's kingdom, they deserve God's blessings. One has to represent a beneficial cause and pray for all God's children so that one may receive God's grace and the things for which one prays. God is always present with those who meet together representing the principles of the kingdom.

IN HIS NAME

For when two or three are gathered together in my name, there am I in the midst of them. Mt. 18:20.

Religion is the chief topic of conversation in the Near East. Whenever two or three people gather together or when two Easterners meet, the first question is: "What is your religion?" Politics have little or no hold on the life of the people. Religious discussions are carried on, not so much because the people are very religious, but because that is the liveliest and most popular topic. During these discussions, the names of God and Jesus are constantly repeated and so they serve as a source of instruction to common and illiterate folk who will sit down and listen. At times, a friendly discussion may end in a heated argument, possibly followed by quarrels and injuries.

Truth always prevails. During and after these debates men and women may be converted. Interestingly, in the early centuries, conversions were chiefly made through debates and not through universities, schools, and churches. Missionaries stood on street corners and spoke about Jesus and his works. Sometimes they were welcome, and as a result of their talks and discussions, many were won to the Christ message. On other occasions, violence interrupted the meetings and the missionaries were thrown into prison. During the trials even judges and governors were given the opportunity to listen to Jesus' gospel of the kingdom.

SEVENTY TIMES SEVEN

Jesus saith unto them, I say not unto thee, Until seven times: but, Until seventy times seven. Mt. 18:22.

In God's kingdom, forgiveness is not limited to seven times but to seventy times seven. The Aramaic text reads: "I do not say to you up to seven times but up to seventy times seventy, seven times." This means an indefinite number of times. God's mercies and love towards people have no limit. God is above time and space. God's love and forgiveness, like the warm rays of the sun, are constantly pouring out into the world. Human beings are likely to trespass against their neighbors many times. But, God's compassion and benevolence are infinite and abundant. As adherents to the kingdom, his disciples were to practice forgiveness, revealing God's nature and power in the community of the human family.

PARABLE OF THE UNFORGIVING SERVANT

Therefore is the kingdom of heaven likened unto a certain King, which would take account of his servants. And when he had begun to reckon, one was brought unto him, which owed him ten thousand talents. But forasmuch as he had not to pay, his lord commanded him to be sold, and his wife and children, and all that he had, and payment to be made. . . Then his lord, after that he had called him, said unto him O thou wicked servant, I forgave thee all that debt, because thou desiredst me: Shouldest not thou also have had compassion on thy fellowservant, even as I had pity on thee? And his lord was wroth, and delivered him to the tormentors, till he should pay all that was due unto him. So likewise shall my heavenly Father do also unto you, if ye from your hearts forgive not every one his brother their trespasses. Mt. 18:23-25, 32-35.

God is a loving, forgiving parent, full of mercy and compassion. According to Jesus, God lets his rain fall on the just and the unjust and lets his sun shine on the good and the bad. His understanding of God was infinite. Jesus knew that God does not withhold forgiveness nor forgive and then take it back.

Jesus just finished teaching that the practice of forgiveness has no limited number; it is indefinite. Thus, it is more than likely that the last verse of this parable (v. 35) was a scribe's addition and interpretation in Matthew's gospel. Jesus would not have interpreted his parable as: "So likewise shall my heavenly Father do also unto you, if ye from your hearts forgive not every one his brother their trespasses." The theme of the parable is about forgiving and the consequences that result from others for not forgiving. God is not the topic or theme of this parable. The point is that forgiveness must be extended everywhere and to everyone. When one jeopardizes forgiveness, a disagreeable payment is exacted, not by God but by other human beings.

The servant who, at first, had begged for clemency from his lord and had asked that his debt be canceled, received pardon from his most generous master. But, when it came time for this servant to forgive someone else, he did not practice forgiveness. Other household servants saw this and wanted justice. Therefore, the master recalled his unforgiving servant and punished him. What we are to understand is that those whose hearts are unforgiving bring on their own painful misery and distressing situations. Human beings invite their own agony. God is there to relieve human suffering, consoling and aiding people to overcome wrongful and harmful actions.

CHAPTER 19

LEAVING PARENTS

And said, For this cause shall a man leave father and mother, and shall cleave to his wife: and they twain shall be one flesh? Mt. 19:5.

The Aramaic word *nishboq* means "separate." A man separates from his father and his mother to live with his wife. Although disputes and quarrels happen quite often in Near Eastern families, family unity is mostly maintained. Seldom do sons leave or even think of leaving parents. Even when they are married and have grown children, they continue to live with them. Death alone parts a man from his father and mother.

There are, however, some exceptions to this rule. If the family relations become too strained, some sons put their wives away and remain with their parents. Others leave their parents and go with their wives. In this case, the family property is divided between the son and his father. To leave father and mother may mean to live apart but under the same roof, and it may also mean to leave the family house and live in another house in the same town. To leave does not mean to sever relationships. After the separation of households, father and son work together, mother-in-law and daughter-in-law visit, and food is sent from one family to the other.

Jesus recognized these strong family ties but pointed out how much better it was for a man to separate from his parents than to leave or divorce his wife. Marriage is sacred. In the story of creation, God created both male and female in his own image and likeness. Therefore, being God's image and likeness, there is no partiality between a man and his wife. They are one and equal. Neither of them can multiply without the other. A man's wife is closer to him than his father and his mother. The marriage union makes them one body.

Moses' ordinance allowing divorce was brought about because of men's hardness of heart. This ordinance made divorce easy for men and difficult and harsh for women. It reduced the status of women from God's image into a worldly possession. Often, men purchased women like one would purchase sheep and cattle.

GROUNDS FOR DIVORCE

And I say unto you, Whosoever shall put away his wife, except it be for fornication, and shall marry another, committeth adultery: and whoso marrieth her which is put away doth commit adultery. Mt. 19:9

The only grounds for desertion and divorce is adultery, for when a husband or a wife commits adultery they break the bond which had united them. Therefore, on the grounds of adultery, a man can divorce his wife and give her divorce papers and marry another. Likewise a woman can divorce her husband on the same grounds and receive divorce papers. She is then free to marry another man. But any man who divorces his wife or puts her away for no cause, makes her commit adultery by marrying another man. And the one who marries her commits adultery because she was deserted without a cause—that is, her marriage bond was not broken.

DIVORCING EUNUCHS

But he said unto them, All men cannot receive this saying, save they to whom it is given. For there are some eunuchs, which were so born from their mother's womb: and there are some eunuchs, which were made eunuchs of men: and there be eunuchs, which have made themselves eunuchs for the kingdom of heaven's sake. He that is able to receive it, let him receive it. Mt. 19:11-12.

Jesus was not opposed to legal divorce, but he was against those who desert their wives without any cause. He was also against lax enforcement of the laws on divorce. Religious authorities seldom upheld them.

Jesus also upbraided those men who deserted their wives and did not give them divorce papers according to the law of Moses. Many Jews, like other Eastern Semitic people, took their marriage covenants very lightly. When they were angry with their wives or did not love them, they deserted them without even bothering to give them proper papers. According to Jesus, adultery was the only grounds for divorce. As the result of the lax enforcement of this law, many innocent women suffered unjustly and were forced to commit adultery when they married other men. These women were still legally married because they had not received divorce papers from their former husbands.

Jesus' disciples thought that their teacher's admonition relative to divorce was too harsh and, therefore, it made compliance difficult. They had been brought up to think that women were inferior. This notion and custom was universal at that time, and still prevails in many lands today.

Jesus' saying does not apply to every man, but only to those who are eunuchs. They are not fit to marry. In Matthew 19:7, he points out that there are cases where a woman can divorce her husband on the grounds of sexual inability. Sometimes men were made eunuchs through force. The Church of the East grants divorce on such grounds. Dr. Lamsa was at one time appointed to examine such cases as these and had to report the findings to the Church authorities.

There are also some women who are not sexually capable of fulfilling the conjugal rights of marriage. In such cases both men and women can apply for divorce.[1]

CHILDREN

Then were there brought unto him little children, that he should put his hands on them, and pray: and the disciples rebuked them. Mt. 19:13.

---

[1]See Mt. 5:32.

240

Usually, little children are loved and cared for in Europe and in the United States. Near Easterners treat children differently than Westerners. Although Eastern men and women love their children, especially sons, at times they discipline them too severely. Children do not have the type of training concerning good manners and cleanliness that children receive in the United States. They are somewhat neglected and frequently form bad habits as they grow. It is common to see children at home and on the streets with unwashed faces and dirty clothes.

When the people entertain an honorable guest, they sweep the house clean before the guest arrives. Then, they send the children and beggars outside with the instructions not to return until the banquet is over. Parents who are kind and gentle with their children send them to a neighbor's home. The host's and the guest's servants keep steady vigilance to prevent undue noises and the entrance of people with soiled clothes and children with dirty faces. When children are permitted to be present, their acts often cause embarrassment and annoyance to the guests. Children not only listen to the conversation but also ask foolish questions and make uncalled for remarks. They would not hesitate to ask the guest what girl he desired to marry if they thought the gathering was for a marriage arrangement. At such times, women sit apart in one corner of the house, listening to the conversation and occasionally casting a secret glance at the honorable guest and those sitting around him.

The custom is different when a holy man visits a town and is entertained. Then, every man seizes the opportunity to present his boys that he may lay hands on them, bless them and protect them from disease. Children know he is a holy man and keep quiet in his presence. In the eyes of Jesus' disciples, Jesus was like a king rather than a prophet. Until the time of his death, they were patiently waiting for him to restore the lost Davidic kingdom. This is the reason they rebuked the children and the people who brought them to Jesus. To these simple men and women who brought the children, Jesus was a a man of God. They did not consider him a political ruler although they, too, had expected the arrival of God's kingdom on earth.

Jesus told his disciples to allow the little boys to come because to such as these was the kingdom of God revealed. These boys were open-minded, free from dogmatic traditions, and did not harbor hatred for anyone. Children know nothing about nobility, rank, or titles. To them all men are just men and not one of them is greater or more important than their own parents. These children knew nothing of political kingdoms or the difference between the Roman Empire and the kingdom of David. In God's kingdom there are no ranks, men of nobility, nor small men, but all are equal in God's eyes because they are all his children. Only men and women who, like children, were free from religious and political prejudices could understand God's presence and kingdom. Jesus also wanted his disciples to realize that children were also future recruits of his kingdom.

WONDERFUL TEACHER

And he said unto him, Why callest thou me good? there is none good but one, that is, God: but if thou wilt enter into life, keep the commandments. Mt. 19:17.

Tawa in Aramaic is an adjective meaning "good, wonderful, well, skilled and righteous." In this case it means "wonderful." When Semites marvel at someone extraordinary, they will call the actor or performer "wonderful." The term *tawa* refers to personal occupation as well as character. They call a skilled shepherd *raya tawa*, and an unskilled shepherd *raya beesha*. A shepherd could possibly be a crook or a murderer but he still will be called a *raya tawa* (good shepherd) because he understands his sheep and knows how to take care of them. When an owner sells an article or animal, he will say *"tawa eleh"* meaning "it is wonderful or good."

This man had called Jesus *malpana tawa*, wonderful or skilled teacher, referring to his preaching and style of teaching. He did this out of appreciation for Jesus. Everyone was astonished at Jesus' eloquent utterances and poetic parables. Even his enemies wondered at this remarkable Nazarene preacher. Jesus was always reluctant to accept compliments and his reply was that "*malpana tawa*" was appropriate only to God, the source of all power and goodness. Jesus' humility and sincerity made him decline any title. He declared that only the Father knew all things. In these lands, holy men often decline honors. Some of them sincerely speak of themselves as sinners and unworthy servants of their Lord. But the more they decline honors and praises, the more people honor them and trust them. (See Luke 10:25.)

TRUE LOYALTY AND SHARING

Jesus said unto him, If thou wilt be perfect, go and sell that thou hast, and give to the poor, and thou shalt have treasure in heaven: and come and follow me. Mt. 19:21.

Obeying the commandments is not enough to help one enter God's kingdom and inherit eternal life. One may not kill simply because of the fear of retaliation. One may not steal, bear false witness, or take false oaths because of the fear of punishment for breaking these commandments. Honoring one's father and mother is not a favor or an act of mercy; it is one's duty.

Those who wish to be mature (perfect), participate in God's kingdom and have eternal life must do something more than just keep the ten commandments. They must work for the kingdom of God, and to do this effectively, they ought to divest themselves of the material interests of this world. In other words, the men who were wanting to learn from Jesus had to sell their sheep and cattle so they could be free to follow him. Surely wealth is a blessing and the rich are God's stewards, administering their goods to God's children. But no one can take care of earthly possessions such as land, sheep, and cattle, and at the same time work full time in God's kingdom, especially in those days.

"Sell everything and give to the poor" must not be understood literally, nor does it apply to all who have wealth. These words were addressed to rich men who wanted to do good things so that they might enter into life eternal. This saying does not mean that everybody should sell all their possessions and give them to the poor. This would be sheer folly. Jesus was not making this a general command. When Elisha followed Elijah, he sacrificed his oxen and destroyed his plough because he could not attend to farming and become a great prophet as he did.[2]

Religious men are supported by what they receive as tithes from their followers. Some of these men are in charge of shrines and receive large incomes which they distribute to the poor. There are no charitable societies in the Near East; the poor are cared for by their relatives and friends, and at times, by pious men. However, many of the priests insist that the gifts should be made to the churches and shrines, rather than to the poor. When the income at these places increased, there was the outcry that the poor were neglected. And some of the prophets went so far as to declare that God did not want sacrificial offerings of animals, but that justice should be done.

This rich young man who had come to Jesus was thinking of becoming an active religious man and had been trained to give to the Temple. Jesus knew where such money went and had seen the luxuries of the high priests. This is the reason he instructed the young man to give his wealth to the poor and not to the temple. Jesus did not mean that all wealth should be given to the poor. Wealth, to work properly, must be shared and circulated and not just accumulated.

THE WICKED RICH

Then said Jesus unto his disciples, Verily I say unto you, That a rich man shall hardly enter into the kingdom of heaven. Mt. 19:23.

The greedy and wicked rich are hated and despised in the Near

---

[2]See 1 Kings 19:21.

East. They are the targets of preachers, prophets, and politicians and the topic of critical discussions among the poor and oppressed. Usually these types of rich men do not acquire their wealth through hard work and honest business. They amass their wealth by unjust means, such as bribery, extortion, and confiscation.

Strange as it may seem, when a man acquires riches, government officials soon promote him. His property becomes exempt from taxation, they grant him certain privileges and often appoint him to collect taxes for them on a profit basis. This practice results in unjust exactions, and the oppression creates discontent and bitterness among the people. Also, when government officials or other wealthy men visit a town, the rich man who lives in the town will entertain them. Of course, this is done at the people's expense, whose sheep and cattle are ruthlessly confiscated and killed by the wealthy to feed the guests. Visitors are also presented with gifts of money, rugs, or other valuable articles that are usually taken by force from the people. The parable that the prophet Nathan related to king David illustrates the greed of these types of rich men.[3]

In times of depression and famine, rich men collect sheep and wheat from their subjects so that their wealth might not diminish and, thereby, their power and prestige be lost. People often say: "God blesses rich men." But many men do not wait for God to bless them; they bless themselves through injustice. These are the kind of men whom Jesus censured, not the righteous rich whom God truly prospers. These unprincipled rich were like Ahab whom Elijah condemned because he had confiscated Naboth's vineyard.[4]

Other types of rich men exist who acquire wealth and property during prosperous years and distribute to the poor in the lean years. They accumulate immense wealth but hold it in trust for the people. Such wealthy men live on the level of the people and in times of famine are ready to share everything and even die with their people who love and respect them. Jesus had friends among the rich like

---

[3]See 2 Sam. 12:1-4 and Lk. 16:19.
[4]See 1 Kings 21:1-20.

Joseph of Arimathea (Ramtha), Zacchaeus and many others. It was not wealth Jesus condemned but the methods of its acquisition and the practice of hoarding riches. Wealth will accumulate in the hands of some people, but they must remember they are God's stewards and should use their wealth for good purposes.

THE NEEDLE AND THE ROPE

And again I say unto you, It is easier for a camel to go through the eye of a needle, than for a rich man to enter into the kingdom of God. Mt. 19:24.

Gamla is the Aramaic word for "camel, rope, beam." One determines the exact meaning of the word by its context. If the word riding or burden appears in the sentence with *gamla* then it means a camel. But when the eye of a needle appears in the phrase then *gamla* more correctly means a rope. There is no connection anywhere in Aramaic speech or literature between camel and needle, but there is a definite connection between rope and needle.

Women, when purchasing thread, often say "it is a rope, I cannot use it," meaning the thread is too thick. Also, there are ropes in every home that the people use to tie up burdens on the backs of men and animals. When the ropes are not in use, they hang on the wall or lay in a corner of the house.

This discussion about rich men may have taken place in a house. Jesus could have pointed to one of the ropes to illustrate what he was saying about the greed of some rich men. "It is easier for a rope to pass through the eye of a needle than it is for a rich man to enter the kingdom of God." There are different kinds of needles in use in the Near East: the tiny needle for fine embroidery, the common needle for sewing, and the very large needle about five or seven inches long, which working men often carry fastened to their garments or attached to the rope. A good sized cord could easily be passed through this needle. It is used primarily for sewing large bags, rugs, and tents woven of goat's hair.

Some biblical authorities suggest that when Jesus referred to the "needle's eye," he meant a little gate in the wall. As there is no such gate in any Near Eastern city called "the needle's eye" where camels have to bend down to pass through, this interpretation is incorrect. Some of the ancient walled cities still remain the same as in the days of yore. They have several large entrances at various parts of the wall. These are the gates through which men, camels, caravans, and animals enter and leave the city. They are the only possible place a camel could pass through.

The word *gamla* is also used in Matthew 23:24, but here it means camel because Jesus was talking about *baqa*, "gnat," and contrasting it with a camel. In this case, both objects were alive and the hyperbole was justified. The use of camel in the earlier reference does not make any sense as a hyperbole. Everyone in the Near East knows that a camel could never pass through a needle's eye but that a rope might at least be forced through a very large needle.

A rope can easily be threaded through the eye of a large wooden needle used for making rugs and tents. But, some parts of the rope would fray and other parts would pass through the needle. Rich men can enter God's kingdom, providing they place God first and share the wealth with others. Rich men are God's trustees. They are entrusted with wealth to be used for the good of all God's children. For one man has been entrusted with wisdom, another with money, another with power to heal the sick, and others with different gifts. They are all God's stewards distributing the abundance of God to everyone.

Such expressions as rope and needle, camel and gnat, are common in Semitic usage, but the comparison or contrast must have some connection, or the illustration would be meaningless. The repetition of some Aramaic words in widely differing contexts is largely due to a limited vocabulary. Aramaic is an ancient language and the gospels were written at a time when language did not require an extensive vocabulary and new ideas were not prevalent.

THE FIRST SHALL BE LAST

But many that are first shall be last; and the last shall be first.
Mt. 19:30.

Jesus' gospel of the kingdom was all-inclusive. He had taught his disciples that God is no respecter of persons and that they must be totally inclusive, treating everyone the same. "If, then, you love only those who love you, what payment do you have? Look, are not they, the tax collectors, also doing the same? And if you greet your brothers only what more are you doing? Are not they, the tax collectors, also doing the same? Therefore, be inclusive even as your Father who is in heaven is inclusive."[5]

Israelites were called first to work and participate in God's kingdom, the great vineyard of God. But, Israel as a whole did not recognize that the kingdom was dawning upon the nation. So the Galileans, other Semitic peoples, and Gentiles began to enter into the kingdom and enjoy its fruits. Israel was to be first and the Gentiles last, but it became reversed.

Jesus was not excluding anyone. People by their own choice put themselves as either first or last. Many Galileans, Samaritans, and Gentiles who were, at that time, looked upon as outsiders, would be first to enter (participate in) the kingdom. But those who were called first and were the heirs of the kingdom would be last. It is not the length of time that qualifies one to enter the kingdom but sincerity and the willingness to serve God first. On another occasion, the chief priests and elders approached Jesus and questioned his authority. After some discourse and a parable Jesus told them: "Verily I say unto you, That the publicans, and the harlots go into the kingdom of God before you."[6] Again, Jesus was not excluding the priests and elders; they put themselves last because they thought they knew and understood God's kingdom and authority.

---

[5]Mt.5:46-48, Aramaic Peshitta text, Errico.
[6] Mt. 21:31, K.J.V.

CHAPTER 20

PARABLE: A MASTER WENT OUT EARLY

For the Kingdom of heaven is like unto a man that is an householder, which went out early in the morning to hire labourers into his vineyard . . . . Is it not lawful for me to do what I will with mine own? Is thine eye evil, because I am good? Mt. 20:1, 15.

The owner of the vineyard paid the laborers whom he had hired last the same wages as those whom he had hired first, simply because it was not the laborers' fault that they were not hired earlier. These men had risen early and had been waiting in the market place, but no one had hired them.

The kind and generous owner of the vineyard, knowing that it was not their fault that they had not been hired to work, decided to pay them the same wages as those whom he had hired early that morning. Although the early workers, the first ones, had worked many hours and suffered the heat of the day, they received the identical wages as those of the last hour.

Part A—WAGES FOR LABORERS. "And when he had agreed with the laborers for a penny a day, he sent them into his vineyard."[1] Dinara was the smallest monetary unit. The government of Iraq still uses dinara, but it has a greater value today. A dinara was equal to about a penny. Some commentators, unfamiliar with labor conditions in the Near East, place a larger value on this piece of money.

The owner of the vineyard paid the laborers a dinara each. This may sound ridiculous and unbelievable to Occidentals who are accustomed to being highly remunerated for their services. Nevertheless, in many of these countries unskilled vineyard workers are now paid only a few cents a day and in Kurdistan and some parts of Mesopotamia, servants and shepherds are still hired for a few dollars

[1]Mt. 20:2, K.J.V.

a year and their food. Before World War I, owners of vineyards hired men for less than a dollar a year and food. A *dinara* may look small in the United States where money is abundant, but in some parts of the Near East, a *dinara* can buy more than a dollar can here in the States. They do not have labor unions in these countries. Laborers work for whatever they can obtain and employers pay what they can afford. Both laborer and employer are just trying to make a living. When a laborer is very poor, his employer takes care of his family during the hard times.

Part B—JEALOUSY. "Have I no right to do what I wish with mine own? Or are you jealous because I am generous?"[2] Jealousy and envy are typical human characteristics. However, Near Easterners are usually indifferent to the possessions of foreign people, but they envy each other. Nothing hurts a man more than to see his neighbor treated with the same favor and respect as he is, especially in the matter of money and wages. Some poor men are happier without help than to see their neighbor receive the same gifts as they.

As there were no clocks and watches in many areas of these countries, there was no way to keep track of the hours. Laborers would go to work at any time they awakened and would leave at sunset. Wages were so small that most field and vineyard owners disregarded the time worked and paid the workers equally, not because they were lenient toward those who had been hired late, but because no one kept time records. These owners knew a laborer depended on the small wages he earned to support his family. This impartiality and generosity of payment often caused dissension, but it was soon forgotten.

Matthew interpreted the parable allegorically when he added the last line about the first being last and the last becoming first. The owner of the vineyard is God and the vineyard is the kingdom of heaven. The early laborers represent Israelites, who were the first people whom God called to play the most conspicuous part in the great living drama and to work in the kingdom. Laborers of the third

---

[2]Mt. 20:15, Aramaic Peshitta text, Errico.

hour symbolize Gentile kindred of the Jews, such as Galileans, Syrians, Edomites and others. Ninth hour laborers were Arabians, Assyrians, and other Semitic peoples. Finally, the eleventh hour workers were the Greeks, Romans, and other European peoples, who were the last to receive God's light through the new gospel. But many who were last became first and all received the same wages.

In God's kingdom social justice and wages are different from human justice and expectations. The message is equality. This parable supplies the answer to the perplexing questions of neo-platonic teaching, the teaching of Socrates, and communism. Jesus upheld free enterprise. The owner of the vineyard had the right to pay the workers whatever he wished. All agreements were made at the beginning before the laborers started their work. In the kingdom the real reward will be according to the services that each person renders regardless of race, color, or the time he began. We must keep in mind that this is a parable that points to God's kingdom. We must not understand it literally.

CUP OF DEATH

But Jesus answered and said, Ye know not what ye ask, Are ye able to drink of the cup that I shall drink of, and to be baptized with the baptism that I am baptized with? They say unto him, We are able. Mt. 20:22.

The mother of Jacob (James) and John was a simple and illiterate woman. She did not realize the gravity of the request she had made to Jesus. Neither the sons of Zebedee nor the rest of Jesus' disciples were cognizant of the bitter cup that their master-teacher was prepared to drink. Jesus' disciples and followers were only concerned over the division of high offices in the new kingdom. They wanted to know who would be the leading figure among them. They did not know that their lord would soon be experiencing crucifixion and that he would begin his glorious reign after his shameful death as a common criminal. They had no idea that to sit on his right hand and

251

on his left would mean to surrender temporal joys and honors and to be ready to drink of the bitter cup of death. Many of Jesus' disciples and followers, in the days to come, would shed their own blood. They would be like sheep, slain for the sake of the new gospel of the kingdom.

Part A—CUP OF POISON. The cup mentioned in this verse refers to the cup of poison that is usually handed to the guest whom the host had marked for death. The sons of Zebedee—Jacob and John—were to suffer and die for the gospel of their lord. Nevertheless, only God could grant the position of sitting on Jesus' right or left hand. Each person had to earn his own place in this kingdom. Jesus could not promise his disciples and followers high places (seats) in the kingdom. They would earn them by drinking from the cup that Jesus was to drink and by being baptized with the same baptism of death that their master was to experience. Jesus was baptized in his own blood and so were many of his apostles, disciples and followers.

Part B—MY CUP YOU SHALL DRINK. "And he saith unto them, Ye shall drink indeed of my cup, and be baptized with the baptism that I am baptized with: but to sit on my right hand and on my left, is not mine to give, but it shall be given to them for whom it is prepared of my Father."[3] "My cup you shall drink" means "the death I die, you will also die." "You will be hated, condemned and put to death because of my teaching and your loyalty to me."

When a host wants to do away with his enemy, he prepares a banquet in his honor, and then he puts poison in the special guest's cup. Kings, princes, and noblemen usually employ cup bearers who will drink of the cup first and also taste the food. Nearly all of Jesus' disciples met with violent deaths. Some met with crucifixion, others suffered death by the sword, and still others lost their lives by an executioner beheading them. They followed their master into the baptism of blood and lost their lives for the sake of a new way of life both here and hereafter.

---

[3]Mt. 20:23, K.J.V.

THE GREATEST SERVES

But Jesus called them unto him, and said, Ye know that the princes of the Gentiles exercise dominion over them, and they that are great exercise authority upon them. But it shall not be so among you: but whosoever will be great among you, let him be your minister; And whosoever will be chief among you, let him be your servant: Even as the Son of Man came not to be ministered unto, but to minister, and to give his life a ransom for many. Mt. 20:25-28.

In the systems of the material world, men fought so that they could become crowned kings and rulers or become heads of State and hold high offices. They did this not so much for the sake of giving humanity peace, justice, and security, or to lead them to a better way of life, but because they wanted to rule, collect taxes, build palaces and fortunes for themselves and their descendants. Jesus' disciples were not to be like the rulers of the world. In this new order or kingdom, a new world system was to emerge.

Jesus taught his disciples that they were to be humble, lowly, meek, and just in their behavior and relationships. The greatest among them was to reveal himself as the least; the most learned one among them was to behave as if he knew nothing. Jesus had practiced these very principles with his disciples. He was not only willing to minister and to serve, but he was ready to die so that those who came after him might live an abundant and everlasting life.

The world had been, for a very long time, in the grip of corrupt politics, unscrupulous systems of priesthood, false prophets, and ideologies that led people astray from the path of God. Jesus taught that the time had come for his disciples to learn to serve and share with one another and entrust everything to God. All honor and glory belong to God only. This kingdom had no overlords, high offices, special ranking positions. Everyone was to serve humanity and reveal a new system of living.

SON OF DAVID

And behold, two blind men sitting by the wayside, when they heard that Jesus passed by, cried out, saying, Have mercy on us. O Lord, thou son of David. Mt. 20:30.

People often used the expression "son of David" as a token of respect and admiration and not necessarily because the person was an actual son of David. It really means someone who is "David-like"; on the other hand, it could also mean a descendant of David. It depends on how the expression is used.

Near Easterners often call gallant men sons of famous kings and outstanding great men who have died centuries before. Jesus called a woman whom he had healed "daughter of Abraham," though she was born two thousand years after Abraham. What he meant was that she was a member of the faith of Abraham or one of his descendants. Mohammed called the Virgin Mary a "daughter of Aaron."

David lived about a thousand years before Jesus. The Jews expected the Messiah to come from David's lineage and to be David-like, if not greater than David. David was a great warrior so they anticipated the Messiah to fight for them, deliver them from their enemies, and establish a universal and everlasting kingdom.

Jesus never claimed to be a descendant of any king or prince. Pharisees and scribes rejected him on the grounds that he was not a descendant of David.[4] They said: "When Christ comes, we will know who he is, and he will born in Bethlehem, David's city." Apparently the Pharisees and scribes and other authorities knew nothing about Jesus' birth, nor did he defend his birth. To the contrary, Jesus quoted Psalm 110:1: "The Lord said unto my Lord, Sit thou at my right hand, until I make thine enemies thy footstool." Jesus was looked upon as a Galilean, and according to religious authorities, he was not entitled to be called "Messiah."

David was the true founder of the Hebrew monarchy. He was a

---

[4]See Jn. 7:11-42, Mt. 22:41-46.

great leader, a conqueror, and a true servant of God. Jesus usually referred to himself as "son of man," meaning "human being." On a few occasions, he was called "son of God." In his humanity, Jesus was a normal man—in his spiritual nature, a child (son) of God.

MIRACLE OF HEALING

And Jesus stood still, called them, and said, What will ye that I shall do unto you? Mt. 20:32.

In these lands, there were many professional blind and lame men whose livelihood depended on begging for money and food. However, there were some blind people who genuinely wanted to receive healing and did not want to remain blind or lame. But there were others who preferred to be left alone so that they could continue their professional begging.

According to the gospel narrative, Jesus had asked these two blind men: "What do you want me to do for you?" The two men replied, "open our eyes." These particular blind men who had approached Jesus were sincerely seeking healing from his hands. He had compassion on them and touched their eyes. Immediately these men could see so they followed him, glorifying God and praising Jesus as a great healer.

CHAPTER 21

COLT AND ASS

And when they drew nigh unto Jerusalem, and were come to Bethphage, unto the mount of Olives, then sent Jesus two disciples. Saying unto them, Go into the village over against you, and straightway ye shall find an ass tied, and a colt with her: loose them, and bring them unto me. Mt. 21:1-2.

People use asses extensively for transportation in countries where modern civilization has not penetrated and where horses and mules cannot travel the narrow roads and ragged mountains. Some families have as many as seven or more donkeys. They keep them in their fields or tie them outside near their doors waiting to carry burdens. If these donkeys have just arrived with a caravan, the owners unload and feed them near the entrance of their homes.

A Near Easterner has his beast of burden just as an American has his car. They are much like taxicabs, ready for hire or for loaning to friends when needed. Government officials and soldiers, traveling from town to town, draft these asses to carry supplies. Noblemen and holy men have the privilege of using the animals at any time. It is quite an honor to lend a donkey to a holy man so that he may ride it. Pious people trust and honor true teachers of God's word and healers of bodies and souls. None of the pious would refuse anything these men may ask. They often say: "Let them take our donkeys, mules or horses. We know they are men of God. They will return them!" An owner of a donkey may also say: "Take the donkey, kill it if you wish, it is yours, you need not ask me."

Everyone who was following Jesus, including his disciples, expected him to restore the kingdom of Israel. Instead, Jesus continually repudiated all talk of a temporal reign. He tried to impress upon his disciples, followers, and some of the people that his kingdom was not of this world. He wanted to enter Jerusalem humbly and meekly, thereby destroying these rumors of an earthly, political reign. (It was on this journey that the sons of Zebedee requested permission to sit one on his right and the other on his left in the kingdom.)

Thus, when Jesus arrived at Bethphage, he sent two of his disciples to bring an ass and a colt from the nearby village. Jesus wanted to ride on the colt. But the young, unbroken colt would not move without the presence of its mother. Jesus understood this, which is why he requested that his disciples bring its mother also. The young colt would follow its mother. A colt symbolizes meekness and humility. Kings, princes, and rulers would have despised riding on a donkey. They would choose a mule or a horse to enter Jerusalem. Jesus rode the colt that no one had ridden.[1] This was a disgraceful appearance. Eventually, people rejected Jesus and lost interest in him.

RIDING ON AN ASS

Tell ye the daughter of Sion, Behold, thy King cometh unto thee, meek, and sitting upon an ass, and a colt the foal of an ass. Mt.21:5.

When Near Eastern kings and princes enter a city, people clean the streets, repair the roads, hang their tapestries from the windows or rooftops of the buildings, and spread rugs on the streets. The people are very lavish and generous on such occasions.

A delegation, composed of the governor, noblemen, and priests accompanied by a large crowd, leaves the city to greet and escort the royal guests. As a token of the city's hearty welcome, the delegation will provide a handsome horse saddled with expensive livery embroidered with silk and gold. The Hebrews used a mule on such occasions. The mule was a symbol of strength[2]

However, the donkey is a symbol of disgrace and humiliation in these countries. Princes and noblemen never ride on a donkey; only

---

[1]See Mk. 11:2; Lk. 19:30.
[2]See I Kings 1:33.

257

the very poor will ride upon one. Nor would they offer such an animal to a distinguished visitor. Near Eastern officials would punish an individual for his heretical views or for some other cause reflecting on his moral character by placing him on an ass and then parading him around town. In many areas of the East, this custom still prevails.

Before beginning on his journey to Jerusalem, Jesus predicted his rejection, humiliation, and death. He knew that he would not receive a warm welcome into the Holy City. The priests were waiting to disgrace him in the presence of the people who expected him to be a king. This is the reason Jesus chose a donkey instead of a mule as the kings of Judah had done. This sudden departure from the custom grieved his disciples, especially Judas, and it engendered fear in many other disciples and followers. (This was doubtless one reason why Judas was led to revolt and turn traitor.) Jesus showed that he did not want a reception as an earthly ruler and that his disciples should not expect a royal welcome from the inhabitants of Jerusalem. On his own initiative, he rode upon a donkey before the officials set him on one.

A group of Galileans who had come early to the Feast greeted Jesus and his disciples when he arrived at the Mount of Olives. They had no rugs or other objects of beauty to lay under his feet. So these Galileans spread their garments on the ground as a token of welcome and loyalty to him and as a rebuke to the religious officials who were shunning him. Little, innocent children began to sing praises before him, unaware of the hostility of the religious leadership. The disciples themselves were shocked when they saw no delegation to greet their master and when the Pharisees wanted Jesus to silence the children who were singing praises..

Jesus' entry into Jerusalem was a political failure. The political leadership and priests of the historic city had totally ignored him. Instead of the governor and the high priests welcoming Jesus and entertaining him in their palaces, his disciples had to seek a place to eat and lodge at Bethany. On Passover evening they had to sleep in the public park of Gethsemane. Nonetheless, his entry into Jerusalem was a spiritual and moral success. He was soon to be crowned an everlasting King. The temporal forces were to fall before the power of the new kingdom. The teaching of the gospel of the kingdom would surpass and supplant the traditions of the elders and religious leaders of the time. A meek man, riding on a colt of a donkey, has no resemblance to a mighty, political Messiah, the conqueror of the Gentile kingdoms. Scripture had been fulfilled. It was predicted that the Messiah would enter Jerusalem in a meek manner, riding on the colt of an ass. Jesus came into Jerusalem exactly as the prophet Zechariah had prophesied.

HOUSE OF PRAYER

And said unto them, It is written, My house shall be called the house of prayer; but ye have made it a den of thieves. Mt. 21:13.

When King Solomon dedicated the temple, he called it "The House of Prayer." He did this so that wherever people would stand before their Creator and pray or worship, they were to face toward the temple and their prayers would be answered. Solomon did not build this house of prayer for corrupt practices of buying and selling animals for sacrifices. Nor did he dedicate the temple so that businessmen could exchange foreign money into temple coins for exorbitant profits and unjust discounts.

The priests and scribes had introduced these businesses into the temple courts for their own material gains. Therefore, Jesus cleansed the temple, which had become a den of thieves, by throwing out all the illegitimate businesses. He also overturned the trays of those who exchanged foreign money for temple coins and the trays of those who sold sheep and cattle for sacrifices. These business did not belong in this area of the temple. The temple was to be a house of prayer.

LESSON FROM A FIG TREE

And when he saw a fig tree in the way, he came to it, and found

nothing thereon, but leaves only, and said unto it, Let no fruit grow on thee
henceforth for ever. And presently the fig tree withered away. And when the
disciples saw it, they marveled, saying, How soon is the fig tree withered
away! Jesus answered and said unto them, Verily I say unto you, If ye have
faith and doubt not, ye shall not only do this which is done to the fig tree,
but also if ye shall say unto this mountain, Be thou removed, and be thou
cast into the sea; it shall be done. Mt. 21:19-21.

Part A—FIG TREE. When Near Eastern men are desiring food and fail to find it, they express their disappointment by making a negative remark. Also when they are thirsty and discover that the well is dry, they will irritatingly speak to the well and may declare: "Stay dry."

For some unknown reason, the fig tree on the roadway had no fruit. Perhaps other travelers had picked all the fruit. Or, perhaps the tree had not produced any fruit that particular season. Evidently, it was the season for figs; otherwise Jesus would not have sought fruit from the tree.

Jesus' casual remark was typically Near Eastern. It expressed great disappointment when finding no fruit on the fig tree. But the lesson that Jesus taught was about faith. The power of faith and prayer is potent. When we sincerely believe that we can overcome an obstacle, that difficulty has already been conquered. But when we doubt, we will not even try to solve the problem.

Faith ignites the force that resides in sincere prayer. Thus, the impossible becomes possible. What one can see in the mirror of the mind sooner or later becomes a reality. According to the text, after Jesus had rebuked the fig tree, it withered much faster than usual. The fig tree served a greater purpose than just producing a few figs. The dry fig tree served as a reminder of the power of faith.

Part B—REMOVE MOUNTAINS. We must not take general statements in the gospels literally. Extravagant and sweeping statements are very common in Aramaic and Hebrew speech but never cause misunderstanding. Semites know that the speaker does not mean exactly what his words are saying. "Removing mountains" means to have the ability to conquer any obstacle or difficulty and accomplish the task.

Jesus was placing his emphasis on the power of faith. The faith of which he spoke cannot be measured. The Aramaic term for "faith" is *heymanutha*. This word may also be translated as "trust." *M'heyna*, a "believer," also means a "trustworthy one." Neither Jesus nor his disciples removed or attempted to remove any mountains. Jesus did not actually mean that his disciples and followers would literally remove mountains. He emphasized trust in one's self and in the power of faith. Therefore, trust in God's power and the worthiness of purpose can accomplish the seemingly impossible. For example, without the determination to succeed, the courage to surmount obstacles, hard work, and absolute faith in God and in others, the vision of the Panama Canal or the Golden Gate Bridge could not have become an accomplished reality.

JESUS' AUTHORITY

And when he was come into the temple, the chief priests and the elders of the people came unto him as he was teaching, and said, By what authority doest thou these things? And who gave thee this authority? And Jesus answered and said unto them, I also will ask you one thing, which if ye tell me, I in like wise will tell you by what authority I do these things. Mt. 21:23-24.

Jesus' authority did not come from anyone of this world. His authority came from God. Neither the Roman government nor King Herod had given him any authority to cleanse the temple (see verses 12-16) nor to teach anything new and contrary to that of the priests and temple worship.

In biblical lands, religious teachers and statesmen, when having to face difficult and challenging questions, instead of answering, will often ask their rivals to first answer a question they propose. Jesus very wisely answered them by asking them a very serious and difficult question which he knew they could not answer: "The baptism of John, from where is it? Is it from heaven or from the people? They then reasoned among themselves saying, now if we say from heaven, he will tell us, Why did you not believe him? And if we should say, From the people, we are afraid of the crowd because they all regard John as a prophet. So they answered saying to him: We do not know. Jesus said to them: Neither will I answer you by what authority I do these things."[3] Jesus was truly a wise teacher. He knew how to answer his adversaries.

ACTION SPEAKS LOUDER

But what think ye? A certain man had two sons; and he came to the first, and said, Son, go work to day in my vineyard. He answered and said, I will not: but afterward he repented, and went. And he came to the second, and said likewise. And he answered and said, I go, sir: and went not. Whether of them twain did the will of his father? They say unto him, The first. Jesus said unto them. Verily I say unto you, That the publicans and the harlots go into the kingdom of God before you. Mt. 21:28-31.

In this parable Jesus places emphasis on action rather than on empty or pleasing words. On another occasion Matthew reports Jesus saying: "It is not the one who says, 'My Lord, my Lord,' but the one who hears my word and does it." Jesus' teaching on the kingdom was not based on creedal beliefs but on a life full of good actions.

The following is an allegorical interpretation of the parable. The man represents God. The first son symbolizes some of the Jewish people who had left the way of God, but later repented and returned to God to do the work of the kingdom. They were the ones who followed Jesus and were working in the vineyard—God's kingdom.

The second son represented those priests, Pharisees, scribes, and people who pretended to be loyal to God's word but refused to do the

---

[3]Mt. 21:25-27, Aramaic Peshitta text, Errico.

work of God. These particular people taught God's commandments but never put them into practice. They taught the doctrine of the kingdom but refused to enter into it. They were also preventing others who were willing to respond to God's kingdom from entering.

Despite this fact, the greedy and corrupt tax collectors, customs officers, and the harlots responded to the teaching of John the Baptist. The scribes, Pharisees, and Sadducees went to see John but did not believe in him nor did they repent. But tax collectors, sinners, and harlots did repent and were working for the advancement of God's reign. It was the same with Jesus. Many of his followers and workers in his gospel were tax collectors, sinners and harlots.[4] Society's outcasts were the first to participate in (enter) God's kingdom.

THE WICKED VINEYARD WORKERS

Hear another parable: There was a certain householder, which planted a vineyard, and hedged it round about, and digged a winepress in it, and built a tower, and let it out to husbandmen, and went into a far country: And when the time of the fruit drew near, he sent his servants to the husbandmen, that they might receive the fruits of it. And the husbandmen took his servants, and beat one, and killed another, and stoned another. . . .But when the husbandmen saw the son, they said among themselves, This is the heir; come, let us kill him, and let us seize on his inheritance. And they caught him, and cast him out of the vineyard, and slew him. When the lord therefore of the vineyard cometh, what will he do unto those husbandmen? They say unto him, He will miserably destroy those wicked men, and will let out his vineyard unto other husbandmen, which shall render him the fruits in their season. Mt. 21:33-41.

---

[4]Modern New Testament scholars debate Matthew's interpretation of this parable, verses 31-32. In reality, the entire parable has come under much scholarly discussion. A reminder: This book is not a critical commentary. Therefore, Dr. Lamsa and I do not discuss the scholarly textual problems. We work with the received text—that is, the text as it appears in our present manuscripts of the New Testament.

The following is an allegorical interpretation: The vineyard represents Israel, the nation and people whom God had called from Chaldea and Padan-Aram and established in Palestine. The tower signifies God's prophets and seers, who were appointed to act as watchmen over Israel. The workers or husbandmen were the kings, priests and other religious authorities who were guardians of their religion.

The first servants who were sent to ask for the fruits of the vineyard for its owner were the prophets. Wicked kings and rebellious priests who had leased the vineyard stoned and killed these prophets.

The second group of servants symbolized other emissaries whom the religious and political leaders of the time had slain. Finally they murder the owner's son, the heir, so that they could inherit the vineyard. But, at last, the owner's anger and wrath will severely punish all the murderous evil doers. The temple was destroyed and many people were slain and others were dispersed everywhere.[5]

THE CORNERSTONE

Jesus saith unto them, Did ye never read in the scriptures, The stone which the builders rejected, the same is become the head of the corner: this is the Lord's doing, and it is marvelous in our eyes? Mt. 21:42.

When a Near Easterner plans to build a house, he first gathers stones and other building materials and cuts beams. He then hires laborers or contracts with builders to construct his house. In the latter case, the materials, especially the unhewn stones, are examined before the contract is settled. Generally the large rough stones are rejected because they are hard to lift and place in the walls. Nonetheless, the owner of the house insists that the large stones be used in the building.

---

[5]There is no doubt that Matthew's version presents a reworked parable. The closest one can come to Jesus' original parable is recorded in the Gospel of Thomas, 65. Of course, the gospel of Thomas interprets the parable from its own perspective also, but it does not have the allegorical view that Matthew presents.

He will argue that it has taken much money and hard labor to obtain them. The builders finally decide to use the large and uncut stones for the foundation and place the largest stone at the corner. It is covered with earth and is hardly seen. It serves a good purpose in the foundation of the wall.

Jesus pictures himself as a cornerstone. Many religious leaders considered Jesus as untrained, uncultured, and irreligious. The high priests and elders, represented by the builders, had rejected the prophet from Galilee. Nonetheless, he was to be the founder of a universal movement and become the cornerstone of a true spiritual structure. His message of God's kingdom embraced peoples and nations of all races and colors.

Usually what men would select, God rejects. And what God selects, men frequently reject. Most of the time, human beings see only the outer appearance, but God's eyes look within. It is not beauty but service that counts. A large uncut stone, buried in the foundation of a building, is more important than a small polished stone high in the wall. It is vital because the weight of the whole superstructure rests upon its foundation.[6]

LARGE AND SMALL STONES—ETERNAL TRUTH

Therefore say I unto you, The kingdom of God shall be taken from you, and given to a nation bringing forth the fruits thereof. And whosoever shall fall on this stone shall be broken: but on whomsoever it shall fall, it will grind him to powder. Mt. 21:43-44.

Part A—THE KINGDOM. God's reign would be transferred from the religious leaders, priests, scribes, and given to other nations. They were to be the new guardians and leaders in God's vineyard so that it might bring abundant spiritual fruit and supply the nations of the world. Many Galilean, Aramean (Syrian), Assyrian, Armenian

---

[6]See Mk. 12:10

religious leaders, and descendants of the ten tribes of Israel, had accepted Jesus' teaching and embraced his message of the kingdom. But many priests, scribes and others had rejected the gospel of the kingdom. Nevertheless, most of the early followers were Jews.

Part B—STONES. Masons in the Near East lack iron and steel tools such as hammers and chisels. Most builders cut one stone with another. Either they lift a large stone with both hands and throw it on a smaller stone to break it into pieces or they break a small stone by striking it against a larger one. This statement in verse 44 is an Aramaic parabolic saying that is still in use among Aramaic speaking people today.

A stone metaphorically means "truth." In Aramaic the word for "truth" is *shrara*. Truth is something hard and strong. This is why Easterners refer to truth as a stone. "Whosoever shall fall on this stone" signifies that anyone attacking this truth (God's kingdom) would be "broken" (defeated). "But on whomsoever it shall fall, it will grind him to powder" means that the truth of the kingdom will utterly destroy whatever it encounters. In other words, error can never triumph over truth, but truth can always destroy error because its premise is false.

Jesus warned his disciples and followers of the extreme opposition his teaching would confront. The gospel of the kingdom would face the hostility of well-organized and powerful religions throughout the world. But he knew that truth would ultimately triumph over man-made doctrines and corrupt forces. Kings and princes of this world who would try to abolish the movement of God's kingdom would be crushed by the stone. This stone was not cut by human hands but by the hands of God. The principles of truth would eventually win out over all materialistic kingdoms. (See Daniel 2:34-35.)

All who would oppose the truth that Jesus taught would only harm themselves and cause the movement to spread more rapidly, for persecution is the very life of a new movement. The kingdom that Jesus proclaimed was based on God's principles which had been revealed to the Hebrew prophets. Therefore, this stone was destined to defeat all false beliefs and ideologies. Truth triumphs whether error attacks it or truth comes against falsehood .[7]

---

[7]See Lk. 20:18.

CHAPTER 22

PARABLE OF THE WEDDING FEAST

The kingdom of heaven is like unto a certain king, which made a marriage for his son, And sent forth his servants to call them that were bidden to the wedding: and they would not come. Mt. 22:2-3.

The term "king" in this verse refers to a landlord (petty ruler) who owns much property, vast estates. In Aramaic people call him *malka,* "king, ruler." Invitations to marriage feasts are issued suddenly. No announcements are sent to those invited; messengers carry the news verbally. Some guests doubt the truth of the invitation and ignore it. Others, due to strained relations between the ruler and subjects, refuse to attend and sometimes conspire against him.

This parable was a direct attack on religious leaders who considered themselves better and more righteous than others. They were the invited guests who failed to come to the wedding feast. They rejected Jesus' teaching, killed him, and proved themselves unworthy of God's kingdom. The Gentiles were then the invited guests to the banquet, and their readiness to accept Jesus' invitation made them a cornerstone for Jesus' gospel of the kingdom.

The following is an allegorical interpretation based on Matthew's rendering of Jesus' parable (see verses 4-10).[1] God, of course, is likened to a King. He prepared a great banquet (a wedding feast for his son) and invited people to attend, but they refused. So the great landlord sent servants proclaiming the invitation.

The first servants are the early prophets whom God sent to the Israelites to invite them to the great feast, but the bidden guests

---

[1]This same parable, as it appears in Luke, is also rendered and interpreted somewhat differently. (Lk. 14:16-24.) Again, this is Matthew's angle of the parable. Reminder: The title to each of the four canonical gospels in Aramaic is *karozutha,* "the preaching." This gospel is "Matthew's Preaching." And so it is with each of the other three canonical writings.

refused to come. The second group of servants symbolizes the latter prophets, whom God sent urging people to return to the way of God, promising them that the coming of the Messiah was near; the day of deliverance was at hand. They too rejected the invitation and slew some servants and mistreated others. In those days, some of the people had gone after the worship of Baal. Others were worshiping the sun, moon, and stars; still others were so hostile to God's way that they mocked some of God's emissaries and killed them.

Finally, the Assyrian and Chaldean kings invaded the holy land and punished the people along with their kings and princes. They killed some of them, carried others away captive and burned the temple, which had become polluted with pagan rituals.

The third group signifies the apostles whom God sent to invite the Gentiles to the great wedding feast. The banquet was all prepared and ready for the guests. The law was written and the books of the prophets were read, but many still refused to attend.

"Highways and byways" refer to the Gentile races and peoples who had not been invited at first and who knew little about God. Since those whom God had called refused to celebrate, Gentiles and pagans were welcome to participate in the great banquet. Now everyone—both good and bad—was invited. Everyone had the opportunity to witness God's reign of justice and peace. The bridegroom represents the Messiah. The marriage feast symbolizes the inauguration of God's universal kingdom—the kingdom of heaven.

A WEDDING GARMENT

And when the king came in to see the guests, he saw there a man which had not a wedding garment: And he saith unto him, Friend, how camest thou in hither not having a wedding garment? And he was speechless. Mt. 22:11-12.

Clothes are very scarce in the Near East. Only the rich have more than one or two garments. Styles similar to those of Europe and

America did not become popular until the middle of the twentieth century. However, there are some areas where people do not know anything about Western styles of clothing. Even when the climate changes, people wear the same clothing. In Palestine and Syria, one seldom sees a change of clothes during the entire year.

A few workers have an extra garment for Sunday, holidays and weddings. It is similar to the one worn daily, but it is kept clean. Except for young men, noblemen, and the rich, who wear different clothes when they are not working, the working garments are worn throughout the year.

It is against Near Eastern custom and etiquette to go to a wedding or banquet without a clean garment. It is an insult to the host. Servants always look at a man's garments before allowing him to enter the house. A man who does not have new or proper apparel borrows it from his neighbor. Borrowing clothes and jewelry is very common. On such occasions, everybody is very helpful and generous. Women lend silver and gold bracelets and necklaces as well as special garments. When the Israelites left Egypt, they borrowed all the garments and jewelry they could obtain from the Egyptians, pretending to need them for the feast. (See Exodus 12:35.)

Some men who have no regard for etiquette neglect wearing a clean garment. They either do not wish to be under obligation to their neighbors by borrowing clothes, or they are too lazy to change. Also, as banquets and weddings are usually held in the evening, men find it difficult and inconvenient to change their garments after work. There is little privacy in a Near Eastern home. Five or six families live under the same roof and it is a problem to dress and undress. Some men would rather be humiliated by being turned away at the door of the wedding feast than undress before the many women in the house. It is not so difficult in the morning when men rise early. While they are dressing, the women are asleep or cover their heads.

The man who was turned away at the wedding probably had a new garment but did not try to change for the occasion. Jesus relates this parable in connection with preparation for the kingdom of God. Men must develop the highest character by reliance on God if they are to enter the kingdom. The wedding garment symbolizes good works and piety. One must dress for the occasion!

LOYALTY TO GOVERNMENT

Tell us therefore, What thinkest thou? Is it lawful to give tribute unto Caesar, or not? But Jesus perceived their wickedness, and said, Why tempt ye me, ye hypocrites? Shew me the tribute money. And they brought unto him a penny. Mt. 22:17-19.

The Aramaic text reads: "Now tell us how does it seem to you? Is it lawful to pay head tax to Caesar or not? But Jesus discerned their cunningness and said: Why do you test me? Hypocrites! Show me that head tax dinara. So they brought him a dinara."[2] The gospels say nothing about the circumstances under which this tax was levied nor do they refer to the reasons the Jews objected to paying such a tax. The Peshitta text correctly states this was a head tax or poll tax and not a tribute. All citizens of the Roman Empire had to pay taxes on property, but the states which were protectorates and retained independence had to pay tribute. This tribute was levied on the people by their own rulers. Hezekiah, King of Judah, paid tribute to Sennacherib, King of Assyria.[3] Tributes were taken out of the royal treasury and collected from the people.

Palestinians did not resent the payment of taxes on property but vigorously objected to paying a personal head tax, especially since the head taxes were paid on sheep and cattle. The Jews regarded paying head taxes exacted by temporal powers as religiously unlawful. They felt their allegiance was to God as the supreme ruler of the State and the payment of two shekels was made to the temple treasury. Jewish kings were the servants of Yahweh but because the Roman Emperors were worshiped as gods, paying head tax was considered idolatry.

---

[2]Mt. 22:17-19, Aramaic Peshitta text, Errico
[3]See 2 Kings 18:14.

271

Today, head tax is still resented in the Near East. Thus, some governments, to avoid trouble, call a head tax by other names.[4]

The Pharisees and Herodians wanted to trap Jesus and have the Roman soldiers arrest him. So they asked him if it was lawful to pay the poll tax to Caesar. Had Jesus said "yes," they would have condemned him as unfaithful to their religion and unpatriotic. If he had said, "no, one should not pay this tax," they would have told the Roman authorities that Jesus was preventing people from paying their taxes. Jesus did not give them a direct answer but asked for a personal tax dinara.

CAESAR'S COIN

And he saith unto them, Whose is this image and superscription? They say unto him, Caesar's. Then said he unto them, Render therefore unto Caesar, the things which are Caesar's; and unto God the things that are God's. Mt. 22:20-21.

This coin was minted at the imperial mint and it bore on its face the inscription and image of Caesar. The temple coin, or shekel, which the Jews offered to God had neither image nor inscription on it. The shekel represented a certain quantity of gold or silver. No other money was acceptable as an offering for the temple; the old temple shekel was the only legal tender. Gentile money was exchanged for temple money. The Jews could not offer silver or gold coins with the images of human gods on the altar of the living God of Israel.

Thus, when Jesus asked them, "Whose is the image and inscription?" they, of course, replied "Caesar's." He immediately instructed them: "Give, therefore, to Caesar what is Caesar's and to God what is God's." The Pharisees and Herodians were amazed at his answer. They had to dismiss the entire matter.

Jesus' disciples and followers, as well as other people, were

---

[4]See Mk. 12:14; Lk. 20:22.

admonished to pay taxes, tributes, and to be loyal to the laws and government of the land. As long as God's kingdom or reign has no authority over people, one must obey the kings and princes of this world.

SADDUCEES

The same day came to him the Sadducees, which say that there is no resurrection, and asked him. Mt. 22:23.

The Aramaic word for Sadducees is *zaduqayeh*, coming from the Semitic root *zadaq*. It means "righteous." The Sadducees emphasized purity of life rather than dogmatic theology and traditions. They had no use for ritual and ceremony but the Pharisees and priests did. They were rationalists in their outlook on life and religion. They wanted peace and prosperity while living on earth. This group was not concerned about what was in store for them in the hereafter, or in the age to come. Therefore, they denied the teaching of the resurrection of the body. Sadducees were content with Roman rule in Judea and did their best to uphold the faith of their forefathers.

Pharisees were nationalists. They believed that the promises which God had made to their forefathers would be fulfilled, if not in this world, then in the world to come. They believed Messianic rule would overthrow the Roman Empire and the Davidic reign would be established in Palestine. They believed those who died without seeing this future kingdom would be partakers of it through their posterity; and, if they died without children, they would be cut off from its benefit. Thus for the Pharisees, the resurrection was an important part of their religious belief, but it was not so for the Sadducees.

NO MARRIAGE IN HEAVEN

Jesus answered and said unto them, Ye do err, not knowing the scriptures, nor the power of God. For in the resurrection they neither marry, nor are given in marriage, but are as the angels of God in heaven. Mt. 22:29-30.

"But are as the angels of God" is a Semitic phrase meaning "Godlike, innocent." God is the Eternal Spirit, and humankind in its spirit is God's image and likeness—good, eternal, and indestructible.

According to holy Scripture, God ordained marriage so that humanity would populate the earth. In heaven there is no need for human reproduction; therefore, sexual union between men and women will cease. They will be spiritual beings, like angels of God, or totally like God.

Some religious teachers believe that life in heaven will be similar to life on earth but much easier and full of joy. They also maintain that people will enjoy everything without having to work. According to this picture, it appears that heaven is a place for idlers and loafers.

Chaldeans and Egyptians believed in another life on this earth. This is the reason that wives and servants of kings and other great men were buried alive with their departed.

Angels are God's counsel and messengers. People usually see angels in dreams, visions, and trances. They have spiritual bodies that can only be seen with spiritual eyes. When angels appear to human beings in visions and trances, they look just like humans.

A SPIRITUAL RESURRECTION

But as touching the resurrection of the dead, have ye not read that which was spoken unto you by God, saying, I am the God of Abraham, and the God of Isaac, and the God of Jacob? God is not the God of the dead, but of the living. Mt. 31-32.

Some of the Sadducees, who did not believe in the resurrection, tried to trap Jesus but had failed. In this instance, they cited the case of a woman who had married seven brothers, one after another.[5] (See verses 24-28.)

Now, all of these seven brothers died one after another. And after having married their deceased brother's widow, they still did not leave any heir. Eventually, the widow died. The Sadducees wanted to know which of the brothers would be her husband in the life to come. They did not understand that in the life to come there would be no husbands and wives.

Jesus also explained to them that the God of heaven is not the God of the dead, but of the living. Abraham, Isaac, and Jacob were not dead; they were living spiritual beings. How could a living God be the God of men and women who ceased to exist? Since God is eternal and indestructible, the soul of humanity is also eternal. Humankind is the image and likeness of God. This was not a fable but a spiritual reality.

The gods of other nations were human beings who were soon forgotten after their deaths. But Abraham, Isaac, and Jacob, though they had departed this life, were living somewhere else. So the God of the Hebrews was the God of the living.[6] The Hebrew concept of death was different than that of the Gentiles and pagans. Moses and Elijah were expected to return and prepare the way for the coming of the Messiah. On the other hand, the God of Israel was the God of all generations, the creator of heaven and earth.

Jesus did not believe in the power of death nor did he think that death was an end, a finality to life. A living and indestructible God would not have created a destructible being. Jesus knew that death had no power over him and that the same God who is the Lord of life is also the Lord of death. (See Mark 12:26; Luke 20:35.)

---

[5]Mosaic law permits a brother to marry and perform conjugal intimacy with the widow of his brother, if the deceased left no heir. After she conceives and bears a child, the brother must raise the child as the legitimate heir for his deceased brother. In the ancient days, when the question of the resurrection was not yet prevalent, the deceased were thought to live through their posterity. Those who had no descendants were cut off from the living.

[6]See Ex. 3:6.

THE GREATEST COMMANDMENT

Master, which is the great commandment in the law? Jesus said unto him, Thou shalt love the Lord thy God with all thy heart, and with all thy soul, and with all thy mind. This is the first and great commandment. And the second is like unto it, Thou shalt love thy neighbour as thyself. On these two commandments hang all the law and the prophets. Mt. 22:36-40.

When the Pharisees heard that Jesus had silenced the Sadducees concerning the resurrection, they gathered together, and one of them who knew the law asked Jesus about the great commandment to test him. Jesus pointed out the two great commandments. The Pharisees were strict in their observances of the Mosaic law and its multiple ordinances and doctrines. Jesus quoted these two commandments from the books of Leviticus and Deuteronomy. As far as he was concerned these two commandments were the core of the Mosaic law. For when one loves God with all one's heart, soul, and mind, then one will love others and there will be no need for coveting, stealing, hating, cheating, lying, and bearing false witness.

Many religious teachers fail to realize that breaking even one of God's laws is the same as breaking them all. Yet, some who are caught stealing or committing adultery may receive severe punishment, while others, who hold high state and religious positions, may lie, covet, and bear false witness but manage to maintain their dignity and receive no punishment.

It is better to abide by the two commandments of loving God and others as oneself. All human problems and difficulties arise because people commit injustices against one another. Human beings need to love and care for each other. If they would put into practice these two commandments, the entire objective and meaning of religion and the law would be fulfilled.

THE TERMS "SON OF DAVID AND LORD"

While the Pharisees were gathered together, Jesus asked them, Saying, What think ye of Christ? Whose son is he? They say unto him, The son of David. He saith unto them, How then doth David in spirit call him Lord, saying, The Lord said unto my Lord, Sit thou on my right hand, till I make thine enemies thy footstool? If David then call him Lord, how is he his son? Mt. 22:41-45.

According to the Jewish concept of the messianic kingdom, the Messiah must be a physical descendant of King David. This son of David was to restore Israel to her former glory. Israel not only prospered under David's reign but also received recognition as a nation from all surrounding peoples and national powers. The division between the Northern and Southern tribes of Israel after David's death strained relations between the ten tribes in the North known as Israel and the two tribes in the South known as Judah. It weakened the nation's aspirations for greatness. Both Judah and Israel lost prestige and finally succumbed to foreign powers.

After the return from Chaldean captivity, a second temple was built with the hope of rebuilding the nation. But all attempts to restore Israel's dignity and power were futile. Many political endeavors were made to free the Jews from foreign yoke, but all were in vain. Israel had come in contact with great empires like Assyria, Chaldea, Persia, Greece, and Rome. Deliverance from these nations called for a nationalistic and courageous leader like King David.

The Jews looked for the Messiah to free them from foreign rule and subjugate the nations of the earth. Therefore, the Messiah must come from the lineage of David. No other Jewish family could take this honor because the messianic promises were too sacred to be bestowed on any ordinary family.

Palestinians were puzzled about Jesus. They did not know what to make of him. They recognized his power as a miracle worker and as a prophet who received inspiration from some authority, but they could not connect him in any way with the house of David or even

277

with the tribe of Judah. This was largely because Jesus was Galilean. These Galileans, although they were members of the Jewish faith, were not well received by the Jews.

Jesus knew that most of the opposition against him was primarily due to his nationality and not to his teaching. He heard them discussing him and so he asked: "What do you say concerning the Christ? Whose son is he?" They replied, "The son of David." Jesus contradicted their literal interpretation by asking them: "How then doth David in Spirit call him Lord? For he said: The Lord said unto my Lord, Sit thou at my right hand, until I make thine enemies thy footstool."[7]

Part A—THE TERM "SON OF DAVID." Jesus knew this scriptural passage was misunderstood. To Jesus, "son of David" meant that the Messiah was to be like David in courage, zeal, and greatness and not necessarily in descent. In the Near East, people will call a celebrated and distinguished man the son of a famous individual who may have died centuries before him. People, on several occasions, called Jesus "the son of David" but not because they thought he was a descendant of David; this was an honorific title people gave to Jesus because he was an outstanding healer. Jesus' argument was simply that the Pharisees interpreted messianic claims from Scripture too literally. After Jesus questioned them and no one could answer him, the scripture says: "From that day no one dared to question him again."[8]

Part B—THE TERM "LORD." In our English translations of the New Testament, both Jesus and the God of Israel are referred to as "Lord." In Aramaic there are two words used for "lord"—*Mariah*, meaning God or the highest ranking "Lord of lords" and *mar*, meaning "sir, master, or lord." The Aramaic verse reads: "The LORD (*Mariah*) said to my lord (*mari*), Sit at my right hand until I put your enemies under your feet." David calls the Messiah "my lord," *mari*.

The reason for the confusion is that Moses had received the name

---

[7]Ps. 110:1.
[8]Mt. 22:46, Aramaic Peshitta text, Errico.

278

of God as *YHWH* but later it became too holy to utter so they used the Hebrew term *Adonai*, "LORD," instead of *YHWH*. (Yahweh is also abbreviated and written as *YAH*.)[9]

---

[9]In the Aramaic Peshitta text of the Hebrew Bible, translators used the Aramaic term *Mariah* for the Hebrew *Adonai*.

CHAPTER 23

MOSES' SEAT

Then spake Jesus to the multitude, and to his disciples, Saying The scribes and Pharisees sit in Moses' seat: All therefore whatsoever they bid you observe, that observe and do; but do not ye after their works: for they say, and do not. For they bind heavy burdens and grievous to be borne, and lay them on men's shoulders; but they themselves will not move them with one of their fingers. Mt. 23:1-4.

The term "Moses' seat" is a metaphor for Moses' authority, i.e., carrying on the tradition. It was also a special seat in the ancient synagogues. The congregation sat on mats or on stone benches. The elders sat facing the people with their backs to Jerusalem. Presumably, the seat of Moses was reserved for the most distinguished elder.

The scribes and Pharisees presided over all judicial matters. They interpreted the law and prophets and rendered legal decisions. They did all they could do to enforce the law and its ordinances, at times to excess. (Obeying religious authorities derives from Deuteronomy 17:9-10.) They also laid heavy burdens—that is, they enacted severe precepts and prohibitions—upon the unlearned and the ignorant making, their yoke harsh; but they themselves did not practice what they taught. They would not lift a finger to remove any oppressive ordinance.

HYPOCRISY

But all their works they do for to be seen of men: they make broad their phylacteries, and enlarge the borders of their garments, And love the uppermost rooms at feasts, and chief seats in the synagogues, And greetings in the markets, and to be called of men, Rabbi, Rabbi. Mt. 23:5-7

The scribes and Pharisees were constantly conscious of their own legalistic positions and the decisions that had been taught by their own great teachers, so much so that many of them could not understand the inner and spiritual meaning of the law. Also, they were more concerned about their long ecclesiastical robes and hems of their garments which made them distinguished and highly honored in the presence of the people.

These men demanded too much honor and reverence from the people. They loved the prominent places at feasts and the best synagogue seats that were on the platform facing the congregation. (Scholars usually occupied these seats.) And they especially enjoyed being called *"Rabbi,"* "teacher"—literally, "my great one."

RABBI AND FATHER

But be ye not called Rabbi; for one is your Master, even Christ, and all ye are brethren. And call no man your father upon the earth: for one is your Father, which is in heaven. Neither be ye called masters: for one is your Master, even Christ. But he that is greatest among you shall be your servant. And whosoever shall exalt himself shall be abased; and he that shall humble himself shall be exalted. Mt. 23:8-12.

Jesus admonished his disciples and followers to shun all hypocritical practices. He instructed them to listen to the scribes when they read holy Scripture but not to imitate them, for they taught piousness but did not practice it. They also enjoyed the honorific terms people bestowed upon them such as "Rabbi, father, and master."

Jesus' disciples and followers were to conduct themselves differently. They were admonished to take the lower seats at banquets and synagogues. The most important among them was to be a servant for others. They were to treat each other as family members and not with ecclesiastical officialdom. These things were new commands that Jesus taught them. He gave them a new order of life that was befitting God's kingdom, where people of all races and social standing were equal in the presence of God. They must put into practice what Jesus

281

had taught them. In this new kingdom—an undivided reality—those who exalt themselves would be humbled, but the humble would find equality with everyone.

Part A—RABBI. The Aramaic term *rabbi* derives from the Semitic root *rab,* meaning "chief." *Rabba* means "great." The final letter "i" in *rabbi* signifies the possessive case; it means "my great one or my chief." At this particular time in Palestine, the term "Rabbi" was an honorific title. It did not refer to the head of a synagogue nor are we to think of "Rabbi" as we do today. Rabbinic schools were not established until circa 200 C.E.

Part B—FATHER AND MASTER. The term "my father" has many meanings in Aramaic and these different meanings are still in use today among Aramaic speaking people. First, it is a term of honor and great respect. A stranger may greet another using this term; a master may call his servant "father." This shows trust and esteem. A father may also address his son as "father." In this case it is one of great endearment and affection.[1] Again, "father, master, Rabbi," are titles that Semites used to convey dignity and distinction. However, sometimes people uttered these terms in an effort to deceive. These expressions were used so much that they often became meaningless and drew the people's thoughts away from God—their heavenly Father.

Jesus stresses God's priority over all masters, fathers, teachers, and leaders. He does not mean to be disrespectful to teachers, fathers and leaders but to put God first, over all leadership.

Part C—ONE IS YOUR FATHER. Near Eastern Semites who are not Christians still have many wives because polygamy prevails in most of the Islamic lands, the exception being Turkey. Family unity is centered in and around the father. In a Near Eastern family there is only one father, many wives, and children from different mothers. Some of the mothers may have been previously married and had children by husbands of a different race and religion.

In the Jewish faith there was but one God. Racial unity and

---

[1] See comment on Mt. 6:9.

interest are based on the one God. This was not so with other races that had many gods and goddesses. Therefore these people were divided and disorganized. Jesus reiterated to his disciples and followers that they only had one Father; they were, in reality, a family and did not represent any ecclesiastic power. People were not to think of them as overlords and neither must they lord it over one another. "One is your Father who is in heaven" means "You are one family."

FALSE PRAYERS

Woe unto you, scribes and Pharisees, hypocrites! For ye devour widows' houses and for a pretence make long prayer: therefore ye shall receive the greater damnation. Mt. 23:14.

In the olden days, people knew and understood preachers to be great by their long and complex sermons, and they knew religious men to be pious by their long prayers. The longer a man prayed, the more he could gain respect, confidence, and admiration from the people; the more complicated and contradictory his teaching, the more praise and respect he received. Therefore, the traditions and interpretations of the elders, scribes, and Pharisees obscured and complicated the clear and simple teachings of the prophets.

A woman did not have many rights in the Near East.[2] Women were denied the right to own property and to sell or buy. Should a husband die leaving no son, his property automatically went to his nearest male relative. If there was a male heir, the woman was permitted to become the custodian of the property on condition that a male guardian was appointed to transact the necessary business for her. Most women selected a priest or a religious man to discharge this sacred trust. As women led secluded lives, most widows found it

---

[2]These customs prevail today in most Near Eastern States. Turkey is the one country where great changes affecting women's rights are now taking place. Also there are many changes in Egypt as well. There is a general movement among women in the Near East, though not at all as it is in the United States.

difficult to know whom to trust. They observed how certain men in the synagogue or church would pray and they made a choice from those who prayed the longest.

Men keenly desired to become guardians of widows and orphans. And, as they were aware of the widows' test, the insincere and dishonest often became the widows' choice. These men would stretch out their prayers to last a long time and put on airs of piety. Then, these clever men would win over the widows so they could steal and embezzle their properties. These men used religion for their own profit and to deceive people instead of helping and uplifting them

Jesus knew all this from close observation. He rightly upbraided the hypocrisy of the undeserving and commended the virtue of the true. Compare his parable of the Pharisee and the publican and his words about the poor widow. (See Luke 18:9 and 21:1.)

SON OF HELL

Woe unto you, scribes and Pharisees, hypocrites! for ye compass sea and land to make one proselyte, and when he is made, ye make him twofold more the child of hell than yourselves. Mt. 23:15.

Terms of speech such as "child of hell" still prevail in biblical lands. One often hears one man tell another, "You son of wicked-ness," meaning "you are an evil person." *Bar-gehenna*, "son of hell," refers to a corrupt person who is good for nothing except to be burned. According to Near Eastern custom, a tree that does not bear fruit is good for only one thing, to be burned as fuel.

Many of the Pharisees, like missionaries of the present day, traveled over land and sea in search of converts. Often pagans who converted would become worse than before. The reason for this is that as members of another faith, they had no education and were immune from many misleading notions and systems invented by religious men who converted them. Many Pharisees had deceived their people through their false piousness. They had cheated widows and orphans and had exacted tithes from even the smallest herbs planted in people's gardens, such as dill and cummin. They had failed to emphasize the important matters of the law—mercy, justice, and forgiveness. The new converts learned the corrupt practices of their teachers and became more corrupt than their religious guides.

FALSE TITHES AND BLIND GUIDES

Woe unto you, scribes and Pharisees, hypocrites! For ye pay tithe of mint and anise and cummin, and have omitted the weightier matters of the law, judgment, mercy, and faith: these ought ye to have done, and not to leave the other undone. Ye blind guides, which strain at a gnat, and swallow a camel. Mt. 23:23-24.

People grew these particular herbs in courtyards and therefore were free from the law of tithing.[3] According to the Mosaic law, only grain, wine, and oil were subject to the law of tithing; rabbinically, vegetables and greens were also included. But the blind teachers of the law had declared the payment of tithes on these herbs and had neglected the most important and weightier matters such as justice, compassion, and trustworthiness.

Tithes on herbs were not important nor did God demand such tithes. What really mattered was compassion and faithfulness. Law and religion were meant to help people and to be a blessing in all human relationships, whether the relationship was personal, social, commercial, or any kind of association. But instead of being a blessing, religious law and ordinances had become a heavy burden for people to bear.

These blind teachers of religion—certain scribes, Pharisees and elders—were so careful in their observances of the least matter in the laws and ordinances, they missed the real meaning behind the law. They refused to walk a few feet more on the Sabbath day and were

---

[3]See Lev. 27:30; Num. 18:12; Deut. 14:22-23.

careful about their daily ablutions, Sabbaths and new moons. But they embezzled property and perverted the law and justice for the sake of a bribe. Truly, they strained at a gnat but could easily swallow a camel. "Strain out gnats" refers to the practice of straining wine through a cloth or wicker basket. This saying is a typical Near Eastern, Semitic hyperbole and there is no doubt that Jesus uttered these words. It was his style of speaking.

CLEANING THE OUTSIDE OF THE CUP AND PLATTER

Woe unto you, scribes and Pharisees, hypocrites! For ye make clean the outside of the cup and of the platter, but within they are full of extortion and excess. Thou blind Pharisee, cleanse first that which is within the cup and platter, that the outside of them may be clean also. . . . for ye are like unto whited sepulchres, which indeed appear beautiful outward, but are within full of dead men's bones, and of all uncleanness. Even so ye also outwardly appear righteous unto men, but within ye are full of hypocrisy and iniquity. Mt. 23:25-28.

In some areas of Palestine and the Arabian desert, where water is scarce and hard to procure for drinking, cups and platters are neither washed nor cleaned. The little bit of food that is left on the platter is cleaned with bread or with spoons. The pots and cups are left unwashed.

However, the scribes and Pharisees complying with legal ordinances or the teachings of the elders at least cleaned their cups, platters, and pots from the outside. It required less water and work to clean these things from the outside than it did from the inside. On the other hand, the outside is generally clean or covered with black so that no one would know the difference.

Likewise, in their conduct, they placed emphasis on the outer part of the Jewish law and religion, instead of the inner, spiritual meanings. They were far more concerned about their long robes, broad garments, their titles, and the beginning of the Sabbath and feasts, than about God's truth which was contained in the law and the books of the prophets.

DECORATING TOMBS

Woe unto you, scribes and Pharisees, hypocrites! Because ye build the tombs of the prophets, and garnish the sepulchres of the righteous, And say, If we had been in the days of our fathers, we would not have been partakers with them in the blood of the prophets. Wherefore, ye be witnesses unto yourselves, that ye are the children of them which killed the prophets. Fill ye up then the measure of your fathers. Ye serpents, ye generation of vipers, how can ye escape the damnation of hell? Mt. 23:29-33

Nearly all Hebrew prophets and messengers whom God had sent to the Israelites met with violent deaths. Kings, princes, and priests had refused to accept their admonitions to turn away from their corrupt works. They mocked these prophets and had them killed.

Centuries later, when these men of God were vindicated by their prophecies and all their warnings were fulfilled, their descendants regretted the actions of their forefathers. They said that if they had been in the place of their forefathers, they would not have killed these messengers of God. These people did not realize that they were the offspring of those who had murdered the prophets and emissaries of God.

Now these people were busy garnishing the tombs of these famous dead prophets. Their blind leaders would do the same thing their forefathers had done. They were subtle like serpents and lacked true guidance from God.

"Fill ye up then the measure of your fathers." People were judged through their parents and ancestors. A good man was always known as the son of a good man. The Aramaic word *bni*, "sons," also refers to "descendants" and "dwellers." These Pharisees were the descendants of the people who had murdered the prophets and had inherited the same virtues and vices of their forefathers. They knew their

287

ancestors did not walk in the way of the Lord. Now they tried to please God by building tombs to the memory of the prophets whom their fathers had slain. At the same time, they continued the identical hostility towards their present day prophets and men of God. They were soon to add Jesus to the list of slain prophets.

Jesus condemned hypocrisy. He did not tell them to continue in the corrupt ways of their forefathers as the King James version of the Bible indicates: "Fill ye up then the measure of your fathers." He pointedly accused them of actually doing the same thing. The Aramaic text reads: "And you also fill up the measure of your forefathers," meaning "you carry on with the same practices as your forefathers."

"You snakes and brood of poisonous serpents!" is an Aramaic phrase and refers to people who are "subtle, deceptive, dangerous, and without guidance." "How can you escape the judgment of Gehenna?" means "How can you escape your own utter destruction?"

ZECHARIAH, SON OF BARACHIAH

Wherefore, behold, I send unto you prophets, and wise men, and scribes: and some of them ye shall kill and crucify; and some of them shall ye scourge in your synagogues and persecute them from city to city: That upon you may come all the righteous blood shed upon the earth from the blood of righteous Abel unto the blood of Zacharias son of Barachias, whom ye slew between the temple and the altar. Verily I say unto you, All these things shall come upon this generation. Mt. 23:34-36

After upbraiding the scribes and Pharisees for what their forefathers had done to the holy prophets, Jesus told them in advance what these men would do to his disciples and followers. They would do worse things to them and incur greater judgment upon themselves.

The blood of all of God's messengers and ambassadors is therefore soon to be required of them. That very generation was to suffer when both the temple and Jerusalem would be destroyed. The days were coming when they would be harassed and mistreated, just

288

as they had mistreated and persecuted men of God. They would suffer at the hands of their Roman cohorts and adversaries.

Zechariah is the son of Jehoiadah, the priest who was later called Barachiah. (See 2 Chronicles 22:11.) Barachiah is his spiritual name, which was given to him when he put queen Athaliah to death, and placed Joash, the son of Ahaziah, King of Judah, upon the throne of his father. Jehoiadah had married Jehoshabeath, the daughter of King Jehoram, and Jehoshabeath hid Joash from Athaliah, who had slain all the princes of Judah. He also cleansed the temple of God and restored the worship of Yahweh.

After the death of Jehoiadah, the princes of Judah conspired against God's religion and returned to Baal worship. Zechariah had warned the people, saying that just as they had forsaken the Lord their God, so would God also forsake them. Then the king had commanded that Zechariah receive just punishment for his warnings and admonitions by stoning him to death in the court of the house of the Lord. (See 2 Chronicles 24:20-23.) His brothers also were slain because they, too, opposed Baal worship.[4]

LAMENT OVER JERUSALEM

O Jerusalem, Jerusalem, thou that killest the prophets, and stonest them which were sent unto thee, how often would I have gathered thy children together, even as a hen gathereth her chickens under her wings, and ye would not! Behold, your house is left unto you desolate. For I say unto you, Ye shall not see me henceforth, till ye shall say, Blessed is he that cometh in the name of the Lord. Mt. 23:37-39.

God, through the prophets and ambassadors, had promised to protect Jerusalem and a remnant of people. But many of the people, their leaders and priests, instead of listening to the prophets and men

---

[4]Some biblical authorities were led to believe that Zechariah, the son of Barachiah, was the father of John the Baptist, who lived about six centuries later.

of God and turning away from their corrupt and destructive ways, slew these emissaries. They were stiff-necked and unwilling to receive any admonition from God's messengers. Their worship of Baal and sensual practices carried them away.

Soon they were to reject Jesus and deliver him to the Romans who would slay him, like the prophets who had come before him. Jerusalem would be stubborn as of yore; the historic city would refuse godly admonition and would not turn away from its corrupt practices.

"Behold your house is left unto you desolate. For I say unto you, Ye shall not see me henceforth till ye shall say, Blessed is he that cometh in the name of the Lord." The reference here is to Jesus' death and resurrection. The religious leaders of Jerusalem had rejected Jesus. The city turned a deaf ear to his message and shunned him as the Messiah. Jesus and his disciples had to sleep in the garden of Gethsemane, a public park for people who had no lodging place in the holy city.

"Ye shall not see me henceforth" means that the people would no longer see him in his physical body, for he was soon to die on the cross as a common criminal. But he was also soon to rise in glory and majesty. He was to conquer death and inaugurate his glorious kingdom.

"Your house is left to you desolate" refers to the city of Jerusalem. It was doomed. The holy temple, the pride of the nation, would soon be destroyed and all hope of the restoration of the Davidic kingdom would vanish like mist evaporates before the sun. Then the people would begin to recognize Jesus' kingdom, a universal state, which was the only answer for all nations, Jews and Gentiles. People who had rejected him would soon say: "Blessed is he that comes in the name of the Lord."

"Cometh in the name of the Lord" is a Semitic saying that means "coming as an ambassador of the Lord." In other words, the Lord God had appointed and was sending this one to deliver a message to the people. An ambassador is a representative of the king who sends him.

The Messiah was an ambassador of God, representing God and

the genuine kingdom of justice and compassion. God had approved of this messenger, whatever he would say or do. In biblical lands, many false prophets and messengers had come in their own name; therefore, their predictions did not come true.

According to Scripture, God had sent Jesus to declare a true and simple way of life that had been revealed to Abraham, Moses, and the prophets. Jesus preached that which the Lord had spoken through the holy prophets. He had come to fulfill the law and the prophets. His kingdom would be from everlasting to everlasting.

CHAPTER 24

NOT ONE STONE UPON ANOTHER

And Jesus said unto them, See ye not all these things? Verily I say unto you, There shall not be left here one stone upon another, that shall not be thrown down. And as he sat upon the mount of Olives, the disciples came unto him privately, saying, Tell us, when shall these things be? And what shall be the sign of thy coming, and of the end of the world. Mt. 24:2-3.

Herod had rebuilt the temple of Solomon to please the Jews and to strengthen and confirm his Edomite dynasty. The temple was even greater in its splendor than the original structure King Solomon had built a thousand years before. The stones were magnificent and the workmanship excelled any other temple that had been known in that century. Thousands of Jews, and even foreigners, came to see the temple and offered gifts on its altar. This colossal temple impressed Jesus' disciples. They did not know that both the temple and the city were doomed. The Romans would soon destroy them both. The ancient ordinance of the daily sacrifice was to come to an end. Jesus, in a sad tone and with a sigh, told his disciples that the day was coming when all the beauty of the temple would be in ruins.

In the year 70 C.E., Titus destroyed the temple. The ruins of this beautiful and immense edifice and of the city remained there in Jerusalem. Thousands of Jews were slaughtered, some were carried away captive, and others were sold in the slave markets. Such was the fate of the once great Jerusalem and the holy temple that King Solomon had built to the God of Israel, the universal God.

Jesus' prophecy was fulfilled when Emperor Hadrian uprooted Jerusalem from its foundations and built a new city, calling it Elia Heliopolis. Today all of these stones of the temple are at Baalbek, Lebanon, about 160 miles north of Jerusalem. Not one stone was left on another. At one time in its past this holy temple had been defiled by pagan practices and Baal worship; during the time of Jesus it had become a den of thieves, developing into a business institution.

"The end of the world" refers to the reconstitution of the world in accordance with the highest ethical ideals that the Hebrew prophets had predicted. Jesus knew this could only come about through an inner revolution that was to take place within every human soul. For the world to be reconstituted, humanity must undergo a tremendous change of heart and mind. But, he also knew that certain national events were to occur. The following sayings of Jesus as recorded in the 24th chapter refer to two major happenings: (1) The destruction of the temple and the holy city of Jerusalem. (2) The final and glorious triumph of the messianic kingdom at the very end of all things.

THE LAST DAYS

For many shall come in my name, saying, I am Christ; and shall deceive many. And ye shall hear of wars and rumours of wars: see that ye be not troubled: for all these things must come to pass, but the end is not yet. For nation shall rise against nation, and kingdom against kingdom: and there shall be famines and pestilences, and earthquakes, in divers places. All these are the beginning of sorrows. Then shall they deliver you up to be afflicted, and shall kill you: and ye shall be hated of all nations for my name's sake. And then shall many be offended and shall betray one another, and shall hate one another. And many false prophets shall rise, and shall deceive many. And because iniquity shall abound the love of many shall wax cold. But he that shall endure unto the end, the same shall be saved. Mt. 24:5-13.

Jesus warned his disciples that false messiahs and prophets would appear on the scene to deceive people. He also knew that after his death on the cross the political situation in Judea would worsen.[1] The Romans would demand more taxes and tributes and those who refused to comply would be oppressed, persecuted, and put to death. There

---

[1]For an account of the fulfillment of these predictions, especially verses 5-8 and 15-22, see Flavius Josephus, *JEWISH WARS.*

would be uprisings and famine, but the end was not yet. Wars and rumors of wars, famine, and pestilence were not the indications of the end but only the beginning of travail.

Usually wars and revolutions create famine throughout the land. During these times, crops suffer severely. Invading forces use green fields for grazing; they burn ripening wheat fields, cut down trees and make vineyards desolate. Owing to this destruction, both people and animals suffer.

Natural catastrophes of drought and locusts also create famine but only affect certain regions of the land. Other parts escape disaster. Inhabitants of destroyed territories die of starvation because the lack of roads and facilities prevent transportation of supplies. Wheat might be abundant only thirty or forty miles from the famine-stricken area but there is no way to transport the wheat. Central governments do not render assistance to their suffering subjects.

Jesus foretold the fall of Jerusalem and that revolutions and wars would precede its destruction. Then, loss of crops, trees, and exhaustion of food supplies would follow the downfall of the holy city and the destruction of the temple. People who were not consumed by famine would die by the sword. (See Mark 13:8; Luke 21:11.)

The Romans would indiscriminately put to death Jews and the followers of Jesus. Many would recant and become pagans just to save their lives. Jesus told his disciples and followers that all of these things were bound to happen and would happen very soon. Many of these things did happen during the reign of Nero, Galba, and Titus. Numerous false religious teachers and prophets appeared among them offering new remedies and some claimed to be the Messiah.

The ardent dedication and love for the gospel of the kingdom that many of Jesus' followers had would cool. Iniquity would abound because false religious teachers and prophets would cause men and women to go astray. These pretenders would introduce materialistic philosophies and notions that were contrary to the gospel of the kingdom. But, as in the ancient days, a remnant would endure all kinds of tribulations, persecutions, and martyrdom. This remnant of true believers would eventually triumph over the corrupt and evil forces that were bearing down on them. These followers of Jesus' message would establish the reign of God on earth through their faithfulness and persistence in practicing the principles of the kingdom that their lord had taught them.

THE GOSPEL OF THE KINGDOM IS THE WITNESS

And this gospel of the kingdom shall be preached in all the world for a witness unto all nations: and then shall the end come. Mt. 24:14.

Jesus' message was God's sovereignty. God must be involved in the affairs of men if there is to be peace and harmony among all nations. Jesus saw that only the gospel of the kingdom, God's presence, among the nations of the world would bring the old order of governing to an end. His teaching was radical and subversive to the usual practices of those in power. It makes no difference if these powers were religious, social, local, or political.

The end would not come until this gospel is first preached and demonstrated to all nations, in all languages and dialects. The end will come, but not even Jesus himself knew the hour when humanity would awaken to the glory and enlightenment the kingdom would bring to the social, political, and ordinary life of people everywhere. Only God knows the final hour.

ABOMINATION OF DESOLATION

When ye therefore shall see the abomination of desolation, spoken of by Daniel the prophet, stand in the holy place, (whoso readeth, let him understand:) Mt. 24:15.

When an invading army besieges a city, its inhabitants take refuge in the citadel, churches, and other holy places. These sites offer the best protection from the enemy. From these strategic points, warriors can defend their city against invaders for months or for very long periods of time. During the siege people cannot leave or enter the city. The water supply is cut off and wells are dug to furnish water for the population, who are also short of food supplies. As the siege continues, conditions grow worse and hardships increase. The most serious situation is the accumulation of filth and refuse that fill the streets and gather in the holy places where people have taken refuge. Near Eastern cities did not have sewer systems and many areas still do not have these systems. Refuse is taken out weekly and thrown into the fields for fertilizing. During war time, this refuse piles high on street corners, courtyards, and around holy places, resulting in disease and plague.

This is what Jesus had in mind when he said: "When you see the abomination of desolation accumulating in the holy place." Jesus had predicted that the fall of Jerusalem was near. The historic city and its holy places were doomed. Roman forces would besiege and capture the city and destroy the temple. The sacred shrines which the people so highly revered would be polluted by the population. Then later, the Roman army would further desecrate these holy places.

In 70 C.E., Prince Titus polluted the holy of holies precinct and, finally, completely destroyed the temple. The invading army brought swine into the most holy area. The Romans were determined to do away with the temple so that they could break Jewish resistance forever. Those who understood the meaning of this prophecy would be able to escape the terrible fall of the city and temple. Daniel had predicted the destruction of the city and the defilement of the temple. The holy temple was polluted several times by Greek and Syrian armies, who offered swine meat upon the altar of God and desecrated all of the holy instruments. Later, Roman Generals entered the holy of holies, but the final destruction did not take place until General Titus marched into Jerusalem.

SUDDEN CALAMITY

Then let them which be in Judea flee into the mountains: Let him

296

which is on the housetop not come down to take any thing out of his house:
Neither let him which is in the field return back to take his clothes. And woe
unto them that are with child, and to them that give suck in those days! But
pray ye that your flight be not in the winter, neither on the Sabbath day;
For then shall be great tribulation, such as was not since the beginning of
the world to this time, no, nor ever shall be. And except those days should
be shortened there should no flesh be saved but for the elect's sake those
days shall be shortened. Mt. 24:16-22.

The impending disaster was to be great and speedy. People would have to flee into the mountains and hide in their caves. Those who slept on the housetops would not have time to come down into the house and gather their belongings and valuables.[2] Those who were working in the field would be cut off from their families and would not have time to go for their clothes. During an invasion, women with infants and pregnant women would have a very difficult time fleeing for safety. Generally invading troops rape and kill these women.

If this were to occur on the Sabbath people would not be able to flee or travel because of the Sabbath restrictions that permitted them to travel only a very short distance. Winter would also be another extemely difficult time to take flight. In other words, they were to pray that there would be no natural (winter) and religious, legal (Sabbath) impediments to their flight. This time of trouble and great tribulation was to be so severe that pregnant women would wish they were barren. And those women who were nursing their little ones would wish that they had never borne their babies. This disaster was to be greater than any in Jewish history, but for the sake of the elect, meaning the pious Jews and followers of Jesus, these awful days of tragedy would be shortened. The slaughter of people during the invasions of Titus and Hadrian was so terrible that the entire Jewish population was nearly exterminated; had the invasion been prolonged,

---

[2]The flat roof of a Near Eastern home is reached by a staircase from the court near the gateway; so that a person escaping in great haste need not go through any of the rooms of the house. He may also run from one rooftop to another since the structures are adjacent to each other.

"no human being" would have remained alive.[3]

FALSE CHRISTS AND PROPHETS

Then if any man shall say unto you, Lo here is Christ, or there; believe it not. For there shall arise false Christs and false prophets, and shall shew great signs and wonders; insomuch that, if it were possible, they shall deceive the very elect. Mt. 24:23-24.

The impending disaster would hasten the coming of many false christs and leaders who would pretend to be the saviors of the people. Many men and women, because of the immense suffering and hardships, would be deceived and would follow these false prophets.

Wherever there were true prophets acting as spokesmen for God, there were also false prophets misrepresenting God and speaking lies. At times, there was rivalry and competition between these two groups. In the old days, some of these false prophets were statesmen and politicians who always took the national side and predicted prosperity and victory. They gained strength and credence in the public eye because they played it safe with their predictions. They would only predict blessings for the nation and calamities on their enemies.

During the reign of King Ahab, false prophets had complete control over the land. God's true prophets were ousted and were no longer consulted as in former days. Kings and princes, who used to rely on these good prophets' sound counsel and judgment, were now imprisoning and expelling them from their country when they predicted defeats and gave warnings. This happened to Micaiah and Jeremiah. (See 1 Kings 22:26-27; Jeremiah 38:6.)

Jesus knew deceitful and lying prophets would come after his

---

[3]The Roman armies under Titus had slain thousands of Jews. They also crucified hundreds of captured rebels and fighters on the hills around Jerusalem. Thousands of men, women, and children were sold into slavery, but a small remnant took refuge in caves and in the deserts.

death. He knew selfishness and greed would dominate and men would be willing to sell themselves for honors and easy living. These deceptive leaders and teachers would preach a new religion in his name and would establish what he had denounced and abolished.

Jesus had told his disciples: "By their works you shall know them." These men would predict prosperity and luxury and encourage people to build temples and shrines, making them forget the gospel of the kingdom and the reasons for which their lord gave his life. Their works would not be the true works of Jesus' gospel. A true prophet is known by his fidelity to God and his courageous stand for truth. (See Mark 13:22.)

THE SUDDEN COMING OF THE CHRIST

For as lightning cometh out of the east, and shineth even unto the west; so shall also the coming of the Son of man be. Mt. 24:27.

In the Near East, lightning is supposed to be the fastest thing in the world, but science tells us that light is the fastest—that it travels 186,300 miles per second. Nevertheless, lightning is the fastest thing our eyes can see in motion. We can not see the motion of light.

Jesus says that his coming will be as fast as lightning. Just as lightning is seen in both the East and the West at the same moment, so he, likewise, will be seen by everyone. Moreover, the events that will precede his coming will take place in rapid succession.

No one will be able to foretell the day nor the hour of his coming, just as no one knows when a thief will come at night. Therefore, his disciples and followers are admonished to be alert and not to be misled by false prophets who, for their own worldly gains, would predict Jesus' coming and thus deceive the faithful. They were to be constantly watchful and ready to greet him when he comes. (See the parable of the Ten Virgins, Matthew 25:1-13.)

CARCASS AND EAGLES (VULTURES)

For wheresoever the carcase is, there will the eagles be gathered together. Mt. 24:28.

Generally when sheep stray, wolves and other wild beasts will attack them. While these beasts prey on the bodies of the sheep, scavenger birds will hover around waiting their turn to devour the remains. Shepherds know where their lost sheep are located by seeing these birds hovering in the sky. They also realize that their sheep have been killed.

Christ foretold that the Romans would destroy the Jewish state. Jerusalem was to fall and the great temple—the pride and center of the nation—was to be demolished. When Rome was finished with its operations in Jerusalem, other smaller nations around Judea would take their turn and gather like scavengers over the defeated nation and devour it.

After the fall of Jerusalem, Jewish enemies would multiply and national calamity would intensify. There is a Semitic proverb that says: "When an ox is tied up and led down to slaughter, the knives to cut off its head are plentiful." The Jews were not only to be defeated by the Roman army who were like wolves, but they were to be humiliated at the hands of neighboring peoples who were like vultures waiting to descend upon the desolate city, which was like a carcass. This prophecy was fulfilled when the Roman General, Titus, conquered Jerusalem and the Jews were scattered throughout the world. (See Luke 17:37.)

The word "eagles" may be incorrect. A scribe may have inserted this term "eagles" into the text to indicate the Romans. All Roman flags bore the image of an eagle. However, Jesus could have said "vultures." Although the eagle is a bird of prey, akin to the hawk, it is not a scavenger. Vultures, however, hover over highways and deserts to find dead bodies. They usually eat spoiled meat which other birds and wild beasts shun. Vultures are true scavengers.

"Carcass," in this instance, is also symbolic of the Jewish race.

The Jews had lost their freedom, and their leadership did not follow precious teaching of the prophets. And now, they were like a carcass ready for the vultures—enemy nations round about them—to devour them. The Assyrians, Chaldeans, Syrians had already devoured the Jewish nation and now they were to be the victims of the Romans.

UNIVERSE SHARES IN CALAMITY

Immediately after the tribulation of those days shall the sun be darkened, and the moon shall not give her light, and the stars shall fall from heaven, and the powers of the heavens shall be shaken. Mt. 24:29.

When the events that will precede the success of Jesus' gospel of the kingdom take place, the whole universe will share in the terrible tragedy which befalls the Jewish nation. In Aramaic, the darkness of the sun and the moon along with falling stars are Semitic forms of poetic figures of speech. These expressions mean that the entire universe would mourn over the terrible human calamity. For example, when Jesus died, the sun turned black. Again, when Alexander the Great died, Eastern writers tell us that the sun, moon, and the stars refused to shine. Commonly, Near Easterners understand such sayings as poetic figures of speech and do not take them literally. The gospel writer reports Jesus saying the stars will fall, and all the powers of the universe will be shaken. "Stars" refer to "great men, emperors, and princes who control the world."

Scriptures also hint that there will be an end to the universe. Some of the stars and planets in our universe may collide and explode. It will be a great calamity—greater than any other catastrophe recorded in human history. Hebrew prophets also made such predictions before Jesus.[4] On the other hand, Scriptures also say the universe is from everlasting to everlasting—indestructible.

---

[4]See Isa. 13:10 and Ezek. 32:7.

A SIGN IN HEAVEN

And then shall appear the sign of the Son of Man in heaven: and then shall all the tribes of the earth mourn, and they shall see the Son of man coming in the clouds of heaven with power and great glory. And he shall send his angels with a great sound of a trumpet, and they shall gather together his elect from the four winds, from one end of heaven to the other. Mt. 24:30-31.

These verses describe a revelation that the reader must not take literally. The gospel writer uses Semitic figures of speech. Jesus' followers will be informed of his "coming" through a revelation; the sign of his coming will appear in the sky, meaning a universal presence. Moreover, he will send his messengers to announce his coming, thereby preparing the way so that his followers may be ready to greet him.

"A great sound of a trumpet" represents an important announcement—Jesus' coming. The phrase "they shall gather together from the four winds, from one end of heaven to the other" is figurative speech. "Four winds" signify the four corners of the earth. Jesus' disciples will come from all parts of the earth. "Heaven" indicates the universe. "To gather from one end of heaven to the other" refers to a universal gathering. Jesus' followers will come from everywhere. *Shemaya*, "heaven," is an Aramaic word and has several meanings: "universe, cosmos, sky" and figuratively it implies "everywhere." "They shall see the Son of man coming in the clouds of heaven" signifies Jesus' triumphant appearance. "Clouds" are symbolic of God's presence. "Coming in the clouds" is also Semitic figurative speech that signifies success, high exaltation, extreme honor and praise. In the ancient world people considered clouds the highest thing in the world. "To come on a cloud" means "to succeed in a mission."

We must remember that this a revelation; we should not understand these sayings literally. For example, heavenly messengers need no trumpet to announce themselves. They come in the stillness of the day and the silence of the night.

Jesus' coming is spiritual; that is to say, he comes in a spiritual body, free of space and time. When Jesus appears, space and distance will disappear and every eye will see him.

FIG TREE

Now learn a parable of the fig tree; When his branch is yet tender, and putteth forth leaves, ye know that summer is nigh. So likewise ye, when ye shall see all these things, know that it is near, even at the doors.
Mt. 24:32-33.

The fig tree puts forth both its leaves and its fruit at the same time. When the leaves and fruit appear on the tree, people know that summer is near. In biblical lands of the ancient world, trees served as calendars. They helped people to know the time for sowing and harvesting because of the blossoming trees, their ripening fruits, and their falling leaves.

Wars, famines, insurrections, revolutions were indicative of the last days; that is, the triumphant day of the Messiah was at the door. The gospel of the kingdom would conquer all opposition and the mission and message of the Christ would be adopted by the nations of the world.

THE JEWISH RACE

Verily I say unto you, This generation shall not pass, till all these things be fulfilled. Mt. 24:34.

The Aramaic word *sharbtha* means "a family, tribe, race, nation, generation, genealogy." In this verse, the reference is to "race"—that is, the Hebrew race or the Jewish people.[5]

---

[5]The Jews at this time were known by their religion. Israel as a State or political entity had come to an end in 586 BCE.

Jesus wanted his disciples to know that they had a great work ahead of them. He knew it would take many centuries before the Jews would understand and receive his message of God's kingdom. Two thousand years have elapsed and only a small remnant of Jews have accepted Jesus' teaching which he taught throughout Galilee and Judea.[6] Throughout centuries, the Jews have played an important role in religion among the nations of the world. They have preserved the sacred writings and a strong belief in the existence of a universal God, which is closely akin to Jesus' teaching of God's sovereignty.

THE ETERNAL WORDS OF JESUS

Heaven and earth shall pass away, but my words shall not pass away. But the day and hour knoweth no man, no, not the angels of heaven, but my Father only. Mt. 24:35-36.

Part A—HEAVEN AND EARTH. "Even heaven and earth will pass away, but my words will not pass away" is an Aramaic figure of speech. It means: "What I say must come true." Semites believe heaven and earth are everlasting. And conversationally, they use phases with heaven and earth and others like it to express the surety of what they say. For instance, they say: "That mountain may move away but I won't move." This style of speech conveys the positiveness of truth, which they affirm with such sayings. The reputation of a prophet is staked on the truth conveyed by his words.

Jesus was not only emphatic in his utterances but he was sure of everything he spoke. He felt this way because what he said was truth and truth is eternal as God is eternal. Truth never changes or passes

---

[6]It was Dr. Lamsa's opinion and belief that the Jews will remain as Jews, as a witness to their Jewish race; but the day would come when those who call themselves "Christians" will truly accept the simple but powerful teachings of Jesus—his gospel of the kingdom. And, at that time, many Jews will embrace the true teachings of Jesus because his gospel is the essence of Judaism—the truth that God had revealed to Abraham, Moses and the prophets.

away. One can erase a mathematical formula but one cannot destroy a mathematical truth. Jesus' words are life, light, and truth. They can never pass away or change. Heaven and earth may change form but Jesus' truth remains forever and unchangeable. His words were often questioned because in the eyes of many of the leaders and some people, he was not an authoritative teacher who would be accepted on the strength of his reputation. Jesus did not depend on superficial testimony but on the inner truth of his message. He expressed his message in the common language of the people and not in abstruse sayings and complicated theological terminology.

Part B—THE UNKNOWN HOUR. Jesus also told his disciples that no one could predict the day or the hour when these things would happen. Only his Father knew when the end of all things would come. Many religious teachers and leaders over the centuries and even to this day still try to name the year, month, and day of the end of all things. But Jesus emphatically said: "No one knows the day or hour not even the angels in heaven."

JESUS' SUDDEN COMING

But as the days of Noe were so shall also the coming of the Son of man be. For as in the days that were before the flood they were eating and drinking, marrying and giving in marriage, until the day that Noe entered into the ark, And knew not until the flood came, and took them all away; so shall also the coming of the Son of man be. Mt. 24:37-39.

When Noah in his day warned the people of the impending disaster, the great deluge, they laughed at him. They were so confident in their materialistic way of life and the prospects of a happy future that instead of turning to God or preparing to protect themselves from the flood, they were planting vineyards, marrying and giving in marriage, not realizing that the end was upon them.[7]

---

[7]See Gen. 7:1.

When the end comes those who trust in the material world and their own judgment will again be caught unaware. They will not accept the true teaching and guidance of Jesus nor will they listen to warnings from those who believe in the gospel of the kingdom and are in communion with God. Nevertheless, no one knows the day or the hour; therefore, one must be prepared.

WORKING IN PAIRS

Then shall two be in the field; the one shall be taken, and the other left. Two women shall be grinding at the mill; the one shall be taken, and the other left. Mt. 24:40-41.

Frequently, Near Easterners work in pairs. Two men take care of the sheep; one is the shepherd and the other is his assistant. The shepherd goes before the sheep and the assistant follows after them to see that none go astray or are attacked by wolves. In the fields, two men plow or harvest; sometimes it is a father and one of his sons. Then, at other times, it may be a master and his servant. A father holds the plow handle and the younger man goes in front of the plow to keep the oxen in position.

In the house, two women will sit on the floor grinding wheat; usually one is an elderly woman who uses both hands to turn the grinder and the other is a young girl who uses one hand to assist the older woman. The younger will also pour the wheat into the grinder from a bag at her side. Blind women are usually grinders. Two other women may make bread; the younger rolls out the dough and the other places it inside the earthen oven to bake.

When an enemy invades and captures a town, all the young women and some young men are taken captive. The invaders will kill the fighters and the elderly women are left behind. Near Easterners respect women of old age and consider it a sin to kill them.

Jesus predicted the fall of Jerusalem. The holy city and the sacred shrines were to be defiled and destroyed, the priestly system and its hierarchy was to end, people would fall by the sword, and young men and women were to be carried into slavery. Invading forces also enter people's homes and take the young girls who may be sitting and grinding wheat in the inner room. They will drag these young women out of their homes while leaving the elder women to starve and die. (See Luke 17:34-36.)

SERVANTS PUNISHED

And shall cut him asunder and appoint him his portion with the hypocrites: there shall be weeping and gnashing of teeth. Mt. 24:51

"Who, then, is that faithful and wise servant whom his lord has appointed over his household to give them food in due time? Blessed is that servant when his lord comes and finds him so doing. Truly I say to you he will appoint him over all that he has. But if that bad servant will say in his heart, My lord delays his coming; and begin to beat his fellow servants and be eating and drinking with drunkards, the lord of that servant shall arrive on a day which he does not expect and at an hour he does not know."[8]

Matthew 24:1-44 deals with the destruction of the temple and the holy city and the glorious climactic coming of Christ. But beginning with these verses a change takes place. Matthew 24:45 through 25:30 begins a new theme and records three parables which do not refer to just the end of the age but also to the end (death) of each one's life. These parables were given to encourage Jesus' disciples to practice the principles of the kingdom so that when the unexpectedness of death comes, they would be prepared to meet their lord without regrets. These parables were also to prepare disciples of any era to be ready to greet their Lord, whether in the end of their personal lives or in the grand finale of all the ages. Chapter 24, verses 45-51 introduces this new theme and prepares the way for the next three parables.

---

[8]Mt. 24:45-50, Aramaic Peshitta text, Errico.

Verse 51 of the Aramaic text reads: "he will severely scourge him"—that is, beat him brutally, tear his clothes and inflict wounds on his body. When a servant is punished savagely, Easterners often say, "He is being cut to pieces." It does not mean to be literally cut to pieces as the King James Version indicates—"cut asunder."

The position of a servant is similar to that of a slave. The master has complete power over him. When servants are disobedient, masters punish them severely and discharge them without pay. The work is divided among other servants until a faithful overseer is procured. No doubt the Greek translator confused the meaning of the word *palagoo* which means "flog" as well as "divide." No master may murder a servant because that would be a criminal offense against the state, but even then the lord of a servant would not have to cut him in two to kill him.

"Appoint him his portion with the hypocrites" means his master may give him a small sum of money when he dismisses him as an unreliable servant. "There will be weeping and gnashing of teeth" is an Aramaic idiom and denotes overwhelming regret and disappointment.

CHAPTER 25

WISE AND FOOLISH VIRGINS

Then shall the kingdom of heaven be likened unto ten virgins, which took their lamps, and went forth to meet the bridegroom. And five of them were wise and five were foolish. Mt. 25:1-2.

Most Near Eastern weddings take place in early autumn or in winter. Usually people have ample time to attend long ceremonial and marriage festivities when they finish with their work. During these seasons, the days are short and as the wedding feast starts in the evening and continues all night, people depend on candles and oil lamps for their light. Butter is the fuel for their lamps.

Near Eastern homes are poorly lighted. Most houses have no windows except for an air chimney on the roof. Commonly, Semites rise early and go to bed early. There is no reading and writing to be done, so there is little need for lamps and candles during the spring and summer seasons. For light during the daytime, people depend on the sun's rays that come through the chimney into their homes. During the autumn and winter, the days are shorter and some work must be done in the evening, so the homes are usually lighted with candles and lamps. In the evening, men and women enter and leave their homes with lamps in their hands. The reason for this is that long, narrow, and dark paths lead to their homes and they can hardly be found without some light.

Candles and oil lamps are prepared before a wedding takes place. Parents of the bridegroom, neighbors, friends, and strangers provide abundant light for the wedding night. For Near Eastern Semites, light is a symbol of happiness and no wedding is properly conducted without plenty of light. A wedding continues uninterrupted, sometimes for seven days and nights. During this entire time, the house is fully lighted. Men and women dancers hold lamps in their hands. Some men fasten candles at the head of their daggers. Visitors,

309

coming from nearby, generally purchase oil at the town where the wedding is to take place. However, there are those who, afraid that they won't be able to obtain oil and candles, bring their own supplies of light for the wedding. As the bride is escorted during the evening when it is dark and because the guests do not know the hour of her coming, some visitors, to their disappointment, find shops closed. Even the oil vendors themselves are waiting for the arrival of the bride. These weddings do not run by the clock. If an evening wedding is announced, it could take place at midnight.

When preparations are completed, a party of men and women are sent to the home of the bride to accompany her to the wedding house. Near Easterners take their time in doing things and never rush. While the bride is being dressed and the guests are entertained, people wait outside with their lamps for the procession. Before the bride and her party reach the wedding house, the bridegroom and his party go out a short distance with lamps to greet the coming procession. And just before they arrive, another elaborate procession of men and women is on its way to greet the bridegroom and the bride.

When the entire party reaches the door of the wedding house, the bridegroom, his bride, and the invited guests go in. The door is then locked because there is no room for all who seek to enter. Even invited guests who arrive late are left outside. They knock at the door, but because of the noise and partying, no one hears them. Servants are instructed not to open the door no matter who knocks. The bridegroom is too busy entertaining guests and cannot be bothered with those who arrived late and are waiting outside.

The ten virgins in the parable took their lamps and oil to greet the bridegroom and bride. The five wise ones, being aware of the emergencies and delays that can occur, especially in procuring water from the scanty wells to bathe the bride and bridegroom,[1] brought extra oil for their lamps. But, the five unwise were negligent and

---

[1] It may take women many hours to procure sufficient water. They must wait at the well until their turn comes to draw water. Therefore, the wedding can be delayed for quite a while.

careless and did not bring extra oil. And when the wedding procession was delayed, all the virgins slept. At midnight the herald cried out with a loud voice: "The bridegroom comes. Arise and be ready!" The five who had been negligent had no more oil and, therefore, could not gain entrance to the wedding feast without lamps to help light the large house. Lamps are important to make the wedding a success. Only those who were prepared entered.

Such is the case with the coming of the heavenly bridegroom and kingdom. No one knows the time and the hour. Jesus emphasized the the importance of readiness for the unknown day of the triumph of his gospel of the kingdom. He likens that day to a Near Eastern wedding in which no one knows the exact hour when the bridegroom and bride will arrive and when the exciting procession will start on its way to the wedding house. Those who have made preparation in advance will have the opportunity to greet him and join him for the celebration. Others who think they are his followers and admirers but made no preparations, or who have waited to the last minute to prepare themselves, will find great disappointment because the door is locked and it is too late to greet the bridegroom.[2]

SERVANTS APPOINTED GUARDIANS

For the kingdom of heaven is as a man traveling into a far country, who called his own servants, and delivered unto them his goods. And unto one he gave five talents, to another two, and to another one; to every man according to his several ability; and straightway took his journey.
Mt. 25:14-15.

When a master or householder goes on a journey, he places his property and business affairs in the care of his servants. Some masters

---

[2]Many New Testament scholars believe that Jesus did not create this parable. The early disciples and followers of Jesus composed this story and put it on his lips so that the new converts would remain faithful. These new converts were to be in a state of readiness in preparation for Jesus' return.

appoint one of their servants as overseer. Others assign duties to each servant according to his ability. Every servant tries to do his best to accommodate his lord so that the master will be pleased with him on his return. None of the servants would dare steal anything because of the jealousy and rivalry that exist among them.

Servants are empowered to act as trustees of the household. They can buy, sell, borrow, lend, and look after their master's family. Although these masters may have grown sons, some of them would rather appoint servants to be responsible for these tasks. The reason for this practice is that many lords are polygamists. When a man has many wives, the house is filled with quarrels and troubles. Each mother would like to see her own son entrusted with responsible duties. It is too much of a problem for the father to make a choice without generating a family feud.

When David was dying, his favorite wife, Bathsheba, begged him to appoint her son Solomon as successor to Israel's throne instead of Adonijah, the son of Haggith.[3] The majority of the people were with Adonijah, but Bathsheba triumphed because of David's affection for her. This change caused the death of Adonijah and David's general, Joab.

Therefore, in order to avoid jealousy and strife between the children and wives, the masters will often appoint servants or strangers as overseers. Servants who fail in their tasks are punished and discharged. But those who serve faithfully are promoted and given greater responsibilities and honors. The lesson here is to accept your responsibilities and opportunities and make the most of them.[4]

The parable of the talents is about God's kingdom.[5] Neo-platonism is a form of socialism and communism that Socrates and his

---

[3] See 1 Kings 1:17.

[4] See Lk. 19:13-24.

[5] Modern scholars of the gospels interpret Jesus' parables quite differently than they appear in the gospels of Mt., Mk., and Lk. They no longer interpret them allegorically. However, this commentary works with the received text commenting on the language and culture of the times. This is not a critical work.

disciple, Plato, advocated and it had spread throughout the countries of Egypt, Palestine, and other parts of the Roman Empire. All races and people who had been oppressed, exploited, and heavily laden were interested in this new foreign ideology. Socrates taught that everything should belong to the state. The rich should be dispossessed of their large land holdings and other forms of wealth. This political doctrine appealed to many poor and landless people who labored as serfs for their wealthy landlords.

Besides all this, the rich were favored and declared tax exempt. They also were allowed to collect taxes and to conscript labor without paying wages. The rich throughout the land were imperialists and oppressors of the poor and laborers. But the citizens of God's universal heavenly kingdom were to be different. They were admonished not to conform to the present system that exploited people.

Jesus instructed his followers to let God's law guide them. They were to uphold the free and just biblical system that the Hebrew prophets taught. Work is a gift of God. Wages are the blessings that are bestowed upon the faithful and worthy laborers. Worldly goods, possessions, and other forms of wealth are the results of one's talent and faith. Therefore, the rich are entitled to all that they have, providing they have not oppressed the poor nor withheld the proper wages of their workers. When wise and hard-working people are deprived of proper remuneration for their labor, they will cease to work.

Poverty is not a virtue nor is there any piety in it. Citizens of God's kingdom are to live life in an abundant and prosperous manner but based on the principles of fair trade for all. They are to multiply their substance so that they may give and share to help feed and clothe the poor, misfortunate, and underprivileged. This is all a part of Jesus' vision of the kingdom of heaven.

Before moving on to the next comment, there is a verse that needs some further explanation. "His lord answered and said unto him, Thou wicked and slothful servant, thou knewest that I reap where I sowed not, and gather where I have not strawed: Thou oughest therefore to have put my money to the exchangers, and then at my

313

coming I should have received mine own with usury.[6] The Aramaic text reads: His lord answered and said to him, Bad and lazy servant! You knew me that I reap where I have not sowed and gather where I have not scattered? Then you should have left my money on the tray and when I returned I would have demanded my own with interest."[7] There is a custom here with which most Westerners are unfamiliar. In the Near East a lord has a special tray or table where money is left so that his servants may take this money and invest it for their lord. Then, at a later time, their lord may call for the interest on the money that was loaned. In this case, the "lazy servant" was so full of fear that he did not even bother to do this simple act so that his lord would gain some interest.

TO HIM WHO HATH SHALL BE GIVEN

For unto every one that hath shall be given, and he shall have abundance: but from him that hath not shall be taken away even that which he hath. Mt. 25:29.

Frequently, a Near Eastern landlord divides his land into lots and rents them to tenants. An oral agreement is made between the landlord and each tenant. As he is the owner of the land, the landlord supplies the seed and receives one-third of the crops produced and the seeds he has loaned. The tenants usually plant wheat.

During the harvest season the proprietor sends his servants to collect his share of the crops and grains. His servants must also observe and report to him how reliable and capable the tenants were in working the land. The landlord must know if the tenants are worthy of any future contracts. Those who negotiate the contracts are also empowered to make any changes that they deem wise and they may also recruit new tenants for any idle and uncultivated lands.

---

[6]Mt. 25:26-27, K.J.V.
[7]Mt. 25:26-27, Aramaic Peshitta text, Errico.

Every tenant reports the condition of his crops to the landholder's servants. Some may complain that the soil was bad; others, that the soil was good but the irrigation system was not sufficient. Still other tenants may have had good lands but did not take proper care of them so their crops were meager. Then there were those tenants who had poor terrain but labored very arduously and produced more wheat than the owner had anticipated.

When the owner receives the reports, he immediately orders the servants to make changes. He will take the land away from the negligent workers and give it to the industrious laborers. In addition, the owner will also take from those careless workers whatever wheat was grown for future planting and give it to his faithful tenants. Thus, the unfaithful were left without seed and land.

Therefore, this saying, "for to him who has, it shall be given, and it shall increase to him; but he who has not, even that which he has shall be taken away from him," was meant for those endowed with certain abilities that they do not use and for those who have few talents but make great use of them. All people have a place and mission in life that are unique. Those who fail to express them lose their place in life. But, to those who are faithful in expressing what they are and have, more is given—that is, the more they express their natural abilities, the more their gifts and responsibilities increase. One's place and mission are sacred because God's share is in them.

THE PARABLE OF THE SHEEP AND THE GOATS

When the Son of man shall come in his glory, and all the holy angels with him, then shall he sit upon the throne of his glory: And before him shall be gathered all nations: and he shall separate them one from another, as a shepherd divideth his sheep from the goats: And he shall set the sheep on his right hand but the goats on the left. Then shall the King say unto them on his right hand, Come, ye blessed of my Father, inherit the kingdom prepared for you from the foundation of the world. . . .Then shall he say also unto them on the left hand, Depart from me, ye cursed into everlasting fire, prepared for the devil and his angels: For I was an hungred, and ye gave me not meat: I was thirsty, and ye gave me no drink: I was a stranger, and ye took me not in: naked, and ye clothed me not; sick, and in prison, and ye visited me not. . . .And these shall go away into everlasting punishment: but the righteous into life eternal. Mt. 25:31-46.

In chapters 24 and 25, the gospel writer reports Jesus as having warned and prepared his disciples and followers by teaching them about: (1) the destruction of the temple; (2) the siege and fall the of the holy city, Jerusalem; (3) the end of the age; (4) the end of individual, personal life; (5) the final judgment for all nations. One must understand that this judgment is based on what the nations did not do for their neighboring nations—that is, not caring for people's needs. "I was hungry and you did not give me to eat; I was thirsty and you did not give drink. I was a stranger and you did not shelter me; I was naked and you did not cover me; I was sick and in prison and you did not visit me."[8] The Hebrew prophets also taught these things.

Part A—SHEEP SEPARATED FROM GOATS. "And he shall set the sheep on his right hand, but the goats on the left." Nearly every family keeps flocks of sheep and goats, for both are needed. White sheep supply the wool for clothing and black goats supply the hair for tents, bags, and ropes. Both furnish the family with milk that they make into butter and cheese, their chief food. Rich families do not use goat milk but keep the goats only for their hair.

Sheep and goats graze together on the mountains and in the fields. Most shepherds dislike goats and sometimes punish them severely because they are wild, troublesome, and difficult to handle. They climb steep places and go wherever they choose. Shepherds are kept busy watching them and fetching them back to the fold. The white sheep are gentle, walk slowly, graze quietly and in an easy manner. The moment the shepherd calls, they hear his voice and obey.

When shepherds bring their flocks to the field, they stand in the midst of the road, back of the fold and separate the sheep from the

---

[8]Mt. 25:42-43, Aramaic Peshitta text, Errico.

goats. Sheep go to the right side of the shepherd on the roof of the fold to be fed with grass before they are taken into the field. Goats go directly through a narrow passage into the fold and no grass is provided for them. On the way to the gate of the fold, the goats see the sheep on the roof eating grass. This makes them fret and they grind their teeth and bleat.

Jesus uses this practice of the separation of the sheep and goats to illustrate the final separation of the righteous from the wicked. According to the gospel writer, the good shepherd—the Messiah/Christ—will separate the righteous from the wicked, just as a shepherd separates the goats from the sheep. (See footnote 12.) Goats represent people who are determined to do evil. They are likened to goats because goats give shepherds a difficult time during the grazing hours.

The judgment is based on the works of good deeds—that is, those who have fed the poor, clothed the needy, welcomed strangers and visited prisoners bringing them food. Those who did these things are the sheep. Those on the left hand will be repudiated because they have done none of those good deeds. They may boast of performing miracles, wonders, and building costly cathedrals, shrines, and temples but they failed to practice the simple gospel that Jesus taught. And finally, the unfaithful will know nothing but regret, wishing they had followed the precepts of the kingdom. On the other hand, the faithful will know joy and everlasting life. They had taken care of people in need.

Part B—PRISONS AND PRISONERS. "Naked and ye clothed me: I was sick, and ye visited me: I was in prison and ye came unto me."[9] *Beth-aseereh*, "prison," is a compound word. *Beth* means "house," and *aseereh* comes from the Semitic root *asar* meaning "to tie or bind." Thus, the Aramaic word *beth-aseereh* refers to a prison—that is, a place where prisoners are bound in chains. It is not just a place of detention where prisoners are fed regularly, pursue their vocations, enjoy games, and study.

---

[9]Mt 25:36, K.J.V.

Near Eastern prisons do not have shower facilities, hospitals, and libraries. Such a place in the ancient Near East would be luxurious for even the rich who had never seen a shower stall until the middle of the twentieth century. Even today, there is no comparison between the prisons in the Near East and those in the West. It is, therefore, very difficult to convey how meaningful this verse truly is. And it is doubly difficult to describe the kind of tortures prisoners experience.

In many Eastern countries, prisoners are bound, hand and foot, in chains. Notorious criminals are treated very harshly. Their feet are put in stocks. The penal house is extremely dirty. It has no sanitary facilities. Dirt is allowed to accumulate. The prisoners are fed just enough bread and water to keep them alive, which prolongs their suffering. Unpaid guards take the prisoners' good garments and their remaining clothes are never washed during the entire time they are incarcerated. The prisoners are beaten at least once or twice a day.

Kind prison officials allow relatives and friends to visit the prisoners and to bring them food and clothing. Usually this is only done after a bribe has been given to the guards. In such cases, the prisoner is, at least, relieved of his hunger. Prisoners who are serving long terms and whose homes are at a great distance suffer incomprehensible privation and misery. They have no visitors and no money to buy food. They die a slow, agonizing death from hunger, cold, thirst, and the unsanitary conditions. Because of these deplorable prison conditions, Near Easterners believe nothing brings greater reward than helping a prisoner who is a stranger. They do this by bringing him food, clothing, and by visiting and comforting him when he is ill. Jesus wanted the principles and practices of God's kingdom to reach into the prisons. Compassion is one of the major principles of God's sovereign presence extended to everyone.

Part C—EVERLASTING TORMENT. "And these shall go away into everlasting punishment: but the righteous into life eternal."[10] "Everlasting torment or punishment" is another Aramaic idiom that carries the same meaning as *gehenna dnoora*, "hell fire." It refers to

---

[10]Mt. 25:46, K.J.V.

regrets that one has for having done evil or for neglecting to do good. This evil or neglect creates mental torment and suffering. One "burns" emotionally and psychologically with regret and anguish.

The notion of "everlasting" derives from the fact that there is no way to remedy the wrong that has been committed. The thought of not having rectified evil deeds—that is, repented—will always continue to plague an evil doer. In other words, time to make amends has passed for the individual and the door has closed never to open again.

According to the Gospel of Matthew, Jesus illustrated this same point when he told the parable of the ten virgins. Five wise virgins, who were alert and made preparations ahead of time, were able to enter the wedding feast and celebrate with the wedding party. Five foolish virgins were regretful and could not join the wedding festivities. They were unhappy and could not do anything to change the situation. The righteous, like the five wise ones, would enter eternal life without regrets or any mental torment.[11] They had helped the poor, clothed the naked, visited the sick, and supplied the needs of incarcerated criminals. They had stored treasures in heaven (good works to help humanity). Eternal joy and everlasting life that they were to experience were not based on extraordinary deeds but on simple acts of mercy, kindness, and compassion—acts that anyone can practice, anywhere, at anytime.[12]

---

[11] In other words, the righteous would die in joy and peace without any mental or emotional suffering.

[12] There is no doubt that the sayings to help the needy originate with Jesus, but these sayings may have been changed to fit a final judgment scene which works well with Matthew's theological theme of judgment throughout his gospel. This also holds true for the imagery of the sheep and the goats. Then, again, Jesus may have been typically using Near Eastern metaphoric figures of speech which we should not take literally. These illustrated utterances of the final judgment are Semitic imagery that describe various behaviors (good or bad) brought about by our own national and individual attitudes and actions in this life.

CHAPTER 26

RUMORS OF JESUS' DEATH

Ye know that after two days is the feast of the passover, and the Son of man is betrayed to be crucified. Mt. 26:2.

The rumors of Jesus' arrest were beginning to spread throughout Judea and Galilee. Jesus himself had been warned from time to time and even cautioned not to go to Jerusalem to celebrate the Passover. Nevertheless, he had to go. He knew that his time had come and he was about to face death on the cross. It was inevitable.

Jesus was to die on the cross so that he could reveal God's power over death and the grave. All through his life and ministry, he demonstrated God's power over sin and sickness. His message of the kingdom was all-inclusive. Prostitutes, sinners, tax collectors, society's outcasts, and the sick flocked to him, finding comfort and healing in his joyful message of God's kingdom. Now he was about to endure the ordeal of crucifixion and death. But his death was also a part of his life and he would show his Father's power in the midst of seeming defeat and failure.

Crucifixion was the usual Roman manner of execution. According to Jewish law, criminals were executed by stoning, burning, decapitation or strangulation. Jesus was to be tried and convicted under Roman law as a political criminal (treason against Caesar). Jesus was Galilean and therefore subject to Roman capital punishment.

The Messiah/Christ was to triumph over death. He inaugurated a new way of life—one of meekness, nonviolence, and loving kindness. The forces of nonresistance and meekness were soon to conquer the world without sword, arrow and bow. The cross would forever destroy the power of death and the grave. Therefore, Jesus was not afraid of death on the cross.

A PIOUS ACT

When Jesus understood it, he said unto them, Why trouble ye the woman? for she hath wrought a good work upon me. For ye have the poor always with you; but me ye have not always. For in that she hath poured this ointment on my body, she did it for my burial. Verily I say unto you, Wheresoever this gospel shall be preached in the whole world, there shall also this, that this woman hath done, be told for a memorial of her.
Mt. 26:10-13.

The acceptance of hospitality from a woman whose character was questionable was contrary to religious tradition, especially at the house of a well respected Pharisee. Jesus' disciples had been raised in the religious traditions of their culture, so the presence of this strange woman seated so near their master was disturbing to them also. They knew that people would criticize her behavior and that it would reflect on them.

Jesus' disciples were also indignant because they thought the precious oil had been wasted. They were thinking that it would have been better to sell the oil and give the proceeds to the poor. They did not realize that the pouring of the oil on their master was for his burial. Jesus would soon be absent from them, but the poor would remain with them.

Jesus readily accepted the woman's hospitality although people considered her a sinner. He had already taught that tax collectors and harlots would enter the kingdom of heaven before the scribes and Pharisees. Therefore, his acceptance of her kind act demonstrated to everyone that Jesus welcomed her.

Society had condemned this woman. Undoubtedly, many self-righteous religious authorities, who cloaked their own sins with their long ecclesiastical robes, had reproached, despised, and even persecuted her. But Jesus received the love and care she poured upon him.

Jesus was so sure of the success of his gospel of the kingdom that he assured this woman of an eternal remembrance for her good and timely act. From then on, her story would be inscribed on the pages of Jesus' gospel and told from one generation to the next until the end of time.

FEAST OF UNLEAVENED BREAD

Now the first day of the feast of unleavened bread the disciples came to Jesus, saying unto him, Where wilt thou that we prepare for thee to eat the passover? Mt. 26:17.

The feast of Unleavened Bread begins on the fifteenth day of *Nisan.*[1] *Nisan* is the first month of the religious year and the seventh month of the civil year. In the books of Moses it is called the month of *Abib*—Spring.[2] Matthew and Mark describe the event as a *Seder*, while John saw it as an ordinary meal. (*Seder* in Hebrew means "Order": ceremony and supper observed in the Jewish home on the first night of Passover. Rabbinic injunction regulates the entire meal. Outside Israel, it is celebrated on the first two nights of Passover.)

Both festivals, Passover and Unleavened Bread (Hebrew: *massot)* are celebrated together, although they are considered as two distinct feasts. Chapters 12 and 13 of Exodus explain both these festivals in full detail.

THE PASSOVER FEAST

And he said, Go into the city to such a man, and say unto him, The Master saith, My time is at hand; I will keep the passover at thy house with my disciples. Mt. 26:18.

---

[1]Nisan is an Akkadian loan word and forms part of the Babylonian system of lunar month names. The Jews began to use this system sometime after their exile in Chaldea. Nisan falls in the spring (March and April). Passover is celebrated in mid-Nisan and it also marks the time of Jesus' crucifixion.

[2]Ex. 13:4; 23:15; 34:18; Deut. 16:1.

During religious feasts, cities become inundated with people. Usually, Near Easterners lodge with their relatives and friends throughout these special holy days. Jerusalem is always overcrowded on Passover day.

Jesus was familiar with the situation in the holy city. Having been in Jerusalem before, he knew about places that provided lodging for men only. For on such occasions, when the city becomes choked with pious Jews and Gentile merchants who had come from foreign lands, people are reluctant to invite large groups into their homes, especially a party of men with no women accompanying them.

In all large cities there are certain inns just for unmarried strangers, foreigners, and people of other faiths. Women are never permitted to work there, nor can they draw water for the foreigners and strangers. However, men work at these lodges and bring water in a sheepskin container. Women will only bring water to families that stay in homes or other places. These women will carry the needed water in earthen vessels which they bear upon their heads.

The Passover—in Aramaic *pesakh*, "the rejoicing"—is celebrated every year in commemoration of Israel's departure from Egypt and release from Egyptian oppression. The celebration takes place on the fourteenth day of *Nisan*.[3] It was an ordinance that Israel was to keep forever. Every Jew participates and eats of the meat of the lamb in memory of the lamb their forefathers had killed when they first celebrated the Passover in Egypt. Their forefathers had placed the lamb's blood on the doorposts to protect themselves from the messenger of death.

The Jews also drank wine during the Passover as a symbol of rejoicing. Salvation for them was wrought through the blood of the lamb. Israel ate, drank and rejoiced. The term "Passover" refers to the event when the destroyer passed over the Hebrew homes and slew the firstborn of the Egyptians.

---

[3]See the previous comment, Mt. 26:17, *FEAST OF UNLEAVENED BREAD*, and the explanation of *Nisan*.

BETRAYAL

And as they did eat, he said, Verily I say unto you, that one of you
shall betray me. And they were exceeding sorrowful, and began every one
of them to say unto him, Lord, is it I? And he answered and said, He that
dippeth his hand with me in the dish, the same shall betray me. The Son of
man goeth as it is written of him: but woe unto that man by whom the Son
of man is betrayed! It had been good for that man if he had not been born.
Then Judas which betrayed him, answered and said, Master, is it I? He
said unto him, Thou hast said. Mt. 26:21-25.

Jesus' humiliating entry into Jerusalem made many of his disciples
and followers feel unsure about their master's messiahship. How could
he be the King of Israel? Their doubts were so strong that many
disciples and followers had left him and even the faith of the twelve
apostles had been weakened. Jesus knew that his faithful twelve would
also desert him and that one of them would betray him.

His disciples and followers, regardless of the constant warnings,
had anticipated a triumphant entry into the historic city. They also
expected that a large delegation of priests, scribes, Pharisees, and
government officials would come to greet him with a white horse and
with salt and bread, which was the ancient custom. But to their great
disappointment there was no such warm reception. This episode
weakened their ranks considerably.

The desertion and conspiracy in the ranks of Jesus' followers
began before their entry into Jerusalem. Not one of his disciples
believed he was going to die. They all looked forward to a successful
mission in Jerusalem, but only a few poor followers from Galilee had
come to welcome Jesus to the feast of Passover. Judas of Iscariot had
already made up his mind to betray his master before their arrival into
the holy city. He thought he had better clear himself and claim
immunity by turning his master over to the authorities.

"And as they did eat, he said: Verily I say unto you that one of
you shall betray me." Near Eastern Semitic men usually let their
emotions show—whether of joy, sorrow, or deep disappointment.

324

Jesus was not afraid to give vent to his deep feelings during the entire meal. At such a fraternal meal, men speak freely and openly. This was a display of typical Near Eastern temperament.

In this land, during suppers and banquets with one another, good friends exchange sop by sharing and dipping into each other's food. It is a token of friendship and loyalty to each other. However, the choice food is always placed before the honored guest, who sends his portions to whomever he wishes.

An Eastern family feels that two dishes and two spoons are sufficient for twelve guests, especially during a wedding or festival where spoons, cups, and dishes are scarce. On such occasions, however, families will borrow from their neighbors. People have no idea about germs and do not know that eating with the same utensil might be harmful. One often sees five or six men sitting on the floor, eating from one dish and taking turns using the same spoon. Strangers are invited to eat from the family dish and use their common spoon, but beggars are excluded and eat alone, using a separate dish and spoon.

During a meal, men often take food from the dish of another group sitting near them. Sops of food wrapped in thin bread[4] are exchanged without the slightest hesitation or embarrassment. Often a man eats half a sop and then hands the rest to another. This may appear to an American as the worst breach of etiquette, but among Semites, it is a token of love between two friends. One bestows great honor on another by eating the other half of the sop or eating from his friend's dish. When enmity exists between two men, they never eat at the same table. When they become reconciled, it is necessary to demonstrate their friendship by eating from the same dish.

Judas was the treasurer. His position was somewhat higher than the other disciples. Or, at least, he thought so. He seems to have been sitting close to Jesus' dish. He could dip his hand in his master's dish and take a morsel. He wanted to make Jesus feel he was still his best friend and he did this so that no suspicion might be aroused among the

_____

[4]Like a tortilla

disciples. Judas did not want his plans to deliver Jesus into the hands of the priests and elders spoiled. He acted as though nothing was happening, but Jesus knew. The master realized that Judas had been behaving strangely and that his seeming friendliness at the meal was to deceive everyone. Jesus could no longer hold his peace. When the disciples insisted on knowing who would betray him, he said that the one who dips with him in the dish is the guilty one. This totally surprised and shocked the disciples, for this act by one of them was a serious breach of Semitic trust.

In Matthew's text the phrase "he who dips his hand with me in the dish" has been construed to mean Judas only. Although possible, this meaning is not true to the normal custom. Dr. Rihbany comments:

> The fact is that according to Syrian [Semitic] customs on such occasions each of the few large dishes contains a different kind of food. Each one of the guests is privileged to reach to any one of the dishes and dip his bread in it. From this it may be safely inferred that several or all of the disciples dipped *in turn* in the dish which was nearest to Jesus. (See Mk. 14:17-20.) The fact that the other disciples did not know whom their Master meant by his saying that one of them should betray him, even after he had said, "He that dippeth with me in the dish," shows plainly that Judas was eating in the same fashion as all the other disciples were.[5]

"Judas, the traitor, answered and said: Maybe it is I, my teacher? Jesus said to him: You have said that!"[6] This is an Aramaic style of speech, meaning "You said it, not I." Jesus had celebrated this feast almost every year of his life. Now it was the last time that he would participate in this religious festival. Therefore, he wanted his disciples to know that when they celebrated the Passover again they were to do it as a memorial to him and not just about Israel's departure out of Egypt. Now he was to become the lamb slain not just for the salvation

---

[5]Abraham M. Rihbany, *THE SYRIAN CHRIST*, pp. 60-61.
[6]Mt. 26:25, Aramaic Peshitta text, Errico.

of one nation but for the liberation of all humanity.

THE BREAD AND THE CUP

And as they were eating, Jesus took bread, and blessed it, and brake it, and gave it to the disciples, and said, Take, eat; this is my body. And he took the cup, and gave thanks, and gave it to them, saying, Drink ye all of it; For this is my blood of the new testament, which is shed for many for the remission of sins. But I say unto you, I will not drink henceforth of this fruit of the vine, until that day when I drink it new with you in my Father's kingdom. Mt. 26:26-29.

Part A—BREAD. Near Easterners consider bread as something more than mere matter. "Inasmuch as it sustains life, it is God's own life made tangible for his child, man, to feed upon," so say Easterners. They think of bread "as possessing a mystic sacred significance." Usually, they will not tell a lie when bread is before them. They also believe that it is sinful to mistreat bread. Knives or forks must not touch the sacred bread. They have to break it with their hands only.

The bread and salt covenant is a strong bond of friendship. To lie and be unfaithful to a bread and salt covenant is to be stigmatized as a base ingrate and untrustworthy person. Among Semites bread has always been eaten with a deep sense of sacredness. There are many expressions in Scripture that testify to this fact: "bread and salt," "bread and wine," "Christ, the bread of life," "for we, being many, are one bread," and "Give us this day our daily bread."[7]

The little group of thirteen men sat down, their feet tucked under them, their hats on their heads, and their shoes removed. It is proper etiquette to keep one's hat on while eating, but it is gross and an insult to sit at a feast with shoes on. Jesus then took the bread, blessed it, and broke it in small pieces. He then distributed these pieces to his disciples and said: "Take, eat; this is my body." This affectionate expression of Jesus was common among Semites at a fraternal supper.

---

[7]See Mt. 6:11, "Daily Bread," p. 98 of this commentary.

Sometimes the men will declare to each other such sayings as: "My life and my blood are for you; take the very sight of my eyes, if you will." They will also use other similar expressions. It was not a strange thing that Jesus, whose entire life was a living sacrifice, should say to his intimate disciples/friends as he handed them the bread and the cup, "Take, eat; this is my body;" and "Drink ye all of it; for this is my blood."

The bread reminded Jesus that very shortly he would be surrendering his body to the cross. The wine in the cup resembled blood, which also suggested to Jesus that his blood was soon to be shed. The wine that usually makes every man's heart light and cheerful was for Jesus a cup of sorrow. That is the reason for these statements. Furthermore, no longer was this meal symbolic of the past, but it became the symbol of the new covenant that Jesus was to seal through his death on the cross.

Part B—CUP. The use of a common cup does not come from custom or from an institution but is due to the scarcity of cups and plates. Today, in those parts of the Near East untouched by Western civilization, it is usual for a family to use one cup. Even in the homes of the rich, the family seldom uses two cups. The cup they use for water is also used for wine. Guests and members of the family drink in turn, passing the cup from one to the other. In Jerusalem and in Syria, people now have many cups and plates. They have special cups for wine and coffee and plates for different foods. This was unknown a hundred years ago, but modern industry has made pottery plentiful and inexpensive in the Near East as in most parts of the world.

Jesus and his disciples drank out of one cup because it was the only one the owner of the house could offer them. Had they been living in parts of the world where cups were plentiful, they would doubtless have used several cups. Nevertheless, the one cup to Semites meant fellowship and fraternal communion. Dr Rihbany says:

> The one who gives drink fills the cup and passes it to the most honored member of the company first. He drinks the contents and returns the cup to the one who poured, who fills it again and hands

it to another member of the group, and so on, until all have been served once. Then the guests drink again by way of *nezel*. (A word difficult to translate into English, some say "treating" but this falls short of expressing the affectionate regard which the *nezel* signifies.) The one guest upon receiving the cup wishes for the whole company "health, happiness, and length of days." Then he singles out one of the group and begs him to accept the next cup that is poured as a pledge of his affectionate regard. The pourer complies with the request by handing the next cup to the person thus designated, who drinks it with the most effusive and affectionate reciprocation of his friend's sentiments. It is also customary for a gracious host to request as a happy ending to the feast that the contents of one cup be drunk by the whole company as a seal of their friendship with one another. Each guest takes a sip and passes the cup to the one next to him until all have partaken of the "fruit of the vine." (See also Mark 14:23.)[8]

At Seder, four cups of wine are drunk, each representing a redemptive last cup of the Seder; hence, Jesus' final statement, "From now on I will not drink from this fruit of the vine until the day in which I will drink it anew with you in my Father's kingdom." This is a Semitic expression of speech meaning, "I will not be fully joyful again till we are all together once more." In this case, the verse refers to the great banquet and celebration of God's kingdom triumphing all over the world. The kingdom of heaven is filled with eternal joy of everlasting life and the ever fulfilling presence of God. "Wine" in Aramaic metaphorically represents "joy, teaching, and inspiration."

"For this is my blood of the new testament" is a blood covenant. The ancient "blood of the covenant" is connected with the rite of circumcision and the Passover (Exodus 12:48, 24:8). Jesus' blood of the covenant refers more to Leviticus 17:11.[9]

---

[8]Abraham M. Rihbany, *THE SYRIAN CHRIST*, pp. 62-63.

[9]Many New Testament scholars believe that the interpretation of the Passover supper as an atonement sacrifice is a later Christian addition to the text. This interpretation "shed for the remission of sins" does not accord with Jesus' basic

SHEPHERD SMITTEN

And when they had sung an hymn, they went out into the mount of Olives. Then saith Jesus unto them, All ye shall be offended because of me this night: for it is written, I will smite the shepherd and the sheep of the flock shall be scattered abroad. But after I am risen again, I will go before you into Galilee. Mt. 26:30-32.

The hymn or praises that the disciples were singing were Psalms 112-117. Immediately after the supper, Jesus and his disciples retreated to a public park on the Mount of Olives. Jesus knew that the lives of his disciples were in jeopardy because of his teaching, so he quoted a scripture to them concerning a smitten shepherd.

When robbers slay a shepherd, his sheep will scatter. This is because they have no one to lead them. They sense the danger, so they run in different directions. Moreover, when sheep smell blood, they become agitated. When a flock is at peace, the shepherd stands with his staff in his hand where all the sheep can see him. His presence comforts them. They know they are safe from wild animals and thieves. Jesus quoted this saying from the prophet Zechariah.[10]

Sheep are very timid. At times, they are frightened even by the presence of strangers. They know the voice of the shepherd, but the voice of a stranger terrifies them. The prophet Ezekiel says, "And my sheep were scattered, because there is no shepherd; and they became food for all the wild beasts of the field."[11] Jesus was the good shepherd of Israel, who had come to gather the scattered sheep, to seek those who were lost, to bind up those who had been injured, and even to give his life for their sake.

When Jesus was arrested, his disciples saw the danger of being implicated, arrested, and probably put to death. So they fled in the

---

teaching of his gospel of the kingdom. Hebrew prophets condemned the Near Eastern sacrificial system that was practiced with the slaughter of animals.

[10]Zech. 13:7; 1 Kings 22:17.

[11]Ezek. 34:5, Aramaic Peshitta text, Lamsa translation.

dark hours from Gethsemane, even as the sheep flee when the shepherd is slain. Some would hide in the city and nearby towns, and others would even deny him and swear that they had never met him or heard of him. Even Simon Peter, his most faithful disciple, would deny him before the cock crowed in one of the adjoining houses near the high priests' palace.

THE COCK CROW

Jesus said unto him, Verily, I say unto thee, That this night, before the cock crow, thou shalt deny me thrice. Mt. 26:34.

Since clocks were not known in the ancient Near East, the shadow of the sun indicated the time by day and the stars by night. Cocks served as alarm clocks to awaken laborers in the morning. Although some homes had no hens, there were roosters in nearly every home. Chickens shared the same room with the families. A board was fastened on one of the walls of the house where the chickens rested at night.

As soon as the light of dawn breaks through the chimney in the roof, the rooster begins to crow. In a few minutes the silence of the night is broken and the entire village resounds with the crowing of the roosters. One can see priests going to church, laborers following them before going to the fields, and caravans resuming their journey. At times, when priests fail to appear at church and laborers at their work, they immediately blame their roosters, just as Americans blame their clocks for being inaccurate.

Jesus' trial before the high priests took place late at night. It was over towards early dawn, just when the roosters began to crow. As there was no other way to indicate the time when Peter would deny him, Jesus said it would be before the cock crowed.[12]

---

[12]See Mk. 14:30; Lk. 22:34; Jn. 13:38.

JESUS' AGONY AND PRAYER IN THE GARDEN

Then cometh Jesus with them unto a place called Gethsemane, and saith unto the disciples Sit ye here, while I go and pray yonder. And he took with him Peter and the two sons of Zebedee, and began to be sorrowful and very heavy. Then saith he unto them, My soul is exceeding sorrowful, even unto death, tarry ye here, and watch with me. And he went a little farther, and fell on his face, and prayed, saying, O my Father, if it be possible, let this cup pass from me: nevertheless not as I will, but as thou wilt. And he cometh unto the disciples, and findeth them asleep, and saith unto Peter, What, could ye not watch with me one hour? Watch and pray, that ye enter not into temptation: the spirit indeed is willing, but the flesh is weak.
Mt. 26:36-41.

Jesus left most of his disciples in one area of the garden of Gethsemane, but he and most likely Peter, Jacob, and John went further into the garden. His heart was in turmoil and heavy. He was so emotional that he could hardly control his tears. The tragic hour was now at hand. Jesus was about to face a trying and difficult temptation. His body was protesting the thought of leaving this world although his spirit was willing to drink from the cup of death.

Prayer was the only consolation for a bitter time such as he was to endure. Jesus prayed aloud while his disciples lay on the ground, dozing in and out of sleep. They had heard some of his prayers and were all grieved and frightened. They had never seen their master so full of deep sorrow. The entire situation was confusing to them. Aside from the three disciples—Peter, Jacob, and John—some of the other disciples were so tired that they slept. They were extremely weary from the mental and emotional exhaustion of the surprising events of Passover week, beginning with Jesus' entry into Jerusalem. The disciples were also physically tired from their long journey to Jerusalem.

Part A—THE FATAL CUP. It is a long established Near Eastern custom that when one wishes to do away with an enemy, he will give a banquet and poison the cup of wine which his enemy is to drink. Such banquets are elaborate and expensive and are intended to win the confidence of the honored guest who is to be the victim. After the meal, the wine is passed and the confidential servant of the host, under unsuspicious circumstances, will hand the fatal cup to the enemy. When the wine is served, every guest is expected to drink without asking any questions. If a guest becomes suspicious, he must either take a chance and drink or kill his host.

Jesus knew the deadly cup he was about to drink would be poisoned because of the religious hostility that was brewing against him. He also knew that, after his feasting with his disciples, the authorities would arrest, convict, and crucify him. Jesus had no choice but to drink the cup or flee from the holy city. This was a trying crisis, so he sought his Father's guidance, willing to abide by the divine decision. (See Mark 14:36; Luke 22:42; John 18:11.)

Part B—AWAKE AND PRAY. "Watch and pray, that ye enter not into temptation." The Aramaic text reads: "Awake and pray that *you may not enter* into temptation."[13] The Aramaic word here is *tiloon,* "enter." It is the same Aramaic term, *talan,* used in the Lord's prayer. The only difference between the two passages is the verbal form of "enter." In Jesus' prayer, it is *"and let us not enter."*

Judas' betrayal of Jesus opened the ranks of the disciples. Before their arrival into Jerusalem, some of his followers had already deserted. The twelve men who stood by him were discouraged and fearful. Judas, no doubt, was very active in creating dissatisfaction and rebellion among his comrades. Possibly he warned them of the danger that would overtake them if their lord was arrested and imprisoned. He may also have suggested that they might meet the same fate as their master-teacher.

Jesus admonished his disciples to pray that they might not enter into temptation. He did not ask them to pray that God would take away the temptation but that they might conquer it. God strengthens those who seek his help to overcome trials and testings. His disciples needed help during this dark hour. They needed to pray so that they might not be tempted, like Judas, who had sold Jesus for thirty pieces

---

[13]Mt. 26:41a, Aramaic Peshitta text, Lamsa translation.

333

of silver. Moreover, their faith in Jesus as their leader was weak. They did not believe that the Messiah had to die so that they might win a victory over evil forces. Again, Jesus' idea of the Messiah was not the same as his disciples.

Jesus' disciples could easily have turned against him as a great deceiver who had lured them away from their religion. Later Peter would swear and curse, saying that he did not know Jesus at all. To many people their life is more precious than their religion.[14]

While they were in the garden, Jesus wanted them to "keep awake and pray" so that they might overcome their fear. He did not ask them to "watch," meaning to offer resistance to the enemy, as the King James Version implies, but to "keep awake." He knew that some of the Pharisees and priests were determined to seize him. Jesus had no intention of resisting them. While a revolt on the part of his disciples might save him from the cross, he knew one of them might be tempted to assassinate him. This is characteristic of many Near Eastern people. No matter how sincere a leader may be, should he meet defeat, one of his followers might slay him. Ishbosheth was slain by his two officers[15] and Darius was killed by his own men after the defeat at the battle of Arbela.

His disciples might have been tempted to put up a strong fight for him, but Jesus wanted everything to take its course so that the Scriptures might be fulfilled. He wanted no other death but that on the cross. (See Mark 14:38.)

Part C—THE BODY IS WEAK. "The spirit is prepared but the body is not strong."[16] Jesus, during his prayer in Gethsemane, was passing through another temptation more severe than in the Judean desert. In the desert, Jesus' body was craving food; in Gethsemane, his body was fighting for survival. Jesus, as a human being, wanted to live. His body was protesting and was unwilling to die. His mind was tormented with the thoughts of death.

---

[14]See Lk. 22:40.
[15]See 2 Sam. 4:7.
[16]Mt. 26:41b, Aramaic Peshitta text, Errico.

Why should he die? What could his death accomplish? Why should he suffer the shameful and agonizing death of a malefactor? But his spirit, the Christ in him, was willing, prepared, and ready to pass through the ordeal of crucifixion so that he could demonstrate that life is eternal and indestructible. He would win a victory over death and the grave. His spirit was willing because the cross was the only way to awaken humankind to end violence, to change hatred for love, to relinquish former life styles for a new way of living, and to open the hearts of men and women to the principles of God's kingdom.

A human being, in physical form, is earthy and loves the things of the earth and the world. But, the spirit also dwells in human beings and is constantly guiding if individuals will heed the prompting of the divine spirit. The body may protest but the spirit is always ready to do the divine will.

It was difficult for Jesus to surrender his life forces. Life is the most precious thing in this world. Thoughts of escape had come into his mind. He had, on several occasions, escaped death before, even death by stoning. But now his time to die on the cross had come. The prophets had foretold his rejection, condemnation, and death. Jesus, as the Messiah/Christ, had challenged the religious teachers and all corrupt forces of his day even though it led to his death.

JESUS STAYS

Rise, let us be going: behold, he is at hand that doth betray me.
Mt. 26:46.

During those last moments in Gethsemane, any rustling of the trees or noises from the city were greatly disturbing to Jesus. He had spent hours in prayer deciding his destiny. Should he die on the cross or leave the place with the eleven men who remained loyal to him? In the past few hours Jesus had gone through inner torment and agony to finally reach his decision. He considered his mother and the sorrow

335

that his horrible death would bring to her. His body was making every protest to escape crucifixion, but his spirit was yielding to the inner voice that came from heaven. Jesus had to struggle to eliminate the physical protests he was enduring. While praying, he heard Judas approaching so he rushed to his disciples and said: "Rise, let us go. He who is to deliver me is coming." Jesus had overcome temptation. He was now ready to meet the arrival of his betrayer and the crowds who came with him.

THE TRAITOROUS KISS

And forthwith he came to Jesus, and said, Hail, master; and kissed him, And Jesus said unto him, Friend, wherefore art thou come? Then came they, and laid hands on Jesus and took him. Mt. 26:49-50.

Judas' traitorous kiss was the greatest sign of hypocrisy and perversion of an ancient, deeply cherished and common Semitic custom. When friends of the same social status greet each other, especially after being gone for a while, they do so with a kiss on both cheeks, "sometimes with very noisy profusion."

The custom of men kissing each other was a natural act in the Near East:

When they [male friends] are not of the same social rank, the inferior kisses the hand of the superior, while the latter at least pretends to kiss his dutiful friend upon the cheek. So David and Jonathan "kissed one another, until David exceeded." Paul's command, "Salute one another with a holy kiss," so scrupulously disobeyed by Occidental Christians, is characteristically Oriental [Semitic]. As a child I always felt a profound reverential admiration for that unreserved outpouring of primitive affections, when strong men "fell upon one another's neck" and kissed, while the women's eyes swam in tears of joy. The passionate, quick, and rhythmic exchange of affectionate words of salutation and kisses sounded, with perhaps a little less harmony, like an intermingling of vocal and instrumental music.

So Judas, when "forthwith he came to Jesus, and said, Hail, master, and kissed him," invented no new sign by which to point Jesus out to the Roman soldiers, but employed an old custom for the consummation of an evil design. Just as Jesus glorified the common customs of his people by using them as instruments of love, so Judas degraded those very customs by wielding them as weapons of hate.[17]

Verse 50 in the Aramaic reads: "Then Jesus said to him: Is it about this that you have come, my friend? Then they approached and seized Jesus and arrested him."[18] When Jesus uttered these words, he looked at Judas' face and saw the weakness of the man who had pretended to be his disciple and friend. Jesus called Judas "friend" because Judas had greeted him with the kiss of friends. And, although Judas was weak and greedy for money, Jesus still counted him as a friend. He did not upbraid Judas at all, nor did he rebuke and condemn him. It was Judas' destiny to betray his lord. That was the part he had to play in the great drama of Jesus' final days. It is no surprise that in John's gospel concerning Judas, we read: "And after the sop Satan entered into him." (John 14:27.)

NON-RESISTANCE

Then said Jesus unto him, Put up again thy sword into his place: for all they that take the sword shall perish with the sword. Thinkest thou that I cannot now pray to my Father, and he shall presently give me more than twelve legions of angels? But how then shall the scriptures be fulfilled, that thus it must be? Mt 26:52-54.

According to John 18:10, the disciple with the sword was Peter.

---

[17]Abraham M. Rihbany, *THE SYRIAN CHRIST*, "Feast and Sacrament" pp. 70-71.

[18] Mt. 26:50, Aramaic Peshitta text, Errico.

337

Jesus prevented Peter from resisting. The latter had drawn a long knife that the disciples carried with them to chop up wood and prepare food. Jesus quoted a great truth from Scripture: "All those who take the sword shall perish with the sword." This is the law of compensation that sooner or later catches up with every person in this world.

Part A—JESUS CONFIDENT. Jesus refers to "more than twelve legions of messengers" in contrast to the "twelve disciples." The Romans commonly kept at least one legion in Palestine consisting of about 6,000 infantry and 600 cavalry. Jesus was confident in God and in the ultimate victory. He knew that God would send legions of angels to deliver him if he should ask for help. Nevertheless, he knew that death on the cross was his destiny and that Scripture must be fulfilled.[19] Jesus, again and again, had tried to impress on the dull minds of his disciples that he must die on the cross; that his death was inevitable. He also understood that the religious authorities would reject him and that his departure from old religious concepts advocated by these authorities would cause his death. He had surrendered his human will to the divine will. He never doubted God and trusted in his heavenly Father to the last moment. The Messiah/Christ had to die on the cross so that he could reveal the hidden truths in the Jewish religion to the Gentile world. Through his death, Jesus would also confirm his teaching, which is based on meekness, forgiveness and loving kindness.

Part B—PERISH BY THE SWORD. Jesus knew many portions of the Hebrew Bible by heart. He had spent the early years of his youth studying Scripture. He knew that those who had taken the sword had perished by the sword. For example, Absalom, who slew Ammon, King David's firstborn, was slain by Joab; and Joab, who slew Abner and Amsa with the sword, was slain by Benaniah with the sword.

This was also true of great empires that had taken the sword; all of them had perished by the sword. Force, like a two-edged sword,

---

[19]See Isa. 53:7.

338

works both ways. Force is generally met by a greater force.[20]

BEFORE THE COUNCIL

But Jesus held his peace. And the high priest answered and said unto him, I adjure thee by the living God, that thou tell us whether thou be the Christ, the Son of God. Jesus saith unto him, Thou hast said: nevertheless I say unto you, Hereafter shall ye see the Son of Man sitting on the right hand of power, and coming in the clouds of heaven. Mt. 26:63-64.

Part A—THE TRIAL. During the trial before the council, many charges were made against Jesus that they might be able to convict him and put him to death. But the testimonies of the false witnesses did not agree, so it was useless and worthless to convict Jesus on their charges.

The people in Jerusalem knew very little about Jesus and his teaching. They knew even less about the differences between his teaching and the doctrines of the priests and their religious leaders. Therefore, Jesus did not answer their accusations. They didn't understand him or his gospel of the kingdom. Even the Pharisees and scribes had taken his words literally. How much more, then, would these false, illiterate witnesses take his sayings literally. There was no use in contradicting them. Other people had heard him making strange claims.

Galilee was close to the borders of Syria where paganism pre-vailed. The gods of these religions had sons and daughters conceived in a human manner. Jesus' teaching was undoubtedly suspected and confused with pagan notions. The Pharisees and priests had been monitoring Jesus from the very beginning of his mission. They had heard people calling Jesus "the son of David." These religious leaders would not tolerate a Galilean assuming such a noble title. Neither could they accept Jesus calling himself "the son of God." To them,

---

[20]See Mt. 10:34.

only a descendant of David could be the Messiah or God's son. The idea of bestowing these titles on a Galilean was ridiculous.

The high priest interpreted Jesus' teaching to mean he was the Son of God physically and in the religious sense that pagans taught. The high priest would not have objected to a Jew calling God his father, because the Jewish concept of the fatherhood of God was spiritual. Jews thought of God as a Father. David told Solomon to look to God as his Father. According to the prophet Isaiah, God called Cyrus, the Persian king, his son.

Jesus did not reply either affirmatively or negatively. He held his peace. Had he replied, he would have had to say *aen*, "yes," or *la*, "no." He used neither word. But, just as soon as the high priest said, "I charge you by the living God that you tell us," Jesus had to answer. He knew his teaching about sonship was misunderstood, so he answered "you say that," meaning "you misinterpret my teaching relative to divine sonship." It also means, "you have said so, not I" or "this is what you say." Jesus never taught that God was his physical father. Nevertheless, the time would come when everyone would "see the Son of man coming in the clouds of the sky and with glory." In other words, they would see this human being (Son of man) sitting at the right hand of God, which means God would be backing him. "Coming in the clouds of the sky and with glory" signifies they would see his mission succeeding with great honor.

Part B—SON OF MAN. The Aramaic term *breh dnasha*, literally translated "Son of man," derives from *bar*, "son," and *nasha*, "man." It has many meanings in Aramaic: "humankind, humanity, human being, a man, an ordinary person, a commoner." When a Semite declines honors and homage, he says: "I do not deserve this honor, I am nothing, *I am just a man*, a simple working man." He will use the term *bar nasha* to express those ideas. Men of rank and nobility are addressed according to their social standing and status. People will call them *mari*, "my lord." People honor and call religious men "*rabbi*" or "father." They call a peasant *bar nasha*—"a man."

The religious expectation of the time was that the Messiah/Christ was to come from the house of David. He was to assume a princely title and was to be known to the people from his birth. Jesus, being a Galilean, could not easily make such royal claims nor could he connect himself with any priestly lineage. Instead of assuming an earthly title in harmony with Jewish messianic aspirations, he referred to himself as *breh dnasha*, "Son of man," which meant a human being, a commoner. He used this term more frequently than "Son of God." It was an answer to those who vainly argued concerning his ancestry and nobility. Furthermore, by this term, he showed that he was no pretender to an earthly throne, but he was to be the suffering servant and give his life for humanity. (See Luke 21:27; John 1:51.)

CHAPTER 27

JESUS DELIVERED TO PILATE

And when they had bound him, they led him away, and delivered him to Pontius Pilate the governor. Mt. 27:2.

Tiberius Caesar had appointed Pontius Pilate as governor of Judea the borders of which were from Samaria to the Dead Sea. The Romans had granted the Jews full ecclesiastical jurisdiction. But the Roman governor had complete political power. Pontius Pilate was the sole representative of Caesar. Ecclesiastical authorities could condemn Jesus to death but they did not have the right to crucify him. The accusations against Jesus were on political grounds, so these authorities could secure a speedy trial, conviction, and execution. The case had to come before the governor.

No doubt Pilate and Jesus conversed in Aramaic. Usually, all civil and military authorities had to learn the native tongue. For example, in the modern world, French and English governors and generals speak the language of the country in which they exercise their rule. In cases where the authorities are unable to converse in the native language, they secure an interpreter for these officials.

Pilate had spent many years in the Near East and knew the Semitic, Palestinian language. Evidently, Jesus did not know any other language. The four gospels do not indicate otherwise. When Jesus spoke in his own defense, he spoke in his native Galilean dialect of Aramaic. Very little is known about the conversation between Jesus and Pilate, which clearly proves no interpreter was present. The few recorded remarks in the gospels were probably reported by the governor's servants or by Jews who were eavesdropping at that time. (See Mark 15:1-2; Luke 23:1-3.)

THE FIELD OF BLOOD

Wherefore that field was called, The field of blood, unto this day.
Then was fulfilled that which was spoken by Jeremy the prophet, saying,
And they took the thirty pieces of silver, the price of him that was valued,
whom they of the children of Israel did value; Mt. 27:8-9.

A field across the valley of Hinnom was purchased for the burial
of strangers and was called *qreetha dadma*, meaning "field of blood."
The writer called it the "field of blood" because it was bought with
blood money for which Jesus was sold and which Judas turned over
to the priests after he realized the terrible act he had committed.

Every town has a separate burial place for strangers, a distance
away from the town. It is separate because strangers may be followers
of other faiths and could not be buried in the usual cemetery. Townspeople commonly bury travelers who die or are killed away from their
homes in the cemetery for strangers without any religious ceremony.

Although Matthew states that there was only one prophet,
Jeremiah, who made this prediction, the quotation itself is a combina-
tion from two prophets. (See Jeremiah 32:6-15 and Zechariah 11:12-
13.) Evidently, the author or copyist made this error. The price of a
man was settled at thirty pieces of silver; the price of a woman was
much less. In those early days, men and women were sold in the
market places to the highest bidder. Joseph was sold in the market
place in Egypt for thirty pieces of silver. Judas sold Jesus for the same
price. The predictions of the prophets were fulfilled.

NOT A POLITICAL RULER

And Jesus stood before the governor: and the governor asked him,
saying, Art thou the King of the Jews? And Jesus said unto him, Thou
sayest. Mt. 27:11.

When Jesus stood before the Roman Governor, Pilate, the first
question the governor asked him was this: "Are you the King of the

343

Jews?" Jesus, with his arms stretched out in bewilderment, replied: "You say that." This conversation was conducted in the Aramaic language. Most Roman officials spoke the language of the people over whom they ruled.

The Aramaic term *at amarat* means "You are saying this" or "That is what you say." Such a subtle, Semitic phrase can only be determined by the facial expression, hand movement, and voice inflection. Pilate understood what Jesus meant. Jesus could have answered with a yes or no, but his reply was more dramatic and emphatic. "You say this" means "I have never said such a thing." Then Jesus added: "Do you say this of yourself or did others tell you? If my kingdom was of this world, I would not have been arrested and brought before you."

The governor understood the tone of Jesus' words and his strong denial of kingship. Pilate kept looking at the meek and haggard man who stood before him. He was amazed at the charge that was brought against this Galilean peasant, so he immediately went to the council and reported that he had examined the man and found no fault in him.

Had Jesus said that he was the King of the Jews, Pilate would have convicted him immediately. But Jesus denied that he was a king and that his kingdom was of this world. Therefore, the Roman governor, wishing to be fair in his judgment, exhausted all means in his power to save the man from Galilee. Nonetheless, the charge against Jesus was so great that, at last, he had to yield to the demands of the Jewish council. Pilate feared that Rome might recall him. The high priests could have accused him of being a friend of the emperor's enemies. On the other hand, Pilate, the representative of the imperial government, did not want to disturb the peace between the emperor and his subjects over a man whose teachings were questionable and whose own people had accused of being the emperor's enemy.

SCARLET ROBE

Then the soldiers of the governor took Jesus into the common hall,

*and gathered unto him the whole band of soldiers. And they stripped him,
and put on him a scarlet robe.* Mt. 27:27-28.

Aramaic speaking people call this kind of royal robe *klamees
dazhoreetha,* meaning "a robe of scarlet" (a color of cloth made in
Lebanon from seashells). Only kings wore this kind of costly garment.
One legend has it that the scarlet robe belonged to one of the
Maccabean kings and was kept in the temple. The high priest had it
put on Jesus to show that they had no other king but Caesar. (Dr.
Lamsa believed that the scarlet robe was one of Herod's old royal
garments.) Near Easterners would take great delight in dressing a man
who had claimed to be a king in royal clothing before he was put to
death. (When Dr. Lamsa lived in the Near East, an Arab Caliph had
done this very thing to a condemned man.) Jesus was wrongly accused
as a political dissenter who claimed to be king.

It is also a common practice in the Near East for kings and
princes to confer royal garments upon their brave and distinguished
men of valor. Degrees, medals, and other decorations are very recent
innovations. The robe was a symbol of authority, honor, and great
acclaim. This custom is also followed by some royal hosts who show
appreciation to their outstanding guests. When King Ahasuerus
honored Mordecai, he commanded Haman to bring the royal apparel
and place it on him.[1]

Scarlet is the symbol of royalty and only rulers and their families
wore such garments. When a new ruler received an appointment from
the emperor, he would receive an official garment. The color scarlet
also stood for loyalty and a willingness to give one's life. Jesus was
accused of declaring himself a king, so Herod mocked him by placing
on him royal garments as one who had just been newly appointed to
a royal position.

---

[1]See Esther 6:8-11.

VINEGAR AND GALL

They gave him vinegar to drink mingled with gall: and when he had tasted thereof, he would not drink. Mt. 27:34.

Vinegar mixed with gall was given to criminals so that their suffering would be less intense while they were on the cross. It acted as a narcotic and helped deaden awareness. (See Psalms 69:21.) Jesus tasted it but refused to drink it. He was thirsty for water. Apparently, Jesus had had no water to drink since his arrest. And, of course, loss of blood also intensifies thirst.

JESUS' TRIUMPHANT CRY

And about the ninth hour Jesus cried with a loud voice, saying, Eli, Eli, lama sabachthani? That is to say, My God, my God, why hast thou forsaken me? Some of them that stood there, when they heard that, said, This man calleth for Elias. Mt. 27:46-47.

The Lamsa translation of this verse reads: "And about the ninth hour, Jesus cried out with a loud voice and said, *Eli, Eli, lemana shabakthani!* My God, my God, for this I was spared! (or This was my destiny.)" [2] Interestingly, the King James Version of the gospel presents Jesus' cry as a question. This implies that Jesus did not understand what was happening to him. It also seems that Jesus felt that God had forsaken him. However, we may understand Jesus' Aramaic cry as a declaration instead of a question: "el, 'el l'mana shwaqthani:[3] O God! O God! To what [a purpose] You have kept me!" Jesus cried out with a deep knowingness of his reason for having lived and for dying. His cry was a victorious one. God did not abandon him. A terse and literal rendering of this cry would be "O,

---

[2]Mt. 27:46-47, Aramaic Peshitta text, Lamsa translation.
[3]Errico transliteration of the Aramaic text

346

God! O God!⁴ To what (a purpose) You have left me!" "Left" in this context does not mean "forsaken or abandoned." It refers to "remaining to fulfill an end or a destiny."

Part A—JESUS' DESTINY. The Aramaic word *shwaqthani* derives from the root *shwaq* which means "to keep, reserve, leave, spare, forgive, allow, permit." "Yet, *I have left (or reserved)* to myself seven thousand in Israel, all the knees, which have not bowed unto Baal, and every mouth which hath not kissed him."⁵ For the same Aramaic word *shwaq* meaning "leave, spare, and reserve" see 1 Samuel 14:36; "forgive," Psalm 103:3, Matthew 6:12, Acts 5:31; "allow," John 11:48; "permit," Luke 18:16. (Aramaic Peshitta text and Lamsa translation.)

The last letter of the word *shwaqthani* indicates "I or me." "My God, my God, for this I was kept" or "for this you have kept me" (or "spared" me) connotes, " it was my destiny to die this kind of death." It does not mean that God forsook Jesus. Nor, is there anything in Jesus' cry to suggest an appeal for help. In his prayer in the garden, Jesus had overcome all his adverse bodily feelings and left the outcome to his Father.

The Aramaic words for "forsaken me" are *taatani* coming from *taa*, "to forsake or forget" (Psalm 13:1, 42:9, 43:2, 44:9, 60:1, 78:7-11, 103:2, 119:140-141 Aramaic text) and *nashatani* from *nashah*, "to forsake or forget." Compare Aramaic—*Manasheh*, Hebrew— *Manasseh*, in Genesis 41:51: "And Joseph called the name of the first born *Manasseh*: For God, said he, has made me forget all my troubles, and all my father's house."⁶

Job also, through all his suffering, had faith in God. No Near Eastern martyr has ever spoken of God's desertion in the hour of suffering. If Jesus had meant that God had forsaken him, he would have undoubtedly used the Aramaic term *taatani* or *nashatani*. The

---

⁴The Semitic word *el* as a verb also means "to help, aid, sustain, succor." Thus, God also means "helper, that is, one who sustains and succors."

⁵1 Kings 19:18 K. J. V. See also Rom. 11:4.

⁶Aramaic Peshitta text, Lamsa translation.

Galileans who were present knew he meant that his destiny was fulfilled. This is the reason that none of his apostles had ever commented on his cry from the cross. Not even the apostle Paul mentioned this cry. He, at least, would not have missed its significance. The soldiers and the Jews standing near the cross did not understand what he said, because Jesus spoke Galilean Aramaic. Had the religious leaders who were by the cross heard Jesus say that God had forsaken him, they would have made an issue out of it and declared that Jesus was definitely a sinner. But they thought he was appealing to the Hebrew prophet Elijah for help. (In Aramaic the word for "Elijah" is *Elia* and is very similar to *Eli*, "God.") Furthermore, Semites would not have believed that Jesus said God forsook him, because they believe that the manner of a man's death is predestined. So when death comes to a man, they believe God is closer to him than at any other time.

Jesus' cry that he was fulfilling his destiny accords with his teaching. During his ministry Jesus had declared and taught that God was a loving Father who was aware even when a sparrow falls. He always felt God was with him. Even when he spoke of his death, he predicted his disciples would forsake him but his Father would always be with him. "You will leave me alone; and yet I am not alone because the Father is with me."[7] On the journey to Jerusalem he said that "the Son of man was to be delivered to the high priests and crucified and rise on the third day."[8] He also told Pilate: "For this cause came I into the world, that I should bear witness unto the truth."[9] ("To bear witness to the truth" means "to be willing to die for the sake of the truth.")

How could Jesus have contradicted all his teaching and shattered the truth and hope of his gospel followers? God was assuredly with him in this hour of agony. Even his enemies who watched him die exclaimed: "He trusted in God; let him deliver him now; if he will have

---

[7]Jn. 16:32.
[8]Mt. 20:18.
[9]Jn. 18:37, K.J.V.

him."[10] In the garden Jesus assured his disciples he could ask God to send angels to fight for him, but his death on the cross was inevitable. He had to drink from the deadly cup to reveal that God had power over death. Jesus' cry was not a confession of defeat, despair, or failure; his words were a declaration of victory and triumph. His mission was fulfilled when he courageously defied the authorities of his day and died a martyr's death.

The Aramaic term *l'mana* has different meanings, such as "what a thing, for what a purpose." It is not in the form of a question, but it is an exclamation of wonder over an achievement when it is accomplished. For example, Esther's uncle had induced her to petition the Persian King on behalf of the Jews, stating she was made a queen for that purpose; that is, it was her destiny. It was unlawful for Esther to appear before the king uninvited. The punishment for such an attempt was death, but Esther, regardless of the severity of the Persian court edict, appeared before the king and besought him for mercy to save her people. However, she was not sure that the king would grant her request. Nonetheless, she realized that this was her mission. "If I perish, I perish."[11]

There is another Aramaic word *l'hana*, "for this," that resembles the word *l'mana* when written in Aramaic. Both have the same sense but *l'mana*, in this case, is exclamatory. Joseph told his brothers, when he made himself known to them, not to grieve because they had sold him. He told them that it was God's will and that it was his destiny to be sold as a slave and taken to Egypt.[12]

When Jesus was on the cross, his tormentors reviled him and called him names because in their eyes he was dying as one who had blasphemed their God. Instead of replying to the insults of the excited crowd, his exclamation was just like that of any Near Easterner today when he is dying an unjust death: "My God, my God, this is my destiny for which I was born. I know I am innocent. Let the people

---

[10]Mt. 27:43.
[11]Esther 4:14-16.
[12]Gen. 45:5.

think what they will, but to me my death has a different meaning." Jesus' words from the cross were addressed to God, his Father, but they were also intended to strengthen the shattered faith of his disciples and friends. They were standing by utterly bewildered, watching him die the death of a criminal. He wanted to remind them once more that this was his destiny and that the Messiah/Christ had to suffer at the hands of his enemies. Jesus fulfilled the role of the suffering servant; nevertheless, he had utter confidence in God.

It was this assurance that made some of his disciples courageous enough to remain in Jerusalem despite the fact that their leader was convicted as a revolutionary. It was this assurance that sealed and fulfilled the Hebrew prophecies of a suffering Messiah/Servant. These Scriptures could not have been fulfilled nor could he have risen from the dead if he had held the slightest doubt in God.

Interestingly, the Assyrian Church still teaches that God was continuously with Jesus on the cross and in the grave. How could God forsake Jesus? If God had actually forsaken him, then Jesus' mission would have been a failure. Pagan gods often forgot their duties to their people and, at times, were asleep.[13] Human parents do not forsake their children at the time of their death. Some of them travel hundreds of miles to be with their beloved at such a time. How could Jesus have thought that God would forsake him?

How could God have forsaken his beloved son who was dying for all humanity? His last words addressed to his loving Father were not: "Father, avenge me" or "Father, save me" but "Father, forgive them" and "O, my Father, into thy hands I commit my spirit." Therefore, in his suffering, Jesus was conscious that God was with him and that he was not deserted. He was not questioning God's wisdom like Elijah had done; Jesus surrendered to God in uttermost faith and confidence. He felt the assurance of the ultimate victory: "My God, my God, for what a purpose I am here!" meaning "For this purpose am I spared or reserved!"

Part B—THE TWENTY-SECOND PSALM. Many New

---

[13]See 1 Kings 18:29.

Testament scholars believe that Jesus was reciting the 22nd psalm, because pious Jews recite this psalm before their death. However, other authorities suggest that if Jesus did recite the 22nd psalm, Matthew would have written: "So that it might be fulfilled which was spoken by. . . ." and so forth.

Again, the words of Jesus were an expression of victory and triumph. He was not quoting from Psalm 22:1, which according to the Aramaic text reads: "My God, my God, for what have you spared me? You have kept my salvation far from me because of the folly of my words." Because he did not realize his purpose more quickly, the psalmist was discouraged and impatient and wondered why God had allowed him to live. This is how Semites talk when they feel that they have failed. They wish God would end their lives. See 1 Kings 19:4, where Elijah "sat down under a juniper tree" and requested that God would let him die.

Dr. Lamsa, in his translation of the Peshitta text, translates verse one of the twenty-second psalm as: "My God, my God, why hast thou let me to live? And yet thou hast delayed my salvation from me, because of the words of my folly." He comments:

The Aramaic word *shwaqthani* which appears in Psalm 22 is rendered "let me live," that is, "spare me" instead of "forsaken me." Easterners when suffering in distress wonder why they live and ask God why he has spared them, and why he has not taken them like their fathers. Near Easterners also use the phrase *l'mana shwaqthani* to confirm one's destiny.

Shwaq also means "to keep," as in Romans 11:4, Isaiah 10:3, 14:1 of the Eastern Aramaic text, and "to forgive," as in Matthew 6:12. It can also be translated "forsake" with the sense of sparing, that is, letting a person live but doing nothing to relieve the suffering.

God forsakes no one. He is mindful of all his children. Nevertheless, sometimes when we are discouraged or suffering, we wonder why our deliverance is delayed and why God does not act promptly. God is patient and does things in his own way. In Psalm 22, the psalmist wonders why he or Israel has been spared to go

351

through so many struggles, and why God has not speedily punished their enemies. Simultaneously he is mindful of God's presence as he converses with him. If God had forsaken him, how could the psalmist converse with God?[14]

A ninth-century C.E. commentary explains Jesus' words uttered from the cross. The title of this ancient scroll reads: *The Testimony [Evidence] from the Book of Commentaries of Lord Ishodad of Merv, Bishop of Hadatha, Beth Naharain [Mesopotamia], 850 C.E., Bishop of the Church of the East.* I have translated a small portion of it. The English rendering appears clumsy because I wanted to retain the thrust and intent of the commentator. As much as possible, I give a word-for-word translation, retaining its original style.:

> The explanation of *'el, 'el, l'mana shwaqthani*: Not at all was he forsaken by the Godhead. Not even during suffering nor during death because the Godhead was always with him—in suffering and on the cross and in death and in the grave; And very God himself raised him in power and in glory as in the psalm of David: For You have not left my soul in *sheol.* And neither have You allowed Your holy one to see corruption.

Another point to consider is that Jesus' usual way of referring to God was "Father." Only on a few occasions, did he use the term "God." However, some biblical experts maintain that Jesus never made this utterance at all. They believe that a redactor (editor) or copyist added these words on Jesus' lips in the gospel text. Again, not all scholars agree with this notion or interpretation. Mark, in his gospel, records the utterance but he uses the East Aramaic dialect for God—*Alaha*—and not *'el.* The simple truth is that God never forsakes anyone, at any time, anywhere! He is with the righteous and the sinner. God is with everyone in joy, pain, suffering and sorrow. God's power and presence are ever working to guide all humanity into paths of compassion, harmony, and understanding.

---

[14]George M. Lamsa, *The Book of Psalms*, p. xiv.

THE RENDING OF THE TEMPLE VEIL

And, behold, the veil of the temple was rent in twain from the top to the bottom; and the earth did quake, and the rocks rent; Mt. 27:51

"Rending" is symbolic of mourning and grief over the death of a loved one or a great personage. Semites rend (tear) their garments when they hear of the death of heroes slain in war or when outstanding people die. David rent his clothing when he heard the news that King Saul's son, Jonathan, and the king himself, had died in battle.[15]

The gospel writer seems to have been overcome with grief when recording the death of his master. The catastrophe was so great, it affected all humanity and, as Matthew points out, nature shared in the sorrow so much so that the sacred temple veil was torn in two, the earth trembled, and the rocks split open. Other gospel writers tell us that darkness was everywhere. This darkness was also symbolic of great sorrow which follows death. These writers were either speaking poetically or the day might have been coincidently covered in heavy, dark clouds.

The rending of the temple veil was also symbolic of victory. Jesus was to unveil all religious and temple mysteries. The Holy of Holies, which was hidden from the eyes of the priests by this veil and was visited by the High Priest only once a year, was now to be opened to all humanity. The mystery of God's presence was revealed.[16]

Verses 52-53 read: "And the tombs were opened and many bodies of the saints who were sleeping in death stood up, and went out; and after his resurrection, they entered the holy city, and were seen by many."[17] Again, the writer is poetically embellishing the events of Jesus' death and resurrection.[18]

---

[15]See 2 Sam. 1:11.

[16]See Mk. 15:38.

[17]Mt. 27:52-53, Aramaic Peshitta text, Errico.

[18]Again, many New Testament experts believe that these verses were a later addition.

CHAPTER 28

MARY OF MAGDALA

In the end of the sabbath, as it began to dawn toward the first day of the week, came Mary Magdalene and the other Mary to see the sepulchre. Mt. 28:1.

This Mary is not the sister of Lazarus (Aramaic—*Lazer*), but Mary of Magdala, a town in Galilee that was far from the town in which Lazarus and his sister lived.[1] Some commentators have confused this Mary with the sister of Lazarus. They think that she was called the Magdalene because she had built a *magdla*, "tower," with the money she had earned by her whoredom. But this is a gross error. In the Near East, harlots never build memorials, nor are they wealthy. Moreover, men and women are often known by the name of the town from which they come. For example, the gospels refer to Jesus as "Jesus of Nazareth" and to Joseph as "Joseph of Ramtha" (called Arimathea in the King James Version of the Bible).

Mary the sister of Lazarus was a pious woman, not a harlot. The name Miriam, "Mary," is very common in Near Eastern countries. There were so many women with the name of Mary that no one can know for sure to whom one may be referring. The gospel writer uses the term "Magdalene" or "Magdala" to distinguish this Mary from the others. According to Mark 16:1 and Luke 24:10, "the other Mary" refers to Mary the mother of Jacob and Joses.

THE RESURRECTION

He is not here: for he is risen, as he said, Come, see the place where the Lord lay. Mt. 28:6.

---

[1]See Lk. 23:55-56.

The Semitic verb for "rise" is *qam*. It has many meanings in Aramaic: "to stand up, to succeed, to rise, to awake, to rise from death." Aramaic-speaking people often use the expression *"qam leh,"* "He has risen," meaning, "He has succeeded, he has come through, or he has awakened." The gospel author uses this very Aramaic term *qam leh* to describe Jesus' dramatic and astounding rise from death.[2]

Although Jesus had repeatedly tried to impress on his disciples that the Messiah/Christ had to suffer and die before he attained glory, and although he explained that he would leave them for a while and return, the disciples could not reason beyond the Jewish concept of the resurrection. They could not believe that Jesus was capable of conquering death, that dreaded enemy of humankind, or of triumphing over mysterious *sheol*, the place over which God exercised no jurisdiction.

According to the religious understanding of that time, this final triumph over all evil forces would follow the coming of the Messiah and establish the Jewish state in supremacy on earth. Jews, like other Semitic tribes, believed in immortality and the resurrection of the soul as the ultimate victory of spiritual forces, but the dead would have to wait until the Kingdom of God was established and all evil overcome.

Many of the Jewish people, and even some of Jesus' own followers, felt that Jesus had not fulfilled the messianic promises. He had not conquered the Gentile nations; how could he have conquered the realm of *sheol*? Jesus' disciples did not expect to see him again

---

[2]THE EMPTY TOMB. According to the text, there were absolutely no witnesses who saw Jesus rise from the dead or walk out of the tomb. When the women arrived at the tomb, Jesus' physical presence (his body) was no longer there. The message to the women was "Now behold, he has gone on ahead of you in Galilee, there you will see him; Behold, I have told!" Jesus' resurrection is based on the appearance of the messenger (angel) to the women and Jesus' own appearances to the women, the apostle *Shimon Kepa* (Simon Peter), the apostles, and to the rest of his disciples and followers. New Testament scholars and historians consider all these episodes, in all four canonical gospels—from the empty tomb to the ascension of Jesus into heaven—as trans-historical or meta-historical happenings.

after he was crucified and placed in the tomb. The women went there because it was the custom. Many of his disciples and followers had decided to return to their former livelihoods of fishing; others were fearfully hiding in bewilderment and seclusion. The tragic events of Jesus' arrest, trial, and crucifixion had happened in such rapid succession that some of them could not even believe their lord had died. They were shocked, mystified, and heartbroken at the sudden, apparent end of one whom they expected to live and reign forever. They were disappointed at the seeming frustration of their dreams for the earthly kingdom. Jesus, in their minds, left them truly orphans.

He had given them a few assurances which, for the time being, seemed like vague promises, but even these served as a consolation for the bereaved followers. They slowly began to ponder these assurances. Prior to this time, they had been thinking of their own selfish ends. The three and a half years of continuous teaching—on how the kingdom would be a different kind of kingdom—had left little impression on their minds. They coveted earthly gains because they had left their occupations to follow him. They expected to become rulers and judges of an earthly kingdom. Now these dreams vanished and their minds were free to contemplate the spiritual side of the kingdom. The "suffering servant of Isaiah" was the new picture they had of Jesus.

Jesus triumphed over death, the enemy of humankind, which can only destroy the physical form. He rose with a new form, a spiritual body—the new Adam, free from all weaknesses and limitations that bind and hold the body to the earth. He was totally transfigured. Now, he could pass through a closed door or move to another location without any hindrance. He had victoriously risen with a glorious body.

His disciples and followers who saw him after his resurrection had also risen to a new power. What, for a time, seemed a dismal failure, turned out to be a triumphant victory. Their master's death had aroused general sympathy and won many new followers. A local event had taken on a national significance. By remaining loyal to him, their fondest dreams would come true. They would sit on his right hand and on his left in the new realm that would encompass all the nations of the earth.

They perceived and understood, as their lord had seen and known, that life on earth was but for a short time and not eternal. The gospel of the kingdom would enrich their lives here and hereafter. Death took on a new meaning. In Aramaic the word "death," *metta,* also means "not present, but somewhere." Death to the Jewish people was a calamity. To his disciples, death came to mean victory. The physical body of their lord had died but his spirit and Christ nature survived. Their lord had given death a mortal blow and immortality a new meaning.[3]

HOLDING THE FEET

And as they went to tell his disciples, behold, Jesus met them, saying, All hail. And they came and held him by the feet, and worshiped him. Mt. 28:9.

Near Easterners bow down almost to the ground when they greet a ruler or high church dignitary. When they are seated, men and women throw themselves at their feet and take hold of the hem of their garments. Some of the popular greetings are: "I throw myself at your feet," "I am less than the dirt under your feet." These Eastern salutations mean, "I am at your mercy." They are also expressions of affection. To hold the feet of a nobleman or a holy man is symbolic of humbleness and submission on the part of the supplicant and, at the same time, it is high homage to the person so greeted.

The messengers at the tomb had told the women that their lord had risen from the dead but they had not as yet seen him. When they did see him, they greeted him with the affectionate Near Eastern

---

[3]Dr. Lamsa believed that the fear of death will ultimately be conquered through a new understanding of Jesus, his message of the kingdom, and his divine Christ nature, and that the resurrection alone offers meaning, reason, and comfort in this life.

custom. They had loved their master and teacher so much that they took hold of his feet. As kissing by women is not the custom in the Near East, they greeted him with the deepest affection and paid the highest homage to him as one who has come through death and returned to them.

THE MOUNT OF ASCENSION

Then the eleven disciples went away into Galilee, into a mountain where Jesus had appointed them. And when they saw him, they worshiped him: but some doubted. Mt. 28; 16-17.

Part A—THE ASCENSION. According to Matthew 26:32, we read that Jesus, before his arrest and crucifixion, told his disciples that he would be in Galilee before them. (See also Mark 16:7.) And John tells us that he appeared to them while they were fishing on the Lake of Galilee.[4] Evidently, all of the disciples had gone back to their homelands and were now following their former occupation, fishing. They had to make a living. They were not fishing for recreation but to support themselves.

In the gospels of Matthew and Mark, we read that the ascension took place from a high mountain in Galilee. But Luke claims that the ascension took place on the top of a small mountain near Jerusalem, called the Mount of Olives.[5] We might note that Luke, a disciple of Paul, had written the Book of Acts many years after Jesus' ascension. The gospel of Mark is a copy of an earlier text of Matthew. Luke's gospel is a compilation from Matthew's gospel and the stories he obtained from eyewitnesses who were still living in his day. Regardless, the most important thing is not the place from which Jesus had ascended but the meaning of the ascension for the disciples. "To rise to heaven" in Aramaic means " to gain in power and influence." ("To

---

[4]Jn. 21:1
[5]Acts 11:12.

358

fall from heaven" means "to lose power and influence.") In Jesus' case, it meant "to become universal in power and influence."

Part B—DOUBTS. Even after Jesus had appeared eleven times to his apostles, some of them were still doubtful or uncertain that he had risen from death. They reasoned that Moses, Elijah, Isaiah, and other prophets had died and were still lying in their graves. Was the man with whom they had been traveling for these three and a half years greater then their holy prophets? Does not Scripture teach that the bars of *sheol* are closed?

On the other hand, the disciples, during these forty days after the crucifixion, had heard many rumors relative to their lord's resurrection—rumors that the women who had seen him were only hallucinating. They also had heard that their master's body had been stolen.

Moreover, some of Jesus' appearances took place when those who saw him were in a deep, ecstatic trance state. Some of the men thought that a spirit had appeared to them. But Jesus told them to feel him, because a spirit has no flesh and bones as they saw their master had. In other words, some of the early disciples of Jesus could not believe the report that Jesus had conquered death, risen from the grave, and was appearing to many of his followers. Peter was the first to declare that Jesus had risen from the dead.[6] The gospel writer wanted both the hearer and reader to know that, although Jesus ascended into heaven, some of his sincere followers still maintained doubts concerning their lord's resurrection. (To this very day, many of Jesus' followers are uncertain about the resurrection of the Christ.)

UNIVERSAL POWER AND THE COMMISSION

And Jesus came and spake unto them saying, All power is given unto me in heaven and in earth. Go ye therefore, and teach all nations, baptizing them in the name of the Father, and of the Son, and of the Holy Ghost. Mt. 28:18-19.

---

[6]See Lk. 24:12 and 24:33-34.

The Aramaic text reads: "Then Jesus approached, speaking to them and saying to them: All authority has been granted to me in heaven and on earth. Even as my Father has sent me, I am also sending you. Now, go, teach (literally—disciple) all nations, and baptize them in the name of the Father, and the son and the holy Spirit"[7] The King James Version does not retain the last part of verse 18: "Even as my Father has sent me, I am also sending you."

Part A—THE UNIVERSAL CHRIST. By sacrificing his earthly life to triumph over all the forces of evil, Jesus had received more power, glory, and honor from God, his Father. Prior to his death, his powers were limited—that is, he always prayed to God to grant his requests. And in some places, he could not heal because people did not believe in him. Now God had granted full authority to Jesus as the Messiah/Christ—ambassador of God. (But, we must keep in mind that the one who sends an ambassador is always the greater one.)

Jesus had conquered all earthly ambitions and temptations. He had complete dominion over all earthly and spiritual forces. After the resurrection, Jesus, the man, was completely transformed in the Spirit and became totally one with God's universality. The obscure prophet from Galilee had become universal. The presence of Jesus as the Messiah/Christ could be felt all over the earth. Time, distance, and space were eliminated. Now people could pray through his name— that is, in his way—all over the world. Jesus was sending his disciples to announce God' kingdom, power, and truth to every nation. Their faith had been restored and strengthened. They were the recipients of the risen Christ and, therefore, were to heal the sick, be they mentally, emotionally, or physically ill. They were to teach and make disciples of people from all races and persuasions to celebrate with them the all-inclusive presence of God. Heaven was dawning on earth.

Part B—BAPTISM. *Mamudita* is the Aramaic word for "baptism." It derives from the Semitic term *amad* meaning "to stand up." Thus, the Aramaic word *amuda* means "pillar." In the Near East, people frequently refer to a teacher's disciples and followers as

---

[7]Mt. 28:18-19, Aramaic Peshitta text, Errico.

360

"pillars" because they uphold and back his teachings. A Semite often says, "he has been a pillar behind me."

Water baptism is a ceremony of initiation that distinguishes certain followers who take upon themselves the pledge of loyalty to the new movement and stand as pillars behind its founder. Water baptism is a simple ceremony symbolizing cleanliness and universal acceptance of the new teaching. Other societies inaugurate their movements by making marks on the bodies of their initiates such as circumcision and other covenants of blood.

Water baptism is an outward expression of an inward cleansing. It also symbolizes the baptism of the Holy Spirit when men and women surrender their bodies and souls to God and pledge to live a new life. John's practice of water baptism was preparation for the baptism of the Holy Spirit. John was the herald of a movement that was to enlist and prepare every individual for the coming of the Messiah and God's kingdom.

Early Church tradition taught that water baptism meant that the followers of Jesus who were baptized were now dead to their former lives and had risen to new lives. Therefore, water baptism signifies death, burial, and resurrection.

(The Assyrian Church has been practicing this form of water baptism from apostolic times. The priest dips the child in water three times, repeating the formula, "in the name of the Father, and the son, and the holy Spirit." They consider a child unclean until the church performs this ceremony, but as soon as the child receives the water baptism, they admit the child into the society of the followers of Jesus Christ.[8])

---

[8] Interestingly, the Trinitarian formula, "in the name of the Father, and the son, and the holy Spirit," was a Church precept. Early Church scribes added this formula to Matthew's text most probably in the beginning of the second century.

GUARDING THE TEACHING

Teaching them to observe all things whatsoever I have commanded you: and, lo, I am with you alway, even unto the end of the world. Amen. Mt. 28:20.

The Aramaic word *ntar* means "to keep, guard, and observe." "Teach them to keep (guard) everything that I have taught you" is a divine command. Jesus in his last hours with his disciples warned them to guard his teachings against false teachers who, sooner or later, would come teaching falsehood in his name. On other occasions he told them: "If you love me, keep my commandments." Jesus always placed great emphasis on doing the things he had taught and not on merely confessing his name, greatness, and the miracles and wonders he had performed.

For many years, Jesus' disciples and their followers adhered to what their master-teacher had taught them and the joyful message of the gospel of the kingdom which was to extend all over the world. But when Jesus' followers began to depart from his gospel of the kingdom and to rely on man-made doctrines, they (the Church) split apart. The true teaching for which Jesus had given his life was supplanted with doctrinal issues that he never taught, and the rapid expansion of his gospel was checked. The progress of Jesus' original teaching is still being hampered today. Personal glory, honor, and material rewards are valued more than the simple, all-inclusive gospel for which Jesus died on the cross. An individual's belief in a set of so-called correct doctrines has become more important than the acts of love, peace, mercy, compassion, and forgiveness which are the principles and foundation of God's everlasting kingdom.[9]

---

[9]One of the best known of the ancient Aramaic speaking fathers, Aphraates, who wrote about the year 337-344 CE.,gives a very suggestive insight into the character of the Aramaic speaking branch of the Christian Church. To Aphraates, Christianity was the revelation of the divine spirit dwelling in humankind, fighting against violence and evil that people do to each other and not philosophical speculation about the nature of divinity and correct doctrines.

JESUS' DEATH AND RESURRECTION

Jesus' death was the key to open the door into liberty not only for his apostles, disciples and immediate followers but for all humanity. His death transcended all physical limitation and extended his spiritual influence throughout the world. The late Near Eastern scholar, Aramaic Bible translator, and co-author of this commentary, Dr. George M. Lamsa, explained Jesus' death in poetic, Near Eastern metaphoric language as follows:

> A glass of water placed in the Sahara contains all the qualities of water, but it is isolated. Ships cannot sail over this small amount of water nor can fish live and swim in it. The moment this water evaporates it becomes an integral part of all water in the air and ocean. Such is it with a [human being] who is alive physically but is isolated spiritually until [he/she] comes in contact with other spirits. This is how Jesus thought of his death. It was an ending to his physical [form] but a larger beginning of his spiritual personality, which was to break through all barriers of isolation and win for him a following of loyal souls from every country and century forevermore. This is what brought him to Jerusalem. His death was the fulfillment of his destiny . . . .[10]

New Testament experts usually interpret gospel writing concerning Jesus' victory over death, his resurrection from the tomb, and his ascension into heaven as narratives of faith and theological compositions. Other biblical scholars believe it is legend. Again, some authorities claim that the disciples were experiencing visions of their resurrected Master and Teacher.

We must also consider the influence Jesus exerted upon his disciples while he was tutoring them. There is no doubt that his charismatic personality and the powerful energies emanating from his physical presence made an everlasting impression on them. This

---

[10]George M. Lamsa, *MY NEIGHBOR JESUS*, "On the Cross," p. 139. The brackets in this quote are my additions

impression was probably so deep in them that they were not aware how much it affected their minds and emotions. It was so acute and compelling that it could not be effaced from their hearts and souls. Their love for Jesus and the love he had for them, in the end conquered their grief so that they could see their resurrected lord.

Jesus' physical presence only half revealed the ultimate meaning of the supreme ethical and inclusive ideals that he personified. Human experience teaches that we never fully spiritually possess the quintessential excellence in those whom we have seen with our eyes and touched with our hands until they are no longer with us. What a physical presence only partly suggests, a spiritual presence fully reveals.

The loss of a beloved in whom the finest principles were actualized stirs and illumines the memory. It also gives free and stronger wings to the soul's most powerful faculty, the imagination. But, we must not think of the imagination as merely a capacity for fanciful flights of absurdities. It is the imagination that has the power to connect us with the spiritual genius of our humanity.

The answer to understanding the resurrection of Jesus lies with the apostles, disciples, followers and the women who experienced him after his crucifixion. After all, they were the ones who reported the astounding event. Before Jesus' death, his disciples and followers did not fully grasp the depth and meaning of his mission and teaching of God's kingdom. They had dreams and aspirations of a messianic kingdom in which they and their lord would rule the nations.

But when the crucifixion took place, all their dreams and political hopes shattered. Their broken expectations and painful loss of their teacher were so great that they soon returned to their old occupations. Nevertheless, Jesus' death began to bring about deep mental and emotional changes within the consciousness of his disciples.

His death began to liberate and expand their reasoning and visionary powers. Because of this devastating defeat and failure, Jesus' disciples would soon experience their resurrected teacher and lord. They now could transcend their former reasoning and begin to perceive things spiritually. Dr. Lamsa describes their experience as follows:

> Waiting [the apostles] in disguise at the *Balahana,* the inn, their powerful, penetrating Oriental [Semitic] imagination pictured Jesus standing before them. In other words, they themselves were raised. Their Lord was really dead and their hopes of the kingdom of earth had vanished. . . . The more they thought of Jesus the better they now understood his teachings. When he was with them they took his sayings literally. Now they saw more clearly. The kingdom of heaven which he had proclaimed was the everlasting kingdom. Earthly kingdoms were to pass away and all peoples were soon to bow down to the Prince of Heaven. The temporal life was to be incorporated with the life everlasting. Their Master had shown them the way. He had gone to prepare them a place in this everlasting kingdom. He had given humanity new hope, and death new meaning.[11]

When this transformation began to take effect within their souls, Jesus, as a living, universal presence, could appear to them in visions and dreams. They saw their lord and teacher as the glorified Messiah. He was with them forever and would infuse them with power and courage. This spiritual influence was so powerful and gripping that the disciples knew Jesus had conquered death. So profound was their experience that they were willing to face death and martyrdom. "He has risen!" was their cry. The risen Messiah/Christ in his spiritual nature belongs to the entire human family in every generation and in every age.

As a human being, Jesus was a simple but profoundly astute and dynamic teacher, preacher, and prophet. The finest and best way one can describe "the beloved man from Galilee" would be to call him, as his own Jewish compatriots did in the Near East, "the son of God." Jesus' source of inspiration was God. And, his faith was in the God of Israel whom he affectionately called "Father." His teaching and apprehension of the nonexclusive, all-encompassing kingdom of God

---

[11]George M. Lamsa, *MY NEIGHBOR JESUS*, "The Resurrection," p. 145.

continues to ignite the hearts and souls of men, women, and children the world over. The Christ lives—"He is risen!"

APPENDIX

A BRIEF HISTORY
OF THE
EARLY ARAMAIC CHURCH

THE BEGINNING

The spiritual movement for the religion we know as Christianity began when Jesus was preaching, teaching, and healing in Galilee. His early disciples and followers were Galileans who became identified with his gospel of the kingdom. People originally called these followers of Jesus, "Nazarenes"; later, they became known as *M'sheeḥeh*, "Christians" (literally—"anointed ones or messiahs"). This faith spread in the Near East along Semitic lines of thought. From its inception and earliest beginnings it remained independent of Western theology and continues so to this very day.

Thaddeus, one of the twelve, and Mari, one of the seventy disciples of Jesus, christianized the kingdom of *Ur-Hai*,[1] today known as Urfa. The geographical location and affinity in language and customs made it easier for the Galilean disciples to approach, first, those Semitic peoples who were closely akin to them. This was in accord with the instructions that their Lord had given them: "Go ye first to the lost sheep of Israel" (the ten lost tribes). These people were taken captive and settled around the river Khabor in Edessa, in Mesopotamia and Persia. The Hebrew prophets had long predicted that the Messiah/Christ would gather these scattered tribes of Israel.

---

[1] A Western Aramaic name. It means "a place of life."

EDESSA

According to Near Eastern tradition, Abgar, king of Edessa, wrote and invited Jesus to come to his city. Jesus promised to send one of his disciples.[2] Interestingly, the Gospel of John 12:20-21, the King James Version, reads that some Greeks wanted to see Jesus: "And there were certain Greeks among them that came up to worship at the feast; The same came therefore to Philip which was of Bethsaida of Galilee, and desired him, saying, Sir, we would see Jesus." But the Aramaic text does not say "Greeks"; it reads *ammeh*, "Gentiles." In Aramaic *ammeh* means "people, Gentiles"—that is, Syrians, Idumeans, and other neighboring Semitic peoples. The word for "Greeks" is *yonayeh*. Assyrian Christians believe that among those who wished to see Jesus were probably men from Edessa. These men spoke the same form of Aramaic as the Galileans.

Eusebius (c.260—c.340), Bishop of Caesarea and the "Father of Church History," stressed the remarkable and rapid spread of Christianity in Edessa from the Apostolic age, the firm foothold which it held in that region, and the importance it played in the evangelization of the countries east of the Euphrates and Persia.

ARAMAIC INFLUENCE FROM EDESSA

Edessa became an evangelizing center in the Near East, as Antioch was in Syria. From Edessa, missionaries went to Persia and other Eastern lands. St. Thomas passed through this famous city on his way to Malabar, India. This city suffered during the Parthian and Roman wars. The Roman Army under Crassus was defeated at Carrhae, 53 B.C.E. In 162 C.E., during the reign of Emperor Marcus Aurelius, war broke out again over the issue of Armenia and the small

---

[2]This tradition concerning King Abgar of Edessa was accepted as authentic in the Near East but widely rejected in the West. It has, however, found defenders even in modern times among both Catholics and Protestants.

kingdom of Ur-Hai, Osrhoene. The Romans were victorious. Seleucia, a large city in Persia, was destroyed by Avidius Cassius' Army. Thereafter, whatever Greek culture was planted in Mesopotamia disappeared and gave way to Aramaic. Greek had been established by the Greek conquest of Asia, third century B.C.E. The change from Greek to Aramaic, in this part of the Near East, took place when Christianity was spreading in Syria and Persia through the Aramaic language.

The Edessan dialect was its language and, as is seen, Edessa became the great literary center of the Aramaic language. Greek totally vanished from the provinces in the Eurphrates Valley with the exception of a few learned men. Centuries after, it totally disappeared from Mesopotamia. The superiority of the Aramaic language in Edessa and throughout Mesopotamia and the influence that it exerted in the Near East is emphatically emphasized by Mar-Yacob Eugene Manna, Chaldean Roman Catholic metropolitan of Armenia. A distinguished Aramaic scholar whose writings are in that language and who is recognized as an authority by Roman Catholics and other Christians in the Near East, he says:

> After Christ, our Lord, the first books which came into our possession, are the Old and New Testaments. That is to say, the version which is called Peshitta. Without dispute it is even earlier than the writings which came down to us from the words of Bar-Dasan, who was living in the latter part of the second century. . ."
> It is well known that they were written in the language of the river (Aramaic). That is the island between Tigris and Euphrates. For it was in Ur-Hai, the mother of cities of Mesopotamia at that time, that the blessed apostles, evangelizers of the East preached at first, and in it was established the first church; and from it by Mar-mari, the blessed, the Christian religion was spread and extended throughout the island, in Assyria, Babylon, Persia, Media, and in the rest of the neighboring countries. And this speech of the river as those from the beginning bear witness was richer and purer

than the speech of the rest of the other parts.[3]

Edessa became a battlefield between Romans and Persians. It was captured in 116 C.E. by the Romans under Trajan, and later in 216 C.E. by Emperor Caracalla. Roman victories and defeats in the Near East in connection with the Parthians and Persians were the chief occasions for the extension of Christianity beyond the Euphrates. The struggle for the control of the fertile and prosperous provinces in Mesopotamia caused continuous warfare between these Empires. The Romans persistently invaded Persia but, in most cases, they suffered heavy losses. Thousands of Christians were taken captive by the Persians. Carus, the Roman Emperor, died in Persia during a campaign. In 260 C.E., Valerian's army was completely defeated by Shapur I at Edessa. Nisibin and Carrhae also fell before the Persian Army, and the emperor was taken prisoner.

Prior to the conversion of Constantine and the treaty between Persia and Rome, streams of captives continued to move towards Persia. Under the Sassanina dynasty, Persians penetrated as far as Jerusalem and Antioch, burning and destroying buildings and taking captives. But while Rome continued to persecute Christians, the Persians tolerated them because they were the enemies of Rome. Thus, while the Christians in the Roman Empire were in hiding, their brethren in Persia were prosperous and well organized. Schools of Christian learning were established in many parts of the Near East, as at Edessa and Gundi-Shapur. Writers like Bar-Dasan, 154-222, Aphraates, 280-350, Ephraim, 4th century, commented on Scripture. Aphraates became bishop of the monastery of St. Matthew near Mosul. This famous writer mentions the New Testament in his native tongue. The council of Nicaea (410 C.E.), confirmed by the bishops of the Eastern Church at the Council of Seleucia, the Persian capital, was after his time.

Persecutions began in Persia in the middle of the fourth century

---

[3]Morceaux Choisis de litterature Arameenne, Premiere Partie. Mossoul Imprimerie Des Peres Dominicains, 1901.

some time after the Roman Empire had adopted Christianity as the state religion. The policy of the Persian government towards Christian subjects changed. They were now regarded with suspicion as allies of the Roman government; but while many martyrdoms took place and church buildings were destroyed, the Church of the East was now strongly entrenched everywhere. Some of the Persian kings were friendly to the Patriarchs of the Eastern Church, and not a few of the princes and high officials had become Christian. Both Persian and Assyrian Christians occupied influential positions as physicians, educators and financiers in the service of the Persian "King of Kings." Nor should it be foregotten that by this time copies of the Scriptures, commentaries, and other writings were widely circulated.

CHURCH OF THE EAST

The Eastern Church played a conspicuous part in the history of Christianity. It successfully withstood both Roman and Persian persecutions. Zeno, the Roman Emperor (east), was persistent in his effort to compel Eastern Christians to accept image worship and the veneration of Mary as the mother of God. And, although thousands of these Christians were killed because of their refusal to accept image worship and the veneration of Mary, the Church of the East remained loyal to its apostolic teachings.

The separation of the Western Church from the Eastern Church at the Council of Ephesus, 431 C.E., left the eastern Christians alone to face the brunt of the invading forces of Islam. Nevertheless, the Church of the East maintained its position and continued to send missionaries to India, China and elsewhere. It continued to increase in strength and growth. It furthermore gained favor from the Mongol emperors who invaded the East in the thirteenth century. The Moslem kingdom of Mesopotamia came to an end. Khalif, Mustasim Billah was killed in 1256 C.E. The army of Hulagu, the Mongol, marched victoriously towards Syria in the hope of capturing Jerusalem. His successor, Abaga, tried to enlist the support of the western rulers, especially King Edward of England, but nothing came of it. Argun Khan, his successor, who was nominally Christian, sent Yahb-Alaha, a Chinese by birth and a Christian archbishop, as ambassador to the courts of Europe and to the Pope. He was received cordially by the rulers and by the cardinals, but as the papacy was vacant at this time, his mission was futile.

The entire situation in the Near East changed in the fourteenth century with the coming of Genghis Khan and Tamerlane. The Church of the East suffered heavy losses in lives and property. Many parts of Assyria were depopulated by the Tartar hordes. Churches, monasteries, and manuscripts were burned and destroyed. Dioceses in lower Mesopotamia and in Persia were abandoned. The catastrophe was so complete that the Church has never fully recovered. Only the Church of the East in the mountain districts of Kurdistan escaped the vandals. Despite all of these happenings, the Church of the East continued intact in Northern Iraq until the World War of 1914. Today, it remains in a weakened and fragmentary condition near Mosul and Bagdad. There also are scattered parishes throughout the United States.

BIBLIOGRAPHY

THE INFANCY NARRATIVES

Brown, Raymond E., *The Birth of the Messiah*: *A commentary on the Infancy Narratives in the Gospels of Matthew and Luke*, New York, Doubleday, Updated edition, 1993.

Meier, John P., *A Marginal Jew: Rethinking the Historical Jesus*, Vol. 1, Chapter 8 "The Origins of Jesus of Nazareth" pp. 205-252, New York, Doubleday, 1991.

Soares, George M., *The Formula Quotations in the Infancy Narrative of Matthew: An Inquiry into the Tradition History of Matthew 1-2*, Rome, Biblical Institute Press, 1976.

Vermes, Geza, *Jesus the Jew: A Historian's Reading of the Gospels*, Escursus: "Son of God and Virgin Birth," pp. 213-222, Philadelphia, Fortress Press, 1973.

ARAMAIC AND SEMITIC STUDIES

Black, Matthew, *An Aramaic Approach to the Gospels and Acts*, Peabody, Mass., Hendrickson, Third edition, 1967&1998.

Burkert, Walter, *The Orientalizing Revolution*: *Near Eastern influence on Greek Culture in the Early Archaic Age*, Harvard University Press, 1992.

Charlesworth, James H., *Jesus Within Judaism*: *New Light from Exciting Archaeological Discoveries*, New York, Doubleday, 1988.
_____, *Jesus' Jewishness*: *Exploring the place of Jesus in early Judaism, New York*, Crossroad Herder, 1996.

Chilton, Bruce & Neusner, Jacob, *Judaism in the New Testament*, London, Routledge, 1995.

Eisenberg, Azriel, *The Synagogue through the Ages*, New York, Block Publishing Company, 1974

Errico, Rocco A., *Setting A Trap For God: The Aramaic Prayer of Jesus*, Unity Village, Unity Books, 1997.
_____, *Let There Be Light: The Seven Keys*, Santa Fe, NM, Noohra Foundation, 1994.
_____, *And There Was Light*, Santa Fe, NM, Noohra Foundation, 1998.
_____, *The Mysteries of Creation: The Genesis Story*, Santa Fe, NM, Noohra Foundation, 1993.
_____, *The Message of Matthew: An Annotated Parallel Aramaic-English Gospel of Matthew*, Santa Fe, NM, Noohra Foundation, 1991.

Falla, Terry C., *A Key to the Peshitta Gospels*, New York, Brill, 1991.

Fitzmyer, Joseph, *A Wandering Aramean: A Collection of Aramaic Essays*, Chico, CA, Scholar Press, 1979.
_____, *Essays on the Semitic Background of the New Testament*, Chico, CA Scholar Press, 1974.

Gibson, Margaret D., *The Commentaries of Ishodad of Merv.: The Gospel of Matthew and Mark* (Aramaic) Cambridge, University Press, 1911.

Hitti, Philip K., *The Near East in History*, Princeton: D. Van Nostrand Co. 1960.

Lach, Samuel Tobias, *A Rabbinic Commentary on the New Testament*, Hoboken, NJ, KTAV, 1987.

Lamsa, George M., *The Oldest Christian People*, New York, Macmillan, 1926.
_____, *My Neighbor Jesus: In the Light of His Own Language, People, and Time*, Philadelphia, A. J. Holman, 1932.
_____, *New Testament Origin*, New York, Ziff Davis, 1947.
_____, *The Kingdom on Earth*, Unity Village, Unity Books, 1966.
_____, *The Holy Bible: From the Ancient Eastern Texts*, San Francisco, Harper Collins, (originally A. J. Holman) 1957.

374

Lawrence, T. E., *Seven Pillars of Wisdom*, Garden City, New York, Doubleday, 1926

McCullogh, W. Stewart, *A Short History of Syriac Christianity to the Rise of Islam*, Chico, CA, Scholars Press, 1982.

Moffett, Samuel H., *A History of Christianity in Asia*, Vol. 1, Harper, San Francisco, 1992.

Overman, J. Andrew, *Matthew's Gospel and Formative Judaism: The Social World of the Matthean Community*, Minn., Fortress Press, 1990.

Rihbany, Abraham M., *The Syrian Christ*, Boston, Houghton Mifflin, 1916.

Stweart, John, *Nestorian Missionary Enterprise: The Story of a Church on Fire*, Kerala, India, Mar Narsai Press, 1961.

Torrey, Charles Butler, *The Four Gospels: A New Translation*, New York, Harper and Publisher, 1947.

Vermes, Geza, *Jesus the Jew*, Philadelphia, Fortress Press, 1981.
_____, *Jesus and the World of Judaism*, Philadelphia, Fortress Press, 1983.
_____, *The Religion of Jesus the Jew*, Philadelphia, Fortress Press, 1993.

Wigram, W. A., *The Assyrians and Their Neighbors*, London, G. Bell and Sons, 1929.

Zeitlin, Irving M. *Jesus and the Judaism of His Time*, London, Polity Press/Basil Blackwell, 1988.

STUDIES ON THE HISTORICAL JESUS

Chilton, Bruce & Evan Craig A., *Studying the Historical Jesus: Evaluations of the State of Current Research*, New York, Brill 1998.

_____, *Authenticating the Words of Jesus*, New York, Brill 1999.
_____, *Authenticating the Activities of Jesus*, New York, Brill, 1999.

Meier, John P., *A Marginal Jew*, *Rethinking the Historical Jesus*, Volumes 1&2, New York, Doubleday, Vol 1—1991, Vol. 2—1994.

GENERAL

Burkitt, F. Crawford, *The Earliest Sources for the Life of Jesus*, New York, E. P. Dutton, 1922.

Charlesworth, James H., *Jesus and the Dead Sea Scrolls*. New York, Doubleday, 1992.

Dalman, Gustaf, *Jesus—Jeshua*, New York, Macmillan Co. 1929.

Dungan, David Laird, *A History of the Synoptic Problem*: The Canon, the Text, the Composition, and the Interpretation of the Gospels, New York, Doubleday, 1999.

McNicol, Allan J., *Luke's Use of Matthew*: Beyond the Q Impasse, Valley Forge, PA, Trinity Press International, 1996.

Renan, Ernest, *The Life of Jesus*, New York, World Publishing, 1941.

ABOUT THE AUTHOR
George M. Lamsa

George M. Lamsa, Th.D., a renowned native Assyrian scholar of the Scriptures, lecturer and author, F.R.S.A., was born August 5, 1892, in a civilization with customs, manners and language almost identical to those in the time of Jesus. His native tongue was full of similar idioms and parables, untouched by the outside world in 1900 years.

Until World War I, his people living in that part of the ancient biblical lands which today is known as Kurdistan, in the basin of the rivers Tigris and Euphrates, retained the simple nomadic life as in the days of the Patriarchs. Only at the beginning of the 20th century did the isolated segment of the once great Assyrian Empire learn of the discovery of America and the Reformation in Germany.

Likewise, until that same time, this ancient culture of early Christians was unknown to the Western world, and the Aramaic language was thought to be dead. But in this so-called "Cradle of Civilization," primitive biblical customs and Semitic culture, cut off from the world, were preserved.

Lamsa's primary training as a boy was to tend the lambs. But, as the first-born son in his family, while yet an infant he was dedicated to God by his devout mother. Years after her death, when Lamsa was 12 years of age, her vow was renewed by native tribesmen, an ox killed and its blood rubbed on his forehead. This vow to God, Lamsa claimed, had always been part of him. "God's hand" he affirmed, "has been steadfastly on my shoulder, guiding me in the divine work."

Lamsa's formal education and studies began under the priests and deacons of the ancient Church of the East. Later he graduated with the highest honors ever bestowed from the Archbishop of Canterbury's Colleges in Iran and in Turkey, with the degree of Bachelor of Arts. Lamsa never married, but dedicated his life to "God's calling." He spoke eight languages and his lowest grade in any subject was 99.

At the beginning of World War I, when Turkey began its

invasions, Lamsa was forced to flee the Imperial University at Constantinople where he was studying; he went to South America. He endured great hardships living there in those years; he knew but three words in Spanish at that time—water, work and bread. As best he could he existed—in the British Merchant Marine for a time, then working on railroads, in mines, and later in printing shops, a trade he had learned while attending college.

After arriving in the United States in his early 20's, Lamsa worked by day as a printer, and by night he went to school. He later studied at the Episcopal Theological Seminary in Alexandria, Virginia, and at Dropsie College in Philadelphia.

It was through his struggles, during these years, with the English idioms that Lamsa gradually launched into his "life's work" of translating the Holy Bible from Aramaic into English. Yet many years were to pass before the world received his translations.

First as a lecturer in churches and seminaries, in halls and auditoriums, before statesmen, theologians, groups of artists, actors and others, Lamsa received recognition as a poet-philosopher and as an authority on all phases of Near Eastern civilization.

It was his own inner compulsion, and the urging of hundreds who heard him, that drove him forward and brought about—after 30 years of labor, research, and study—his translation of the Holy Bible from a branch of the ancient Aramaic language that the earliest Christians used. (It is known fact that Jesus and his followers spoke Aramaic.)

There were times that he was temporarily stopped in his translations when the idioms in the manuscripts could not be given correct English equivalents. It was Lamsa's firm belief that this translation from Aramaic would bring people closer to the Word of God and would facilitate understanding between the East and the West. For forty years, he produced commentaries and many other works based on the Aramaic language. The last 10 years of his life, Dr. Lamsa tutored and prepared Dr. Rocco A. Errico to continue with the Aramaic approach to Scripture. He left this earthly life on September 22, 1975, in Turlock, California.

ABOUT THE AUTHOR
Rocco A. Errico

Rocco A. Errico, Th.D., D.D., is the founder and president of the Noohra Foundation of Santa Fe, New Mexico. The Noohra Foundation is a nonprofit, nonsectarian, spiritual educational organization of Aramaic biblical studies, research, and publications. Dr. Errico is an ordained Unity minister, lecturer, author, Bible authority, translator, Aramaic instructor, educator, and spiritual counselor.

For ten years he studied intensively with George M. Lamsa, Th.D., world-renowned Assyrian biblical scholar and translator of the *Holy Bible from the Ancient Eastern Text*. Dr. Errico is proficient in Aramaic and Hebrew exegesis—Old and New Testaments—and in the customs, idioms, psychology, symbolism and philosophy of Semitic peoples. Errico has translated the Gospel of Matthew from Aramaic into English. He is also fluent in the Spanish language and has translated the four gospels into Spanish.

Dr. Errico holds a doctorate in Letters from the College of Seminarians, The Apostolic Succession of Antioch and the Church of the East—American See, a doctorate in Philosophy from the School of Christianity, Los Angeles, a doctorate in Divinity from St. Ephrem's Institute, Sweden, and a doctorate in Sacred Theology from the School of Christianity, Los Angeles. He also holds a special title of Teacher, Prime Exegete, *Malpana d'miltha d'lahu*, among the Federation of St. Thomas Christians of the Order of Antioch.

Dr. Errico serves as a professor of Biblical Studies in schools of ministry for many denominations and is a regular feature writer for Science of Mind magazine, Los Angeles. He formerly served as an editor and writer of *Light for All*, a religious magazine. He has held advisory positions with many boards of ecumenical religious organizations. Dr. Errico lectures extensively throughout the country and is widely known for his numerous radio and television appearances.

Under the auspices of the Noohra Foundation, Dr. Errico continues to lecture for colleges, civic groups, and churches of various denominations in the United States, Canada, and Mexico.

Contact the Noohra Foundation for a complimentary catalog of Aramaic Bible translations, books, audio and video cassettes, and a brochure of classes, retreats, and seminars. Those interested in scheduling Dr. Errico for a personal appearance may also contact:

Noohra Foundation
ˌ045 E Don Diego Ave
Ꞅe, NM 87501

ˌ com

Faʌ.

Noohra Foundation web-site: www.aːˌ   ⅃

4480H S Cobb Dr SE # 343, Smyrna, GA 30080
NOOHRA FOUNDATION
Ph: 770-319-9376, Fax: 770-319-9793
email: noohrafnd@aol.com, www.noohra.com

380